Musings of
BAREFOOT BANKERS

Lessons from
GROUND ZERO

Moorings for
FINANCIAL INCLUSION

Musings of BAREFOOT BANKERS

Lessons from GROUND ZERO

Moorings for FINANCIAL INCLUSION

FOREWORD BY

Dr.K.C.CHAKRABARTY

Deputy Governor, RBI

Varanasi Bhaskara Rao

Reprint: 2017 with corrections

Published by :

BS Publications
A unit of **BSP Books Pvt. Ltd.**
4-4-309/316, Giriraj Lane, Sultan Bazar,
Hyderabad - 500 095
Phone : 040 - 23445605, 23445688
e-mail : info@bspbooks.net

ISBN : 978-93-85433-22-1 (HB)

Dedicated to

My Parents

FOREWORD

The world today is undergoing a period of the most rapid acceleration of what Joseph Schumpeter alluded to as 'creative destruction' in the history of the financial sector. In the process of creative destruction, new constructs emerge. It is precisely when an old paradigm crumbles and the new one is not yet fixed in place that we get great bursts of creative thinking. This is perhaps such a moment.

This indeed is a transition time in banking. Perhaps the most talked about, yet least understood, transition has been in the area of information technology and information application, distribution and processing technology transitions hold the key to the shift to virtual banking which is prompted by the desire to have low cost operations. Most new financial services are in fact based on technology creating ways to do them.

While the financial sector policies in India have long been driven by the objective of increasing financial penetration and outreach, the goal of universal inclusion has eluded us. What we need today, therefore, are new approaches to financial inclusion that build on the lessons of the past, but also involve trying out newer approaches and instruments. Importantly, this also requires a change in the mindset of policymakers, practitioners and other stakeholders alike to figure out and put in place effective ways of reaching out to hitherto un-reached and under-reached segments of our population.

Reserve Bank of India's recent policy initiatives and responses have also prominently focused on inclusive growth. This signals an earnestness on the part of the central bank to make optimum use of emerging technological tools as also drive the idea that the poor are eminently bankable. We have encouraged banks to use IT-enabled financial inclusion by leveraging on the smart cards/mobile technology. Business Correspondents of banks are making extensive use of hand-held devices/mobile phones to reach banking services to remote villages, and especially for Electronic Benefits Transfer of NREGA wages and social security payments. This has been very successful in some parts of the country and some pilot projects are underway in most states of the country.

Put together, there is thus tremendous opportunity on the way forward for reducing costs of banking business by increasing volumes. Information technologies and the innovations they enable are strategic tools for enhancing the value of customer relationship. They reduce the costs of financial transactions, improve the allocation of financial resources, and increase the competitiveness and efficiency of financial institutions. Most importantly, aided by such IT interventions, a dedicated posse of barefoot bankers has been able to get around the difficulties that the brick and mortar bank branches have historically faced in reaching out to the remote corners of our country,

It is in this context that Shri Varanasi Bhaskara Rao's rather evocatively titled book "Musings of Barefoot bankers" emerges as a significant and well-timed effort. These episodic recalls and first person accounts from Ground Zero seek to reflect the heart and soul of the earnest efforts of a band of committed service-providers.

At a time when every effort need be made to drive home the efficacy of Financial Inclusion as a win-win opportunity for the poor, for the banks and for the nation, Shri Bhaskara Rao' book turns out to be essential reading for anyone who is interested in the life-altering experience of unleashing the "fortune at the bottom of the pyramid". I wish the author and his book all success.

Dr.K.C.CHAKRABARTY
Deputy Governor, RBI

September 8, 2011, Mumbai

CONTENTS

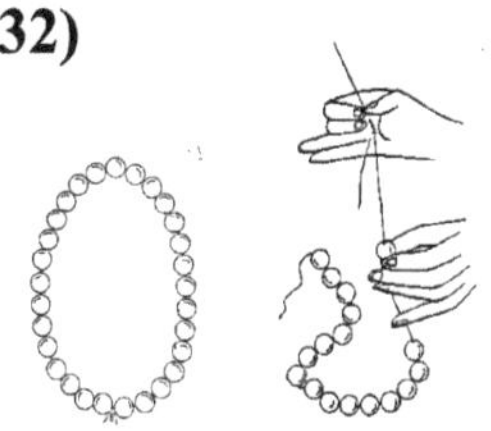

* * * * *

PROLOGUE

Life is an unending series of experiences and learning. We learn by *acting, reflectively* thinking, and *testing*, (It is an ART) what we believe in. Testing is taking risks, the risk of failure, loss to the individual and the institution for which he acts and tests. There are gains both to the individual and the institution provided there is reflection and correction on the basis of experiences and experiments. Gandhi's life was full of experiments and attempts to draw the right lessons from them. In the pages that follow, you'll find some of my experiments and experiences and those of several other managers.

I put them down in the hope that the managers and administrators of Banks and the Government may learn something from these experiences and experiments.

I called them 'episodic memories' which psychologists take them as one type of mental material that influence an individual's actions. The critical incidents serve as case-lets for class-room discussion using case method.

They are history. Stefan Zweig wrote in the foreword to his book, 'The Tide of Fortune':

> Like Nature, history, which is the spiritual mirror of Nature, assumes infinitely diversified and incalculable forms. It laughs at method, and contemptuously disregards laws. Now, like water, it seems to flow towards a goal; at another time it pursues chance happenings that are the sport of the wind… till a *dramatic instant* comes when crowded spheres are generated in a flash… it is only in these explosive incidents that their significance becomes unmistakable'.

Nationalization of banks was the *dramatic instant* that came to us. Experiences of bankers should become history through documentation. Then the personal histories together will become part of country's banking history in its struggle to eradicate poverty. It also traces the emergence of the barefoot banker and his qualities and skills.

It contains Managerial Insights, the result of my avid reading of management literature.

Political Economy – Rhetoric and Reality, is the outcome of reading staple news-breakfast information - the reports, editorials, articles and developments in political economy of the country. The report on Financial Inclusion and the committee's recommendations have been main focus till, one *'chance happening':* I came across the book 'The Great Speeches of Modern India' (2011) which made me turn to pre-independence rhetoric.

Career options in BFSI Sectors

I have included a note on *Career options in BFSI sectors* based on the talk by Sri Vepa Kamesam, MD, Institute of Insurance and Risk Management to the students of BFSI sector for the benefit of student readers. The illuminating talk outlines the job opportunities in the financial sector which is one of biggest beneficiary of reform process which started in 1993. The same reform process brought about what is termed as Financial Inclusion. It is not limited to India. Several other countries both developed and developing countries have started the Financial Inclusion process. It is said 'the more developed a society is, the greater is the thrust on empowerment of common person and low income groups.'

Private and public enterprises are beginning to see the potential market for micro insurance.

90% of the Indian population – some 950 million people – are not covered by insurance and signify an untapped market of nearly $ 2 billion.

This enormous "missing market" is ready for customized life and non-life insurance, but first, serious mismatches between the needs of the insured and the insurers must be overcome, pitting priorities against profits.

UNDP Study

The committee on Financial Inclusion in its report wrote 'Micro insurance in conjunction with micro savings and micro credit could go a long way in keeping this segment (people at the bottom of the pyramid) away from the poverty trap and would truly be integral component of Financial Inclusion'.

This book has something to offer to the professionals of non-banking. Financial and Insurance professionals as well. The challenges are similar to all BFSI professionals – in designing and developing products, reducing the transaction costs and delivery systems etc.

WHAT THEY SAY - CRITIQUE

There is another unusual thing about this book. I gave hard copies to some eminent persons for their observations and suggestions for change. Little did I imagine that these dignitaries with whom I had interacted during my career in the bank, would commend and comment in such evocative, educative and eloquent language.

With the result, I have included them in the beginning of the book under the heading 'What they say' to pass on the advantage of their experiences and exposition to the readers. These diverse perspectives put together will give an emerging picture of India's growth and finance. I feel that the reader will richly benefit from their words of wisdom.

NET GAIN

What they say and mean is a NET GAIN: Need, Essence, Timing of *Musings of Barefoot Bankers* and General Appraisal of, India's Need, which enhances the net worth of the book itself. More importantly it reveals to the reader Dynamic, Interdependent, Multilevel reality of India (DIM reality).

It is also a net gain to the reader who may not skip this section 'What they say'.

Architecture of the Book

Dr. Prasanna Kumar in his critique wrote, 'what makes the book particularly enjoyable is its architecture, imaginatively designed and interestingly interspersed with illustrations, photographs, anecdotes, aphorisms–all conveying a message'.

Acronyms and boxes are not only ASIDEs - Away, Short, Informative, Deliberate, Excursions; but also AIDs –Alternative Idioms Designed to help different kinds of readers. Readers are familiar with presentation of diagrams, graphs, tables and boxes which are very much part of expository writings.

Illustrations

The illustrations are unusual. 'Cartoons and fables are for children', some think. If we equate 'children' with learners, age is no bar to learn from illustrations. I have used them in the class-room with telling effect. I have always kept teaching – learning processes in mind while writing texts.

The illustrations, and drawings are neither decorative pieces meant to attract the reader; nor are they caricatures that ludicrously exaggerate the distinguishing features; nor parodies or satires held up to ridicule. They are there as pictures that convey the images the narrators held while recalling the past events.

We will see how five types of mental material is put together in two forms of thoughts, one imagistic and the other propositional in Part-III. The latter form of thought is called personal constructs, how one constructs the world in one's mind. The cases reveal imagistic as well as propositional forms of thoughts. Hence there is a need to illustrate the images they might have had as they narrated their personal histories/stories. The artist and the author had to recreate them together imaginatively.

I expect this volume will be a resource book for class-room discussions. I present below two boxes by way of examples.

What type of learner are you?

According to the proponents of NLP for teaching and learning – there are 3 kinds of (V-A-K) - Visual, Auditory, and Kinesthetic learners.

Visual people 'see' things and decide by how things look to them; auditory people 'hear' the ideas and decide by how things sound to them; kinesthetic people 'feel' and experience vicariously what is being read and decide by do's and don'ts suggested in the text.

All people are a combination of V-A-K, their pie-diagrams vary. More visual reader and less auditory, he or she will read rapidly and memorise by visual association. They scan, skim and skip to speed up comprehension of what is being read. The auditory element in the visual people will prompt a second reading at a later time as and when the need arises. The kinesthetic, the slowest reader, may capture do's and don'ts.

If the reader is more auditory than the other two orientations, he will PULL (Proof reading, Underscoring, Lip-movement, and Loud-reading are the things they do the text skipping the cartoons). They like lengthy discussions. As these orientations are not rigid, it is hoped, the auditory reader might use the techniques – scan, skim and skip the text and read again to their heart's content. There after, my appeal to the visual and kinesthetic elements in the reader whose preferred style is auditory, to spend time on the caricatures drawn by a professional artist appreciating the messages; I intended to pass on to the reader. The cartoons save a lot of words. Among thousands of words there are a couple of hundred pictures and a few diagrams worth studying at leisure, at least.

In the end I have to stress, as a trainer for over three decades my preference has been to aim my work at the students and the teacher at all stages of life. Life long learning has become imperative in the 21st century.

Inclusive Rhetoric

Core of 12th Five Year Plan is Inclusiveness – A Report

'11th five year plan experience has shown that higher economic growth rates do not by themselves bring inclusiveness or a reduction of inequalities'.

'Although the previous plans did have elements of inclusiveness, the significant difference in the 12th five year plan is the recognition that inclusiveness has to be at the core of the plan'.

'While all growth would lead to some reduction in poverty, the share of the poor in the fruits of growth has been meager'.

'There is a need to include the characteristics of inclusive growth in the strategy and focus on social and economic factors in the policy measures like providing *infrastructure* for the remote places and access to political power is equally important.'

These are the statements reported to have been made by eminent people in a Lecture Meeting in IBS.

So goes the rhetoric from the economists and intellectuals. If this rhetoric has to become a reality you need barefoot professionals from banks, insurance companies, agricultural science, technology, NGOs and extension managers and so on. More importantly they have to work together synergistically so that we see 'faster, more inclusive and also sustainable growth'.

Varanasi Bhaskara Rao

Career options in BFSI Sectors

A career in **Banking, Financial Services and Insurance** commonly referred to as **BFSI** sector is not all about money, but it is close. For young educated ambitious students like you obtaining a degree is just the beginning. What is left is to take a closer look at available options measuring sectors which have the greatest need of professionals. The BFSI industry is multifaceted, offering a variety of positions catering to a number of different skills and interests. Financial services have multiple sub industries encompassing niche opportunities. The key to individual success is to research, locate and land the financial job that has the greatest compatibility with your skills and interests. The same is true for professionals seeking a change in service and who want to take a shot at financial sector.

A career as a BFSI professional today is vastly different than it used to be years ago. Stockbroker, financial planner, investment banker, insurance underwriter and **Actuary** are just a few examples of jobs that may be chosen when pursuing a career in BFSI. As BFSI grows year to year, being accurate and up to date with financial information and financial techniques is essential when considering a career in BFSI.

The economic reforms of 1991 involving Globalization, liberalization and deregulation have changed India unrecognizably.

Among the biggest beneficiaries of the reform process in India has been the financial services segment - Liberalisation has brought in new products, new services, new players - all of which have resulted in multiple choices for financial consumers and loads of business to Financial institutions. Furthermore, the stage of economic growth that India is going through is expected to see a growth in the BFSI segment estimated at 1.5 times the GDP growth-underscoring the continued attractiveness of careers in financial services.

Financial markets across the world are getting integrated and complex due to technological advancements of most of the erstwhile closed economies. **The Indian stock market** is on the roll. **Insurance industry** has been coming out with latest innovative products to suit customers needs. **Internet** has touched almost all aspects of our lives. The internet has emerged as a convenient channel for these service providers.

Banking sector is also witnessing changes. Banks are eyeing retail segment as it offers immense opportunities. However, on the governance front, the sector is facing multiple challenges like: increased competition, rising customer expectations, and diminishing customer loyalty. **Mutual funds** are also competing with commercial banks in the race for retail investor's savings and corporate float money.

> "The financial sector is now poised for a quantum leap and the challenges are so vast that they will fulfill the aspirations of **the innovators, the workaholics** as well as **the researchers** from all streams of society. Those who join the finance sector in the take off stage will dominate business and trade worldwide for decades to come."

Employers value the analytical skills and the training in the latest financial methods and technology to meet the challenges.

Risk Management

Financial institutions particularly banks and insurance companies have been aligning their Risk management architecture to international standards. The area of Risk Management needs professionals with of high standards of knowledge.

The old stereotype financial officers do nothing but crunch numbers all day is fading quickly. Thanks to computers which do the number crunching, finance officers now spend their time assessing reports generated by computers. The CEO of Coca-Cola said: “The secret isn’t counting beans, it’s growing more beans”. Thus the need has increased for *intelligent, dynamic communicators* and *analysers* in all aspects of the financial world. It is your call: your world.

Sd/-

Vepa Kamesam, M.D.,
Institute of Insurance & Risk Management
Former Deputy Governor, RBI &
Former M.D., SBI.

Who is Who of '*WHAT THEY SAY*'

M.Gopalakrishna, IAS (Retd.)
Former Chairman, SCOPE, Former Chairman, Rural Electrification Corporation,
Former Director, Institute of Public Enterprise

S. Narayanan, IAS (Retd.)
Former Indian Ambassador to the WTO, Geneva

Prof.S.Ramnarayan,
Professor of Organizational Behaviour at Indian School of Business, Hyderabad.

Prof. T.V.Rao
Chairman, TVRLS, Ahmedabad

Prof. Krishna Kumar
Former Director, Indian Institute of Management, Kozhikode.

Dr.Anil K. Khandelwal
Former Chairman & Managing Director, Bank of Baroda

Sri M.Balachandran
Director, Institute of Banking Personnel Selection, Former CMD, Bank of India.

G.Nagamal Reddy
Former MD & CEO of Tamilnad Mercentile Bank Limited
General Manager, (Retd.) Bank of Baroda

Prof. V.S.Prasad
Former Vice-Chancellor, Dr.B.R.Ambedkar Open University &
Former Director, NAAC.

Dr.A.Prasanna Kumar
Director, Centre for Polity Studies,

Prof.S.Ram Kumar
Director, Entrepreneurship,
Kerala Veterinary & Animal Sciences University

V.V.N.Simha Rao
Freelance Facilitator of Voluntary Organisations (Retd.) from ECIL,Hyd

R. Bhanumathi,
Trainer in a Public Sector Bank

Administrators

India has to ensure food security, water security, economic security, environmental security and above all, livelihood security for the country and its growing population. Our five-year plans have invariably talked about economic growth with social justice leading to the creation of an **inclusive society**. Such a society must provide for **Opportunities**, building of **Competence** and capacity to utilize the opportunities and provide **Accessibility** to the opportunities leading to **Social inclusion.**

We have now reached a situation where agriculture is in crisis. News papers daily carry reports about difficulties faced by farmers due to, low yields leading to abandonment of agriculture and farmers suicides.

We are witnessing a digital divide between the literate and illiterate, the urban and the rural, the rich and the poor in India. This is often referred to as the India - Bharat divide. The banking sector has to play an important role as a prime mover of economic development and bridge the gap. Financial inclusion is essential for economic development which must ensure that every citizen is a bank account holder. Financial inclusion is not merely extension of banking service but full utilization of the banking services for savings, credit and insurance purposes. This should lead to the economic, social, political, cultural and overall growth of the individual. Appropriate financial instruments have to be developed in tune with the individual requirements of the clientele.

While, banking facilities are extensively available in urban areas they are still not adequate in rural areas and do not cater fully to the requirements of agricultural investments and development of micro, small and medium industries, and for development for requisite infrastructure in rural areas. This requires provision of knowledge connectivity, physical connectivity and electronic connectivity in the rural areas.

In the above context, there is need for a re-look at rural banking which should provide the 'last mile connectivity' to the last person in the village. It appears that financial inclusion in terms of supply side push has been reasonably successful in the banking sector but there has not been adequate demand pull to back it. It is here that barefoot bankers who carry the message of "no frills" banking can play a major and important role in ushering in an inclusive society.

New initiatives which are appropriate and suited to the local conditions are required. While we talk about global issues, we seem to have forgotten that local issues ultimately turn out to be global issues. Local issues can be solved only when bankers are both 'focal' and 'vocal' about them.

One of the primary tasks of barefoot bankers is to educate the farmers and illiterate account holders by providing them good advice. Education in banking must provide for enlightenment about opportunities, enablement to utilize opportunities, empowerment to take decisions and elevation of the standards of living of the rural folk. Bankers have been trained to understand "men and matters" and "men who matter". They will now have to deal with men and matters and to do so, become "men with mettle" Only then, can they convert policies into practices and produce the desired results.

As 40% of the experienced bank staff would be retiring very shortly, there is imperative need to not only recruit but also train a large number of banking personnel to meet the needs of 70% of the rural population who are not yet securing the advantages of banking. In the above context, Sri V. Bhaskar Rao, an experienced banker and trainer, has rendered yeoman's service by compiling a very thoughtful book with practical wisdom and knowledge which can be applied to live situations with great success and benefit.

Volume- I of the book "MUSINGS OF BARE-FOOT BANKERS" published in two volumes by Sri V. Bhaskar Rao is a very useful addition to the literature on practical banking in rural areas. Part– I gives as many as 31 real life case studies under the title, "episodic memories". Part - 2 talks about the emergence of barefoot bankers (like the barefoot doctors of China) under the heads of (1) evolution of rural banker and training needs (2) Corporate communication and communication skills and (3) "*Yagna*", the spirit of rural banking. (4) Managerial insights into reflections and conceptualization of rural banking

Volume – II is in two parts., (1) An outline of political economy which talks about both the rhetoric and the reality. (2) Financial inclusion and future of banking and their tall rhetoric and trivial reach.

The author has clearly brought out the **concepts** of banking, the **context** in which the concept has to be applied, the **content** of the concept, the **connectivity** and the **communication** skills necessary so that problems can be solved satisfactorily. The book emphasizes both the concept of 'Know Your Customer' as well as the importance of 'customer-centricity' and its relevance in banking, convenience banking and nation building. The book comes from a thinker, teacher, trainer, author, motivator and communicator with four decades of banking experience and is bound to be a good reference book and bible for aspiring bankers working in rural areas. I am sure personnel of rural banks, NBFCs and Micro finance institutions will benefit a great deal by reading the book and putting its suggestions in practice. This book should be available not only in every branch of the banks but also on the shelves of libraries in management institutions, engineering colleges and in the hands of avid readers.

The book provides inspiration to rural bankers who have to operate at the bottom of the pyramid and also reap the fortune at the bottom of the pyramid. The book talks not only about the need for working on the bottom line but also to work beyond the bottom line i.e. for the planet, profits and people. The book encourages both intrapreneurship and entrepreneurship in banking. It provides not only glimpses and **'sights'** of banking but also deeper **'insights'** which leads to creativity and innovation. A thoughtful reader will recognize that 'sights' lead to insights which lead to foresight. In other words, we have to link the past with the present and lay the foundation for a sound future. The book delineates and provides ample foresight and emerging opportunities where the concepts can be put into practice.

One of the welcome features of the book is the background material on the development of the banking sector and the exposition of ethical values and moral issues that should be followed in the banking sector. The index of useful Acronyms will be a real boon for students and trainers alike. The illustrations and cartoons are realistic and provide graphic description of situations and persons that one encounters in rural areas. Between the lines, we see how the concepts of 'need' and 'greed', 'green' and 'ever green' revolutions have to be held in balance by the societal ethics and fear of punishment.

Shri Bhaskara Rao's emphasis on the development of the individual, his ideas and ideals and the need for personal transformation for improved performance is both timely and relevant. Shri Rao believes in the process of dialogue, discussions, deliberations and debate before taking a decision. His stress on individual proficiency, team efficiency and organizational effectiveness to fulfill national objectives is the hall mark of the book. He believes that with correct orientation, training and mentorship of barefoot bankers at the grassroots level we can bring about rapid social transformation, economic development and universal human welfare. His concept of the barefoot banker is that of a person who is a "one-man army" "a one-stop shop" and a real friend in distress.

It is up to the banks, the bankers and the authorities to draw useful lessons from the book and benefit by putting them in practice. I compliment Sri V. Bhaskara Rao on his painstaking efforts in driving home the truism that bankers have to do their "home work", put in "hard work", put in "smart work" build "team work" and "network" with all members of society to bring about rapid economic transformation in India and enable it to take its rightful place in the global arena. I commend that this book be prescribed for orientation courses for bankers and other professional involved in rural development in India.

M.Gopalakrishna, IAS (retired)
Former Chairman, Rural Electrification Corporation, &
Chairman, SCOPE, A.P. State Financial Corporation,
Director, Institute of Public Enterprise,

The critical role played by the banking sector in our economy is too well known to need any elaboration. It is widely acknowledged that one of the reasons for India emerging relatively unscathed during the recent financial crisis is because the public sector banks are a predominant part of our banking system. However, it will not be realistic to assume that our public sector banks are contributing to the development of our rural economy to the extent one would expect them. In spite of significant expansion of the banking network in the rural areas, the mindset and the approach of a large number of banking functionaries is substantially urban-centric even today.

I recall the 1970s when I worked as District Collector in two different districts of Andhra Pradesh. That was the period when, following the Nationalization of major banks, both the Central Govt. and the State Govt., looked upon the public sector banks to play a significant role in the implementation of various Govt. programmes meant for the poorer sections of society, especially those residing in the rural areas. The Govt. of India introduced the Lead Bank Scheme under which a particular nationalized bank took the lead in fulfilling the credit needs of a district and also making available loans to poorer sections for various bankable projects in that district. The Govt. of Andhra Pradesh established a number of corporations to facilitate tapping of the resources of the banking system for implementing development programmes, especially those designed to help poorer sections in rural areas. The district collectors were designated as Chairpersons of the District Level Coordination Committee (DLCC) under the Lead Bank scheme and were given the responsibility to ensure effective implementation of Govt. sponsored programmes. I used to spend considerable amount of time in chairing DLCC meetings and following up with different bankers implementation of decisions taken in the DLCC meetings. This was imperative since the resources available for developmental projects in the district through Govt. budget were rather meagre compared to the resources the banking system could make available under various schemes.

In spite of my offer of complete support of the district administration by making necessary manpower available to the bank managers for making credit available to various developmental schemes in different parts of the district, the response of bank managers, in general, was lukewarm, except in the case of the Lead Bank managers. The banking functionaries from banks other than the Lead Bank used to take the position that their bank had the Lead Bank responsibility elsewhere and hence could not pay much attention to my district. However, it will not be fair not to acknowledge that there were outstanding exceptions to this. These officers from banks, other than the Lead Bank, participated actively in the DLCC meetings, made commitments, influenced or pressurized their head offices and honoured their own commitments. My own feeling at that time was that baseless fears about lending to the poor coloured the thinking of many young and bright banking professionals. These professionals did not have adequate knowledge about lending to the rural poor nor have they been trained adequately in areas like communication and collaboration. Of course, things have somewhat improved since 1970s; however, the inherent bias against rural areas, especially rural poor, is still there in the banking system and one major developmental challenge facing our country is to make the banking system overcome this bias. The district administration and the banks have to work together, as before, if this challenge is to be met successfully.

What Shri Varanasi Bhaskara Rao through his book titled "Musings of Barefoot Bankers" has tried to suggest that "Barefoot Banker" should become a reality and they should be equipped adequately through training to face the challenges of rural banking. Shri Bhaskara Rao with whom I had the pleasure of working when I was the Collector of East Godavari, was an ideal "Barefoot Banker" in his younger days. The book *Musings of Barefoot Bankers* is in five parts. In the first part, a number of cases or episodes are described in detail, based on the field experience of a number of young and energetic bankers, who were from a bank, which had no Lead Bank responsibilities in the district to which the case/episode relates. In the second part, the emergence of "Barefoot Banker" soon after Nationalization is dealt with. In the third part, the author links managerial concepts to the cases and episodes covered in the first part. The fourth part deals with political economy aspect by reproducing extracts from various newspaper reports and other sources during the relevant period. The fifth and last part discusses financial inclusion and future banking. The organization of the vast material available in this book is understandably unconventional, since Shri Bhaskara Rao, who is a banker, trainer and author all rolled into one, has tried to make the book instructive as well as interesting without losing sight of the main focus.

The basic conclusion Shri Bhaskara Rao arrives at is that, while technology can be of some help, without a dedicated band of "Barefoot Bankers", it will not be possible to achieve financial inclusion. Unlike early 1970s, there are a number of young and highly focussed banking professionals today who appreciate the significant role financial inclusion can play in transforming our rural economy. What is needed is to motivate them and to equip them to take up the challenging role of "Barefoot Bankers". It is in this context I feel Shri Bhaskara Rao's book is making its appearance at the right time. The book fulfills three functions. First, it is a source of inspiration to all those who believe in the concept of "Barefoot Bankers". Second, it initiates the process of equipping banking professionals with the required knowledge to take up the role of "Barefoot Bankers". Third, it sensitizes the general public, especially those interested in rural development, to the issues arising out of the interface between banks and the rural poor.

I am sure Shri Varanasi Bhaskara Rao's book will motivate, inspire, enthuse and guide banking professionals who are committed to make the concept of financial inclusion a reality and a vehicle for transforming the economic and social landscape in our rural areas. Equally, for the general public, it will provide insight into the enormous potential of "Barefoot Bankers" for bringing about fundamental transformation in our rural landscape.

S. Narayanan, IAS (Retd.)
(Former Indian Ambassador to the WTO, Geneva)

Professors of Business Schools

It is quite evident that the writing of this book must have been a labour of love for the author. The first section presents stories or case illustrations that he has painstakingly compiled from a number of managers who have operated from rural branches of a nationalized bank. Subsequent sections introduce and discuss a wide range of concepts and ideas from a variety of sources. The author has proposed frameworks to interpret experiences of barefoot bankers – managers operating at the cutting edge of rural banking, and derive useful insights from those ground realities. The cartoons are a valuable addition – they aid comprehension and give the book a 'friendly' look. Thus the book explores a unique set of resources, and is distinctive in its character.

The book makes more sense as a volume that brings out ground realities of inclusive agenda of banks. These experiences are valuable in exploring how policies ultimately translate into practice at that cutting edge.

Prof. S.Ramnarayan,
Professor of Organizational Behaviour at Indian School of Business, Hyderabad.

The future of India depends a lot on its people. All over the world people are looking towards India for talent. The rest of the world imagines India to be the next super power essentially because of demographic dividend, as the country enjoys the unique advantage of having largest young and productive population. The median age being 25 years India can be a real super power if all its millions of people are talented. This could turn out to be a myth if it turns of out to be mere numbers without talent. This is the real fear India has to face.

The economic advancement and talent development, research has demonstrated, are interlinked. Talent development, also termed competency development or human resource development is intimately linked to economic development and poverty eradication. One makes the other happen. However it is not automatic. It has to be preceded by government interventions. HRD interventions are done through the institutions like educational institutions, hospitals, corporations, banks, insurance and other financial bodies, etc. The role they play in the health of the State is crucial.

Financial institutions play a great role in translating economic and poverty alleviation programmes into reality at the grass-roots.

As reforms era has reached a crucial stage where fruits of growth have not reached the vulnerable sections of society, the rural poor and farmers, Government of India have made commercial banks play vital role in making Financial Inclusion – 'a process of ensuring access to financial services to all irrespective of their current social and economic status' – mandatory.

The commercial banks are 'advised to consider setting up farmers' training centres, rural development, and self-employment institutions for developing skills among farmers/rural entrepreneurs for effectively managing assets financed believing lending to the poor is viable and profitable marketing strategy. This is consistent with modern concepts in marketing discipline such as internal marketing treating employees as customers. Peter Dunne and Barnes observed in their book 'Internal Marketing – Directions to Management': selection must screen potential employees utilizing an approach that will enable the identification of congruent values, cooperative nature, and a service orientation.

Financial Inclusion, that is, reaching out to the un-reached and should be seen as 'Diversification' – going to new markets with new products. The kind of push banks and other public sectors institutions gave to technology should be given to HR.

This book helps pointing out many eye opening lessons for barefoot bankers to participate in this great revolution India may go through. The book reveals that the concepts are always there in India from the pre-liberalisation era. However, their relevance has increased in the recent times. The book has illustrations from the past and will be a great help for the future generation of bankers. Any one who is committed to the country might find it useful.

I congratulate and compliment Varanasi on bringing out such a great piece with wisdom coming borne out of experience..

Prof. T.V.Rao
Chairman, TVRLS, Ahmedabad – 380 015

The author Mr. V. Bhaskara Rao (VBR) was my colleague in the staff college of a public sector bank for over 4 years. We shared the room and ideas regularly. I was a senior core faculty and he was a senior operational banker with more than 25 years' experience in bank branches. He used to share with great excitement and conceptual knowledge his experiences as 'barefoot banker', an identity he found now. Instead of restricting the narrations to own experiences, he collected similar, diverse, experiences and presented them as episodic memories case studies for organizational learning. For every concept that we as core faculty articulated, Mr.Bhaskara Rao had a practical case to cite. Despite his age and long practical experience, he was quite at home with conceptual bases for managerial action.

I remember the case 'Malgudi Bank' he wrote jointly with me, first published in Vikalpa, journal from IIM, Ahmedabad as 'Janata Bank' case. It was a much discussed case – a case about a bank manager who became a victim of middleman's manipulations, risking thereby his career. There after he wrote cases regularly for class room discussion one of which 'Snakes and ladders' found place in the book of cases in organizational behaviour 'Managerial Dilemmas' published by Tata McGraw. Nearly 26 years later I find that he has come out now with this work speaks volumes about his commitment to a cause what has come to be known today as Financial Inclusion.

When I was going through the manuscript which he sent to me for feed back, I recalled at once our sharing ideas in the shared room. We had first met in an executive programme that I was conducting. Six months later when he joined us at the staff college, we found him repeatedly referring to McKinsey's 7S model, which he had read while convalescing for an ailment. It had penetrated the practitioner's head and also in mine, perhaps because both had worked in the industry and were looking for integrative models for managerial action. He at once saw the change management with 7S model in mind was ideal for nationalized banks. He was arguing then, and now through this massive work that consideration of 7th S – the shared values, is missing in majority of the cases in practice. *Shared values, Shared vision and Shared mission are the concepts that are often not understood by both senior management and the grass roots managers. We often hear of mission mode and everything is called some mission or other. No mission will succeed without people working with missionary zeal.* It is the same holistic approach with all the inter-connection between all 7Ss – Strategy, Structure, Systems, Staff, Skills, Styles, and Shared values that he has taken now to present in this volume.

I see in this book his reference to Kolb model of balanced learning, which he was using regularly before the courses started to impress upon the practical oriented people to use conceptualization of their own experiences reflectively observing their own day to day performances. Cases and cartoons, acronyms for check lists were VBR's strengths in class room instruction. His participants – middle aged manager and direct recruit officers relished alike his presentation of complex concepts in simple and vivid visuals and acronyms.

I commend this book to all professional students, besides bankers. The illustrations and acronyms are amenable for power point presentation admirably.

Prof. Krishna Kumar
Former Director, Indian Institute of Management, Kozhikode.

Bank Chief Executives

It is a well-known fact now that in spite of impressive GDP growth, the fruits of progress has eluded the rural poor. The continuous decline of contribution of agriculture to our GDP growth is a telling example of how our policy makers in the melee of growth have missed out on this key sector. No wonder one can clearly see two Indias – the first India residing in metro and urban sectors enjoying the fruits of development and the second India living in poverty in rural areas. In this context, the recent emphasis by the policy makers on financial inclusion is a welcome initiative.

Again financial inclusion does not mean distribution of money to rural poor but to first create financial literacy and create a cadre of inspired rural bankers with right attitudes. The book 'Musings of Bare foot Bankers' hits the point very well. The book conveys the essential points in a very readable and understandable manner through graphics. The author Mr Varanasi Bhaskara Rao is a banker, author and a thinker. This is a rare combination in the tribe of bankers who are mostly obsessed with creating numbers. Bhaskara Rao who was my colleague in Bank of Baroda Staff College for over 10 years was always a passionate thinker and a popular trainer. He experimented in early 80s with the concept of quality circles. Post retirement he has continued to think and write more productively is evident by the number of books that he has written.

In a large organization with network of branches operating in diverse environment in a mission mode, follower ship assumes greater significance. The freedom and entrepreneurship that exist at the top is also required at the bottom – grass-roots level. Academicians and case writers for long have focused their attention on the Chief Executives.

This book looks at the bottom of the pyramid and not at the bottom line. The Committee on Financial Inclusion argued that 'lending to the poor raises *interalia* issues of attitudes towards the poor as viable and profitable customers'. The committee recommended (R.No.14) 'a system of incentives/disincentives for performance and non-performance to achieve desired levels of financial inclusion for change of attitudes.

There are many young men and women who look for challenge, opportunities to learn and freedom and independence in their careers. With over 40% of bank personnel retiring in the near future the banking sector can attract the right talent, enterprise, commitment that is in good supply to achieve the objectives of financial inclusion. It is in this context this volume written by my ex-colleagues is a must read for the career conscious youth, managers in the middle in the upward movement in banks.

The cases he compiled are from his own personal experience besides the experiences of a few others he collected to identify the common thread that runs through the beads of bright spots – successful efforts worthy of emulation. He gave them an identity – BAREFOOT banker – a role model generalized. They serve as cases for study in the class-room in MBA classes and in all training establishment in banks in particular.

In subsequent parts he discusses implications to managements by presenting inputs from the literature that surfaced in the last two to three decades. It serves as reading material for discussing the cases in Part-I. The discussion would have been incomplete if he had not put the whole matter in the context of Political Economy – the Rhetoric and Reality since British times. Being not an expert on the subject he just presented gist of reports and articles that appeared in the print media in the past two years.

As Chief Executive of two public sector banks I know the problem of implementation of the mandate given to banks by democratic government is problem of human resources management and development. Mr. Bhaskara Rao, a true HRD man by nature focused more on the human resources than on the technology or profitability. Technology has certainly enhanced capability in financial delivery but it is the dedicated men and women who leverage technology to maximize performance with profitability. Being a voracious and versatile reader he could read between and beyond the lines to present such a book.

Dr.Anil K. Khandelwal
Former Chairman & Managing Director, Bank of Baroda

The title Barefoot Banker is an anachronism. I, like many would tend to, was put off as I believe that for carrying banking service to a new generation of untouched customers, new set of Skills and metamorphosis in attitude were required which indeed were more than being 'bare footed if not sophisticated. But after reading of contents one would discern that perhaps the author is making a point. Financial Inclusion, the challenge *before* banking industry, compel us to look at the past when some banks conceived holistic approach - Gram Vikas Kendra of Bank of Baroda and a few others of the kind were such non-conventional ways to reach out to under privileged segment of society for not just lending but aiming at economic development. A team of qualified and dedicated bank men moved around (during those days when mobile banking vans were yet to be introduced) to provide services at doorsteps. The motto was "our money with our advice'. Agricultural specialist officers who worked under the umbrella of branches with a committee decision making process was yester years' successful model for coverage, access, and delivery of services under financial inclusion mission.

These initiatives were designed for a sustainable economic development of rural area touching upon households engaged in

Farm and Non-farm activities serving land owners and labourers alike and providing an array of financial assistance for productive, trade and consumption needs. I dare say that the MFI model of today was practiced in a way more benign through these Gram Vikas Kendras. The success in my opinion was more by making credit not only accessible but affordable and backed by non monetary inputs including technical advice, propagating adult literacy, social hygiene, etc. The onsite service attempted today through Banking Correspondents and Banking Facilitators was enabled through 'cash collectors' who collected cash not just for recovery but deposits too.

But much of the success can be attributed to blending with the new breed of young officers by senior officers like the author Mr. Bhaskara Rao who took to rural banking for the first time in their career. It is this blend of job knowledge with aptitude that is required even toddy. The Banking Correspondents, Banking Facilitators and the personnel who have to man banking services in rural areas have to possess the right blend of product knowledge and service aptitude.

There is added advantage of technology today. The ubiquitous technology will certainly enable the strategy to happen much more rapidly. 'IT matters but individual initiative matters more'. That is the argument put forward by my colleague.

We at the Institute of Banking Personnel Selection notice that more and more qualified young men and women of diverse disciplines are seeking banking career for the challenges it offers. These new entrants and the existing bank staff with a long service ahead will greatly benefit serving in rural and semi-urban areas which gives *greater* opportunity for autonomy and independent decision making. Such an opportunity enables faster growth and development in the individual. Many of my ex-colleagues have shared their early experiences in rural and semi-urban areas with nostalgia and satisfaction which Mr.Bhaskara Rao painstakingly has compiled and theorized to identify a neo banker, a role model worthy of emulation.

This book will give a glimpse of 40 years of initiatives taken by the banks and inspire the *career* conscious young men and women who will be sensitized to the emerging opportunities and challenges with right perspective. From that angle the attempt of Mr. Bhaskara Rao's publishing this book is timely and appropriate. Even wider audience like those who are engaged in rural development programmes as also the researchers would find the reading stimulating.

Sri M.Balachandran
Director, Institute of Banking Personnel Selection,
Former CMD of Bank of India

What is needed is the conviction of the Bank officers to work in rural areas and not by compulsion, The Managements of Banks should select such people who have not only got a rural background but also the mindset to understand the problems of the people living in villages and have empathy towards them and their needs. *They should be given incentives, preference in promotions and necessary training to make the Financial Inclusion a success, otherwise this will be another scheme doomed to failure like many other schemes of Government of India.* This is the need of the hour for the Banks not only as a requirement of the Government but also as a *business opportunity*. Future of the country lies in villages and similarly, *Banks will have to look to the villages for their future business growth.* Hence, it is in the fitness of things the Bank

Chairmen understand this and take initiatives for *recruitment of right people* for this special job. I sincerely believe that it is going to be the Banks in rural and semi-urban areas which are going to play a crucial role in alleviating the poverty of this country. The time has come for such a change and no lip sympathy for agriculture will help any one, neither the Banks nor the agriculturists. If at all farmers suicides have to be stopped it cannot be done by giving more and more subsidies but only by making them self dependent, by providing loans at reasonable rates and affordable terms by the people who understand them and their activities.

This is the theme of 'Musings of Barefoot Bankers'.

G.Nagamal Reddy
General Manager, Retd-Bank of Baroda
Retd. MD & CEO of Tamilnad Mercentile Bank Limited.

Professors of Political Science

Mr. Varanasi Bhaskara Rao, combines rich experience as a banker, social sensitivity for human development, wide scholarship and good communication skills. This is a formidable combination which resulted in this book of inclusive knowledge for inclusive banking, under the title of "Musings of Barefoot Bankers". *Barefoot is symbolic and is used* here to describe the role of bank managers in rural areas who sometimes do '*Padayatra*' (walking on foot) to meet people and understand their problems. This symbolism is very appropriate to describe the role of bank managers in rural areas.

This is a very insightful study on rural banking, made in the frame work of *inclusive knowledge.* It has case studies under the title of 'Episodic Memories', describing field experiences of bank managers. There is discussion on emergence and spirit of rural banking. The managerial philosophy is discussed under 'Managerial Insights'. The broad currents of political economy and quotes from Vedas to sayings of Vivekananda, Tagore, *Gandhi, Nehru and Indira Gandhi were extensively used to explain and understand* the *context* and practices of rural banking of India. The sayings of Greek and Western writers including modern Management Gurus like Peter Drucker were also extensively used at appropriate places to deepen the understanding of problems in rural banking in India. The unique methodology adopted by Mr.Varanasi is to explain the particular with the help of general theory in a broader context. *This linkage of particular experience of rural bankers with the general framework of social transformation is the strength of this work.* The impact of liberalization, privatization and globalization is taken note in examining the activities of rural banks. This study helps in appreciation of ground realities in developing appropriate policies and programs for banking for financial inclusion.

The Episodic Memories and their analysis in subsequent parts is a great resource material for development of human resources in banking sector. The presentation tools used in this work are very effective as learning techniques. Extensive use of illustration, drawings, cartoons, anecdotes, parables and acronyms makes the work *a* commendable one in corporate communications.

I *compliment* Mr.Varanasi for his 'Spontaneous Optimism' to use his experience and knowledge to make a difference.

Prof. V.S.Prasad
Former Vice-Chancellor, Dr.B.R.Ambedkar Open University &
Former Director, NAAC.

Mr. Bhaskara Rao's credentials are sound. He has inherited from his father values and ideals of the freedom movement which was multi-dimensional in Andhra desa where as early as 1923 the first commercial bank and in 1925 the first insurance company in this part of the country were started by Dr B.Pattabhi Sitaramayya Congress and later President of the party.

When Prime Minister Indira Gandhi nationalised banks claiming credit "for helping the poor farmer and small trader" Andhra Bank's Chairman Mr K.Gopala Rao then reminded the nation that such a laudable initiative had been made in Andhra by Dr Pattabhi Sitaramayya four decades earlier! Bhaskara Rao's father, committed to Gandhian ideals, had worked for the promotion of insurance.

What makes the book particularly enjoyable is its architecture, imaginatively designed and interestingly interspersed with illustrations, photographs, anecdotes, aphorisms – all conveying a message to the bank and its customers. Shri Bhaskara Rao does not entirely depend on his experience and achievements only but catches up with modern developments, particularly the awesome changes ushered in by technology. He makes it a point to convey a message to the larger society and tips to youngsters and bankers in achieving their goals. His effort to combine tradition with modernity, skills with values and business with philanthropy is both commendable and timely. That enhances the value and utility of Shri Bhaskara Rao's book..

Dr.A.Prasanna Kumar
Director, Centre for Polity Studies,
Former Rector, Andhra University

Professor of Veterinary Science

"Barefoot Banker" is a wealth of wisdom. Though it talks about the real life experiences of a Banker in rural setting, it will be a delight for anyone interested in rural India. Through various interesting anecdotes, the book gives an insight into the building of livelihoods of people in the rural sector, and reminds that a committed personnel can definitely contribute to the changes in villages, thereby to the development of the Nation. It talks about communication, management, sociology... which could be good examples for people who practice – bankers, agricultural officers, veterinarians, rural development officials..

All these people play change agent role if they bring necessary dedication, values and skills together with pertinent knowledge. The book wants the bank manager to collaborate with bankers, agricultural officers, veterinarians, rural development officials… to bring about a concerted change in the rural areas.

Prof. S.Ram Kumar
Director, Entrepreneurship,
Kerala Veterinary & Animal Sciences University

Freelance Facilitator of Voluntary Organisations

If I venture saying bank staff, in general are not 'customer friendly', no one would take any objection. In particular those staff who are to deal with the needy and the rural poor, my observation finds a place.

The Grameena Banks who are essentially set up in rural areas are no different. Even the look of 'Grameena Bank' does not attract clientele. There are exceptions to the general as in any other sphere.

Sri Bhaskara Rao's 'Musings of Barefoot Bankers' vividly presents the self-fulfilling feeling of those bank officers who on their own reached out to the farmers and artisans in the field. It is clearly brought out through numerous case studies how quite a good number of officers with large heart, won many a heart of the local people. Sri Bhaskara Rao went on to analyse and theorise based on such experiences, that this approach can be a model for any bank manger posted to rural areas.

Unfortunately, the present day urban oriented instruments like 'gold loans' and 'car loan mela' 'house loans' lure the young bank officers to learn such activity, which ensure performance results and thus management's appreciation we have paradox as in our country: Arjun Sen Gupta Committee on unorganized sector recorded 834 million Indians live on Rs.20/- a day or less. Tendulkar Committee pegged the poverty line at Rs.447 a month, or about Rs.15 a day, at 2004-2005 prices. Aruna Roy, member of National Advisory Council said 'it reflected the government's lack of empathy for poor (The Hindu, September 21, 2011)'. Not withstanding such reports, it is a grass-root reality that we have large population in absolute figures, is poor in rural and also in urban areas.

I have seen large numbers of rural women in dire need of support. Welcome trend is formation of SHGs.

Good number of schemes, 29 in all ministries put together are there to serve the poor. Execution chain depends on the role of banks. It is the 'Barefoot' bank manager who can be central actor – says Shri Bhaskara Rao in so many ways.

V.V.N.Simha Rao
Retd from ECIL,Hyd

A Trainer's Litmus Test (RBM)

To test the efficacy of cases in the section Episodic Memories of 'Musings of Barefoot Bankers', I selected, 5 cases in the Induction Programme for Direct Recruit Officers who had only exposure to metro and city branches, expecting one. For want of time the participants of the programme were asked to read and brain-storm ideas. The list of concepts is given below:

RESULT/LEARNINGS

1) Relationship beyond banking. 2) Think out of the box, you are the Brand Ambassador 3) Credit is a rope through which farmer can prosper 4) Turn around right 5) Understanding the problem 6) Taking initiative 7) Building Team, & Involving Team members 8) Revamping infrastructure 9)Marketing 10) The case study removes the perception of the farmers that banks are nationalized but not managers 11) The Branch Manager setting himself as a role model by staying in the village, attending office early, building team, involving team to address the issues of the farmer 12) Take initiatives and be ready to walk the extra mile 13) Improving social and organizational skills 14) Make a difference.

The test was made at the end of two week programme in which they were exposed to banking and marketing concepts. It proved that the modern youth are capable of conceptualizing concrete experiences of others.

There is a paucity of real life cases. As these cases are real life, short and crisp, I feel we can use them gainfully with confidence. They serve a variety of purposes: knowledge inputs and value orientation and better understanding of ground realities. They can be used more effectively in 'Orientation' and 'Refresher' programme to bring about attitudinal changes and revising mindsets. 'Financial Inclusion' is another area where these can become main teaching material. Even in generalists training programmes, they can be used to stimulate their thinking and creativity.

R. Bhanumathi,
Trainer in a Public Sector Bank

* * * * *

SECTION – I

INTERNAL MILIEU

INTRODUCTION TO VOLUME I

The ability to introspect critically and place an experience or an event in a larger framework is a ***sine qua non*** *for learning, whether of individuals or organizations.*

A large proportion of positive activities, as Lord Keynes puts it, depend on ***spontaneous optimism*** *rather than on mathematical expectation.*

- Managerial Dilemmas
By Prof. S.Ramnarayan & Rammohan Rao

Bureaucracy both facilitates and inhibits progress. It seeks to regulate body politic. It was the Government's decision that the nationalized banks go to villages and serve the masses, the hitherto neglected sectors of the society, with bank credit.

Some enthusiastic risk-bearing intrapreneurs among managers got better of the inhibiting bureaucracy. Narrators do so at great personal risk to their careers. Some of us achieved results in spite of bureaucracy with charisma. Those who followed the rule book drifted and did nothing. They preferred doing nothing rather than doing something and being blamed for it. They were not really playing safe. They are removed and posted to positions where no risk was involved. But their careers may not flourish. There is something similar to the fellow who committed a theft and was sent to jail. There he played cards and cheated the inmates. He was thrown out of the jail! This is what bureaucracy achieves.

These intrapreneurs, officers with entrepreneurial streak in a bureaucratic large scale organizations share their experiences.

Book I consists of 3 parts. Part I comprises of Episodic Memories Divided into 4 sections. Pioneers, Followers, Miscellaneous, and Agricultural Specialists.

Pioneers – are those officers having been promoted from clerical cadre and posted in the rural and semi-urban areas. They went with their families and lived as one in the local society.

Followers – these are experienced clerks / cashiers who worked under the Pioneers and did outstanding work when they were promoted and given a chance to work for rural development.

Miscellaneous – are the rest of the experiences mostly narrated on phone. Some of them wrote in fictional style.

Agricultural Specialists – these are the officers who joined the bank as direct recruit officers with specialized knowledge on farming and extension work. Supported by the structure, Gram Vikas Kendra or Village Development Cells with systems and field staff and also vehicles have done admirably keeping in view the concept *our money with our advice.*

Part II is identification of Barefoot Banker and his qualities, skills and functions.

Part III is the background material separated from the cases in Part I deliberately so that the class room discussion is not coloured by my thoughts. Instead I present some developments in management science which do not reach the grass-roots manager expeditiously. The teacher and the taught may still make use of the material and ongoing developments.

SCOPE

The episodic memories serve as cases for classroom discussion where a chunk of reality is brought into the classroom for discussion, analysis and synthesis. The SCOPE of the cases:

Study of Rural Banking – Emergence of Barefoot Banker
Corporate Communication and Skills of Barefoot Banker
Organizational Learning and Knowledge Management
Poverty Alleviation and Financial Inclusion
Entrepreneurship in Organizations

A large proportion of the cases are positive experiences based on spontaneous optimism and not any mathematical calculations.

Analyzing Organisational Effectiveness
The 7S McKinsey Model

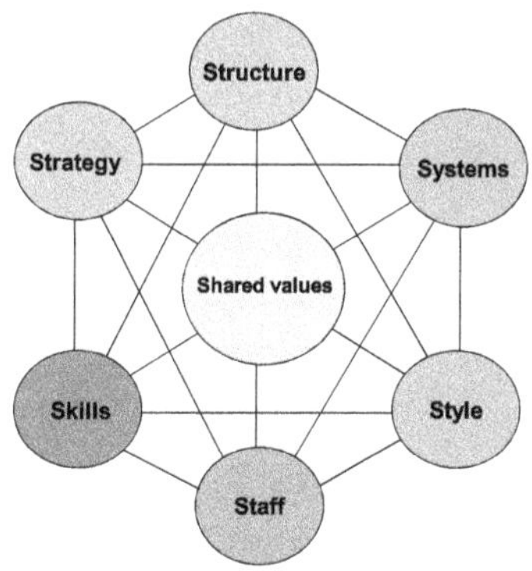

Interconnectedness is an important feature of this model

Rural Development Network

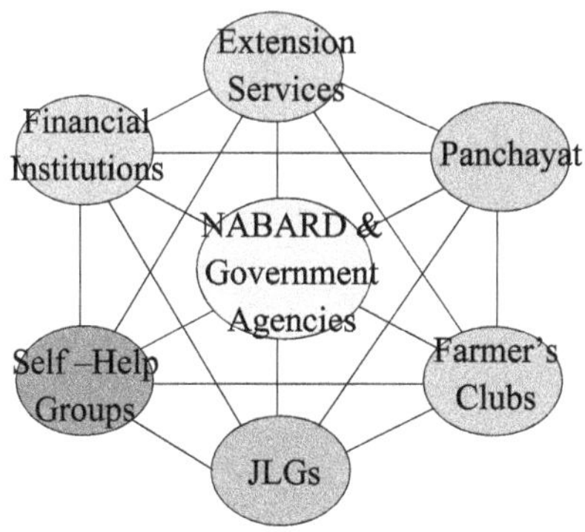

* * * * *

MUSINGS OF

BAREFOOT BANKERS

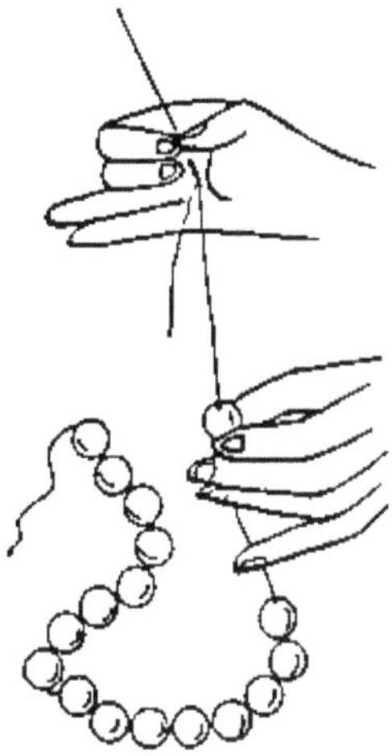

PART-I

EPISODIC MEMORIES *Running* THREAD

T	Tenacity
H	Hard Work
R	Responsibility
E	Enterprise
A	Altruism
D	Dedication

SECTION – I PIONEERS

Case 1

A Tribute–One Barefoot Banker

*"Sam Gachchadwam Sam Vadadwam,
Samvo Manansi Janatam"*

Rig Veda

(Let us walk together; let us talk together; let us understand together)

Venkat was asked to man a one-man branch of the bank in a village. He was given a cashier-cum-clerk, that made the two-men branch in actuality. He was paid servant allowance who attended to his personal work and bank's work. The premises was office-cum-residence and the safe-room of the office was the bed-room of the residence. No watchman, no armed guard. The family members, his wife and widow mother were the watch and ward. He was given no other perks or allowances.

What is more important was he had no job-description expressing duties and responsibilities. Everything was oral communication, if at all there was any, it was from the Regional Manager.

Organizational theories tell us that under such circumstances, '*the shaping of role-behaviour is influenced by three kinds of demands: Personal Demands, Social Demands, and Organizational Demands.*

Personal Demand of Venkat

A commerce graduate he joined the bank as a clerk in late 50's, passed C.A.I.I.B., got promoted to officer cadre and had displayed confidence as a desk officer in Advances section. Personal Demands include *education and previous exposure*.

Social Demands of Venkat

Social Demands are inter-personal demands. By nature he was sociable and very much interactive. He was not like the proverbial banker who keeps his eyes and ears open and mouth shut. Instead he could make others shut their mouth, by shouting at them. What we did not know was his ability to learn and willingness to learn. We'll come to it later.

Venkat's interpersonal skills apart, his knowledge, and other skills and experience played part. His personality and values were revealed in the trying circumstances – his ability to '*strike a rapport, establish high quality inter-personal relations with key members of the work group, and generate supportive behaviours*'. It is not merely with workgroups but also with the groups of people who matter in the village.

Organizational Demands

It is here one might say that the demands from the higher authorities were far from being unambiguous. The circulars from Head Office gave him only the targets – no. of accounts and disbursements made to agriculture and other weaker sections. For these ends the circulars generally do not spell the means. The means were left to the individual who occupies the role.

The higher authorities were under pressure from the Government to show results. Even to them the results meant targets. One of the measures the higher management took was to open rural branches and post middle aged officers like Venkat and wait for things to happen.

While addressing the Chief Executives of 14 nationalized banks, the Prime Minister, Indira Gandhi exhorted the bankers thus:

'I know banking is a conservative and staid profession; but people's aspirations are rising and the bankers must rise to meet their heightened expectations. I know that expectations run ahead of capacities to fulfill them.'

The Heads of Banks nodded, some applauded, others had their doubts unexpressed, lest their heads might roll. The prudent banker amongst them wondered about their fiduciary responsibility in dealing with other people's money. A prudent banker should observe *'how men of prudence, discretion and intelligence manage their own affairs in regard to the permanent disposition of their funds considering probable income, as well as probable safety of the money involved'.* (1830 Massachusetts Court definition)

However, they knew that the Prime Minister knew it, as could be seen from her opening remarks. All they had to do was to reconcile. Building capacities as referred by the Prime Minister takes time. Motivating the grass-roots Managers and re-orienting them to the new roles is not an easy task. The impatient Government of the people want results, immediate and tangible. Of course it means exceeding the targets put before them.

Government Initiatives

Government has taken several initiatives like formation of NABARD, Credit guarantee scheme and other measures to encourage the bankers which were first reported in the newspapers and came in the form of circulars much later. Venkat had been reading the reports, articles and editorials and made his own self study. He had to make a difference and that was his *personal demand.* He could make things different by his leadership and other soft skills. He was intelligent enough to read between the lines of both the reports and the circulars from the head office. The signals were far from clear – green, red or amber, nobody knows.

Venkat made a difference

Some of his colleagues adopted different style. Some behaved like the shoe company salesman who found that no one wears the shoes in the area and hence no scope. But Venkat was like the second salesman who saw the same thing but with different pair of glasses. He thought there was tremendous potential if only we teach people to wear shoes. There were others who did pretty little and were transferred back to the city which was what they wanted. It is like the fellow who committed a theft and went to jail; in the jail he played cards and cheated the inmates and he was thrown out!

But Venkat is a different man. He wanted to test the hypothesis that money given to the villagers is both safe and income generating. It is a viable proposition. He must prove it. He believed in Dr.Johnson's dictum – it is better to trust and be cheated than not trust at all. Venkat trusted and went ahead with positive thinking. This is what Lord Keynes meant when he said that 'a large proportion of positive activities depend on *spontaneous optimism* rather than on mathematical expectations.'

Farmers' Despondency

He went, he saw and now he had to conquer. He had hurdles to overcome, battles to win. But his first hurdle was that the farmer was not responding to the bank's initiatives. Repeated cyclones made the soil unsuitable for the cultivation of their staple crop-tobacco, which had been fetching good returns. Returns from agricultural operations must be attractive to the farmer to re-invest. Rich farmers may take a holiday for a season or two. The small farmer was in distress. Fifty percent of agriculture output in India comes from the Small and Marginal Farmers.

The real purpose of Nationalization was to help innumerable small and Marginal Farmers to raise their incomes with *timely credit* for investment in agriculture. Venkat had a new role to play-Barefoot Banker. He must embark on *padayatra* the Gandhian way of understanding the peoples' problems. Gandhi did not invent *padayatra.* He re-invented the 'wheel' of understanding in ancient times.

Let's walk together, let's talk together, let's understand together. We have its poor imitation in news channels, now. You have to walk in the fields, in the open spaces with an open mind; under the trees, away from homes and bank premises, talk as equals to understand the situation.

Its aim is *collaborative problem solving.* Farmers know farming, they have their past-experiences–but only traditional wisdom. Science and technology is searching for improved methods of cultivation, better seeds, equipments, cropping pattern etc. A farmer in distress needs information and Venkat can't provide it.

There was no Internet in 1969. Nearby Agriculture College, Bapatla was a good source of information. But district administration must help them. So he led a delegation of farmers to the District Agriculture Officer and obtained valid information – they must change to cotton. Venkat was thrilled but not the farmers. He must use the skill of *persuasive reasoning.*

Venkat I knew as a clerk could shout at any one who opposed. He must have un-learned this dysfunctional habit of raising the voice. He began using the skill of *personal disclosure.* He appealed to them that the bank opened the shop with high hopes. There was no reason why any prudent banker should ever think of opening a rural branch, much less at their village with such negative people. He could have lived in the cities happily.

The emotional appeal worked on some. He had a few supporters to his idea of cotton crop, a new venture; a few were ready to take risk. With them he went on *padayatra* to all the villages in the area. He began *articulating exciting possibilities* – high return for small risks taken. The number of early adopters was rising.

Having enlisted the early adopters he did not wait too long. He offered novel incentives: clean loans, bridge finance, on the lines of credit facilities given to industrialists. He had ample experience in class banking, product development and innovation, what was left was to convince his superiors, an organizational demand.

The higher ups had no knowledge of what this barefoot banker was doing. They had to rely on him. He had the independence, freedom and autonomy, necessary for decentralized decision making. He knew the way, how in the past his Manager in Chennai was exceeding his authority and used to write to the head office to ratify his decisions. He did the same thing with success. But the Regional Manager kept mum, – it was his style. Wait for results, if they were positive, well, he could confirm all actions done at grass-roots. If the results were bad the axe could fall on Venkat for indiscretion.

Fortunately for Venkat it worked in his favour. Each farmer who borrowed Rs.5000/- brought back Rs.50,000 or more. By next season those who migrated returned home to grow cotton with the bank's financial help. The late adopters joined in the village fell in line. The branch grew by leaps and bounds.

Entrepreneurship

Any other person would have thanked God. Venkat, an agnostic that I knew, would have patted his own back for what we call *entrepreneurship.*

He left the place on his onward journey in the banking career which was cut short by a massive heart attack in 1981 in Chennai. It was the village representatives who were the first to arrive at Chennai to attend Venkat's funeral. This is what the barefoot bankers get-the gratitude of the multitude. There have been many, ever since, who are all remembered with great reverence for a long long time for the role they played.

Karma Yogi

What these barefoot bankers do is yajna in the true sense of the term, altruistic action, done for the welfare of the society without seeking personal rewards.. They perform karma raised to the level of yajna.

* * * * *

Case 2 – First Person Account - BVS

I passed B.Com and joined LLB when I casually applied for DRO (Direct Recruit Officer) post in a Karnataka Bank and got the appointment after an interview. I think I was selected because of my extracurricular activities in school and college. I was in Boy Scouts in school and into N.S.S and N.C.C. in college as group leader.

I worked in Udipi and Mangalore. My father wanted me to be with him in Chennai and therefore I had to change the bank accepting a clerical post. But I was posted to Kakinada . I was fortunate to work under two good bankers and served the branch from its inception. The branch being small, trying to establish itself, I could learn all the work in all the departments. Soon I discovered that I was good at *relationships*. The branch progressed rapidly and within three years I was promoted to the officer cadre. I was sent to Vizag to assist in the organizing of a new branch there. From that time onwards I was identified as an expert in making arrangements for a new branch. On a number of occasions I was deputed to the branch opening. The Gujarati bank systematically expanded their branch network in A.P.

My first posting as Manager in rural branch came as a boon in 1968 (Yeditha). It was an experimental one-man branch. I was given a servant allowance of Rs.50/- and my residence and the branch were one and the same, My wife became the Bank's unpaid 'employee'. Though she was not doing any writing work, she accompanied me in outdoor work for deposits mobilization! It was women folk, the decision makers, observing *purdah* that made my wife's contribution significant. Thanks to the quick growth, the branch became a full-fledged branch. This experiment was the most rewarding experience in my early career. I was awarded for work in service, loan recovery, and public relation. ***I was instrumental in getting telephone and tar road for the village***.

I spent money from my pocket on the domestic servant more than what bank allowed because of my natural *disposition of generosity*.

The village life is different from the urban life. I had to adapt myself to the new situation. As a bank Manager who commanded a special place in the village I had to meet their expectations. I went beyond their expectations by *organizing picnics, tournaments in badminton, volleyball and elocution contests on topics like 'savings'*. I impressed upon the influential land lord to donate money for the *improvements of the infrastructure for the school*. The thatched shed turned into a near-comfortable building. I derived *pleasure in the community service*. Branch had no strict timings, it was like day and night bank. Recalling those wonderful days itself is an elixir to me.

From Yeditha branch, a rural branch with name and fame I went to Barkatpura, Hyderabad branch where I worked for 6 years and made it an 'outstanding' and 'best managed' branch and won special increment. I was the only man who got it in Andhra Pradesh.

In 1978 I was asked to open 4 rural branches in a span of 1½ months. Inole, Zafargadh, Narmetta – all under lead-bank scheme – and Kadipikonda were opened.

Though I had completed 4 years rural service I was again posted to a rural branch. *I did not hesitate to go. Wherever I went I went with family and I never did 'up-down' although I could have easily done* because Kadipikonda branch was actually situated in Kazipet which was 2 hours journey from Hyderabad and is like a small town with 10000 or more Railway employees living and a small market developed around the Railway Station.

I found marked difference between Yeditha and Kadipikonda areas. In Yeditha the farmers were rich cane growers linked to Chelluru sugar factory. There was no Lead Bank scheme or DLCC meetings nor were there any targets for weaker-section.

Kadipikonda was in a backward district. Lead Bank scheme was in force. Agriculture was not developed. Farmers were small and marginal farmers who grew rice and jowar under rain-fed cultivation. I started canvassing for deposits from the rural areas, Railway employees, small businessmen, shop-keepers, and improved the branch in all fields within a short time to the satisfaction of the Regional Managers.

I contacted missionary people – St.Gabrial School, Church and Archbishop of the area for deposits with considerable success. Villagers and farmers approached the branch for loans for agriculture and other occupations. I requested them to get their names registered through Revenue Officials and Lead Bank offices. I *educated* them about the advantage of bank loans provided they repaid promptly. They responded well. They were very sincere and I had happy experience financing the rural people. The staff strength increased, customers increased and branch progressed and earned good reputation. *My staff cooperated very well.*

An event I cannot forget was when the area Bishop came to dinner to my home. When I invited him, his assistants raised their eyebrows but to the surprise of every one the Bishop accepted the invitation. There was a large gathering on that day in my house. He blessed and appreciated my social behaviour and politeness. I was thrilled with joy.

The then Chief General Manager, of South Central Railways visited the bank once with his family. I requested him to open an account and he readily obliged. I was very honest and sincere in duty and in discussions with all.

More than 70% of our advances were to the farmers and the rest for small borrowers. Yet I had to face an *unpleasant situation*. One day the MLA came to our office with a list of 100 names and asked me to grant loans. I told the politician to route the application through revenue officials so that they would forward it to the bank, but he would not listen. He wanted the loans to be sanctioned within a week and threatened me with dire consequences. *I kept my cool* and he went away. Subsequently the Regional Manager phoned me and asked me to come to Hyderabad Regional Office. It seemed the MLA complained that I insulted him, a peoples representative. But the RM told the MLA that I was not a man to insult any one, leave alone an MLA. That was the *confidence I enjoyed from the higher authorities*. I was, in fact, complimented for tackling the situation well.

During my stay between 1978-82 the branch earned 'best performance shield' which is given for alround performance. I got a transfer to Visakhapatnam, a high potential area. I realized from these transfers that a Manager must adjust to the area of operation and different postings to different areas will enrich his life.

PS : Gratitude Over-Whelming After Four Decades

B.V.S. happened to visit Yeditha after a lapse of forty years. News of his impending visit spread in the village, spurring the villagers into a frenzy of activity. Vow! What a reception was accorded to him! He was welcomed with the traditional

NADASWARAM and was led to the town hall where he was felicitated. Speaker after speaker waxed eloquence, recalling his innovative banking schemes, the benefits reaped by the villagers and the consequent upliftment of the village.

The entire episode----the welcome, the felicitation and the eulogy---was a testimony to the warmth and gratitude of the villagers and their recognition of his selfless and innovative services.

The second generation beneficiaries were not far behind in recognizing and acknowledging the services of B.V.S. A middle aged man narrated how he reaped the fruits of MINOR ACCOUNT SCHEME started by him.

If a minor account is opened, the account holder [minor] used to be given an incentive of a slate and pencil. The gentleman referred to in the episode, argued and fought with his mother to get his Rs. 5 to open the account and get pencil and slate free.

Episodes like this serve two purposes -it is the greatest publicity to a bank or an organization. It also gives a boost to rural banking and restores the villagers' faith in the banking system.

It saves the rural masses from the clutches of private money lenders who suck the meager finances of the innocent villagers. More important, the warm glow of the gratification and recognition are rewards that go a long way in lighting and lightening the banker's life.

- Author

Case 3 – First Person Account - SVS

I took charge of the rural branch in the year 1975 which was opened in 1969 as a one-man branch under the base urban branch to support it. I was not going to a strange place.

As an accountant of the base urban branch supporting the one man branch, I was fully involved in the opening and subsequent support.

My predecessor, the late Mr.Venkatanarayana created history about which there is a tribute in this volume.

With his hard, sincere and selfless work the first Manager of the branch was remembered and loved so much by the people of the area that when he died, many from the village had voluntarily gone to his place to pay their last respects to him.

To take over charge of such a branch is not easy. The customers and villagers used to wonder whether I would live up to their expectations. In my 4 years of service there I could establish myself as a benefactor in equal measure. What is more important, the bank's name established in the minds of all the villagers. Change of Manager would no longer work on their minds. There was continuity in the image of the bank we both worked for.

Crop Failure

The people who grew cotton had got good returns and the next year almost all the people in and around the area started growing cotton. But in a few places people also started growing food crops due to the inclusion of the area under the Nagarjuna Sagar Ayacut. With this their requirements had gone up and we were obliged to extend higher loans to meet their agriculture operations. By then the Cotton Corporation also started functioning from the nearby urban places. They expected good production that year, but unfortunately due to untimely rains expected yields were not seen, not only that year but also for the next 2/3 years. During 1977 there was a very big cyclone which devastated the crops. Looking at their plight I undertook extensive survey of all the 40/45 villages coming under the branch by going from field to field to assess the damage of each person, for which I literally took *Padayatra* through the field walking every day about of 20 km and submitted my report to higher authorities informing them of the alarming situation and of further help required by the farmers for survival, which could be done by converting the existing seasonal loans into long term loans and extending additional loans for their seasonal operations. While this was being processed by the Regional Office, the Central Office had sent instructions to extend further loans and convert existing loans into term loans.

The farmers felt relieved and started raising further crops. They got the required help from the Bank in their difficult days and they voluntarily came to me and promised that they will not only repay their seasonal loans and the installment on the term loan promptly, but also give adequate deposits to the branch if they get good returns. The situation with some of the farmers was so bad that they did not have enough money even to feed their families, for which I provided them with clean loans repayable out of the crop sales.

In 1979 I was transferred from the place and the next year there was bumper crop and the farmers fulfilled their long pending promise to keep their surpluses in the bank deposits. They told the then Manager that it was an act of gratitude towards me.

During my tenure there I not only helped agriculture but also helped in setting up new small scale units, providing assistance for small business, small entrepreneurs, self-employed people and downtrodden people to enable them to earn their livelihood, and any other financial assistance suitable to the area of operation, individual or group requirements. Though there was no specialized cell for agriculture. I was undertaking almost all the scheme covered under that programme, and other Governmental programmes.

I was not only a Manager but also an adviser and was required to guide them in their daily problems. I was also taken as an advisor on the board of their Montessori School. Literally they recognized my service so much that during their Silver Jubilee celebrations they invited me to their village after I retired from service and felicitated me. Even today, 30 years after my leaving the place they invite me to their village once a while to seek my guidance in certain matters. Recently I was invited and they showered their affection on my family with their hospitality. They expressed that they had not come across such straight forward, yet strict and sincere Managers like me and the late Mr.Venkatanarayana, the first Manager of the branch. Such was the love and affection. They even tell the other Managers about the style of working of both of us. Hearing this the present Manager, when I recently visited the place, invited me to the branch and sought my advise for improving their business, which I gladly did.

My stay at the branch was not all that smooth as I had encountered a few problems during my working. One day while I was processing Govt. sponsored loans, BDO called on me and threatened me that he would tarnish my image by going to press if I did not consider the loans to some of his own persons outside the bank scheme, as well as under government schemes. I told him that he was at liberty to do anything but I would not yield to such threats as I was required to implement the bank and governments' scheme and I was answerable to only those two authorities.

It was really a challenging, innovative and pleasurable assignment in spite of some inherent risks involved in it. I still cherish my four years of stay among such nice and lovable people of those villages. Even today I feel glad that my sincere, hard and selfless service to them has been so much recognized by those people, but it pains me to realise that the same was not recognized by my own Bank. These are only a few of my experiences and I do feel that many of the Managers working in various rural branches must have had their own experiences, rewarding and satisfying.

PS

In 2010 the branch celebrated 40th Anniversary which was taken up by the villagers themselves. Over 500 farmers attended the function in a function hall. It was graced by bank's Regional Manager and NABARD officials. On the occasion many Managers of the past were remembered.

BANK 40th ANNIVARSARY

* * * * *

Case 4 – First Person Account - KBN

Timely Credit

It was in August, 1996 after retirement from Bank's service, I shifted to my own house situated at Poranki-Vijayawada Rural. Bank of India Poranki Branch is nearer to my residential place.

I had chosen to open an Savings Bank account at BOI, and visited the Branch. I requested the counter clerk for savings bank opening form. Hearing my request, another employee of the branch greeted me and introduced himself as a customer of my bank, to whom as Manager of semi-urban Branch, I sanctioned Education Loan for his son's studies abroad. I could recollect and enquired about his welfare and that of his son. He informed me that by availing the loan of Rs.2 lacs his son completed his MS in the US and had also secured a good job. He also informed me that the loan was granted *at a crucial time-- just one week before his son's departure to US to join the University.* Though he was an employee of another Bank, due to procedural delays he could not secure loan from his own bank in time.

The boy could repay the loan within 1½ years of his securing a job in the US. His family could join the category of "High Income Group". Father of the boy used to enquire about my welfare and used to convey 'New year greetings' every year for about 8 or 9 years.

Follow up Relations

I feel, after repayment of loan by the party, the bank should have a mechanism to follow-up by sending new year greetings, advising various deposit schemes for NRIs, and may also seek their cooperation in getting deposits.

Out of the way service

An Engineer employed in BSNL had a bank account with our bank. He used to maintain savings bank account in his name. Whenever he came to bank he used to discuss in general the service at our bank and used to convey his satisfaction. He informed that he was due to retire in one year and would continue to stay at Vijayawada in his own house. One day he called at the bank after banking hours at about 4.30 pm and anxiously enquired for sanction of a loan to meet his *wife's heart operation.* He offered gold ornaments as security and the medical expenses were to be paid before 8 pm. The cash transactions were closed and the closing of cash was being attended to by the staff. When I approached the staff and apprised them of the customer's request they readily agreed to help him by sanctioning and disbursing of loan. He received the loan amount at 5.30 pm and proceeded to the hospital to take care of his wife's health and by-pass surgery costing Rs. 90,000/-.

The customer expressed his gratitude and thanked the Bank's staff after successful operation of his wife. He appreciated the gesture of the bank in providing timely financial help, thus saving his wife's life.

Subsequently on his retirement he deposited the retirement benefits into our bank's deposit account after adjusting the gold loan. This engineer introduced some good accounts of his friends/ relatives and became an ambassador of the bank.

I may add that he invited me to his retirement function arranged by his staff and introduced to them, by saying that he was grateful to the Bank's assistance for his wife's health which contributed to a happy retirement.

This type of appreciation of Bank's services gives a long-lasting satisfaction to staff involved.

Social Banking

Loan for family / social obligation:

A retired Engineer who used to work for Irrigation Department living in 'Krishna Lanka' Vijayawada approached the Bank for opening of Savings Bank account. He had two sons – one working in Hyderabad in a private firm, and another chemist working in Autonagar, Vijayawada. He used to deposit certain amount, saved from his second son's salary in the new savings bank account. During discussions he used to tell us that his elder son had two daughters but had no financial stability. And it was his responsibility to perform his grand daughter's marriage. One day he approached the Bank and informed that his grand daughter's marriage has been fixed and the savings in the account was inadequate and he required a loan of Rs. 1 lac. He offered the security of property of Krishnalanka house worth over Rs. 6 lacs. The issue was considered by the bank and a loan of Rs. 1 lac was sanctioned to meet his grand daughter's wedding expenditure.

He appeared trust-worthy as he could maintain his family after retirement as Engineer; he was known for his probity, sincerity and hard work and never accumulated illegal wealth from his position while in service.

After three months he visited the bank and informed that his second son had secured a job in a good pharmaceutical company with a decent salary of Rs. 10,000/- a month, and assured the bank that he will be able to clear the marriage loan within a year and as promised the loan was repaid with 10 months. This was not the end of it. He made his son to open a monthly Recurring Deposit account with substantial amount for a period of 5 years or so. Bank's timely help made their family to route their banking transactions, with our bank.

The underlying principle is this---the more we share, the more we have.

We have to treat the whole family, their current and future requirements and all types of financial needs as if the bank is personified of friend, philosopher, and guide rather than treating the applicant as just an individual.

* * * * *

Case 5 – First Person Account – VBR (Episodes 1 to 15)

Episode 1

On the fore-noon of 10th December, 1973 I arrived in Warangal to open a new branch of our bank by the end of that month. It was by accident I met the Vice-President of the town's rotary club on the train from Hyderabad to Warangal. He invited me to a seminar their club organized on the subject, 'banks before and after Nationalization. I went to the meeting well before time to get acquainted with elite of that place. I was surprised to see a large gathering including the press reporters. The seminar started on time and speaker after speaker began criticizing the government. The bankers among them were no exception. Four years after Nationalization of major banks in 1969, it was a general understanding; that depositors' money is thrown in the name of social justice. The audience lustily responded to the speakers' sarcasm and sometimes scathing remarks.

I felt sad and was eager to get a chance which I got at the end with a condition that I should be brief. Brief I was. Referring to one speaker, a banker who said that 'credit is the hangman's rope as the French proverb says, that's what banks are offering'; I added it was a rope, alright, but not meant to be hangman's.

Bank credit is a rope that facilitates the farmer to draw water from the well to irrigate his fields and prosper, and not meant to hang himself.

'Our money with our advice' is motto with which we give credit. The challenge is challenge of extension work. In this mighty task we need the help of voluntary organizations like the rotary club to educate the rural borrowers to put the credit to proper use'.

CORPORATE COMMUNICATION IN ACTION

I put the matter with logic and emotional appeal. The local press gave ample coverage next day. It gave me and my bank a head start.

Episode 2

Thanks to this introduction and press follow up, I was able to meet people in their places for my business development with ease and without a business card.

Almost all enquired about the credit squeeze by RBI. Some of them who were known as 'exporters' were worried that without bills purchase limit the business in Warangal would come to stand still. It was during these conversations that I came to know the complexity of environment in which I was going to operate. The town has a well regulated grain market. Farmers from the hinterland bring their produce - Chillies, Cotton, Pulses, etc – to the market in carts early morning and the commission agents strike was a price and the packing is done and by evening the commission agents sold them to the exporters who booked the wagons, obtained waybills, invoiced them on buyer's all over the country and got their bills purchased by banks. If banks did not finance these bills, the whole market used to come to a standstill and the poor farmer suffers in the end.

All other banks had put an embargo on financing that season. As I was wondering what to do under such circumstances I received a circular from our head office that the credit squeeze did not apply to Bill Purchase limits.

That was a golden opportunity which I encashed with the help of my regional authority who gave enough discretion to go ahead and capture this business opportunity. There were some problems regarding staff and cash management etc which I could sort out and made good business that season. I became a savior. Others followed little later.

The connection between farmer and the trader and the role of banker, who must keep the interests of farming and rural development, were firmly established in me. I was learning from experience.

Episode 3

Commission agent was the source of information. Bills Purchase facility to exporters – the middle men – was a traditional indirect finance to the agriculture which I grasped interacting with the market.

But I had to mobilize deposits. I was told that commission agents kept their surplus funds in the banks during off season. So I contacted the biggest agent Mr.Nagalingam to secure some deposits. It turned out to be something different. That made a lot of difference to my strategy in the next four years.

He was a money lender with a difference. During season I visited him and saw him busy; he was with farmers crowded in his home-cum-office – talking, calculating, recording and negotiating and also lending certain amounts as advance before the exporters settled the amounts after receiving the money from banks.

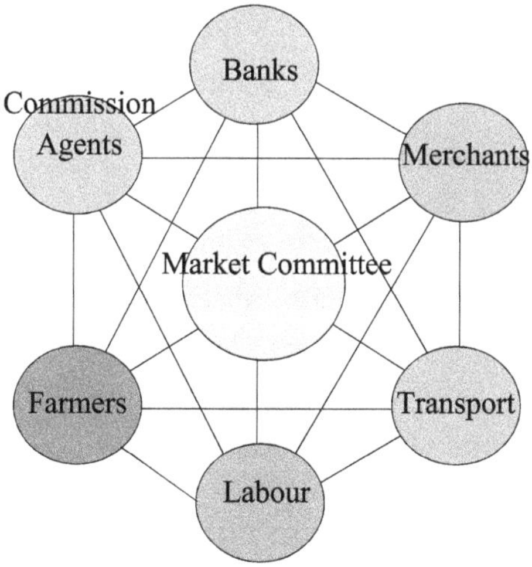
Banks
Commission Agents
Merchants
Market Committee
Farmers
Transport
Labour

Fifteen days was the time limit. His focus was on small and marginal farmers who considered him with high regard. They have been doing business with him for several years. There was certain bond between them. But now Nagalingam regrets that banks have spoiled the cordial relations by offering direct finance to the farmers. He told me that the town is talking about me. 'They see that you want to help the farmers in a big way. You can take a few lessons from us and be careful in the help you want to do' he said. He said that his community of commission agents has been financing the small farmers without asking for all the records banks ask for. "You have a cumbersome procedure of pre-sanction and post-sanction, scale of finance and kind component and cash component".

He knew all the terminology. He cautioned me not to burn my fingers as most of the other bankers had. 'There are hundreds of suit filed cases in the District Court', he said.

I went to him for deposits, instead, I got sermons. 'I don't waste money on vakils and courts. I have a few rules. Every year the farmer brings produce to the market. I earn my commission on the produce sold. A farmer brings more and more produce year after year. I know from my records who is a progressive farmer, who is not. I give a loan limit three or four times the commission I earned. My customers remain loyal to me. I trust them and help them to my capacity. But there are some whose needs are beyond my capacity.

I want you to help them; I can suggest a few names. They all belong to Thammadappali village. They are settlers. It is an interior village. I don't want to know whether they own the land or they are tenants. I know you can't do as an employee of the bank. You can take your precautions; I assure you about their honesty and ability to produce and generate income'.

I kept quiet most of the time. I was getting a lead and clarity about my strategy hence forth. Nagalingam and his ilk are a source of inspiration and information.

Information opened the gate to the rural world

Field visit of the Manager

Episode 4

To cut the long story short, I went to Thammadapalli and gradually adopted 16 villages in the neighbourhood all interior hinterland whose farmers were connected with the regulated market at Warangal in 1976 two years after the opening of the branch and in the emerging political setup in force. That was the time when the bank management encouraged us to adopt villages. But I had to deviate from one norm – 10 miles radius from the branch. I took up cluster approach and ARDC refinance. My memory goes to how I got diverted to weaver's plight.

I discussed the idea of village adoption with farmers who were not ready to the idea of mass-banking-financing every one in the village. I sought their help in identifying some from weaker sections to which they suggested weaver community. A young fellow suggested that the bank may consider agricultural labourers too. The plight of the weavers was worse than the agricultural labourers who got their daily wages. Most of the younger generation weavers had migrated to Sholapur, Bhiwandi, and Surat to work in textile miles. The older people were living hand to mouth and were being exploited by the master weavers. The idea of master weaver made me recall what happened to a fellow banker. What follows is an episode within the episode.

A Scape Goat

A dedicated and prudent banker who grew from ranks received a circular from the higher authorities that he should finance 100 loans on Gandhi Jayanthi day under DRI (at 4% interest) to the poorest of the poor. He was in a dilemma whether and how he would find 100 beneficiaries within a fortnight's time. He shared his anxiety with a valued customer who happened to be a master weaver, a *lungi* exporter. The master weaver suggested that he would bring poor weavers whom he might finance. The prudent banker has another worry, the verification of end use to which the master weaver's master mind came up with an idea. The loan of Rs. 1000/- can be given to the beneficiaries for purchase of yarn which the valued customer would supply and the amount could be credited to his own cash credit account and that he would guarantee repayment on monthly basis.

The whole arrangement the inspecting officer later found was defeating the very spirit of DRI loans. The 4% benefit was cornered by the rich middle man! The Manager was subsequently punished afterwards by the bank for having colluded with the customer to divert the benefit from the poor to the rich.

I became cautious. I must have long term plan for the weavers I thought. They must have superior looms and become independent. They could make material which the villagers in the area could buy from the weavers of cloth independent of the master weaver's strangle-hold. Right then what I thought I could do was to buy yarn in bulk and distribute. Later on I could think of upgrading technology. First they must borrow and repay and cultivate the banking habit. The rich farmers in the village wanted a particular variety of dhotis and sarees which were not made in the village because they were not of finer variety. I organized the weavers who needed the particular yarn and few changes in technology with the help of the government department. Needs of both the rich and the poor had been woven into the fabric of a self-sufficient village. It was an extension work without which bank credit would fail. 'Local production for local consumption.' Who said it? Gandhiji.

PS: *A local vernacular daily reported that a group of rich textile owners from Surat belonging to Warangal district are starting Rs.200 crore textile park in Manikonda to employ 2000 weavers.*

These men 40 years ago left as youngmen from their villages for Surat 40 years ago in search of employment, now coming back to pay back, with upgraded technology. Reversal of migration I contemplated in 1976 has come true only after 4 decades.

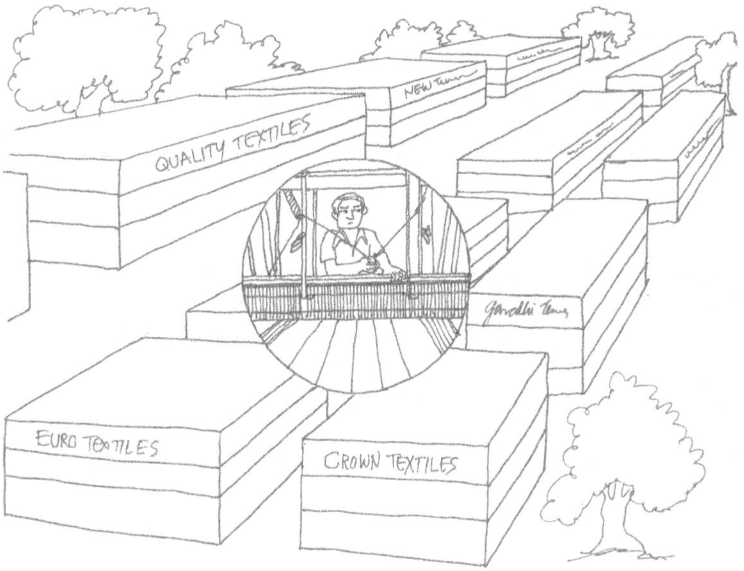

Episode 5

The government sponsored poultry units of 55 birds under live stock production programme popularly known as LPP. Scheduled Caste members of Thammadapalli wanted dairy animals to which the SFDA and Animal Husbandry department did not agree because they were interested in poultry units because of direction from the central government. They argued that the graded animal may not survive in the local climate. Moreover to rear a graded animal the beneficiary needed training for which the department was not ready. So they had to accept the poultry scheme.

Later, KVIC approached the farmers to take up biogas plant with 25% subsidy from them as incentive. KVIC chose this village because of our bank's presence. A group of farmers approached me for financing for biogas plant to biogas plant to whom the idea was sold by KVIC officers. They were ready to create simple mortgage in favour of the bank which, I thought, could be extended to all loans including crop loans they have been already availing from us. I took the opportunity to introduce graded animal through gobar gas scheme.

Episode 6

Next it was L.P.P. programme in villages-Joint Screening of applicants for a 55 bird poultry units for S/Cs and other weaker sections. Whichever may be the agency that gives subsidy, margins or credit the task of collection of applications fall on the village level worker who later was designated as V.D.O. – Village Development Officer under the block development officer (B.D.O.) of the *Samithi*. Today these posts are called Mandal Development Officer or MDO and VDOs. When our bank designed Village Vikas Kendras a new post was created. They were called cash collectors, an unimaginative title. Soon the name for the post was changed to agricultural assistant.

CREDIT CAMP

The list of beneficiaries was prepared in consultation of the *Sarpanch* and *Panchayati Raj* officials. The BDO was a smart officer. He had other targets to be achieved. One of them was vasectomy, a forceful campaign. The smart officer combined granting of loans from the bank. He excluded from the VDOs list all those who refused to undergo operation. This I came to know in the joint screening, when some poor people complained to me that their names were not included. I promised I would consider their cases at the end of the day's screening work. But their subsidy and margin money was linked to bank credit. I had to argue with the government official and got all eligible names are included. But there was limitation for poultry units, and hence some other schemes had to be identified to be screened at a later date.

Slowly I was learning the politics of weaker sections finance. Because I was determined to overcome every kind of obstacles; I did not lose heart. On the positive side I had learnt a great deal about the conditions in the village both social and economic. Family planning was good for them but not good the way the programme was taken up. I had read literature on the concept of change agent. He has to achieve results in spite of bureaucracy by sheer charisma. He has to play several roles, - collaborator, re-educator, emancipator, diagnostician, information specialist, builder of teams, leavener, evaluator: The interviews in the villages were very rewarding.

There was one, Ramu who did a somersault. 'I don't want birds, I want goats'. BDO sprung to action. He pushed Ramulu, told him to move out and called the next person. I had to stop him and told Ramu that he should meet me later. I made it my policy that no one should be denied credit even if he does not fit into any scheme.

The Deputy Director (Animal Husbandry) in the team told me that there was no subsidy for goats because RBI did not want to encourage loans to buy goats. When I asked for rationale some one quipped that 'goats were thieves'. They destroy plants and trees. Then *Sarpanch* came to the rescue of Ramu. He said he is going to buy the goats from some one in the village and the population of goats is not going make any change.

We completed the work of interviews and broke for lunch. When the government officials wanted to leave the place soon after lunch, I insisted that I must visit beneficiaries' homes. Birds need a decent place to live in the already poor hut. As we were inspecting the place next to their dwellings Ramu stopped me to show his hut.

'This is my house, this is my wife, and this is my son (10 year old) and these are the two goats I have he said.

'Give me 3 more goats. The boy can manage 5 goats, I don't have money to buy and give 3 more goats'. Some one said, 'you fool, you don't get subsidy'. His innocent reply was, 'I don't want subsidy, I want goats'.

I felt he was saying 'I want to live'. He added, 'my wife and myself go to work in fields of the farmers. This boy is wasted on two goats'.

In the year 1976 I did not think of the boy's education. Today we insist that he must go to school, but things in backward rural areas are no better even in 2010. Today the family would have migrated to far off places as construction workers. NREGS is an alternative in spite of all its malpractices the governments are struggling with.

Ramu came to the bank next day and got a loan of Rs.600 for 3 goats without subsidy or margin. He repaid with in a few months. I left Ramu to his fate. There are thousands of such stories, which the bank Managers had tackled and took spot decisions in those days, on which there was no data available with banks.

Episode 7

Before I adopted the villages in 1974, we had a District Collector who was a conferred I.A.S., a very senior, belonging to Y*adav* community. He, with the help of an MLA who belonged to the same community, started about hundred occupational and caste based cooperative societies of shepherds in the district. There was thus RBI approved scheme of 20 ewes and ram economically viable and bankable especially for the weaker sections among shepherds.

The scheme was meant for people from shepherd community, those who had no sheep and the person must belong to the community. Two villages 10 km away from the bank were allotted to my bank. The Collector wanted me to inaugurate the scheme.

I secured the services of my Bank's Agricultural Officer in Hyderabad for sanction and disbursement. The MLA arranged, for grand function in the village with the Collector as the chief guest. MLA made a political speech and the president and the community head of the predominantly shepherds village with no farming community, and a few piggeries and toddy tappers made speeches.

The head was also the richest shepherd, virtually controlling the entire village. Interestingly the whole stock of sheep had gathered along with the scantily dressed villagers for function.

It was a treat to my eye, as I never have had a panorama of sheep and shepherds, head-bending sheep and half naked shepherd and their typical dress code. It was quite an impressive display of live-stock wealth. The stocks always move together as one entity from one field to another field and are reared and hired collectively. Who owns and how many is difficult to say. All the dignitaries including the chief guest, the District Collector had a group photograph, with sheep included. Both the bureaucrat and people's representatives exhorted the members of the society to make the best use of bank credit and prove their credit worthiness. Bank's Agricultural Officer then explained the salient features of the bankable scheme and the purpose of uplifting the poorest among them. The scheme was meant for those unfortunate members who did not own any sheep.

Such individuals should make separate application to the bank. So saying he sat down little imagining that he was throwing a bomb shell. The president of society sprang to his feet and said in a firm voice.

'It is a common saying that shepherds are fools. I am surprised that bankers are worse than us. I can't understand the wisdom in giving loan to fellow who has no sheep at all. (He pointed to one particular person in the group). 'His father gave 50 sheep to him and he has none today. My father gave me ten sheep and I have now two hundred sheep. Whom do you lend, me or that fellow who squanders? Sir, let me make it clear to all here, give us Rs.50,000/- and leave it to us the task of distribution. We will repay in full with interest.' 'Don't split the community. Give the loan on our terms'.

Then I insisted that the bank would like to know where they are going to buy the additional flock and that they have to buy from Nellore breed only. The president did not like the idea. He defended that Nellore variety would not survive in their place. Then we came down to purchase of Rams, at least dozen of them. The ewes could be bought locally. The MLA played his politics and finally we yielded and gave Rs.50,000/- which they repaid promptly after two years, economic uplift of the weaker lot was left to the society's leaders and elders. I have no data about the upliftment of the poor.

A villager from another community confided with me that the money was used for money lending and that was how income was generated.

One more society we financed on similar lines from where recovery became a Herculean task and it was outstanding for years.

Episode 8

In 1976 I turned my attention to the urban poor in this semi-urban centre after 1975's thrust given by the government to the so called informal sector which employs largest number of people who largely borrow money from the private money lenders. The Sivaraman Committee on informal sector observed.. 'Innumerable small farmers, marginal farmers, artisans, small retail traders, petty vendors, hawkers, vegetable and fruit vendors and a host of self employed persons, is peculiar to a vastly populated country like ours'. There was another report by a banker – Thakkar Committee Report who looked at bank credit to the informal sector. Banks started special cells with field staff and simplified procedures and appraisal by means of schemes and simplified documentation.

It was a run-a-way success in attracting the small people who had been accustomed to borrow at 30 to 40% interest rate. The money lenders, I found, were the richer among them who had grown by their own enterprising qualities in course of time. They exploited the small fish in their own trade eg. vegetable and fruit vendor and street hawkers.

They lend and collect the installments back on a daily basis. Their recovery was always almost 100%. The field staff introduced by the bank brought to bank wealth of information and the complex nature of the strangle-hold on the poor people. The money lenders felt threatened by banks entering their domain with 4% interest. We had also found that these enterprising middlemen-money lenders were under the control of the office bearers of the association of petty traders.

I was aware of the system of Multani micro lending. These Multani Association of money lenders in the cities like Bombay were discounting hundis (clean) with banks as refinance. Today we find MFIs getting a line of credit from banks.

The purpose of Nationalization of banks was to eliminate these middlemen and lend directly to the each individual. We have a name for it now – Financial Inclusion.

The small borrower cell was inaugurated by the District Collector who became our spokesperson for the initiatives we had taken. The popularity of the bank grew by leaps and bounds.

The Collector, one day, requested me to come to his office and put a proposal before me. 'Look Mr.Rao, I have received Rs.50,000/- from Social Welfare department to be used for releasing bonded labour. Each released labourer is to be given Rs.1000/- to rehabilitate himself. We have decided to give them one cycle-rickshaw instead of cash. But these people must cultivate thrift habit. I want your bank open Savings Bank accounts and let your field staff collect everyday a small amount and credit into their accounts'. I said, 'Our field staff collects only the loan installments and not savings for which I need permission from higher authorities.' 'But I have a suggestion to make. I shall give them loan for buying cycle rickshaws and the field staff would collect the installments on a daily or weakly basis. The administration may deposit Rs. 1000/- each in the savings account or fixed deposit. The beneficiaries will be allowed and be entitled for the amounts when the loan amount is fully recovered! The section head who was also present in the chamber of the Collector was prompt to tell us that the rules did not permit. There would be audit objection, he said.

The Collector was sold to the idea. He told the Assistant that he would take care of the audit objection and that they would put through the novel scheme. The collector had his target achieved and the bank got a bulk deposit and weaker section target accomplished. On January 26th 1977 the scheme was launched with fan fare. I don't know if there was an audit issue for the Collector but the bank inspector felt that the Manager had exceeded his authority! Spot and novel decisions could put the bank Manager in a spot!

Episode 9

During my joint screening I found that many small and marginal farmers applied for purchase of plough bullocks. After some negotiation with the government and the beneficiaries I changed these applications into loans for digging new wells and deepening the existing because I was advised by ARDC officers not to encourage plough bullocks loans.

My strategy was to combine village adoption financing agriculture, allied activities, and government sponsored schemes and formulate a project under ARDC (Agricultural Re-finance and Development Corporation) which later became NABARD because that would validate my efforts and ensure transparency. For the ARDC to approve the minor irrigation schemes would require Ground Water department clearance and the same was not forth coming. The applications were sanctioned in all other aspects in one village – Konachalam and ready for disbursement. I was planning to visit Ground Water department office in Hyderabad to get the clearance. Visiting officers and chasing papers had become part of my routine. If this was cleared then REC (Rural Electrification Corporation) would do their part to electrify the adopted villages.

As I was wondering what to do, a phone call came from the Project Officer, SFDA (Small Farmers Development Agency) with a request to bail him out. This was not first time he asked for my help. A few days before the Secretary Mr.Sankaran (who passed away recently) of Social Welfare department came to the place to visit a village adopted by SBI to inspect the common well of dalit families. It was a Sunday and SBI Manager was not in town. SFDA officer who had to take Mr.Sankaran to the village wanted me to accompany him, which I did. I requested Mr.Sankaran to visit our villages but it did not happen. On another occasion this it was the Cabinet Minister, Rural Development was visiting the place and a loan mela was to be organized. In those days these were known as credit camps. At that time Congress party was ruling in the State and Janatha Party at the Centre. The Congress must prove that they were pro-poor. An ex-communist, the minister was known for his integrity and I knew it. Hence I wanted to cooperate. But there was a hitch. The village I chose was having a Communist *Sarpanch* and it was also much more interior than other villages and there were no motorable roads. Only a petrol jeep can take us to the place. BDO was adamant. I was helpless because me and the Collector decided that in these camps only processed applications should be considered. It appeared the minister himself welcomed my suggestion. Still the Ground Water department clearance was must for the sanction.

I traveled to Hyderabad in SFDA vehicle and contacted Ground Water department and sorted out the issue which is the next episode. For now, about the loan mela which had given tremendous fillip and reinforcement to me and my bank, first I had to clear the doubts of the BDO who was apprehensive that the Sarpanch with Communist background would not cooperate.

I contacted the Konachalam Sarpanch and requested him to reassure the BDO. The *Sarpanch* told me that in the history of the village not even a District Collector had ever visited it. If a Cabinet Minister were to visit, he could not do otherwise than make the occasion memorable. He did justice to his promise. About 3000 people gathered. Neighbouring village rich farmers came in tractors and bullock carts in large numbers. The minister and his retinue were delighted to see the

grand reception. The dais was arranged and further a seat was provided to me which I refused because I thought it not wise to share the stage meant to be a political meeting.

The meeting started promptly with the welcome address by the *Sarpanch*. He did not mince the words: 'Minister is here because of the Bank Manager…' The Congress MLA took credit for Congress and Indira Gandhi who nationalized the banks. Then the minister stood to speak. He was not allowed to proceed because they wanted the Bank Manager to speak before him. I declined at first but the minister had to persuade me to speak; otherwise he said he may not be able to speak. I yielded and was very brief asking the crowds to make the bank Nationalization a success by making best use of money borrowed and repay in time. Then the minister spoke and the speech was most memorable to me. He said: 'I have never seen such expression of gratitude to a Bank Manager in my entire political career. I wish other Bank Managers emulate his example. I wish all Bank Managers visit this block and see for themselves the exemplary work done by this service-minded banker'. He added in typical politician's style that 'if the Bank Manager were to contest for elections, his opponents would lose their deposits.' He was quick to add that may not be interested in politics. Later on, I was told, this minister spread my name and my banks name wherever he went in the state.

Episode 10

Jagadishwaraiah, a coconut merchant doing business next to the bank's premises had a Recurring Deposit which matured. After taking cash of the principal amount he asked me to remit the interest to Lord Venkateswara of Tirupati. He agreed to my suggestion that he would get equal amount of *punya* if he donates it to the poor. I told him that there were some poor *rickshaw wallahs* who are very prompt in repaying their installments for the loans obtained from the bank. 'The coming season being summer' I said, 'I will spend the interest amount on buying sun-hats and present them.' He readily agreed and I made Jagadishwaraiah to present the hats to the prompt borrowers in an impressive meeting with staff and a few customers. I sent a press release to the District Public Relation Officer who got the news item published in the State level vernacular daily.

Jagadishwaraiah was thrilled to find his name in the newspaper. He came running with the newspaper and said that the Lord was pleased. But a few other traders around the bank were not so pleased. They complained to me that I was being partial. I promised the aggrieved customer that they would get their turn. But there was one big customer who threw a cheque on my table and asked me to spend on the poor borrowers. I had to refuse the offer telling him that my intention was to see that the donors do it themselves as partners in the schemes for poverty alleviation and self employment. While our bank was gaining popularity with the have-nots, the well to-do were under the impression that banks were throwing their money to the poor for whom they had nothing but contempt. I, used those occasions to address both the rich and the poor explaining banks intention.

Episode 11

Rickshaw loans were given only for brand new rickshaws, by making payment to the dealer. But I had to deviate from the rule in the case of Sayalu who has been plying in the city for a few years a used rickshaw not for passengers but for carrying vegetables to the market. He approached our field staff who denied credit for second hand rickshaw. He wanted to buy the rickshaw which he had taken on hire basis.

He came to the bank and directly requested me to consider a loan for Rs.500 to enable him to buy the same vehicle and he would pay Rs.2/- per day to the bank and clear it in less than a year. I allowed the loan outside the schematic lending. He brought the owner to the bank to receive Rs.400/- and the balance he kept for repairs.

He repaid the loan within 6 months but continued to remit into his S/B account and went on accumulating the savings up to Rs.2000/-. We did not notice it till he came to me with a new request. This time it was a much bigger test for us. He wanted a loan of Rs.2000/- to buy back his land which he sold and migrated to the city. I was actually delighted at the prospect. This was the unarticulated aim of rural development. Those who migrate to the cities and towns because life was unbearable in the villages must eventually go back to where they belong-to the land and cultivation. I had powers up to Rs.8000/- to lend for unsecured advances temporarily but the purpose was long term. He would not be able to repay in the near future and there was no scheme for buying the land. It was also cumbersome to verify the transaction which involved going to a place which was not one adopted village. Both my joint Manager and me agreed to give because of the honesty of the hardworking poor fellow.

We told Sayalu to bring back the sale deed after registration and keep it in the bank. After a week Sayalu came back deposited the entire money because the deal was not struck. The price was too much. So, he reconciled himself to carry on as second hand cargo rickshaw rider. By coincidence about the same time the Director Social Welfare Department Hyderabad visited our branch to compliment us on various schemes we had taken up. I told her Sayalu's story when she (Director) asked me to send a photo of Sayalu with Rickshaw.

We obtained and sent a copy to her in Hyderabad. The Department runs a magazine titled 'Andhra Pradesh' in which the Sayalu story with the photo was published. As a Manager I came close to the conditions of poverty and diverse nature of its faces. We can't design bankable schemes for everyone. Only Managers should use discretion with courage and compassion.

Episode 12

Narasamma, vegetable vendor who was regularly borrowing Rs.300 at one time repaying in 90 days, approached the bank for a loan of Rs,.1000/- after about a year.

The staff found no rationale in asking for such a jump when her operations did not warrant the Rs.1000/-. Then she approached the peon to convince the Manager about her honesty and that she would repay in one year. When the matter came to me I asked the peon to go to her house and find out her living conditions and the real reason for the increased loan amount. The bank staff was concerned about the place of business and not any other details. There was no KYC in 1970s. He came back to tell me that they were not very poor people and that they live in a tiled house which was badly damaged and she was asking money for repairs to the house. He felts he was the only earning member. We did grant her loan for 20 months duration as per the scheme. The inspector could not find out any irregularity.

It was difficult to separate the productive needs and the consumption needs in poor families, urban or rural. Total needs based on repaying, capacity with longer period for repayment. The honesty can be presumed. That is what a benevolent banker does.

Episode 13

Cheralu was one of the cycle rickshaw borrowers from a neighbouring rural area belonging to S/C category. He was one of those who was rewarded with sun-hat by the coconut vendor for his promptness. He approached the bank during the tenure of loan for an additional loan of Rs.200/- for repairs. We had no scheme for contingencies. After the interview with him the bank peon came and told me that the real reason was daughter's marriage. I called him back and gave the loan under the newly introduced Consumption Loan scheme. He then, had to pay daily Rs.3/- in place of Rs. 2/- installment to which he agreed. Had the bank not given the additional loan he would have had to beg, borrow or steal' as the phrase goes. He might even sell the asset. Marriage is sacrosanct to all, for the poor man it is much more.

What is most interesting was that the fellow came to bank and paid in full the second loan with in a couple of days after the wedding. He received cash presents, part of which was enough to repay.

These small events made all the staff members share the same values I cherished. It is better to trust and be cheated, than not trust at all. (Johnson)

Episode 14

One day the peon told me that Krishna who borrowed to buy new cycle Rickshaw was seen plying an old one. Obviously he sold off the new one and was plying a hired one, we thought. I asked the peon to catch him and bring him to the bank. The staff interrogated him and extracted a promise that he would pay off the entire loan or else he would be handed over to police.

Caught in the MIRE

M – Miserable

I – In deep debt

R – Recurring medical expenses

E – Emaciated state

It was only a threat but they thought that the truth will come out. One of the field staff members accompanied him to find out his home and living conditions to report to me. They came back to me saying it was a gone case. 'We can forget about the loan recovery and the man. He has a sick wife, bed-ridden and an invalid sister. He was the only earning member in the family. He had sold the rickshaw for medical expenses. No two cases are similar. It is for such cases that Credit Guarantee scheme is required. We have to-day, health and medical expenses schemes and many other government schemes.

Episode 15

In course of L.P.P. identification and credit camp I often came across cases like this one. The camp used to be conducted in the open. Everybody knows everybody's problems. There is no secrecy in villages. I used to summon the entire family to the extent possible. After clearing a few applications one fellow burst out; I have changed my mind. Don't ask me questions. I want a loan of Rs.2500/-.

I will repay without fail. We are a family of honest people. Give me cash; the government officials asked him to step aside and make way for the next man. It was always men we were considering, not women. But in these camps wives accompanied men. Now it was the turn of the wife to appeal to me. She said Rs.2000/- is enough. 'We spend Rs.500/- for deepening the well. One of our bullocks is dead. We will sell it off and buy a pair. We buy a bag of urea.' After a minute the man adds 'I have to repay a few hand loans'. This is the reality – ground reality. No one scheme will fit all of them. The family was already mired in poverty and indebtedness. No single scheme is going to get the family out of the rut. The poor man, always, had been borrowing. At any point of time he was indebted before he came to the bank.

* * * * *

Case 6 – Narratives – GP (Episodes 1 to 9)

Episode 1

I was posted as a Branch Manager in a small Rural Branch during the period of post Nationalization of banks.

Within a week of my joining duty an aged man, who was a small borrower from one of the adopted villages of the bank approached for a loan limit of Rs.500/- for duck-rearing purpose under DRI scheme.

When I enquired about him, I came to know that he had borrowed previously for 5-6 times with a loan limit of Rs.500/-. Knowing his promptness in repayments, I insisted that he should get a loan limit of Rs.1000/- so that he would raise his income for the family, but this great man refused to accept the offer for fear of default. At last, he availed the loan limit of Rs.500/- and continued with his prompt repayments.

One morning, before opening of the bank, a young man, son of the borrower, conveyed the news of death of the father and wanted to settle the balance amount in the loan account (i.e. about Rs.250/-) before the funeral function. His son conveyed that his father should not be a defaulter to the bank and the message of the defaulter would spread in the village and spoil their family name. He has settled the balance amount and took the counter-foil and showed it to his villagers for evidence of 'no dues.'

The entire staff members paid tributes to this old man, by participating in the funeral. *This message spread throughout the village and the bank got very good name and prominence.*

Episode 2

Sincerity is remembered by farmers and poor villagers.

Here is an incident; but an astonishing one. When I was Branch Manager in a rural branch I had extended all help to village farmers and small business people.

After three decades of service in the bank I had just entered a temple with my family members one evening at about 6 pm. I approached the nearby shop keeper and requested him to look after footwear of my family members.

Without looking at my face the shopkeeper was telling that he had heard the voice which was familiar to him.

Immediately he recognised me and showed all out help as he has grown from a small street *vendor* to a big *shopkeeper/owner* because of the help extended by me and staff three decades back.

Street Vendor to Shop Owner

Episode 3

In the early period, no bank had any specific schemes for agricultural sector as feared default. But most of the villagers treated the Branch Manager as a friend, philosopher and guide since the Branch Manager alone could sanction loan and release the funds in time. Timely assistance' gained importance among villagers.

When a farmer approached the bank for a loan amount of Rs.5000/- for laying the pipe line for lifting the water through his neighbour's land, the Regional authorities instructed the branch that there was no scheme for this purpose. In order to save the standing crops as a *permanent solution*, the branch considered the loan amount and helped the farmer for laying the pipe line for lifting the water for irrigation and the scheme was implemented, later on various agricultural schemes for lending purpose were formulated, one among which was minor irrigation. The bold and timely action of the Branch Manager was appreciated by district authorities and farmers from all villages. Rules have to be bent to serve people. Rules may not be violated but timely actions with utmost honesty gained good-will among rural masses. Branch Manager and staff are always respected when they visit the villages after two or three decades. There is no need to restrict the lending activities by quoting prescribed rules/sections.

Episode 4

'A friend in need, is a friend indeed'- is true. The timely assistance plays a great role and creates a psychological effect among all sorts of borrowers in a village where a bank's branch functions with devoted, sincere, honest and hard working staff members. No rigid rules or bank's procedure, or book of instructions are to be effectively followed except playing sympathetic role or with a customer sense in all developmental activities.

A *dalit*, a very small borrower, with half acre land holding, with little primary education, approached me one day at the bank after *office hours* i.e. after 5pm and requested me to sanction a loan amount of Rs.500/- without any NOC certificate from Primary Co-operative society and other documents relating to the land holding for planning paddy. The period of transplanting was over and the plants in the nursery would not sustain for transplanting, if delayed.

Noting the urgency of the small farmer in the village, a crop loan amount of Rs.500/- was sanctioned on the next day, out of sympathy and need and the amount was given in full, as cash against instructions. After a gap of 3 months, the borrower came to the bank in the evening and conveyed the happiness about the yield of paddy in his land and settled the loan amount in full. He was so grateful to the bank and spread the message to all farmers that the bank was so helpful if all are honest in repayments and the customer was a good ambassador for the bank. The timely assistance is an important message to all the bankers serving in the rural areas.

An experienced and aged District Co-ordinator told the farmer that the banker was the only person who could lend on the spot; others were following lengthy and unwanted procedures. It is a great lesson that all staff members learnt. After two or three decades of service, each member of the staff had occupied the executive position in the bank/other banks.

Timely help and devoted service never go waste/in one's life and always "learn to treat others in the same way you would want them to treat you".

Episode 5

On 28th April, 1978 at about 1.45 pm, at the closing time of business hours two persons entered the premises and requested the cashier to exchange cut-notes of ten rupees. As usual the dedicated cashier of the branch requested them to join the cut notes by offering gum. Within a short time one of them pretended to offer pasted cut notes to the cashier. But he pulled out a big and long knife and threatened the cashier and asked him to hand over the entire cash lying with him. The cashier quickly closed cash drawer and that time the second person inside the premises took out his revolver and threatened all the staff to raise their hands.

The cashier was threatened at knife point by the other standing at the cash counter but no one reacted to their threats. They were very much upset and the person with the revolver fired one round which hit the abdomen of the sub-staff (peon) and tried to escape from the premises. But in a *swift action*, lifted the chair and hit the gunman forcibly. He tried to escape along with the third person who was waiting out side on a motor cycle. The villagers caught them with the help of the bank staff. A passerby who helped in catching the dacoits was stabbed in the back. Subsequently with the help of villagers' both the injured were admitted in the hospital and they recovered. The Bank and police honoured the bank staff for their bravery, protection of money and customers' jewels.

The bank staff must always be alert and agile and must identify a customer from a stranger; vigilance is the key.

Episode 6

Generally in rural areas the farmers, artisans, labourers, small business people have the tendency of making payments to the cooperative society, banks as a *second option* (second priority) for self needs/requirements, when money comes to their hand after the harvest. If they want to make payment to the bank, they want an assurance/guarantee. Bankers supposed to sanction the loan immediately.

This had been the tendency for long before Nationalization of banks.

In one of the rural branches we suffered a lot because of more than 60% to 70% bad debts. The farmers were not *aware* of the advantage of bank (loans); did not know how to utilize the services. A few farmers were also *dodging* useful defaulters.

One day, a leading farmer enquired about the small machine kept in the bank i.e. the ultra violet machine that was kept for detecting alterations and forgery of cheques and drafts. I explained the use of the machine.

But (mischievous) staff members told a farmer that the machine was installed at the branch in order to find out the 'truth' from the village borrowers (lie detecting machine) who availed the loans. They said, 'if the machine shows white light, the customer is honest' if blue (ultra violet) comes out, the farmers are telling lies about crops, money realised etc.

The farmer was afraid and spread the wrong message in the villages in bank's area about the '*Truth Finding Machine'*

All defaulters realized the truth and started making payments. The recovery was more than 90% and had its own effect. The false 'threat' rectified, the people responded admirably.

The staff learnt a lesson and started responding honestly, sympathetically and genuinely.

Episode 7

The so called 'prudent banker', an experienced *metro* banker who always entertained negative thoughts, a hatred (probably) for the destitute human beings who are suffering their past *karma.*

He had no kindness without which you cannot play any role in rural areas. It is virtual antipathy he suffered from. In addition, his competence in decision making was in question. With the result the rural people, farmers, businessmen and self-employed were vexed with the man.

The branch was on the verge of closing. However, a few of the farmers did not stop coming to the bank. A leading farmer approached the 'prudent' Manager for a crop loan. The clever and evasive Manager devised a novel way to reject the loan application.

He asked the farmer to have a close look at his face and tell him which of his two eyes is artificial and which one is the natural eye. If the farmer succeeds in answering correctly, he would get the loan! Perhaps the Manager did not calculate the risk he was taking.

The already vexed farmer told the surprised Manager correctly that the Manager's right eye was artificial for he did not see any life in it. But more was to come. He told the unhelpful Manager that his left eye, is reddish, and reveals unsympathetic nature of the man.

The Manager kept his word and told the farmer that he was prepared to sanction the loan. But the farmer was not prepared to take it!

Episode 8

A branch in Tamil Nadu on the border of A.P was serving villagers of both states. One leading farmer from across the border wanted to deposit harvest proceeds in the branch. Those were the days when it was difficult even to get a deposit of Rs.5000. The man made many enquiries to ensure the safety of the money and liquidity i.e. prompt withdrawal of money deposited. Banker used to think of trusting the villagers. But villagers had their doubts about the solvency of banks.

The Branch Manager and staff visited his house and found him to be a very wealthy person and highly respected in the village. The visit paid dividends.

The man brought a basket of mangoes to the branch next day at 3p.m and handed it to the cashier. Beneath mangoes there were bundles of cash! After receiving the deposit receipt the farmer-asked whether he could withdraw the next day! Assurance was not enough. He could probably test the bank. The bank had to keep sufficient cash balance always for such contingencies.

Episode 9

Purpose of Nationalization, as we all know, was to raise the standard of living of rural poor with bank credit. In spite of the laudable intentions the benefits of government initiatives were not reaching the poor.

Hundreds of loans for the purchase of buffalos were given with 25% subsidy from government agencies with a tie-up arrangement and resulted in hundred percent recoveries. Every body was happy. But nature can play truant spoiling man's designs. Draught during summer made it difficult to procure the feed for the animals and food for the farmers. The Manager summoned his staff and brainstormed solutions to meet the crisis which he saw as his own and his banks and his staff's. There was unanimous decision-grant a term loan of Rs.500/- to buy fodder/grains from outside (1981/82). That saved the lives of animals and their owners. The branch also arranged for whole sale grain supply so that the poor man and poor animals were saved.

Leading from the front (Action)

Leading by consensus

* * * * *

Case 7 – Narratives – GKR

I had an opportunity to work in Shadnagar as an Accountant where the Manager was an Agriculture officer. I used to go for post-sanction inspection to the fields of farmers.

Although the bank financed for paddy and other crops, the farmers used to grow-mosambi, guava, and mangoes to a limited extent. Our bank did not have any scheme for horticulture at that time. I discussed the matter with the Manager and we began financing for horticulture under known schemes like land development. This deviation helped us develop good business.

In 1980 I was transferred to a rural branch in a backward district as Branch Manager. By this time the bank had a scheme for horticulture. I adopted just four villages and took complete responsibility of servicing them by identifying the needs of both the rich and the poor. I educated and motivated the progressive farmers to take up horticulture keeping in mind the climate and water scarcity of the area. I used my Agricultural Officer for it and clubbed it with my own exposure to it in Shadnagar area.

Along with rich farmers, I encouraged small farmers who were hard working and sincere. These farmers could reap good returns and some of them even bought wet land under tank irrigation.

I had also an obligation to finance weaker section under DRI-for piggery and other sponsored schemes. This helped the branch make profit because head office paid the branch the difference in interest for normal advances. I took initiative and prepared the list of DRDA beneficiaries in my four villages and asked government agency to go by it. They were happy to accept it.

I ignored my superior's unusual restriction on my freedom. I do not wish to speak about it beyond this. My business in 1980 crossed 1 crore. I was transferred to Kolkatta as a punishment with out reason. I had to leave the place abruptly without formal handing over charge to the next Manager. At the intervention of the Officers Association I got a posting to Cuttack.

There I was given the task of setting house keeping work that was in arrears for six years. I cleared it in 3 months. Then I was asked to go to Rourkela and take up house keeping - pending for 12 years. I resisted the posting but the zonal head persuaded me to take up the work but I put some conditions. A few staff members were suspended for malpractices without whose help I could not clear the arrears of work. I called the erring staff to the guest house where I was staying and told them that if they promise to help me in clearing the arrears, I would try and get lesser punishment for them. I had received help from employees union also. I made the zonal head accept my proposal and enquiries were conducted and completed as I desired. It took me just 4 months to complete the task and in return I bargained for a transfer to my native state. I was looking forward for retirement so that I could go back to my native village and start *horticulture.* Some jealous officials in the bank, tried to tarnish my image but they could not because I always honest and asserted my rights.

Now even after 13 years of my retirement, I represent the association of horticulturists in Mahboobnagar district. I must thank the bank for whatever I am now. I arrange meetings and invite agricultural scientists to discuss with farmers their problems and suggest solutions.

* * * * *

SECTION – II - FOLLOWERS
Case 8 – Narratives
Present day Managers

The most important change in the branch system of a bank is technology even in the rural area.

Most operations have been computerized. In the early days the biggest problem of mass-banking was the manual work of book entries and documentation and balancing books which the inspecting officers found it next to impossible to verify in the stipulated time. Most-documents remained unfilled. There were some improvements like non-banking working day when the staff could complete back log when the customer transactions were not allowed. With the computerization this non-banking a working day became paid holiday to a few. But the dedicated Managers and the team used this day for visits to villages and meeting people. They needed leadership qualities to get all the staff members involved in 'barefoot banking'.

I have included the sharing of those who were committed to the task of rural development. We can divide the present day rural Branch Managers into two categories. One set of Managers talked at length about the good work they have been doing with positive results which was their rewards. The others were not as enthusiastic to share their experiences as much as the first category. Interestingly the former group was Managers of rural areas where the agriculture is progressive with assured irrigation facilities and favourable monsoon. The latter are from rain fed and drought prone areas. The former easily accomplish their targets and even mobilize deposits. Even their lending to weaker sections was satisfactory. Most importantly their motivation came from the high percentage of recoveries. Even in the area of SHGs financing there had been very good results till 2009. Now they were worried (2010). Till 2009 the MFIs presence was very small. There are branches in East Godavari district of Andhra Pradesh who have financed 600 to 800 SHGs – first dose, second dose, even third dose–as they call repeated financing. They may soon introduce credit card system, a running account with repayment and drawals and minimize the interest burden. The burden of SHGs visiting bank in large numbers, women with infants and small children to execute the renewal of documents may be reduced. They are slowly taking courage to finance the tenant groups without security. By and large there is enthusiasm and pride and satisfaction of helping the cause of elimination of poverty.

But the real poverty is in the rain-fed, arid lands with vast majority of small and marginal farmers and agricultural labour.

Though they say that they were doing their duty, they feel there was no charm in working in such rural backward areas. They have more challenges with few rewards. Their biggest worry is that with poor recoveries, no deposit growth and non-achieving the targets, their career prospects were in jeopardy. If the management appreciated their difficulties and look at the hard work and sincerity they have been showing, they don't mind doing their part and would like to leave results to god.

They all speak of all staff working as one team, helping each other complete the task. Almost everybody attends to customers with consideration for their plight. At times when they had to do time bound lending, recoveries, re-scheduling or agriculture debt relief (ADR) work they worked day and night literally. All of them agree that the old system of specialized cells with exclusive field staff, agricultural officers etc. were the best part of the earlier schemes.

They do speak of the branch's history and the predecessors about whom the new Managers learn from the sub-staff who remain in the branch for decades like permanent fixtures of the branch. All Managers without exception told me that they used them as 'information specialists' of the branch; what they know even regional offices do not know. They speak of one Manager, in most cases, the first Manager as one who made a great impact on the villagers.

They made a distinction amongst Managers who lived in the village and won the people's admiration. But most of those who commuted daily from the city were not spoken very high of by the sub-staff or the villagers. Then there were those who neglected the branch and left the branch in bad shape. They also speak of men who lived in the village and restored the image of the branch.

There have been some who maintained and never increased loan portfolio. They were pre-occupied only with recoveries. There were a few who went to villages organized *gram sabhas* to educate and negotiate. There were those who, with agricultural background and qualification attracted the farming community's attention as a guide in agricultural operations.

One Manager is said to have given gold loan in the midnight to save a marriage. The bride's party could not arrange for cash in time. The groom's party wanted to walk out when the Manager called his cashier and arranged for cash. Next day both the parties thanked the Manager though it was irregular in every sense of bank's policy and procedures and practices. The people in the area remember the Manager even after 20 years. The Manager took voluntary retirement vexed with the frequent transfers including out of the State transfers. When I contacted him to give more details about the incident which earned him the status of god he requested me to spare him. He refused to speak about it.

In the same branch the present Manager told me that though the villagers don't speak of it, there was a Manager who had close relations with a local influential person and granted loans-all benami transactions; the money raised was shared by both the persons. They became bad debts and villagers slowly revealed the truth. Nothing can be hidden in the rural areas. Everybody knows everybody else. Before the bank authorities came to know of it the Manager had retired and the loans were written off through ADRs. All sins are washed out by the affirmative action of government. There are others who were summarily dismissed but the man was reinstated through court order.

There are Managers who have been working in different rural branches even beyond the mandatory number of years for different reasons. A few continue because the place is the outskirts of urban area from where he could commute. These places on soon become part of the city still carry rural, label. They prefer the rural branch because they have become experts in agricultural finance. Others want to avoid out of State posting. For all purposes the family and children's education and aged parents-are variables that come into decision making. They are not keen on getting promotions.

There are some agricultural graduates who enjoy doing their professional work in doing agriculture extension work keeping themselves in contact with the professional peers in governments and university. They are ready to take up any initiatives and innovations the bank keeps trying. The management invariably use those branches – be it farmers clubs, consultancy counters or financing joint-liability groups. Recently, one had Manager told me that they celebrated the 40th anniversary of the rural branch in a marriage hall which was attended by over 500 farmers. It was also graced by NABARD and government officials who praised the bank. When I discussed continuity of good work – image etc he quipped that his branch has always kept the bank's flag up by several predecessors till date. Another bigger public sector bank which opened their branch in the nearby village had to remain second all these 40 years. I have included in this book two of the earlier Managers stories of this historic branch.

* * * * *

Case 9 – Narratives – Srinivas

'I have taken over charge of this branch one year 4 months back as I had to undergo compulsory rural tenure for at least 2 years. I am not an Agricultural Officer, but I have gained considerable insight into the problems of the people of the rural area because I have taken it with a positive attitude and intention to gain experience serving in the rural areas. Now I know the problems of the people here and I feel I am doing my service adequately.

This is a single crop, paddy, area with a few tenants and others as owners of the lands. Some time back the government gave lands to the landless whose needs also are met adequately. I have now a lady Agricultural Officer, a direct recruit officer with one year experience. I have been financing as per targets all the government sponsored schemes, particularly Self Help Groups of women. The District Collector instructed his men and machinery to assist the bank in recovering the loans. The experience is very good.

There is seven level in the promotion, maintenance and control of SHGs'.

'Recently our branch is selected on an experimental basis for Village Consultancy Cell. It is a counter which is a single window counter to meet all the needs of the farmers other than credit needs. The objectives are manifold, demanding additional staff strength of right quality. Yet I feel this is an opportunity for me to improve the image of the bank which is already quite high. We have also started farmers club on the foundation day on 20th July'.

P.S.

During his predecessor's time the District Collector was so much dissatisfied that he threatened to see that the branch is closed!

Author

* * * * *

Case 10–Narrative

Manager of another Bank

I met a Chief Manager of another bank, a post graduate in agriculture who had 25 years of service, concurred with me that almost all villagers were honest and if banker trusts them, they will trust the banker.

'Trust does not mean promises but keeping up promises. Willful defaulter is the name bankers gave them. We borrowed the phrase from the cooperatives. In most cooperatives – primary producer societies, the management committees were in the hands of dominant communities who cornered all the facilities. They were the people who capitalized on the principle 'all for each and each for all' with hypocrisy and double standards.' It was a case of fish rotting from the head. This legacy was passed on to the SHGs and JLGs as well. Even among the women the same masculine dominance seems to have crept. He narrated to me that 'when he took charge there was one pending case of a defaulter, small farmer. 'My predecessor obtained permission from the Regional Office to file suit and handed over this one as urgent and left' he shared.

'I kept the matter pending for one month during which time I contacted and interacted with him with consideration and compassion. He came with a story as to how he got into trouble with the predecessor who was vindictive and branded him as willful defaulter and an obstinate fellow. I asked him to forget the past and if he pays his ducs, I would consider fresh loan and restore normal relations. He agreed and the matter was settled amicably.'

'We may not blame any one for such casualties. But the banker must rise above such pettiness and be magnanimous is the lesson both of us drew from our experiences.'

* * * * *

Case 11 – First Person Accounts AVL

"I took charge of the branch in the year 1995. Earlier I worked as cashier for 3 years from 1978 to 1981-in another branch opened at the same time in the same backward area. As a cashier, I used to complete the work in the cash department first and later attended to other clerical work.

I was very much interested in attending to field work and accompanied the officers whenever it was possible. I feel the people in the area were honest but innocent and ignorant. The farming community was limited to a village or two. There were other communities engaged in sheep rearing, piggeries and toddy tapping for their livelihood.

After a lapse of 15 years I became the Manager of this branch and was shocked to see in what a bad shape the bank was. Bank's image was very low, there were over dues and time-barred debts. The reasons were many. The branch had the good and the bad and the indifferent Managers. The first Manager was "GOD" to the villagers. There were a few bad Managers according to the villagers and / or the senior management. It was the indifferent Managers, the self-centred, passing the time kind, commuting from the city daily who created a problem and did more damage to the bank's image than the bad ones. In fact they made the bank non existent for the villagers who stopped visiting the branch. But I do not blame the Managers completely. There was another reason for the situation.

A few years ago, naxals blasted the bank premises which was housed in Panchayat Office in the village proper. With the permission of district authorities the branch had to be shifted to a small town, 15 to 20 kms away from the village. The branch was out of sight for the villagers and hence out of their minds.

In spite of repeated requests from both the villagers and District Collectors, nothing happened in this regard. The indifferent Managers behaved more like official liquidators as if the branch was closed. Whenever a new Manager comes the word goes to villagers, reviving their hopes. In the case of indifferent Managers, they encountered cold reception and nothing happened further. When I took charge, a few farmers from the villages walked in with fresh proposals. The government had been regularly announcing some bankable schemes with subsidies and margins etc.

Taking the cue from the government initiatives these farmers were approaching the bank. Having understood that official liquidator style did not and would not work, I changed my style leaning more towards lending.

But there is one temporary sub-staff who has been working in the branch and who is a native of the same village, Mr. Achari, started cautioning me saying that the applicants were from the same family of earlier defaulters whose loan amounts have already been written off. While making a note of his advice, I began perusing village level record books and keeping a list of early defaulters. The previous Managers were concentrating only on their recoveries, *suspending lending altogether*. I focused my attention on fresh lending. I decided to give loans and attract the villagers to the bank again. I used to tell the callers that I would visit the village the next morning and requested them to call others to revive their connection with the bank. My second objective, which was always at the back of my mind, was to get in touch with all those defaulters and ensure some recoveries. It was achieved because when we reached the village the next morning at 7.00 a. m. All the defaulters were there eagerly waiting to talk to me. They openly apologised for their mistakes and they expressed a wish to re-establish their connection with the bank. They started giving a lot of explanation for their past behavior and I gave them a patient hearing and started negotiating for recoveries luring them with proposals of fresh and higher loans . At the same time, I disposed of the eligible applications in quick time.

That was demonstration enough for all the villagers that I keep up my word. The transparency worked wonders. More and more people fell in line by making payments in to their overdue accounts. By the time I left the place I could recover even written off debts to the tune of Rs. 2 lakhs! I believe that there was a credibility gap, a phrase I learnt in the training programmes, between the bank and the people whom we often brand as willful defaulters.

During this period I took the bank to the village by carrying cash up to Rs. 5 lacs at a time to the village using public transport at great personal risk. I could do all this because of the exemplary cooperation from within the branch – my staff who worked with a spirit of service and commitment. We were a cohesive team consisting of newly recruited young people. It was a brief but a memorable period in my career which is going to end in another 5 years."

* * * * *

Case 12 – First Person Accounts PSN

I joined the bank in 1984 as a clerk in Gujarat. After 10 years I had an opportunity to compete for all India Officers' position. I secured the highest mark in the written exam at the zonal level. I was lucky to get a chance to work under a most competent officer who guided me in my job.

I was posted as Planning Officer and the superior gave me ample freedom. There was no system of seeking help from the Head Office Planning Department. It was good in a way because I could take the initiative and innovate in improving the branches' profitability through systematic study and planning. I studied the potential from the environment with the help of the Branch Manager and Officer. I made field visits for assessing the area potentiality. Even the branches appreciated my work for it helped them in preparing their strategies on the lines we suggested. Some areas had potential for NRI deposits and other areas for savings and term deposits. There was clear direction of efforts for the branches for the first time.

I discovered I had natural flair for data collection and in depth studies. I enjoyed every minute of original work I embarked on my duty with the motivation of superiors. It involved a lot of hard work, touring and late-sitting in the office. People like me who had no influence with the local leadership had to accept the role. It was a blessing in disguise because there was greater competition for the planning slot.

Two years later I was transferred to AP my native State – here again I was posted in Regional Office. This time I was asked to take up recoveries. I was lucky to have, a very senior, experienced officer, a doctorate in agriculture who initiated me into the rudiments of recovery portfolio. To my good fortune RBI introduced a scheme OTS – One Time Settlement, a simple but effective step. It was mandatory for banks to advertise widely about the scheme. I was briefing Managers of branches of AP where the NPA was to the tune of Rs. 250 crores. My immediate superior was a brilliant officer who is now a General Manager. His approach towards the NPA clients was very conciliatory. He spoke with concern for the client. The client approach, empathy and sympathy combined had helped the bank recover sizeable amounts under the scheme. I used to fix the dates, intimate Managers to mobilize the defaulters to assemble in the branch premises. For negotiating settlement, I always believed that Branch Manager's cabin was the best place where we have 'own court advantage'. It has a psychological impact. Bank must have 'king' status ready to pardon, condone, and yield, for compromise. 'we give them the last chance' approach. First I ask the other person to spell out how much he was ready to pay.

They used to quote in most cases amounts higher than what we expected. That was the quality of the offer, RBI gave us through OTS. The offer had to be more than reasonable if we are serious about getting rid of the headache. All traders do it. Why not banks. Banks spent huge sums on lawyers' fees, court fees, and litigation with rigid stance.

I was again lucky I was in recoveries section at such a historic point of time. Per day we used to settle 30 to 40 cases, some of them started as far back as 1978 – suit filed, decreed, lying unexecuted for the banks had better things to do than spending money on 'the dirty job'. I did not consider recovery as dirty job. I took it in the right spirit and followed diligently the set procedure. Results followed; that was sufficient for a man like me who had come from a middle class family and laying great emphasis on contentment and duty consciousness. I have still nine years of service. I said the postings were not sought after by me. I did not take any sides or tried to use the influence of 'extra-constitutional authorities'. Again I was asked to go to Gujarat. This time I was 'shunted' to a rural branch as second officer which was a loss-making branch. My thoughts of days as Planning Officer came back to me. I took the new post as a challenge.

I stayed in the village of about 2000 population. The Manager was living on the first floor of the bank premises. He belonged to Maharashtra and he was looking for a transfer back and hoping that I would take over and allowed me the freedom to study and improve the performance of the branch. The other staff gave me full cooperation. During my stay of 8 months I was the defacto Manager with the Manager frequently going on leave. His absence helped me in a way. People came forward to tell me about their perceptions. He was helping only one community people, others therefore went to other banks, about which he was completely oblivious. I had time from 8 am to 8 pm to meet some affluent families of different castes and talk to them. They were quite open to me and there was free flow of vital information as to why they were boycotting the bank which was opened in 1970. This was the fate of the branch in 2001. At the end of the talk I asked them to start operating the account which they readily agreed to do.

I had another advantage. I spent long years at Navsari where I had a neighbour whom I met and told him that I was posted to such and such village branch. It was a joy for both of us because they had some relatives 'Desais', one of whom was a highly respected Principal of the High School. Networking helped. I was meeting them regularly in the village. They were only too glad to give all the assistance. They treated me as one of them. The Principal became quite close to me. He was a highly respected man and he came along with me to introduce me to important persons of the village. In no time I became one of the villagers.

The company the Manager keeps makes all the difference for the image of the Bank

In the meantime I had turned my attention to large number overdue accounts. Most of them were those of tribal population. I became an expert in OTS. I started the work. We sent 300 letters of compromise to which there was immediate response from 100. *I gathered from them that the earlier Manager was very aggressive and threatening and therefore 'we did not pay the dues'*, and a new man and new schemes are welcome. *They also told that the Manager was a friend of local MLA and between them all further loaning was done to only one community.* All OTS clients were granted fresh loans as per the scheme by me. The branch came into profit. Then something like a jolt came to me. I was transferred to Bulsar Regional Office. They wanted a good Planning Officer.

They could not think of a better man than me. Am I a recovery expert or planning expert? Which one? Only others decide. My job is to accept whatever comes my way.

OTS negotiation in action

I became a pardeshi who came and left.

* * * * *

Case 13-Narrative

A Cash Collector Recollects

I hail from a traditional depressed community, graduated as village contractors during my grandfather's time and town and urban contractor in my father's time. I was born and brought up in ever growing capital of Hyderabad.

Soon after graduation I joined a progressive and innovative bank as a 'Cash Collector' in Village Vikas Kendra (VVK), a new set up and an organization within an organization. Therefore, I did not enter the traditional bank of high counters and army of pen pushers. It was my good fortune that I joined this bank in 1978. I was in that post in one place for nearly 5 years which I cherish even to this day. During that period I did post graduation in Public Administration in the distant mode which gave greater clarity to the grass-roots role that I was performing in a bank. On the first day of joining, the Manager, a kind hearted man, gave me keys of a motorbike and a list of borrowers whose loan amounts became over-due in Rajaram village. I was asked to seek guidance from my senior cash collectors how to reach the village which was nearly 30 km from the district head quarters.

I went there with anxiety and with thoughts more vague than clear. As told I went to *Panchayat* office and contacted the *Sarpanch* of the village. I had no previous experience of a village set up and the authority of *Sarpanch*. I gave the list of borrowers. He at once sent word to them and they all assembled in due time. I was observing the whole mechanism and the influence of *Sarpanch*. They came, but none paid their dues. Fortunately on that day no body denied the loan. They made their promises and they were recorded in a village-wise register with their signature. This was a procedure I learnt on the job to practice with diligence. I took leave of them. I have a natural courteous behaviour, probably; I got through my up-bringing for which I must thank my parents. This won me the villagers' affection in spite of their being defaulters. I began with trust in the unfortunate.

'Trust builds trust' is what I experienced.

Even after 5 years in that position and several hundred interactions with villagers who were cursed with droughts and pests and ignorance I have not lost faith in my assumption or conviction towards the mission of the bank. There is no willful defaulter in those days and even now if only the bank continued *with the kind of link we Cash Collectors established between the branch office and the beneficiaries.*

I do not say all is well with the villagers now. There are factions, groups, extremism etc. I used to hear some *Sarpanches* tell me not to grant loans to some people giving their own version about their character. I used to listen, smile, and keep quiet. When these maligned people, particularly, the weaker sections approached for some facility or the other in the office we did entertain their applications without any bias or prejudice. In fact their repayment was more prompt than those recommended by the *Sarpanches*. Politics are inevitable and I have studied the subject in my post graduation. It had a bearing on my conclusions. The seeds of tactful but transparent behaviour were sown there which I had been reaping its benefits in the career till date. Some times my Officer or Managers used to accompany me to the village when the villagers were very liberal in their praise for me. In fact at the end of my tenure in 1983 the *Sarpanches* forum passed a resolution seeking BDOs and District Collectors intervention to stop my transfer. After I left the place for Hyderabad and became a clerk, the new Manager at that branch recommended for me for a special increment. Because by that time bank abolished granting special increments, the Chief Manager, Hyderabad handed me over a letter of appreciation of my good work in a small function arranged for it. I received appreciation both from the beneficiaries and the management. I left my Cash Collector role happily with positive thoughts.

A decade later in 1993 I was posted as Manager in one of the branches in the same *mandal* where I had worked for 5 years. This branch had a checkered past. The branch had no VVK structure or Cash Collectors. By then village adoption was replaced by Service Area concept. It was a couple of years before it was blasted by extremists. The branch was ultimately shifted to *mandal* head quarters, a town with Railway Station, and it was in this place that I was posted as Manager. I felt nostalgic and I began visiting some of the old villages. I was happy to notice a sea change in the surrounding area-the improvement in standard of living, health, education, agricultural operations, dairy etc. I believe it is a silent revolution brought about by the bank from the 1970s to this day. It was visible to my naked eye.

Some of my predecessors had done outstanding work here. There were some black-sheep both among Bank Managers and the farmers. But I must mention the name of Surendra who was with the bank for more than a decade as helper. I say helper because he was not a permanent sub staff. He has been serving with the bank all through, almost from its inception. Being a boy belonging local family he knew every one by name and their background. He had been advising the Managers about the credit worthiness or otherwise and the family history. I took him along with me whenever I visited villages. He was a tower of strength to me and the bank. If this branch had the support of VVK and cash collectors [1983 their designation was changed to Agricultural

Assistant; they should be given more dignified and more appropriate designation], the people of Service Area would have progressed a great deal more effectively and more efficiently without hiccups.

Money Lenders Style

Bank Representative Style

Bank representative always gave his list to the *Sarpanch* who in-turn used his own style of village *dandora* to assemble all at the *Panchayat* office.

Case 14 – First Person Accounts SRG

I was the Cashier of a rural branch and I had put in 7years of service in this branch in Guntur district. It was a one man branch comprising of a Branch Manager, a cashier\clerk and a domestic servant. Though, rural banking was a little known concept in those days the efforts of Sri Venkat, the first Manager of the bank, yielded rich results and the branch flourished. I also remember another great personality, Sri Tella Krishnamma Choudhary, a M.L.A., who was instrumental in opening this branch in Pedanandipadu, which would have otherwise gone to Amravati

The simple rural folk extended unstinted help and co-operation to the bank employees and always treated them as a part and parcel of their families. The bank never lagged behind in returning their favours and worked 24/7. Loans were disbursed till late in the evening. The farmers too trusted the bank and handed over the cash in our houses to be deposited in their accounts. The farmers had to work from dawn to dusk and quoting rules or sticking to bank hours would go against their interests.

In village the families are close knit and people live as one unit. Everyone knows the background, family history and financial position of everyone else. We too were taken into their fold and partook of their joys and sorrows, participated in general festivals as well as personal celebrations, weddings, naming ceremony etc. Many a time we used to discuss and analyse their financial problems. We counselled them wherever it was necessary. Our intimacy grew, friendship paid rich dividends. To cite an example, excess money was paid to some villagers while disbursing loans but was returned promptly once they realized the mistake the other villagers volunteer and rush to their house and make them return the money. On one occasion, when a local youth misbehaved with my family members the local *Panchayat* President warned them so strongly that they were scared to even look at me in the eye or at my family members for the rest of our stay there. The heartening aspect of episode was that, the President warned them on his own, without receiving any complaint from me.

Our Bank also extended help in establishing a degree college at that place thereby enabling the youth of the village as well as the youth of neighbouring villages to pursue higher education there itself.

The sincerity, hard work and innovative approach of Branch Managers like Sri. Murthy, Sri. Sarma and many others who continued the good work of the founder Manager Sri.Venkat made the branch one of the most successful rural branches in South India.

Relationship banking and beyond

* * * * *

Case 15 – Narratives – LR

At 20 Lakshma Reddy joined the army because he was poor in studies according to himself. That was in 1974. He served in the army at Sikkim, Kashmir and other North Indian areas.

Like all soldiers he was self disciplined instantly obeying orders given by the superiors. Hard work and bravery were his forte. He got married in 1977 and his wife had to bring up their children alone with her parents' support.

After 16½ years service he got an option to retire. He could have continued the military another 5 years. But he made the decision to opt for retirement while he was still young so that he could seek employment as an ex-serviceman in any public sector undertaking. He got armed guard job in SBH in Warangal, his native district. After serving there for four months he came to our bank which, according to his perception, had a better standing. It turned out to be a good decision because after about 5 years he became a jeep driver, a better job than a stationary guard.

He was posted to a village branch, in Guntur, a forward district. In that branch the bank's novel structure – VVK was set up and jeep driver was part of a team of dedicated work force with jeep, motor cycles and Agricultural Assistants an Agricultural Officer-all under the supervision of Manager. There was committee system for loan sanctions. There was a lot of exchange of information among all the members of the team. The branch had 25 years of reputation with some of the Managers doing exemplary work for the cause of rural development. I quote:

"I was more than a driver and was interacting with the villagers who were always hospitable to the bank staff. To better

my future I completed 10th class and was elevated to the post of Agricultural Assistant some of whose duties I was already performing. I am now attending to clerical work besides out door duties. I had a feeling that I was serving the nation through my bank service. In the year 2000 I was transferred back to my native district, rural branch as an Agricultural Assistant.

The village branch was operating from block head quarters after it was blasted by Naxals. I had seen three Managers and adjusted to different superiors all of whom used my services well.

In 2003 I was transferred to the present rural branch in the same district. During this period I was promoted as Special Assistant. I was actually doing the work of Cashier, Special Assistant, and Agricultural Assistant besides doing most of the out door work. Here also I have seen many Managers who had appreciated my 'all-rounder' role. I have another 4 years service left and I have no desire for any more elevations and wish to settle in the neighboring town. I have three daughters whom I educated like sons: first one is MCA married and happily settled in Siddipet; second daughter is studying B.Sc. (Ag.) and the third is in MBBS stream."

Whether it was intentional or not, all his daughters' specializations are important for the rural development to which he devoted his service.

To a specific question Lakshma Reddy replied that many small vendors who borrowed in 1977/78 from his bank have now become *karodpathis* in Warangal city but the same cannot be said of the poor farmers who struggle in villages in drought prone and rain fed areas. He feels agriculture has not become a paying proposition in spite of bank credit in over 30 years! Who will respond to this reality?

De-facto Manager

* * * * *

Case 16 – Narratives – JS

Here we find the travails of a rural Manager who is pro-poor because he hails from a family who made a successful journey to senior management cadre.

He joined my branch in 1974 as Cashier. I met him after a lapse of 3 decades and was surprised and embarrassed when he told me:

'I've always admired the way you helped the cause of upliftment of weaker sections of society. I longed that you would involve me in your activities. There was one particular instance when on 15 Aug, a national holiday, you got the District Collector distribute cycle rickshaws to the released bonded labour. You also asked the officers to join in but they did not turn up for the function. For them a holiday was more important than service to the cause of the poor.'

He also shared with me some of his experiences in rural service.

Encounter with a willful defaulter who had naxal connections.

His loan amount was outstanding and the debt was getting time-barred. He got his name included in the government sponsored list for a larger loan amount. I deleted his name because he was a known defaulter. First he threatened me with dire consequences, and later came back to the bank with a wealthy guarantor. As my staff cautioned me I yielded to his pressure and agreed to consider giving him a loan with the guarantee offered. After a few hours the guarantor phoned me saying that he gave the guarantee under threat from the naxal connection. I told the guarantor that he could not go back on his surety. I discussed the matter and we jointly brought pressure on both the parties that the old loan will be first liquidated with the proceeds and only balance amount would be paid to him. Thus I saved old debt which was getting time barred. We impressed the person that he would be eligible for any future requirement without the stigma. That's how we solved the tough problem on the spot.

Working with a team spirit and negotiating with a divergent groups are rare skills developed only in the face of such situations – a unique gift offered by a rural branch alone.

An award won by the branch for showing the highest average in savings bank balances for the entire State came as a pleasant surprise to me. Thanks to the international airport being developed in that area, lots of land in the surrounding villages was taken over and compensation paid in cash. My staff and I were required to keep the cash counter open and receive large sums into SB accounts. A backward branch had become prominent on the bank's map.

High risk area of operations

This is another case of staff working as a team for the bank. Such things are done at personal risk and administration that awarded them now would not protect them if things go wrong. A cashier could have refused legitimately, and the administration need not have called for explanation from the person.

'I was alone in the office and someone came with Rs.48 lakhs to deposit. I asked the party to bring it the next day. And the deposit had gone to another bank!

I had financed SHGs (women) and SHG (men). There was cent percent recovery in the former and not in the latter.'

This was a general trend and I probed for the reasons. The Manager told me that there was greater unity among women and the amount of the loan did not exceed Rs.30 thousand each time. In the men's group the unity was less and also amounts were in lakhs of rupees. The former used more for consumption purposes and the latter used for agricultural operations. Purpose, quantum, solidarity are the variables, reasons, for good or bad recovery.

The principle, 'All for each and each for all' is common. I think it is more than what we attribute to gender; it is the quantum of the amount and purpose. Yet, there is another factor that is emerging now. Micro Finance Institutions as alternative source for borrowing. Although MFIs charge very high rate of interest, the burden is less as long as the amount is small.

* * * * *

SECTION – III MISCELLANEOUS

Case 17 – Kidnap - SRG

Sometimes, life is stranger than fiction, with its many twists and turns, thrills and adventures. As we look back we wonder 'Did this really happen to me'? I would like to share one such experience with you-the unforgettable incident of the Naxalites kidnapping me during my tenure as Branch Manager, Narmetta. It was in the year 1990, this spine chilling and nerve-wracking incident took place. But before I embark on my narration, I would like to acquaint you with the social background and economic scenario of the place in seventees. The rural folk were unaware of banking and various Government schemes that help them through banks, but MMR*, its 3rd Manager had rendered an excellent service. Direct finances to agriculture and agriculture related services by our Bank had brought the Bank so close to the rural folk that everybody felt that it was their Bank, a guide and a well wisher that promptly came to their rescue in times of need. Government waived loans up to Rs10, 000 to agriculturists and our branch was the one which took initiative to implement the programme under the directives of the Central Govt. thereby helping the farmers a lot.

It was a Naxal dominated area and the village was like a fort for them. One had to be very careful in one's behaviour and talk. A single word or a simple action of anyone was sufficient to ignite their fury and to brand him as their enemy.

---

* There is a first person account of MMR in this Chapter.

On the fateful day of kidnapping, i.e on 4th Dec.1990, the Bank started functioning as usual. Some members of staff were on leave and only the Cashier and myself and one sub staff were on duty. Suddenly, at around 11a.m.we heard some commotion outside and on enquiry learnt that ANNALU, [Naxals] have arrived and were forcibly closing shops and offices in protest against the arrest of their central committee member. We understood the situation and closed down the shutters and stayed inside the branch as the branch had no other exit. After 15, 20 minutes, a group entered the premises and started banging on the shutters and windows, demanding that they should be let in.. The banging on the shutters grew louder. We had no option but to let them in.

Immediately 15 to 20 youth rushed in, some of their members ran upstairs to find out if there were any employees or their family members hiding there. They enquired about the Manager and we tried to hoodwink them saying the Manager was out of station; but they did not believe us .Soon they identified me as the Manager.

Two able bodied persons stood on either side of me and ordered me to go with them. After taking me a few yards they blindfolded me and took me to an unknown destination on a motorbike. I was in between two persons. I was given the information that they were taking me as well as some more officials in retaliation for the arrest of their member. I kept silent on realising the gravity of the situation. After 3 hours' ride they removed the blindfold and I found myself in a forest.

I was handed over to another group of their *dalam*. It was a thick forest with a very narrow path along which I was dragged mercilessly.. I was exhausted, starving and almost on the verge of a nervous break down. By 4 p.m. we joined a larger group of *Naxalites* with three more people who were kidnapped like me.

After a short break we resumed our journey. Pitch black night, freezing cold, zig-zag pathways among bushes, fear of the unknown and uncertainty gnawing away at our hearts, we had little hope of survival. I drew strength from the deep springs of spirituality which I inherited from my forefathers. With abundant faith in the Lord and a stout heart, I was prepared for the worst.

We had a long walk of 15 kms and at around 2 am we reached a partially harvested maize field. Some people were already lying down there. We were forced to squeeze in between those people and sleep. Early next morning the hide out was again shifted. The kidnapped were also separated. The Naxalites had a very good network and intelligence and well built communication system. I was alone with the leader and a few of his members.

On the third day of my capture, I came to know that the supporters, family members and associates of the arrested leader attacked the police station of the village and in the ensuing fight and police firing, a protester was killed. One of the Naxal members, in an uncontrollable fit of anger tried to attack me, but was stopped since there were no instructions to kill me.

At one time I engaged one of the guards in conversation. I began explaining how the bank did welfare programmes for the poor. I explained that nobody will volunteer to work for uplift of the poor if they do like this. The man kept mum for quite sometime and told me to shut up and said, 'we are not against you personally, we have our demands'

Meanwhile my wife approached the Employees Union and Officers Association to get me released. The human rights leaders were approached. Through the media appeals were broadcast. Bank management also plunged into action and approached the top brass of police. The combined efforts of everyone, the grace of God and the release of the Naxal leader, earned me my freedom. I was set free on the eve of 7th Dec. After walking a distance of 5 km, I reached a remote village and the villagers helped me reach the Hyderabad road–a road to freedom.

Two able bodied persons stood on either side of me and ordered me to go with them.

One of the Naxal leaders members, in an un-controllable fit of anger tried to attack me, but was stopped since there were no instructions to kill me.

* * * * *

Case 18-Story-1
Biogas for A Bright Future-KKN

Asha was married to a bank officer. She then moved to a remote village-Mosali in Surat District from Delhi where she was brought up. Quite apprehensive of comforts in the remote rural village she was pleasantly surprised to see piped gas connection. Some industrial estate must have been nearby she thought before someone told her that it is 'gobar gas'.

"What? Gobar gas? That shit of a gas?" she roared not realizing that she was right even in her anger. The very thought of preparing food in the kitchen gave her a feeling of nausea and suffocation as her mind was occupied more with the ingredient of the gas than the ingredients of the food that she had to prepare. She was almost into tears when she opened the pack of vessels that her mum and her clan had so affectionately packed for her during the 'bidayi' with all modern gadgets full of best of aluminum, brass, copper and silver. All these have to interact with that ---- of a gas she thought and more tears came out of her eyes.

Poor Asha had to adjust virtually A to Z. No newspapers, TV (TV means television she explained to some of the locals), or for that matter company of any educated lady, and in the matter of daily chores no bread, tooth paste, powder leave alone samosa or chat. In the matter of dress too what was considered conservative in Delhi was not an acceptable form of a dress in the village to a bahu. Mercifully being an officer her husband was provided quarter that was considered 'pucca' construction and had many luxuries like an independent bathroom.

As Asha went out to fetch water from the well, she had her first interaction with the village folks. All watched her with awe and vied to pull water out of the well, even as she controlled her irritation at being made an object of exhibition in their looks. Some of them stretched their brains to convert their Gujarati thoughts in to Hindi, even as Asha tried to rush back with the bucket of water to her house. En route she also had an encounter with stray cattle and stared at them thinking of the unwanted product that they are capable of delivering.

Her husband being an Agriculture Officer in the bank slowly explained to her the affection that the people are capable of unlike the uncaring metro neighborhood. The benefit of pollution free life, fresh vegetables, rice and wheat free from fertilizers, fresh milk and fresh.... Stop it. I know the fuel is also fresh and pollution free she snapped even as her husband had a snigger at her continued aversion for the gobar gas.

As Asha continued to struggle with kerosene stove, her husband offered to take her to some of the successful bio-gas projects. As the word with G was replaced by bio, she felt a mild sense of relief. Biogas means 'domestic or commercial gas obtained by treating naturally occurring materials' explained the specialist and Asha felt comfortable though the last three syllables 'naturally occurring materials' continued to give some discomfort. As she heard more on treatment process and waste management she started realizing that the fuel that is entering her kitchen is not raw and dirty as its origin appear. Added to this was the envy of the villagers on the privilege of the officer's wife using a gaseous fuel unlike the dried raw variety that majority in the village use as fuel. Next day when Asha went to fetch water she did not see any offence in the looks of the locals and also tried to touch the back of the cow in reverence as most Hindu women folk do.

Two decades later she had proudly displayed 'cow' as logo for her outlet and had a banner prominently displayed "biogas fuel station- the stop for pollution free ride" in the suburb of Delhi.

Story 2 – Raja and Raja - KKN

Raja had a very unhappy beginning to his career. He reported in a godforsaken village in Gujarat and did not know what to do. A massive hall of a closed ginning factory with tin shed was his residence, with a couple of equally disgruntled colleagues for company among humans and rats and occasional snake among non humans. Being designated as 'Agriculture Officer' in the bank he had no other go but to live in the village. It was almost three decades ago when TV and PC were unheard of even in towns. Far away from his native Bangalore, the distance, separation from home, loneliness and the alien culture all added up to his misery.

Next day as he went to take bath in the common well people stared at the 'foreigner' and children giggled at his lungi. His Tamil accent of Hindi added to the comedy. Life was getting miserable to Raja till he met another Raja. Rajabhai D Parmar was the name of the five year old kid who wished him good morning in chaste English and offered barter. Barter of language.

The elder Raja under compulsion to learn Gujarati was willing to share his English. The little Raja started bringing various items of toy and learnt the names of animals and the elder learnt the names of vegetables and grains in Gujarati. Their relationship slowly grew with the elder choosing to play rubber ball cricket and trapping a field rat and the little Raja reciprocated as he soaped the cloths and brought food for the elder. Sheer innocence of questions on both sides helped the relationship to blossom. The younger was inquisitive about the eating manners, dressing, cosmetics and the hugeness of Bangalore city and the elder Raja though very literate was too ignorant of Gujarati customs and village life.

Raja had a motorcycle given by the bank and the little one was all too familiar with all the accessories and took upon himself to clean the vehicle everyday. The elder Raja had the benefit of the boy accompanying him everywhere. It was joy ride for the boy and a valuable guide to the man in the course of his inspection in the fields. The boy however felt as if the vehicle was given more to him than to the officer. The possessive approach of the boy made Raja feel all the more attached to him. It was then the elder decided to get idli made for the boy.

Apart from the recipe he also fetched the moulded vessel from his native. Almost the entire village assembled to see idli getting ready and tiny Raja was the most inquisitive of all to know the color and shape of idli. It was a damp squib of an idli party for little Raja as the elder had spoken so much of missing it he thought it to be as colorful as faluda and as attractive as an ice cream in appearance. It was just a rice cake in a barren white color though as a consolation, sambar the side dish was a much better item for everyone to have.

Memories were fresh in the mind of Raja even after two decades as he was elevated as Regional Manager (Western Region) that included Gujarat under his jurisdiction. His first thought on posting was little Raja. He vividly remembered the boy who cried on his leaving the village on his transfer also bringing tears to his eyes. At the earliest opportunity he made a visit to the village only to find none recognize him. People were busy with TV and PC. There was no knowledge gap between the city and village unlike his days.

Things had changed so much that none in the village branch knew that Raja started his career there. Incognito he wanted to visit the branch and much to his amazement remained so. Suppressing his disappointment, he went ahead with his review of performance, secretly searching for any customer by the name of Raja. He also searched during the course of visit to fields for a person who could be Raja. Somehow he did not want to share the fact that he started his career in that village.

It was Gujarat, Rajasthan and Maharashtra that were part of his jurisdiction. The biggest issue he had to settle was the issue of officers who were posted out of their native place. Though Raja had not forgotten his experience, the pressure of work and the responsibility to discharge his duties made him take a sterner stand on requests for transfer. Though drowned in the pressure of work, he also concentrated often in that village of his, both searching for Raja or other familiar names who could give a lead to the little Raja. As the time came for his leaving the place after a stint of three years, he was very disappointed and the HR head was after him to complete posting of transferee officers from other states.

Raja was not happy to handle this work on the verge of his leaving and hence was irritated whenever a posting decision was sought. When he was in the heat of his irritation, one officer barged in with a transfer request and was shouted to 'get out and the man almost on the verge of tears begged "Sir, I am RD Parmar, please post me to Mosali branch". It took a while for Raja to realize that transfer is sought to the place where none want to go even today and as he recognized the man requesting it, he had a very pleasant surprise. It was Raja whom he was searching among the customers.

Story 3 – Buffalo Loan - KKN

Ram never knew that banking could change so much in one decade. He also did not envisage some of the activities that he would be required to perform under the 'banking activity', holding a rope of a buffalo for example. He left India when banks were just nationalized and returned after a decade. When he left India, banking was largely meant for the educated and the elite, more so he thought having worked only in the elite of the then metros Bombay. He returned to India after five years tenure each in Belgium and Fiji islands, and was posted to Delhi as in charge of 'Northern Zone'.

What Ram did not realize then was North Zone includes Madhya Pradesh and that Madhya Pradesh has many rural branches. It was the time the ministers were busy proclaiming 'loan melas' and giving 'loans in a hurry' that too to the have not's was considered KPA of many bankers. The loan of course was to buy utility items by the villagers. Buffalo being more than a utility item was busy getting filled under the column Loan for: in the application forms. Again being an item of a prestigious loan in the village, it also attracted onlookers with the building festive atmosphere adding to the pomp and show that ministers chose to participate and inaugurate.

Ram landed in India not realizing all these intricacies of rural loan portfolio, and being a function attended by the state minister was rushed to the function immediately on landing in Bombay. Tired of jetlag and the midnight train to Bhopal and journey in Indian roads in the rural area Ram was in a totally confused state and was seeing a different world. As his car arrived the gathered villagers hooted and whistled in excitement, much to his amusement. As the minister came and formal introductions over, the function started even as the bewildered Ram stared at the rough wooden chairs on a shaking stage quite in contrast to his star hotel meetings.

As the proceedings proceeded in Hindi it added to his confusion, but the frequent clapping and whistling suggested that the bank officer is articulate enough to handle the show. Ram was asked to get down from the stage even as the rousing chorus of joy of the villagers added to his confusion. "Bains number eke" (buffalo No1) announced the officer and the seller loosened the rope for the buffalo to march on. It was almost like a parade for about 100 feet even as the villagers clapped in jubilation. The buffalo was made to stop near Ram who squirmed in discomfort as the buffalo looked as if it chose to come out of its bath half way through. The buffalo too was reciprocating discomfort to stand next to a man who was in no way fitting that environment in his suit. Since the cameraman wanted them together both compromised with a grudge. The claps were slowly getting frenzied and the buffalo was on the verge of breaking free. The bank officer commanded to hand over the rope of the buffalo to Ram, who wondered what are they up to?

'Borrower number 1 Bharat Yadav' was the announcement that raised the tempo of the clapping. The minister was feeling at home, the villagers in never before enthusiasm, the bank officer in one more "on duty loan mela", the borrower happy, seller happy, only Ram and the buffalo were not comfortable with each other as well as the atmosphere. After a round of disquieting swing by the buffalo, a chide to the owner to control and a bewilderment to Ram, came the announcement of grant of loan.

With cameras clicking Ram handed over the rope to the borrower symbolically granting the loan. It was huge celebration in the village for the whole day; a huge immediate relief to Ram with a whole day of introspection as to what all are in store in the coming days of banking that is nationalized.

* * * * *

Case 19 – In First Person

Story No. 1 – KVD

Gandhi Jayanti and Vijaya Dasami

Her thunderous voice pierced the calm of the house, reverberating through the silent house; her eyes blazed in fiery indignation; her anger reached a crescendo. My wife yelled at me 'this is male chauvinism, pure and simple. 'You want to go out on a festival day. Leave me to my kitchen and this endless drudgery. Do whatever you want. You have no consideration, no concern for me.' My father, who has been a silent listener to her tirade, came slowly inside. Scared that he too would be swept off by her angry deluge, called me aside and asked me what the matter was. I told him, 'today is 2nd October, Gandhi Jayanti. Since it is a national holiday, my Manager has planned to visit the nearby villages and talk to the villagers. I have to accompany him.'

My wife stormed in again 'look at him today is Gandhi Jayanti; today is Vijayadashami also' He should be able to spare at least one day, a festival day with the family. When there is no time for family, no celebration, no festival, no enjoyment he should not have married me. That Manager calls him and this Clerk jumps at the proposal.' The thunder and lightning were portents of an oncoming storm that threatened to engulf us at any time.

My father slowly walked back to his easy chair on the verandah – I followed him, meek as a lamb. I felt at least my father should know what we were doing. I explained to him, 'Today is Gandhi Jayanti as well as Vijayadashami. Moreover it is a Saturday.[2-10-1976] Tomorrow being Sunday, we have two consecutive holidays. My Manager is an idealist. He says helping the downtrodden, neglected segment of the society is alone paying a real tribute to the Mahatma. The govt. is ready to help the downtrodden classes with many schemes. The District Collector promised a handsome subsidy of fifty percent. Today being the most auspicious day we are sure our efforts will be crowned with success. So we planned to go out.'

My father argued 'all this talk is fine and beneficial for your Manager. He will be in the good books of his superiors. He will be appreciated, may get a promotion. But I don't think you will gain anything from this.'

I was dumbstruck - true I may not reap any benefits, may not earn a single rupee. I may squander a precious holiday following my Manager but after that I have to sit at my counter, making entries in the debit and credit columns while he takes credit for all the good work done, but I expressed my readiness to go with him. Though a Clerk I have my self respect and must try to keep up my word. I thought I also heard the small, little voice of my conscience telling me that I should help and educate the needy. But the storm on the domestic front was scary and unnerving. To go or not to go was the dilemma. Finally the pendulum swung I went. Once again my father interrupted my thoughts asking what exactly we proposed to do in the village. I tried to explain to him the many schemes the government was trying to implement through the banks.

My father had another genuine doubt 'you give loans but if your villagers do not, cannot repay the loans the bank will go into a big loss'

'True' said I. 'But out of the 100 people who have taken loans, even if 20 people repay the loan, they are eligible for a higher loan amount. When they avail this they prosper and their standard of living goes up. This can be an eye opener for the rest, who may come forward and repay the outstanding loans, the number of defaulters becomes less and less once they understand the banking system.'

My father seems to have understood. He gave me the go ahead signal with the assurance that he would take care of my wife's temper tantrums.

'Most of the surrounding villages that we had to visit were situated in deep valleys surrounded by lush green forests rich and replete with fauna and flora. But the tribals who lived there were the rightful heirs to this wealth and unaware of their rights. Nor did they have the resources to turn this wealth to their benefit. They struggled to earn a paltry sum and felt happy if they could get enough sustenance to stay alive. Often they fell into a debt trap [a death trap] of the middle men who exploit them unscrupulously. A little financial help could go a long way in uplifting these men and women. Government was ready to help them through banks. We were instrumental in this, a link between the tribals and the Government. Only problem is that we need to gain their confidence.' My father was silent, probably trying to digest what I told him. I decided to go with my Manager and assist him in whatever way I could.

A healthy seedling embedded in the fertile earth, bursts forth as a smiling sapling. So also our efforts, rooted in the lofty ideals of Bapu, nurtured by our sincere efforts to help the society, bore fruit. We explained to each villager the schemes of the bank, the loan facility, the benefits of prompt repayment and the disadvantages to defaulters. I handed over the loan applications to the village assistant asking him to return the applications at my house after filling in the necessary details.

I returned home, a cheerful song on my lips; but as soon as I entered the house, the song died out. An impregnable silence confronted me - impregnable, intimidating and hostile-a lull before the storm. The food was served in the same silence-an eloquent silence that spoke volumes about the displeasure of my wife. After dinner she retreated into her fort of protest, leaving me to my confusion and worries.

Next day I took my father and kids to the nearby park and returned home as it was getting dark. A great surprise awaited me. My wife, all smiles, greeted me at the door. My confusion got confounded when she dragged me inside. She said a man; Bukya Naik came from the village. He told me what you people were doing yesterday in the village. He was praising you so much before going he told me that I was really lucky to marry a man like you. He also said, 'till yesterday we lived a hand to mouth existence. But these people changed all that. We can actually plan, think of tomorrow. May God bless you.'

I looked at the portrait of the Mahatma smiling and understood the real meaning of his words

A selfless man is really happy because he thinks less of himself.

In First Person Story No. 2 – KVD

A rural Bank Manager has to do a tight rope walk. The branch is small and the work light. But the moment the Manager takes over the charge he becomes the victim of a two-pronged attack. The villagers do not rest till they know the ins and outs of the Manager-personal as well as official. He has to learn and conform to the norms and traditions of the village. His behaviour and movements are closely watched .He should feel the pulse of his customers, the villagers, accommodate them and in the process may have to forget the office hours or schedules. On the other hand, he has to realize the ambitious schemes of the superiors and see that the bank prospers.

I took charge of such a rural branch the work was not heavy, though. Real work used to start only after the office hours. One such evening amidst the gathering darkness, I was sitting at the bank, regurgitating sweet and bitter experiences of the past few months. I came out of my reverie when my Cashier said,' 'sir, we better close the cash for today. It is getting late.' I was surprised to note that we had been working in dark-the sun had gone down long back, and there was a power cut. Immediately we started packing up for the day. Suddenly, Kusumaiah, a prosperous, well known farmer of the village barged in, upset and tense, anxiety writ large on his face, Without any preliminaries he said, 'You must lend me Rs.30,000. My father-in-law is critical. He is in the hospital and has to undergo surgery immediately. Even then there is no guarantee of his survival. But I cannot leave him to his fate. Try as I might I could not get the money anywhere. You must help me.'

I did not know what to say. Though Kusumaiah is prosperous, he lived with his in-laws, in their house. The legal rights of the property were vested with his wife. Was it wise to give a loan after bank hours, without any security? I could understand very well what the frantic gestures of my cashier indicated. But it was a small place and maintaining good relations with every one was vital though a delicate task. Life was much more precious than Rs.30,000 and how could I stand between the two? Rural Banking is not walking on a tight rope, it is walking on a razor's edge.

Finally I decided to take a risk, paid him the money after taking his signature on the documents, ignoring the disapproving looks of my cashier. I tried to keep my fears at bay, telling myself my P.F account was the only security.

That night I did not sleep a wink–I tossed and turned and thrashed on the bed. Will I be able to tally this account-an impulsive, perhaps foolish, though humanitarian act of mine against the rules and regulations of the bank. Bank had empowered me with the custodial rights of the deposits but, cannot permit the indiscriminate advancing of money to anyone. Lost in these thoughts I slipped into a disturbed sleep for an hour or two, but woke up very early the next morning. As I was staying in the nearby town, I caught the first bus to the village. I had to cross Kusumaiah's house to reach the bank. As I neared the house I stopped suddenly. My adrenalin started flowing, the blood raced through my veins, my pulse quickened, my hands and legs became numb; I saw a shamiana in front of the house, heard sounds of wailing coming from inside. Both were self explanatory–the inevitable, the unwanted had happened. My days in the bank are numbered I thought.

After 3 days Kusumaiah's son came to me and called me to his house. I saw a light at the end of the dark tunnel and followed him quickly. His wife thanked me for the help rendered though her father could not be saved. She was very gracious and offered to part with her gold, to be kept as security against the loan. I heaved a sigh of relief, congratulated myself and made a silent prayer to the Almighty.

On the heels of this crisis came March, the most dreaded month when the Head Office writes our horoscopes, when we have to meet the annual targets, receive bouquets or brickbats, an appreciation, a promotion, or a reprimand. I calculated and was startled to know that I was 3 lakh rupees away from my target, too long a distance to be covered now. My spirits were at the lowest ebb, only a miracle could save me. Suddenly I heard the voice of Kusumaiah, calling me.

'Sir is something wrong? These days you are so worried, so lost'.

I said 'we cannot reach the target for this year. We are short by 3 lakh rupees.'

He was lost in thought for sometime and then seemed to have come to a decision. He said, 'I will meet you tomorrow by 7 p.m. Don't close your ledgers.'

I saw him next evening with three and a half lakhs to be deposited in his account. I wanted to hug and kiss Kusumaiah. He laughed at my excitement, and slowly walked away.

My branch not only reached the target but also crossed it, thanks to Kusumaiaha. I basked in the appreciation of my higher ups. Bubbling with enthusiasm and cheer, I went to my friend's house to express my gratitude. I found him busy in conversation with a stranger and overheard the latter telling him, 'Sir, you have to repay the entire amount you have taken. My *Seth* specifically asked me to convey this to you. 'Kusumaiah assured him that it would be done so and packed him off. Then he saw me and told me in a matter of fact tone,' 'this man is working for the money lender in the town, from whom I have borrowed the money and deposited in my account.'

I was flabbergasted as the truth slowly dawned on me .....he took a loan for a higher interest rate and deposited it to pull me out of the deep waters. Choking with emotion I tried to thank him. He dismissed my words saying, don't make a mountain out of a molehill, sir. I borrowed money and deposited it in my own account. You risked your career, your future prospects by giving me the loan....after the bank hours, without any security. We are the beneficiaries since the bank is here, but you are no less...you are millionaires....all our money is with you.' He smiled benevolently at my confused expression.

The quality of mercy is not strained

It droppeth as a gentle rain from heaven

Upon the place beneath. It is twice blest;

It blesseth him that gives and him that takes.

* * * * *

Case 20 – Titbits

Phone Facility

One rural Manager allowed the villagers to use bank's land line in those days when there were no mobile phones.

This helped him develop business. Gradually he extended the public phone facility for incoming calls too by sending word to the particular persons.

One day a caller told the Manager who received the call 'I am committing suicide please inform my parents' and put down the phone. After some dilly-dallying the Manager ignored the message. Next day the police came to the branch and started interrogating the Manager. Soon the word went round in the village and the elders in the village confronted the police and sent them away saving embarrassment to the bank and the Manager. 'The caller had actually committed suicide and the last call was traced to the bank' hence the interrogation.

On the villagers' advice the incoming calls were stopped but the Manager carried on as usual. He never informed the management about the incident to avoid complications.

Emergency Gold Loan

The same Manager went out of the way to sanction gold-loan for Rs.2 lakhs on a Saturday evening after business hours. The loan was sought for medical expenses for the borrower's daughter-in-law who was admitted to a Super Specialty Hospital in the state Capital. On Monday morning the man returned the cash saying that the patient died by the time the man reached Hyderabad.

The question in the Manager's mind was 'had I not granted the loan what the whole village would have thought of me?'

Even this incident, he did not inform the higher authorities. Aviation accidents take place for external reasons or internal reasons. A black box is designed to find out what went wrong. There is no black box designed for rural branches. The controlling offices have no means of finding out the truth to fix the accountability.

They found one method – anonymous letters. There are always aggrieved persons inside or outside the bank to debunk whatever Manager does, the decisions and actions – are based on his reasoning, gut feelings and mood which he himself may find it difficult to explain.

* * * * *

SECTION–IV
AGRICULTURAL SPECIALISTS
Case 21 – First Person Accounts
JB

At the out set I thank you for choosing me to share my experiences as Rural Branch Manager way back in 1984-1985 where I worked for 1½ years.

After joining the Bank as DRO (Agr) in 1981 in Gujarat, I worked in Vyara Branch (SU) as Agricultural Officer and in 1984 I was transferred to A.P and posted to the village after GKR left the place abruptly as Branch Manager.

Though I belong to A.P, I was new to the environment of a rural branch that too as a Branch Manager and there was nobody to hand over/take over of the branch formalities as I had relieved the Officer who was on deputation temporarily. I had to manage alone, new to branch and the hinterland.

Immediately after taking charge of the branch I started studying branch portfolio and avenues for business development. For business development I had to go and meet people in addition to meeting prominent people of the area in the area. Because of my nature I could soon make friends with them.

The operational area of the branch comprised of 4 villages where the main occupation of the people was agriculture, growing major crops like Cotton, Chillies, Paddy etc. and the cultivation depended on bore wells or rain fed crops.

Under allied activities the farmers were taking up Dairy, by bringing buffaloes from Krishna Dist. The agriculture operations were carried out with bullocks and mechanization was in the initial stages. Armed with this information, I formulated mentally a strategy of extending credit for dairy, mechanisation, and minor irrigation etc.

Though we were extending finance to the needy farmers directly as well as under Govt. sponsored programmes, the recovery of loans was a problem because of crop failure and dry conditions prevailing in the area.

Recovery Camp

There was hardly any habit of saving among majority of farmers due to the above reasons. We had attempts to educate them in thrift habit. We have conducted several loan melas and recovery camps and of the two there was lot of political involvement in loan mela and poor response to recovery camps and this I feel was due to lack of awareness and proper education among farmers. [Note: It is Mandal Development Officials who are involved in loan melas. But it is Mandal Revenue Officer who attends the recovery camps. MROs are very busy in administration.

To summarise my experiences I felt:

- that the area was very backward
- people were illiterate
- lack of Infra structural facilities
- lack of marketing facilities for the farm produce/ un-remunerative returns for the farm produce.
- dry area /no perennial source of irrigation
- Naxalite prone area

No thrift/savings habit and not much concern for loan repayment which led to lot of over dues in the Branch.

* * * * *

Case 22 – First Person Accounts GRB

I hail from a poor orthodox family in a village with high moral values. My father was an Ayurvedic doctor and a strict disciplinarian. My mother was a devoted and committed wife who died in Jan 2010. I studied Agriculture and obtained a diploma related to Storage, Entomology and Post Harvest Technology. I worked for Shaw-Wallace as Sales Officer in West Godavari district for 3 months and later for ICRISAT Patancheru as a Technical Assistant for Pulse Entomology Programme, with Dr.Reed, an International Scientist and jointly published papers two times in 1976 and 1977. (Red gram and Bengal gram)

In 1976 I applied for M.Sc and also for the bank job. I was interviewed for two days in succession, one in Rajendranagar, Hyderabad, next for the bank job in Chennai. I was selected for both. I consulted my professor who had selected me for M.Sc. He advised me to join the bank. I must share how I was selected for bank officer job. The interviewers asked me why I chose banking. I gave an emotional reply. I told them I studied Indian economics in which I read that the Indian farmer is born in debt, lives in debt, and bequeaths debt. Through bank service I can do something to alleviate his poverty by releasing him from the clutches of the money lender. I could see that one person who was from Agricultural discipline was touched by my out burst.

I joined in Bhimavaram branch of the bank where I learnt the rudiments of banking under the late Mr. Murthy. After two years I was transferred to Eluru. Both are in West Godavari district where I had worked as Sales Officer in Shaw-Wallace company, both the places are near my native place. In Eluru I had a Manager who was tough but fair, from whom I learnt a great deal. These two gentlemen together with my father shaped my personality. Eluru Manager gave me full freedom and whatever proposal for agricultural finance was recommended by me was accepted by him. Even when I recommended a quantum of finance which was beyond his powers he sanctioned at once and wrote for confirmation to higher authorities. It appeared that the Regional Manager and this gentleman were not seeing eye to eye and to inconvenience him I was transferred to a village branch in a backward district in Telangana area which was contast to the prosperous district I was leaving. Initially I was apprehensive of the role I had to play in an interior village in a rain fed area, with scanty rainfall. I stayed there for two years which was more memorable than any period in my entire service 34 years so far.

I was 25 and I went there one week after my marriage. I took my wife along and stayed in the village itself. I must share my feelings. I reached the place from Eluru by train and a bus to the godforsaken place. That was how I felt. In the bus I travelled, some goats and sheep were the co-passengers. I could not make out the language people spoke though it was Telugu, my mother tongue.

As I mingled with people I gained confidence and I found the people were so good and nice to me. I started imagining how as a Manager with education in agriculture and specialized knowledge I gained in ICRISAT should help them. I started day dreaming of helping small and marginal farmers and the poor agricultural labour. I recalled how I got through the interview when I emotionally articulated my conviction of helping the rural poor get out of the clutches of money lenders.

The area is surrounded by Thandas – tribal habitats. Most of the crops were rain fed. They needed upliftment, not mere finance. I began assessing their requirements in concrete measure for improving crop production and bringing social development–cultural change in their lives.

I learnt more about their problems interacting with them daily by engaging them in talk. Once they became free and expressive I could get an insight into their problems. What these conversations revealed was that I should play a social reformer more than any other lender who may have come to release them from the sharks of real money lenders. This is the meaning of a development banker, I thought, cropping pattern, irrigation requirements especially of the small holdings in command area of our branch which is quite large. I took immediately the following steps:

1. Assessing the credit requirements of the farming community-short term and long term. Crop loans/major crops – Paddy, Jowar, Groundnut and Sunflower.

There were some over-dues to the bank. I approached them with the proposal that their currents needs would be met if they clear their loans taken earlier.

There used to be a practice of *pyrvikar,* the middle man acting on behalf of the farmers which I broke. This paid dividends. As farmers responded I fulfilled my promise without any delay. Others followed suit. That 'actions speak louder' than words came true. I was happy that the strategy worked very well.

2. Apart from this action oriented strategy I used to visit the villagers, lambadas in Thandas in particular straight to their cultivated area when the crops were grown. With my research background and experience I used identifying zinc deficiency and guided them with my technical knowledge for improved cultivation. This was the strength which I brought to bear on my role.

They no longer looked up to me as a Bank Manager but as a friend, philosopher and guide. It was no fault of my two predecessors who were commerce graduates and of urban upbringing that they could not give this kind of service. This worked to my advantage in my performance which reflected in the outcomes at the end of the first year of my two year tenure.

During this period I attended 'Branch Management Programme for Rural Managers' at bank's appex college which came a year too late. Neverthless, could share my experiments with other participants who came from all over India. For a conscious learner like me these programmes had a great impact on my thinking. More than that what I did in that year found acceptance at the organizational level. Earlier in 1977 I had attended an induction programme for Agricultural Officers which gave me a sense of purpose. I used to give *package of practices* to be adopted for increasing crop production by usage of HYV (High Yielding Variety) seeds and also adopting the latest scientific practice methods of cultivation. All these things I could do because of agricultural extension background and liaison with Samithi President of the block who helped in the release of fertilizers, seeds and implements to the bank borrowers at subsidized rates. This Samithi President's contact helped me in my role as Branch Manager in a variety of ways and manifold.

2nd year in The Place

My focus shifted to the Government Departments and agencies and I secured subsidy release in time and other measures. I used my influence as a Manager to get maximum electrical connections to bank's poor customers for minor irrigation programmes. The District Collector gave orders for sanction of electrical connections for the finance we made for new wells and electric motors or for deepening old wells. Groundnut and other crops were raised with well water. I had become their family member during this period. The job satisfaction I got was immense. It is not a wonder to say that some of these farmers attended my daughter's marriage at Hyderabad in Aug 2009, travelling a long distance – 26 years after I left the place.

One Moment of truth in the period 1981-83

I used to go to the villages for meeting the borrowers/field inspection/end use verification in the early morning time or evening time. In between I used to attend office work from 10.30 to 4.30 pm. That was my routine in those two years.

I recollect that, whenever I visited the tribal areas, the lambada thandas all villagers used to recognize me. I can't forget it nor is it an exaggeration to say that the children aged between three and ten ,playing at the primary school, or bore well or near the *panchayat racha banda*, , used to get up, stop their play and look at the YEZDI motorcycle and me and shout with pleasant excitement, saying 'bank sir has come'. That was the immediate response in almost all the areas of my operation. I was just 25 then.

I also recollect that whenever I was going to the fields, borrowers wearing a turban in a Telangana tradition used to greet me normally and start talking to me. In case they were under the influence of toddy, then they would greet me with folded hands and would never open their mouths. When I used to make any casual enquiry about their welfare, they would say in a low tone, 'Sir, my condition is not good, tomorrow I shall meet you,' in his regional accent. That was the respect and regard I enjoyed in those days. I will never forget their deferential attitude. As promised, next day they used to come to the branch and interact normally.

There was one occasion 1982 in Alwar Banda Thanda a tribal colony near Thimmampet. (The locality is on the way to the railway station. Railway station was the samithi HQ.) One Mr.Banoth Jagru S/o Hatya aged about 60 years used to come to our branch. His elder brother's son aged 25 yrs was working as a Cashier, Banoth Harilal in SBI, in the nearby town. There was a property dispute between Mr. Harilal and Mr. Jagru. Incidentally Mr.Harilal used to come to our branch for his crop loan and he also had one Recurring Deposit account.

There was a dispute between Mr. Harilal and Mr.Jagru regarding water supply from the joint well and they had exchanged heated arguments. In an irate condition both parties had tried to manhandle each other. As a result of which a case was filed in Wardhannapet P.S by Mr.Jagru against Mr.Harilal. That had happened sometime back.

Poor Harilal was nervous and frightened as some body had warned him that he might loose his job if arrested by the police. He immediately rushed to the police station and met Mr.Narsaish the then Sub Inspector of police and pleaded with him to save his job.

Incidentally Mr.Narsaiah was known to me and remembered me for the help in his marriage alliance / negotiation / and arrangement of *purohit* for performing his marriage six months back.

Immediately Mr.Narsaiah SI of Police informed Mr.Harilal against whom a case was filed, that nothing was in his hand but suggested to him to approach the 'bank sir' (i.e. me) as he was influential in Alwar Banda Thanda where Mr. Jagru stays and certainly chances were there for Manager influencing Mr. Jagru to withdraw the case.

Early morning Mr. Harilal came to my residence. It was hardly 7 am and I was to drink my morning coffee. All of a sudden Mr. Harilal came to my house and fell at my feet. I was surprised. Then Harilal requested me for help. For a moment I was in a dilemma whether to interfere or not. What role had I to play? If so, how? I got the answer. Then I assured that I would help.

Immediately I sent one person with a message to Mr.Banoth Jagru to come and meet me immediately. On my request Mr. Jagru and his wife came to me on a bullock cart. I informed him what has exactly happened and finally I could infer that the issue had a remedy. I convinced Mr. Jagru that after all Mr. Harilal is young and emotional but he is his nephew. In a moment of anger he had reacted but was not a big issue nor did he have any bad motive. It is pardonable and Jagru may withdraw the case as Mr. Harilal's job was at stake. At last Mr. Jagru and his family were convinced and the issue was solved amicably and the case was withdrawn.

Next day Mr. Harilal came and met me and expressed his gratitude. He was literally in tears. This particular incident made an indelible mark on my life because it taught me that the rural Bank Manager has a vital and important role to play in the social lives of the rural people, especially agricultural farmers. Banker is a friend, philosopher and guide in social, economic, and all aspects however young he might be.

Arrival

Departure

* * * * *

Case 23 – First Person Accounts GAK

After completing my post-graduation in Agriculture with Specialization in Extension Education, I joined the bank as an Agricultural Officer.

My First Posting

I joined as Agricultural Officer at **Nellore branch** in mid 1982, just before the June closing, an entirely new world for a science student, and enjoyed the experience of sleepless nights in tallying the books and finding out the differences

After the initial working in various departments of the branch, I was into the much-awaited Agricultural Finance Department; the previous Agricultural Officer (a native of Tamilnadu) was about to be relieved, as I have been posted there. The Agricultural lending was scattered in almost 30 villages, all over the district up to distance of 100 kms, with only 4-5 villages having more number of accounts; the portfolio was also small (when compared to Model I VVK) and the recovery percentage was only around 18%

Nellore District has been the traditional rice bowl of A.P., as the name itself denotes growing single paddy crop followed by the legume crop under the tanks/canal irrigation and two paddy crops /legume under filter points, besides these, sugarcane was also being cultivated in some pockets of irrigated area, with the district having a cooperative sugar factory nearby in Kovur which is just on the other side of the river Pennar parallel to Nellore town.

After joining the branch, my main objectives were

1. Increasing the recovery in Agriculture.

2. Increasing the Agriculture portfolio.

Slowly, I started getting myself involved in the serious banking business of lending and recovery, attending Block level and District level meetings. It was observed that the main / one of the reasons for over dues were not maintaining *regular contact* with the borrowers /villagers and liaison with the Government Agencies and Sugar factory officials. As the days progressed, the borrowers understood that if the payment is regular or if there is a crop failure [not by drought, but due to the unseasonal cyclones which hit Nellore district the previous three, four years continuously] finance would be sanctioned / renewed within no time. With this understanding recovery started improving.

During the course of time, it was observed that there was one ledger which had only 15-20 accounts and the total amount of the ledger was less than Rs10000/- with the letters DRI. The clerk connected to Advances Department informed me that for meeting the target we had to finance certain accounts under the above scheme. I had been provided with Hand book of Agricultural Finance Schemes which has guided me about the Differential Rate of Interest and the eligibility criteria.

Training

During the above period, after working in the branch for 3-4 months I attended the Induction-cum-Branch Banking for Agricultural Officers, which helped me in getting acquainted with the situation, as I started correlating the little experience I had to what is being taught.

I was fresh from college, having studied day in day out, about Rural Development and also having conducted an evaluative study on the "Impact of Adult Education on the Farm Learners (farmers)" as project work for the thesis, coupled with the observation that most of the weaker sections were, in-fact, not getting the benefit.

Tenant Farmers

I observed that the village Kodurupadu with its hamlets Girijanapalem, Harijanapalem, Arundatipalem and Gavalapalem were having tenant farmers who were allotted land under the CJFS (Coop. Joint Farming Society) each varying from Ac 0.150 cents to Ac 0.300 cents by the Government. I observed that they were cultivating groundnut, but were taking loans from money lenders/brokers as they were not in the habit of approaching the bank may be due to their unawareness or other inhibitions. I started giving crop loans starting from Rs.150/- to Rs300/- depending upon the crop Paddy / Groundnut / Blackgram / Greengram / Vegetables. The scale of finance at that time was ranging from Rs 800/- to Rs 1000/-per acre. Even when most of the tenants were financed, more than a 100 of them, the outstanding amount was less than Rs 30000/- which was equal to one big crop loan but that "Pavala" (Twenty five paisa) vaddi with only revenue stamp for DPN and unstamped hypothecation deed helped these people, as they were not made to spend anything. My branch head advised me to check whether I was increasing the work without profit to the bank. I convinced him about the Banks 1% commitment for DRI lending. This gave me *immense satisfaction*, as more than 100 tenant farmers were brought under the gamut of banking.

The repayment was proper and some tenants farmers were paying in sums of Rs 25/-, Rs30/- on weekly/fortnightly, whenever we visited the village, thereby retaining entire proceeds of crop for themselves. This had improved the recovery position as we used to convey the information to other borrowers that these tenant farmers are regular in repayment

During the course of Branch inspection by inspection officials, we took them for inspection to these villages, the inspecting officer told me that the poor farmers appreciated our work and held us in high esteem which gave me and others immense satisfaction.

The recovery was also good, not only because of the follow up but because of the *social pressures, recognition, identification of the tenants by the bank officials, and extolling for regular repayments whenever we meet them, and asking others to emulate their example.* Besides we started getting good amount of deposits from the farming community as our acquaintance with the villagers started growing.

In the three years span I had the satisfaction of meeting the objectives of increasing the agricultural advances and improving the recovery to 54%.

As a Rural Branch Manager

In the month of August 1987 while I was working at Rajamundry, I was identified to head the Rural Branch at Kateru village near Rajamundry, East Godavari District. Before my selection, my Branch Manager had informed me, about the proposal of selecting me as the Branch Head. As I was working in Advances Department, I had some information about the village and was reluctant to take up the assignment for the following reasons.

1. There were many suit filed accounts at that time including those of the then village Sarpanch and some important leaders of the village
2. The Ex-Sarpanch was banking with us and enjoying advances limits.

There was rivalry in the village, regarding the branch location whether it should be inside the village, or in the ex-Sarpanchs street. Most of the villagers were the supporters of the Sarpanch belonging to a regional political party and were not willing to step into the street.

"I knew the area like the back of my palm. I was a best suited to head that branch." After hearing about these problems from me, my Branch Manager informed the Regional Office that I knew the ins and outs of the locality, I will be best suited to head that branch.

I took charge of the branch on 20.9.1987, and observed that

1. the branch had been opened without any publicity – 3 months earlier on 24.06.1987, as there was opposition from the villagers for opening of our branch since another Bank's Cluster branch was already operating in the village.

2. the total deposits was only around Rs 20000/- with no advances.
3. only a temporary branch head was functioning at the branch on rotation basis (every week one Manager was deputed from nearby Rajahmundry/ Hukumpet branches to act as Branch Manager) and the Head Cashier posted was already promoted as officer and was about to go on inter-zonal transfer. The villagers had misgivings about the stability and continuity of the bank and hesitated to open and operate their accounts with the bank.

Turn Around

During the 1st week of my posting, I observed that there were only 1 or 2 Vouchers per day and some times there were none and the branch staff used to credit / withdraw Rs 10/- from their accounts to show vouchers.

The infrastructure was poor-there were no cash cabins or counters, only two rooms were provided and the cashier made payments from his table.

Going out and meeting people

I started moving with the villagers, after identifying the big farmers of the village as a confidence building measure.

Though East Godavari District produces about 10% of A.P Food grain production and the river Godavari flows adjacent to the village boundaries, and the village had rich black soil, water was not available for cultivation as the village is located at a higher plane. Tobacco is the main crop in the village, followed by Paddy, Sugarcane and other crops which were grown using borewells. Since it was the end of September, the crop has already been financed by the other bank and we had to wait for the next season to finance; and also to wait for deposits till the next harvesting season. The only option was to finance loans under pledge of jewels which we started on 2 days a week basis.

Tactics

One Dhal mill was located on the outskirts of the village belonging to the merchants of Rajahmundry. During my visit to the Dhal mill and discussions with the merchants I was informed that they were getting DD's from Andhra Bnk at 50% of the commission rate by depositing Rs100/- and Rs50/- notes and since they were getting currency of Rs.10/- and Rs.20/- more they are not able to remit the same and also that DD's were available only in the evening.

As we did not have sufficient work for Head Cashier and the Sub Staff, we offered to give them the same concession for entire amount of deposit with a condition that they should deposit maximum of 10 bundles of Rs 10/-/Rs20/- comprising of upto 50% deposit along with bigger denomination for which they agreed.

We started issuing DD's and cashier used to sort the cash till afternoon and remit the amount to Rajahmundry branch after meeting out the Jewel Loan disbursements. The villagers started feeling that there was activity at the branch. Out of the Jewel Loans disbursements the farmers from nearby villages used to take cash and the local people started depositing the same in SB and to use as and when needed as the assayer for gold valuation used to be available for 2-days in a week and the villagers started banking with us.

The following incidents helped in building the image of the branch.

1. Invitation to Wedding

One of the residents of the village of Kateru (who was a medium size farmer) gave an invitation for the marriage of his son at a place called Raghudevapuram which is almost 25 km from Kateru and the marriage was at night around 11.30 pm.

I started for the marriage at around 10.00 pm and as I was nearing that village my Yezdi motor cycle tyre got punctured. I started cursing myself (at the thought of attending a marriage of some unknown person) and I parked the vehicle on the side of the road. A person was watering his field. I introduced myself and told him the trouble I was in. He gave me his bicycle and helped me reach the marriage venue, 2 km away. At the venue, the villagers saw me coming on the bicycle and enquired. After hearing about the incident and about my attendance at the marriage in the midnight, the matter has became talk of the place and after attending the marriage they arranged a car for me and a tractor to carry my motorcycle to Kateru

Invitation to wedding capitalized

Next day, I got the deposit from Mr.Surya Rao and he said that neither his banker nor the bride's family banker attended the marriage whereas I attended and aroused his sentiments and made him come to the bank. He also told us that there was a discussion and general agreement at the marriage venue among most of the villagers and friends and relatives from the surrounding villages to bank with us. It is not difficult to win over rural-folk.

2. Relationship beyond Banking

As said earlier, there was rivalry in the village and the branch was opened in the area where one group was dominant and the other group was not banking with us. During the discussions, we came to know that the youth of the village used to play ball-badminton. We (Head Cashier and myself) mobilized a group of youngsters and started playing badminton by motivating the youth of one group and after a few days opened another court for the other group and used to play with both the groups. After some time both the groups started knowing that we meant sport and business and that we were not for any one group.

Invitation to rural factionist youth

Through this movement with youth, we were able to know about the villagers, as to who sell/purchase land, their stature and the background which helped in the improvement of the business. Youth of 1987 now influential middle aged still recall those wonderful days, I am told after 20 years.

3. Total Requirements:

Crop loans - (one season made the difference) Earlier a group of farmers of around 4-5 families (15-20 a/cs) used to avail crop loans from Rajahmundry branch and the majority was availing loans from another bank. As said earlier the major crop in the village was Tobacco and the produce had to be sold to the Tobacco Board and payment was made through cheques. The loan amount and name of the lender recorded in the Tobacco board pass book. It was observed and found out that most of the loans sanctioned by the bank were only for Rs 5000/- and they were coming for Jewel Loans. When enquired, the farmers informed that if any body wanted more loan, they had to wait for fifteen days to one month as the sanction has to come from Regional Office.

At that time the scale of finance for Tobacco was Rs3000/- and a farmer having a Tobacco barn (5 acres) was eligible for a loan of Rs15000/- and for ½ barn (2.5 acre) an amount of Rs7500/-. Hence the farmers were going in for Jewel Loans. During the farmers meetings we made a propaganda about scale of finance and the amounts we could give, etc. without waiting period (the branch lending powers for crop loan was upto Rs.30000/-). The crop loans portfolio picked up and one season made the difference, and almost all the farmers started coming to us.

4. Customer Relationship Management:

During the Branch inauguration, a Puja was done at 6.30am and branch inauguration took place at the same time on 24.06.1987. One day before the inauguration, we officers from Rajahmundry branch went to village for inviting the farmers for inauguration.

At that time, one well dressed farmer, who was influential in the village, informed us that he had opposed the opening of our branch in the village and petitions were sent to RBI and all the farmers were customers of the other bank and that bank was doing good service to everybody and so they did not want our bank in the village. It so happened that after three months, I took charge of the branch and was told that he was a progressive farmer and even the Central Tobacco Research Institute (CTRI) used to bring officials for visits to his farm and also that he and his brothers were getting substantial compensation from the Government for the A.P.Paper mills land.

When I approached him, he told me point blank, that he did not want to bank with us as he had been ill-treated by our Rajahmundry Branch and that he was against the opening of our branch and he was getting VIP treatment from the other Bank. After a week in the evening, I visited him at his farm next to the river bund after parking my vehicle on the bund. On seeing me he stated that he did not want to see me. I said that I have not come for the deposit. I told him that I was a Post Graduate in Agriculture and came from Paddy cultivating area and that as I have been told about his progressiveness in farming and I wanted to know about Tobacco cultivation. He took me inside the farm for a short visit.

I used to visit him regularly once in a week / 10 days and the discussion went on from cultivation practices to other aspects. After about 50 such visits and almost one year by which time rapport was built, he said that he was getting first cheque of Rs 7 lakhs I had not asked anything, as he was not willing to open an a/c with us. Now as there was very good bonding between us I left the decision to him. He was pleased and he gave the cheque and also helped us in getting the funds of his brothers.

He owned land on the main road of the village, through which all the buses upto Seethanagaram used to ply. He offered to construct the premises for the branch and till date the branch is in the same building.

A man, who had sent petitions for not opening a bank, has become the landlord of the branch.

During those days, the annual closing was done in December and in March 1989, the banks Balance Sheet was for 1year and 3 months and the branch had shown profit and the controlling office was appreciative of that as most of the Rural branches in those days were making losses.

During the year 1989-90, the branch was adjudged "Best Performing Branch" in the Region among the rural branches.

It is through small steps and building relationships, more than banking and attracting the youth that we could build long term business relations. This is now named as Customer Relationship Managements leveraging, of course, technology.

* * * * *

Case 24– First Person Accounts MMR

"I joined the bank in the year 1978 as Agriculture Officer and was posted to Kakinada branch; Kakinada is the district head quarter of East Godavari, a forward district in every respect.

It was a lucky beginning for me because I was exposed to DLCC meetings under Lead Bank scheme. Andhra Bank, the lead Bank was always encouraged my participation. The lead bank officer made sure that I attended the meetings, by informing me over phone in advance. This was because of my active participation in every meeting.

It gave me insights into the banks' role in rural development and the purpose of Nationalization of banks. That's how agriculture graduates and post graduates had entered into a rewarding service and career. I could reach to the high echelons of bank's hierarchy due to my early career opportunities.

The Chairman of D.L.C.C. the District Collector was a very dynamic young man from whom I learnt the concerns of the district administration in *pushing* through the government programmes. He used to say that he spent a lot of time with bankers. In those days some Collectors were so vexed with the negative attitude of Bank Managers, that they said banks were nationalized but not their Managers!

The lack of initiative, I believed, was due to lack of independence, freedom, and autonomy of the Bank Managers in general. For everything they wanted clearance from higher ups. I was secretly entertaining a dream 'what I would do if I were to become a Manager'.

There were work-shops and panel discussions organized. Our Rajahmundry Branch Manager was participating in those work shops on special request from the Collector. He had established a name for himself for his work in a backward district earlier.

During my stay at Kakinada the Rajahmundry in charge and myself V.V.K. (Village Vikas Kendra) went to Elamanchali to survey for a branch to be opened. There I was exposed to an NGO, BCT engaged in rural transformation. Development is a mild word to describe the kind of work they were engaged in. With this background I went to branch which was opened in 1978. It was one of four rural branches opened in a span of three months for the first time in a backward district, thanks to the efforts and initiative of our district head quarters Manager who later became Branch Manager of Rajahmundry. It was a bold decision by the bank. The Manager went from a backward district to a forward district and my case was reverse.

On a rainy day 4th August 1981 I reached the village branch housed in a two room tiled house of Gram Panchayat. The village was a remote place. Only one state transport bus used to ply for four times a week from the nearest town. The village being remote, the Branch Manager was given an official residence in the town. The branch had a four member team, a Cashier, a Clerk, a Peon and the Branch Manager.

On the day of my joining, I was shocked to find the bank hardly did any business. I started analyzing the prospects of improving the image and the business of the bank. Some of the impediments for the development of the bank were: Manager resides outside the village, the villager's do not believe that he is one of them and can help them. The two Managers who worked before me never stayed in the village. The villagers treated the bank as a chit fund company and the Manager as an agent of chit fund company who comes in the morning at 11.00 am and leaves by 4.00 pm collecting the cash in a bag. Other staff staying in the village engaged themselves in small business activities forgetting that they were the employees of the Bank.

The borrowers, mostly agriculturists, had not been paying the dues, thinking that they had to pay additionally for the renewal of their accounts. There by the entire portfolio had become overdue with a recovery percentage of 5 to 6 %. A proposal for the construction of new premises was sanctioned by Head Office but was not executed. The farmers were progressive in nature and were cultivating Cotton, Chillies and other commercial crops in the Black Cotton soil fields.

Being an agricultural graduate I could make out the available potential in financing and also recovery by timely approach and follow up.

Steps taken:

- Timely reporting to the Office before commencement of office hours and assigning the work to the cashier and regular meetings with the villagers. Organized *gramsabhas* and explained the schemes of the bank for financing and various deposit schemes.
- Took up with land lord for construction of new premises for Bank building with Manager‘s quarters.
- Meanwhile internal inspection of the branch commenced and was completed and my was work appreciated.

The villagers started believing that the bank would do some thing for them and started coming to the Bank.

I requested the Regional Manager to transfer the Clerk as there was no work in the branch and requested for substitute to be provided after a year when the branch business was developed. It was immediately done and the cost on establishment reduced.

When I took over the branch in 1981 it was in a bad shape worthy of closure with the permission of RBI. The villagers would not have been as unhappy for it, for they could get another bank there. That was the sorry state of affairs. The officers posted had neither the dynamism nor knowledge of agriculture or meaning of rural service.

The first thing I did after joining the branch was to stay in the village with my family. I put my young daughter in Fatima residential school in the town. I had new building constructed with banks help for residence cum office. Later for the comfort of the staff we had extra rooms constructed for them to live in the village itself. That was a clear message sent to villagers in and around the place. They started responding. It had become 'our bank' in their minds. Then using my knowledge of agriculture I could gain the confidence of the farmers, particularly small farmers. I did not neglect the weaker-sections, the landless and others who were engaged in other occupations. We met our obligations with the government sponsored programmes.

Although VVK was established in 1978 at District Head Quarters branch which was supposed to give support to all the four branches, I did everything on my own.

Things happened:

The Land lord started the constructing a building at the bus stand road little outside the village. With in five months the building was complete and the furnishing was provided by the Zonal office Chennai. The branch looked better than a city branch. The branch was shifted to the new building on 12 May 1982 by the Zonal Head. The budget meeting of district branches was held at District Head Quarters branch where I promised the management a growth of 100% The then Area Head asked me to do whatever I could, 'there is no target for me' he said.

By the year end I did more than 100% in deposits and more than 75% growth in advances with a recovery of 95%. I got the Managers residence constructed by the land lord and I shifted to the place in the following year. I had also advised the land lord to construct two portions for the Staff members at the backside of our building and both Head cashier and the peon were also staying in the compound.

I introduced Jewel Loans for the farmers on shifting to the new premises which has picked up very well and boosted the crop loan portfolio very much. I had also introduced the Locker facility in the village for safe keeping of the gold and jewellery ornaments for the customers.

The Bank was treated with high esteem by the Government officials and the local president of the *Panchayat* used to tell in the farmers meetings that our Bank is the only Bank of the poor and needy people and all other banks in the block are working for and at the behest of affluent people. There was not even a single complaint on the working of the branch during my stay and the Bank was considered as sacred as a temple in the village and set an example in the area.

I stayed for a total period of four and half years as a successful Manager. I was also promoted to Scale II at that branch. The staff strength has increased to 5 and it *had become a training centre for the new recruits for learning rural banking.* I also proudly say that the Agricultural Officers on training at Hyderabad had visited the branch for a case study on recovery of tractor loan accounts.

I also acknowledge the recognition of the management for the development of the branch. The Chairman & Managing Director had visited the branch in the year 1984 during the platinum jubilee celebrations of our Bank.

I rose to a Deputy General Manager's position at the Bank; still I feel it is not because of my other assignments at places like Jubilee Hills, Overseas etc but due to the hard work rendered by me with dedication and sincerity at this small village branch.

I acknowledge the support and encouragement of the colleagues- particularly the head cashier and sub-staff members but for whom I could not have shown the results. Still I feel I had constructed the home with the strong foundation laid by these two staff members, who stood behind me as rocks in the business growth.

Face lift to the bank

Uplift for the village

* * * * *

Case 25 – First Person Accounts NSP

I joined a Nationalized Bank in 1982 as an Agricultural Officer. In my 28 years of banking career I served in various geographical areas.

I experienced banking life in Metro, Rural, Urban and Foreign branches. I have also worked in almost all the departments of the bank. I specialized in rural banking for 11 years and moved on to Information Technology (13 years including 3 years for establishing and running the IT system at overseas subsidiary).

My Background

As I hail from a rural agricultural family, I used to go to the fields and extend support to my father when I was young and thus learned the hardships of a farmer at a very young age. As I grew older, I could visit the fields only during vacation and began to understand why people term Indian agriculture a gamble.

Nature's fury coupled with man made problem plays havoc in the lives of farmers. Heavy rains, drought, crop diseases, pests as well as increased input costs, fall in prices at the harvest time, delayed implementation of plans or financial help from Government - all take a toll on the farmer's life. To cite an instance, the A.P. Government planned to construct an irrigation project to supply water for crops over large areas covering many districts. Assuring this water facility, Govt. advised the agriculturists to level and develop their rain fed lands to suit canal irrigated crop. Land Mortgage Bank provided them with the necessary finance. However, the promised water supply did not materialize for a long period, forcing the farmers to sell their lands to repay the loans to LMB & PACS. My family was also a victim of this delayed and unfulfilled promise by the Government. The suffering and nightmarish experiences that my family went through made an indelible impression on my mind.

Opted to work in Rural Area

My rural background and the insight into the sufferings of rural folk made me readily accept the post of A.O in the Bank. But my first posting at Hyderabad main branch did not give me any satisfaction as most of my time was spent in obtaining revival letters (LADs) from the borrowers of various villages or in attending to suit filed loan cases. So I opted to work in a rural branch though rural service was not compulsory for a banker in those days. I was posted to rural branch in a backward and drought prone area.

I tried to follow the advice of my predecessor and a few self laid principles to be a good rural banker.

- Create awareness and educate people to use the banking facility to the maximum.
- Do not yield to any outside pressure which harms the image / prestige of the bank.
- If the bank cannot provide the required financial assistance, inform the applicants immediately, so that they can make alternate arrangement.
- Educate the people about the benefits of prompt repayment so that more schemes may come.
- Field inspections should be thorough at various stages especially before sanctioning the loan and during the disbursal.
- Prompt sanctions / disbursal are essentials.

- Be pro-active for natural calamities and insurance claims.

These guidelines helped me in carrying out my duties and helping the rural customers. From the 'Treasure Trough' of my experiences, I would like to share with you a few pleasant, cherished memories.

I educated the customers on the necessity of clearing overdue loans so that they can be the beneficiaries of 2nd dose assistance under Central Sponsored Program, for minor irrigation.

The beneficiaries who cleared the over dues were 36, out of whom 32 belonged to Scheduled Caste. The D.R.D.A officials were surprised and verified the ledgers and records to confirm the loans were fully repaid. They identified the individuals too, going round the villages and making enquiries. Fully satisfied that the list was genuine, they released the subsidy within a week.

The bank won the appreciation of the officials as well as the villagers. After about 3 years of service at that branch I was transferred to lead the Special Agriculture Kendra at district headquarter branch.

Revival of a branch

Another incident stands out distinctly in my memory. In Dec'90, a naxalite was arrested by police in the village where I served earlier and in retaliation, about 16 Government Officials, from and around the village, were kidnapped. One of them was an officer from that branch. The branch was closed for 3 months. The customers grew panicky and desired to withdraw their money. The branch reopened in March'91, but with in a brief spell of one week, the staff expressed their inability in running the branch due to fear complex. At this stage I was requested to run the branch for some time till alternate arrangements were made. Though I had fever at that time, I went there and took the charge of the branch on 23rd March.

Deadline for ADRs

My first priority, on joining the branch was to submit the Agricultural Debt Relief claims to RBI by 31st March. I did so on 30th March through Zonal Office, though it called for a lot of concentration and effort. Agricultural Department from Zonal Office was in constant touch with the branch during this period. Once again my efforts brought laurels to the bank as the relief claims were finalized and submitted in spite of all the problems faced by the branch and benefited many customers. I glowed with inner satisfaction for a job well done.

Cooperation from villagers

Since no officer was willing to take charge of this problematic branch, I was advised to continue as incharge for longer time. I took up the challenge willingly and ran the branch with minimum staff (one cashier and one sub-staff) but with the maximum co-operation from the villagers as they realized finally how beneficial the bank was to all of them. *The same people who kidnapped one of the officers, escorted me to a distance of 20 km in a subsequent situation during those six months, as they saw trouble brewing in that area due to the arrest of one of their leaders.* In spite of many odd situations, the branch was brought on track and it started functioning smoothly.

Trouble – shooter - role

Now another challenge came my way. On 2nd Aug' 91, another rural branch was blasted by Naxalites. Valuables were shifted to one of the branches at district headquarters leaving furniture and many old records at the branch. Permission was taken from the District Collector to shift the branch to a nearby semi-urban area. This branch also remained closed for three months. I was assigned the task of shifting, re-opening and running of the branch. I used the good will of customers of the previous branch and completed the shifting smoothly, without taking police protection though it was suggested by higher authorities.

Soon after reopening of the branch, I was approached by the Govt. officials to take up the pending joint screening of applications for Govt. Schemes in four villages. I did this in the shortest possible time in 3 villages and displayed the selected list in their Panchayat offices before leaving the joint screening meeting. I convinced the officials / villagers that if our short listing (of any one) was not acceptable for any reason, the same should be conveyed to the Bank within a week or else the list would be considered final.

We encountered a strange situation in the fourth village. The list was finalized and displayed in the Panchayat office. But when we were about to leave, a group of people started complaining against Government officials. In spite of my telling them repeatedly that I was a bank official and their complaints, if any, should be relevant to banking, they persisted in their complaints and told us that we should at least listen to them.

Finally, I advised them to come to the bank and air their grievances. Only then did they allow us to leave the village. But the Govt. officials were scared and expected trouble from the villagers. I told them to come with us. When we just came out of the village, we saw two tractors approaching us filled with people who were armed with sticks.

I was scared out of my wits when I saw them. Are they going to attack me? How do I protect myself and the Government officials to whom I gave all sorts of assurances? I gathered my wits and put up a brave front and approached them.

On enquiry I came to know that these people were coming to our rescue since we got delayed in the village. Tears of joy welled up in my eyes. These people considered me, accepted me as one of them; took upon themselves the responsibility of protecting me. My heart sang with joy and gratitude. My faith in the inherent goodness of mankind was restored.

My few months service earned the goodwill and affection of these people; Long back, their counter parts (my native villagers) in Adilabad district used to run away on seeing any LMB / PACS vehicle since they had no way of repaying their debts and dreaded the officers. It is a long and memorable journey from there to here! Given a chance, I would like to serve in a rural area once again, which gave me abundant love, satisfaction and a sense of achievement.

* * * * *

Case 26 – First Person Accounts NG

I joined the bank as Agricultural Specialist-DRO in 1990 and there was no looking back since then. It was highly significant to me as well as to my father. Throughout his life my father had been loyal, honest and hard working agricultural labour who later by dint of his hard work acquired and cultivated land of his own. We belong to a tribal family. My father never wanted his children to toil like him.

His dreams were fulfilled when I graduated in Agriculture from Tirupati.

I was a sportsman too, played volley ball for the State and won gold medal in pole vault. After completion of my degree I stayed in the village and formed Girijana Youth Association. As President of the association I sponsored sewing machines for 20 women tribals and SBI Atmakur sanctioned loans under self-employment scheme. Simultaneously I tried to educate the tribal children.

My first hand experience of economic constraints, the neglect and indifference shown to the tribals and a strong desire to help the downtrodden , made me look forward to banking., especially rural banking. *Banking has never been a profession for me; it has been a passion.* I worked for the first 7½ years in Gujarat, first as Agricultural Officer and then as Branch Manager. I brought a turn around of my branch and won appreciation of my superiors.

I worked for 3 years as in charge of Priority Sector (Agriculture) in the Regional Office when I had an exposure to the functioning of different branches and the working style of different

Managers. I also had an opportunity to attend State level meetings and Hyderabad dstrict level meetings and also special meetings convened by NABARD along with regional heads. At times I attended the meetings alone.

For another 3 years I worked in a city branch and then in the year 2004 I was posted to a rural branch in a backward district in AP which was in existence since 1978. Around 38% of the branch's advances were bad debts – known as non-performing assets-NPAs. Having gained diverse experiences in 15 years of my service, I had a fairly good idea about what I was supposed to do during my stay, .

As a student of agriculture I knew the significance of farm finance to the Bank Manager without which the banker could achieve practically nothing in the village branch. Moreover as a tribal who had seen generations of neglect by the educated, urban, dominant community, I knew my priorities. **Bank funds must reach the depressed and deprived classes in rural area.**

Thanks to government initiatives, these people got some development loans but the banks did not give production loans without which they could not repay the development loans. All these years many of my predecessors never looked at the real problem of financing the poor.

Moreover whatever bank targets were achieved, it was through financing the rich farmers who cultivated cash crops, neglecting the poor farmers and their needs. I knew the bank I was serving was a progressive bank with pro-poor policies. It is only the individuals who were not translating the policies into action. ***I must make a difference***, I thought. The bank's flag must fly high for everybody to notice.

Little did I imagine that I was running a risk at a place where majority of my colleagues did not share my values and thoughts. I never knew that they would be closely watching my every move.

First thing I did after joining the branch was to keep the media and middlemen out. I was rather blunt to them which earned me some enemies.

Immediately after my taking over charge, there was pressure from political workers of left parties to re-schedule the agricultural loans as per the Government directives. Myself and my staff had to work day and night to prepare the list of 1617 default borrowers. We had to attend to those who came to the branch to repay their dues and those who had to open SB accounts because I insisted on every borrower opening Savings Bank account before availing the loans. We allowed S/B account transactions up to 3.30 pm and there after till late into night we allowed people to repay and become eligible for fresh loans. It was a Herculean task-calculating interest, granting fresh loans and obtaining documents in which every staff member assisted. If you are sincere, people automatically extend cooperation. The rural branch was shifted to the town because the Naxals blasted many rural branches and the rural premises,. When the town people watched us working in the nights, the image of the bank improved and the flag of the bank was flying high in every sense.

I must mention the special support I received from a sub-staff member. He rendered excellent service. We spent 45 days exclusively for recovering agricultural loans, renewals, fresh appraisals, sanctions, disbursement and also pre and post sanction inspections. *The higher ups hardly knew what was happening in the villages, same was the case in many other rural branches.*

Fortunately for me the Deputy Regional Manager visited the branch and understood that we were understaffed, and struggling to cope up with work. *He sent reinforcements from the neighboring branches causing disturbance to those branches.* Probably this special favour done to me was not appreciated by other Managers who were among the colleagues eagerly expecting something untoward to happen to me as I was causing a heart burn to them. I targeted to reduce the NPAs to 5% from 36%. I fell ill on 20th Sep 2004. I also promised shelter to the farmers who could not return home due to rains. There were some who were attacked by bears and had to be sheltered. After the bear attacks there was greater pressure on us to complete the work during day time. Those who remained had to be provided shelter in the Manager's quarters. At that time I was living alone.

During 2004-05, all accounts were computerized and that received top priority.

Now we started moving into villages and documentation was done in the villages particularly for SHGs. In some remote villages we combined field visits obtaining applications and documents to save TA & DA and actual transportation expenses for the staff. Within two days we completed all formalities in the villages. We worked up to 11 pm at times to complete the work of SHGs. That became necessary because of the late return of the women from the fields. It is worth noting that the villages we served have become distant places because of the shifting of the branch after Naxals blasting the branch.

The villagers offered us shelter over night, but we declined and returned to town risking our lives.

I had another duty to do as an agricultural specialist. I had to recommend right mixture of pesticides and insecticides to the cotton growers. I even inspected the disease conditions of the crop for 15 days before recommending the exact mixture and dosage. I had tried the mixtures in my backyard in Hyderabad before advising farmers. An inappropriate recommendation of the use of pesticides/insecticides would have made me accountable to the farmers. These are the routine risks in the life of a rural Bank Manager. If he is not a specialist he would not take those risks. That is his good fortune.

Farmer's Clubs and SHGs

There were three FCs before I went to the branch but they were clubs of progressive farmers who were concerned only with getting loans and showed no interest in developmental activities.

I started 2 clubs for the scheduled tribe one exclusively for tribal women and other for tribal men in two *Thandas* in the month of May 2006. AGM, NABARD inaugurated the women's club and at the suggestion of AGM, we granted a tractor loan to the President of the club. NABARD sanctioned each club Rs. 5000. A fund was raised and the money was kept in F.D.R. in the name of the President.

Many groups were formed even before I took charge. Even 6 to 8 year old SHGs did not get any financial assistance from the bank! They distributed the corpus fund and continued with thrift. I verified their records and observed that they had no idea of what SHG was. I had to clarify to the group members that, among other things, poorest of poor should get first priority in the 'help'. Gradually all members' incomes should go up for productive activities. I had monitored the progress of more than 100 SHGs.

We arranged purchase of dairy animals from West Godavari dist. for SHGs. *I always avoided loan melas and involvement of government officials just for the sake of publicity.*

Farmers began approaching me for advise on technical matters like pest control. I gave advice only when I was confident. I suggested what was practical. I advised borrowers and *non-borrowers.*

There were 200 SHGs formed in 1998 but no linkage was established with the bank. I took up that work. I took up every government scheme and created awareness and made SHGs avail their rights fully. I trained a few farmers and asked them to train other farmers because I could not spare time for all.

Timely irrigation, timely ploughing, applying fertilizers, insecticides, harvesting, would reduce the cost of cultivation and increases the production. This is the benefit the farmers got by having a Manager background in Agriculture.

SHGs were not functioning the way they should. I reactivated some of them. Proper education, maintenance of books, recording of minutes, was necessary. Because of poor functioning of the SHG they could not be linked with bank credit. I helped them in all these respects. It was time consuming and tiresome. I watched the groups for their regular repayment. For good SHGs we enhanced the limits. We had in all 160 SHG at the end of 2005 and added 130 SHG in 2006. Today most of them were eligible upto a loan limit of Rs 5 lakhs.

Looking back I think the factors that motivated me to do what I did for which I received appreciation letters from the very same higher management who had put a blot on my character for acting the way I did, as under:

1. The area was under drought for previous 5 to 6 years and small and marginal farmers had started *migrating*. The administration might have argued that it is the government's responsibility.
2. This branch had been making loss ever since its inception (30 years)
3. There were proposals of merging the branch with another branch 30 km away. Already due to naxal's problems, the Service Area moved away by 10 km to the new premises.

Now it would have add by another 30 kms. *Bank may have gained but what about the thousands of the poor whose hopes the bank had raised?*

4. I wanted to take my chance. I toured all the villages in the Service Area and canvassed for Savings Banks Accounts. I educated people about the bank's worries which they alone could solve by using services for mutual benefit. 'Start repayments and become eligible for fresh loans' was my main plan. I saw concurrence in many of them wherever I went along with the sub-staff member who was my tower of strength. A few repaid the loans with interest. I processed and granted fresh loans to them which had demonstrative effect on others who followed suit. Mutual trust was re-established, within a week.

There was an unusual rush that I had to cope with. Farmers from various villages visited the branch in hundreds, loanees for repayment and non-loanees for fresh assistance. Since all of them are dalits or tribals or other depressed communities, I had to respond with sympathy. That was the compulsion. It resulted in 24/7 service in which *the staff responded with equal zeal.* But the administrators who had no empathy for the tribals and downtrodden would question my compulsions.

I had another worry. Among the crowds there were a few naxals, I was told. They were watching the situation. This was an important dimension considering the past history of the branch.

I had to negotiate with the crowds because of uncontrollable situation. I had a strategy which worked-dividing the farmers into two categories. For time consuming work, they were asked to come after 3 pm. The result was that I could recover Rs. 90 lakhs reducing net NPA (bad debts) to Rs. 60 lakhs resulting in Rs. 4.5 lakhs profit by the half year.

Extension Services

In August 2004, there were welcome showers but they blocked the roads. About 70-80 farmers were allowed to stay back in the bank. Women with children were also fed. That was the time I could discuss vocations, cropping pattern, crop rotation, irrigation, pest control etc. I had a feed back on their problems and suggested solutions. At that time they did not know that I was an agriculture graduate.

I took greater responsibility and risk. Later I visited their farms. After educating them on farming I started reforming on matters of banking. They had wrong notion of banks and banking because of the influence of politicians and middlemen and even input dealers – all with selfish and narrow interests.

Quality Support from the Staff

I spared one week specially for small and marginal farmers, land less labourers, SHGs mainly to educate them on banking discipline. To face the rush at the branch my entire team – Accountant, Cashiers, Sub-Staff and temporary staff member did excellent team work. Seeing the plight and anxiety of the poor folk they would have done the same anyway,. It was a human response, it could not be otherwise. Sometimes they worked till next morning. There were doubting Thomases who were never in such a situation.

I had one Sub-Staff who is now promoted and posted elsewhere as a Clerk. He had potential to grow in the bank based on the foundation he had. He was loyal and hardworking. We have identified bonded labour and rehabilitated them with financial assistance for self-employment. During kharif season I convinced the farmers that I was sparing for them my time instead of going to rich for deposits or approach government officials for parking funds with the bank. I lost no opportunity to educate them to remain loyal to the bank.

During next kharif season in June 2005 the farmers voluntarily deposited their surpluses.

I raised the deposits from Rs. 3 crores to Rs. 5 crores, advances from Rs. 2.72 crores to Rs. 8.3 crores, and profit to Rs. 26 lacs as on 31.3.06. NPAs stood at 5%. Based on my performance I got excellent, all round performance award for 2005-2006.

Ironically for the good work I had done I suffered humiliation at the hands of administration for minor lapses which they did not consider in the overall perspective. The reasons were more of organizational politics than factual.

What I did not anticipate was that the local money lenders and some political elements could not swallow the rising impact of tribal population in the area rising and deciding things independently. *They formed a group and made allegations against me.*

Adding fuel to the fire my successors who found their jobs tough stopped paying attention to the loans I had granted. One successor told the villagers that I would be out of service for the things I had done for which there was no approval of higher authorities. The money withheld in F.D.R. as a security for the old loans was released to them and further loans to the old clients were stopped.

Because of the false estimation of my performances by my successor and changed regional management attitude the image of the bank suffered and my name was tarnished. A set back to my career was due to fate than any thing else. But my conviction in financial inclusion is intact.

BANK

* * * * *

Case 27 – First Person Accounts KK

I was transferred to Warangal branch to head the proposed Village Vikas Kendra (VVK), sometime in March, 1978. Village Vikas Kendra was an innovative concept introduced by our bank to increase its reach in rural areas.

An innovative concept

Our bank was the first commercial bank in India to implement the rationale behind the Nationalization of banks in letter and spirit. As early as in 1974, the bank came out with an innovative scheme of helping the poor in promotion of their livelihood in urban areas through the small borrower cell (SBC) concept. SBC cells were opened in many urban centres including Hyderabad.

Enthused by the success of SBC concept, the bank replicated the model in rural areas through Village Vikas Kendras (VVK) which were attached to branches in rural areas. Three types of models were planned based on the extent of the area of operation, presence of the bank in the command area and the number of customers served by the branches in the area of operation of the VVK Model-1 would cater to the needs of 100 villages, model-2 for 50 villages and model- 3 was planned for 25 villages. Adequate human resources were proposed for each model. VVK was headed by an experienced Agricultural Officer having good exposure in rural economy and agricultural finance. Additional Agricultural Officers were posted based on the business generated by the centres.

The main tasks of the Officer-in-charge of the centre were to plan, implement, monitor and evaluate the business plans, providing technical advisory services to the beneficiaries by utilizing the human resources effectively. The Officer-in-charge would be assisted by an Officer and Cash Collectors. The main responsibility of Cash Collectors was to recover the bank dues in addition to originating applications for financial assistance. VVK had a loan committee headed by the Branch Manager with the Officer-in-charge as committee member. On many occasions I headed the committee in the absence of the Branch Manager. The loan committee was scheduled to meet once a week to consider the applications received during the period.

The committee concept was new at the branch level. I found the experience gained as a committee member, useful, in the later part of my career. I headed various committees in my career like Revamping Training System (1989), Committee on e-Training(2004), Committee on Manpower Planning for the Central Office (2002), Finance Committee on Selection of ATMs for the bank (2005) etc.

Comparison of VVK model with Grameena model of Dr.Mohammad Yunus (1976):

VVK model envisaged covering of all households in a village including the poorest people, and where the beneficiaries did not own any asset, the collateral was not insisted upon. This was the reason why the majority of beneficiaries were from weaker sections namely Scheduled Tribes/Castes. VVK had also encouraged group borrowing to improve recovery.

Grameena Bank on the other hand aimed at covering the poorest people, who could not provide collaterals to secure financial assistance. Group formation was one of the important features of the Grameena Bank concept.

Background of Warangal VVK

The first centre of VVK of Model-1 category was inaugurated on 2nd October 1977 at a place in Tamilnadu coinciding with the birthday of Mahatma Gandhi. This was followed by Warangal, also Model-1 category was inaugurated in March 1978.

The branch was making a steady progress in helping farmers in one block of the district since its inception in 1975. The branch conducted a survey with the help of the district administration and Lead Bank and formulated an area plan for extending agricultural finance in about 16 villages. The plan was sent for approval to the then Agricultural Refinance and Development Corporation (ARDC). The area plan subsequently became the basic plan of action for the VVK. The operational area was increased to cover 100 villages to suit the requirement of the VVK model-1. Lendable schemes and village wise plans were prepared. A comprehensive perspective plan for the next three years was in place by the time the centre was inaugurated by the branch.

Adequate infrastructure and staffing was proposed for our VVK. In other words it was a branch within a branch exclusively meant for integrated rural development in the adopted villages, proposed to be achieved through bank finance and technical advisory services.

The centre was inaugurated by the then District Collector Mr. S.Ray at a grand function held at the Zilla Parishad Hall and was attended by the departmental heads of the district and others including some of the beneficiaries.

It was attended by nearly 700 villagers from adopted villages. A small exhibition was arranged by the villages, KVIC, & Z.P. The bank had its own stall We got an artist to draw two or three cartoons. The Collector while inspecting the exhibition made a comment on the title. Credit was a rope to draw water from the wells to irrigate, not a rope to hang one self. The same was beautifully caricatured by the artist from the university.

The Collector asked the Manager to place some bank representatives at the stall to explain the caricatures. He asked the Manager, 'are you scaring away people? Please take care that the message goes clear and certain'.

But the Manager was focussing on the second cartoon in which the artist depicted **reversal of migration**. Thanks to establishment of VVK the people who migrated to town and cities were happily returning home.

Loan cheques were handed over to the beneficiaries by the district collector. Bank's then Regional Manager, stationed at Madras (Chennai), presided over the function.

The district collector praised the efforts of the Bank to reach the rural masses through the concept of VVK and assured his cooperation whenever required by the bank. The inauguration was a grand success and was prominently covered by the press notably by the Hindu and the Deccan Chronicle*.

---

* The Hindu of 23rd March 1978 carried two column report.

My reservations

However, I had my own reservations about the success of VVK since the staff members selected for the centre were *essentially bankers*, who were not exposed to this kind of concept before. I had expressed the same in my conversations with the Branch Manager and the Regional Manager. I also had the opportunity to present my views to the Zonal Manager during a seminar held at Coimbatore. He, however, assured me that all possible assistance would be provided.

Taken by storm

The concept of VVK had received considerable attention of other bankers. Even academicians evinced keen interest in the concept. I made a presentation on VVK at the seminar organized by the local University on rural development and highlighted the difference in approach in normal lending by a bank and that adopted by VVK model. 'The Hindu' prominently covered my presentation.

My Role

I was an agriculture Science graduate. I had also the benefit of serving in the rural areas as Agricultural Extension Officer ***(Zirayte Madatgar)*** for two years- 1966-68, in Domkonda Panchayat Samiti, near Kamareddi in Nizamabad district. I joined the State Department of Agriculture soon after my graduation in Agriculture in 1966. The main responsibilities of the post was to supervise and guide the village level workers (VLWs), providing technical guidance to the farmers, arranging inputs viz. seeds, fertilizers and pesticides to the farmers, planning and implementation of village level and block level agricultural development plans, participating in Panchayat Samiti and Zilla Parishad meetings etc. Among the notable challenges I faced during my tenure at Domkonda, I would like to mention the special campaigns handled by me for introduction of high yielding varieties of seeds and controlling of pest attacks on Maize crop. Thc area was so backward that farmers viewed spraying of insecticides with suspicion. Those were the days, when any epidemic affected the crops; the farmers used to go to the village deity (temple) and pray for protection from pests and diseases.

However, it was a rich experience for me as I was exposed to rural life and dealt with issues relating to agricultural development at field level. My interactions with farmers and others engaged in rural development were highly rewarding.

I also had a two month stint with the National Seeds Corporation (NSC) in the summer of 1966, propagating the use of high yielding varieties of paddy in East Godavari district. NSC had just then introduced hybrid seeds of paddy like IR-8 etc. in Andhra Pradesh.

I, therefore, thought that the rich experience I had in my earlier assignments would be useful to my new role as Officer in charge of VVK.

This was for the first time a commercial bank was entering the area of rural financing in an integrated manner with focus not only on extending credit but also on the technical advisory services. As VVK in charge, my role was also to provide guidance to the beneficiaries in their areas of operations like advising the farmers on ground water norms, new high yielding varieties, pests and diseases, arranging soil testing etc. Efforts were also made by me to create linkages between the beneficiaries and the bank's customers dealing in agricultural inputs and agricultural commodities. I had also arranged the services of technical personnel from the government departments mainly, Agriculture and Animal Husbandry for sorting out the problems of technical nature of the beneficiaries. Block Development Officer, lent a helping hand to my efforts to popularize the activities of the centre.

(i) Involving Government departments

I headed the centre for two and half years, implementing the plans prepared for the villages adopted by the bank. The first year experience had been highly rewarding, since for the first time many of these villages were covered by a bank extending credit and other services. In the beginning, the beneficiaries were getting the attention of the government departments, block development officials and non officials as they were all involved in the efforts of VVK to make the concept a success. District Rural Development Agency (DRDA) and Integrated Tribal Development Agency (ITDA), the two important wings of the government in rural development, had collaborated with VVK in providing subsidy and margin money to VVK borrowers. Khadi Gramodyog Board was actively supporting VVK in reaching out to village artisans like potters, carpenters, handloom weavers, blacksmiths etc. The board provided subsidy/margin/ seed money wherever required. Even District Child and Women Welfare Department had shown its interest in the villages covered by VVK, as perceptible change had appeared in the area. VVK, therefore, *successfully brought together most of the government departments dealing with developmental activities, in its pursuit to act as a change agent in the rural areas of the taluq.* This had immensely benefitted the area, all because VVK was standing out as a financial institution with a difference.

(ii) License for new branches

As a result of the activities of the centre, carried out with zeal and enthusiasm, bank could secure licenses from RBI to open four branches in the district. This was largely possible due to the support extended by the district administration.

(iii) Formulation of schemes

The taluq had no major irrigation source and depended largely on rains received in the kharif season. Small segment of farmcrs had irrigation wells. Therefore, VVK gave priority for increasing the minor irrigation potential by sanctioning loans for sinking /development of wells and purchase of pump sets, mostly oil engines as majority of villages did not have power connection. When state Electricity Board floated Rural Electricity Bonds in

1979-80 for the electrification of villages in the district, VVK formulated a scheme of helping farmers to contribute to the Rural Electricity Bonds. VVK sanctioned self liquidating term loans to more than 1000 farmers for buying electricity bonds. The loan amount was adjusted out of the maturity proceeds of the bonds. Thus VVK helped many villages in its area of operation to get power connections for agriculture purpose.

The impact of financing community irrigation wells (CI wells) could be gauged from the fact that for the first time, beneficiaries belonging to weaker sections brought substantial part of their land under irrigation and raised irrigated crops. I felt that this was one of the noteworthy successes of VVK.

(iv) 'Well done' say internal auditors

The functioning of VVK in the first year was highly commended by the internal auditors. VVK had recorded an excellent growth in loans sanctioned and disbursed and excelled in recovery of the current dues. It even registered tremendous improvement in recovery of old dues.

VVK had adequate staff to meet the work load in initial stages. As business expanded in terms of volume and geography, a need was felt for some more trained staff. The centre had a four wheeler vehicle and motor cycles for Cash Collectors. Field operations were mostly attended by the Cash Collectors and myself.

State Bank of India soon followed our pattern and started Agricultural Development Branches (ADB).

Impact

The impact of VVK's activities was quite visible with large number of wells adding to the irrigation potential in the area. On 26th January, 1978 the District Collector was reported to have stated in a public meeting that the drought funds had lapsed because of VVKs massive 'well digging' activity! Many beneficiary farmers were able to raise paddy crop without much difficulty in the kharif season. Some of them could even raise second crop although to a limited extent. The road from a distance of 10 km. was seen dotted with small poultry farms financed by the VVK. The biggest impact was seen on the face of the weaker sections particularly Lambadas. They could come to bank on their own without middlemen and talk to the VVK staff. That was not the case before. The frequent interactions with the VVK staff helped them in gaining confidence to perform their own business with the bank without depending on others.

Though two years was a very short period to assess the impact of VVK, the following factors, according to me, had affected its performance later on.

1. Ambitious planning: 100 villages were to be covered under VVK as per the plan. However, about 30 villages were only covered due to operational problems like inadequacy of field staff etc. There was a lot of pressure from the district administration and people's representatives to extend the coverage. However this could not be done.

2. VVK plan envisaged covering of all the households in the adopted villages. This could not be achieved since many of the farmers were defaulters of cooperative societies which made them ineligible to seek loans from VVK. Multiple financing came in the way of spread of VVK activities.

3. Though district administration had agreed to provide necessary infrastructure like roads and power connections to wells, nothing had happened, resulting in slowing down of VVK activities. Further, not much assistance was forthcoming from the government departments in providing

technical services. Even VVK staff was not in a position to provide such services to all the beneficiaries, due to inadequacy of trained staff. The initial enthusiasm shown by the district officials gradually petered out. The transfer of the District Collector, Shri S.Ray had its impact on the involvement of government staff.

4. Some faulty schemes like 50 bird poultry units, one animal dairy units etc., found to be inadequate to raise the income levels of the beneficiaries. This resulted in mounting over dues. *However, the Child and Women Welfare Department which was implementing applied nutrition programme for the weaker sections, observed improvement in the health of the children in the beneficiaries' families who availed of the above loans. This could be due to the fact that the beneficiaries might be consuming whatever they could produce with the bank's assistance.*

5. Lack of effective supervision coupled with faulty schemes led to mounting overdues in all the schemes, particularly in animal husbandry related schemes. The increase in operations in the second year was much more than what the existing infrastructure could manage, and was responsible for slackening of the human effectiveness resulting in the above disturbing trends.

6. Waning of interest on the part of the bank management had in a way contributed to the downgrading of the experiment. *Selection of proper human resources for VVKs was not given due importance resulting in VVKs being pushed to the back and then into wilderness.*

I was transferred in December, 1980 to head the new branch at Mallipudi located in prosperous Godavari delta in West Godavari district.

When I look back at what happened during my tenure with VVK, Pratapgadh, two things come to my mind regarding my own contribution to the success of VVK in the initial years.

1. My educational background and the experience, I gained during my stint with the State Government had greatly helped me to adjust myself to my role as VVK incharge. This was further enhanced by my exposure to hard core banking since my joining the bank in 1973. This exposure gave me the necessary insight and inputs to lead the team from the front and organize the human resources at my command to meet the challenging job at VVK. It was no exaggeration to say that all my colleagues at the VVK, were trained by me and I had the satisfaction to see them delivering goods as long as I was there.

2. The eagerness of many of the beneficiaries to utilize the opportunities provided by VVK to improve their own livelihoods had made me to commit myself to the success of VVK as long as I was at the helm of the affairs.

Learning Lessons

The tenure taught me many lessons on management of resources, both human and others, project management with human face and leadership to deliver the goods to meet the expectations. These experiences helped me in enhancing my own effectiveness in all my endeavours in the next 25 years, till my retirement in December, 2005.

* * * * *

Case 28 – First Person Accounts NR

Best part of my career, which is close to my heart, was during my tenure as In-charge of Village Vikas Kendra, which is a special cell meant for all-round development of villages and villagers.

The place was Rajahmundry which consisted of both dry tracts and delta lands. This has given me very good opportunity to understand the rural population and their needs, their simplicity and their affection.

Even before I took over the VVK, the cell had established a good name among the rural public especially in the adopted villages giving me a very good launching pad. I had all the necessary infrastructure such as vehicles, manpower and full support of the branch staff. Most of the people whom I approached to give financial assistance, were small and marginal farmers and agricultural labourers, for improving their incomes. There was no activity that was not felt eligible–for financing from a small sum of Rs.400 for a fisherman to purchase a fishing net to a few lakhs of rupees to establish a dairy or poultry farm were our lending activities.

In all the 33 villages we adopted, we could build and strengthen the faith of the people in the Bank by positively responding to all their genuine and bankable needs. An atmosphere was created where any villager could walk into the Bank or meet the officer for his requirement. In those days there was no such thing as "Financial Inclusion" but our Bank practiced the same philosophy of involving every family in the banking activity for their betterment. Bank was well identified as their well wisher which will take care of not only their productive needs but also their consumption needs. Kendra had the liberty to consider such loans as long as repayment was not in jeopardy. There was flexibility in our approach and speedy response.

Taking advantage of the developmental objective of VVK, we could successfully implement various schemes benefiting individuals and the community.

In the uplands, we along with District Rural Development Agency (DRDA) could implement community bore-well scheme for many small and marginal farmers very successfully. This made all such farmers, who could not afford to dig a bore-well on their own, to have irrigation through the community Bore-wells. Similarly, the agricultural labourers were getting loans for purchase of two buffaloes to supplement their daily wage income through sale of milk. Another activity for such daily labourers was small poultry unit with a capacity of 500 birds.

Small vendors of fruits and vegetables, small petty shop owners were all given loans to suit their requirements. There was microfinance without the MFIs private money-lending in-disguise. Whenever any borrower defaulted, we developed a practice where the villagers would assemble near the Panchayat office or any other common meeting place and call the defaulter for recovery. If he would not pay within the given deadline, the *villagers themselves will sell the buffaloes or other assets created out of Bank loans at the market value and credit the amount to the loan account of the defaulter. If there was any shortfall the guarantor would volunteer to make good that amount, without any grouse, as they knew that only then the Bank would be able to give further loans. With this kind of recovery culture, there was no hesitation for the Bank officials to lend within a reasonable time.* SHGs were unheard of in those days and yet there was moral suasion.

Another reason for the success of this model was involvement of Bank staff and their field visits and understanding the activities of the applicants which is very essential for any lending activity. The villagers, small and big, prospered alike according to their capacity and hard work. Looking to the success of these few, others also took up new activities leading to all-round progress of the area. Loans for cycles for the vendors, cycle-rickshaws for rickshaw pullers, and many small ticket loans were given *without looking at the cost and time involved, making everybody feel that this was their bank* and which naturally made them feel grateful to the Bank so that they pay their loans without default in spite of problems that might come to them temporarily. Most of the loans were unsecured. We took risk, though small, many a times but we never failed. With the number of people transacting with the Bank increasing day by day our satisfaction and confidence levels also grew leading to more and more involvement and participation in the activities of VVK.

Brotherly affection

The best example of the success of our VVK can be narrated through an instance when I went to one of the villages after almost 30 years people gave a ceremonious reception and felt *as if their own brother had come back*. All this without any advance notice which goes to prove the gratitude and the affection, these people had for officials who help them in their hour of need. It was an unforgettable experience for me and I am sure no big industrialist or businessman ever remembers a Banker for 30 years. Unfortunately such faithful and innocent people are not getting the deserved assistance from the Banks to the desired level today.

What is needed is the conviction of the Bank officers to work in rural areas not by compulsion, The managements of Banks should select such people who have not only got a rural background but also the mindset to understand the problems of the people living in villages and have empathy towards them and their needs. *They should be given incentives, preference in promotions and necessary training to make the Financial Inclusion a success, otherwise this will be another scheme doomed to failure like many other schemes of Government of India*. This is the need of the hour for the Banks, not only as a requirement of the Government but also as a *business opportunity*. Future of the country lies in villages, similarly *Banks will have to look to the villages for their future business growth.* Hence, it is in the fitness of things the Banks understand this and take initiatives for *recruitment of right people* for this special job. I sincerely believe it is going to be the Banks in rural and semi-urban areas which are going to play a crucial role in alleviating the poverty of this country. The time has come for such a change and no lip sympathy for agriculture will help any one, neither the Banks nor the agriculturists. If at all farmers suicides have to be stopped it cannot be done by giving more and more subsidies but only by making them self dependent, by providing loans at reasonable rates and affordable terms.

Case 29 – First Person Accounts SSR

I came out of the university with graduation in M.Sc (Agronomy). My first choice was a bank job- Direct Recruit Officer (DRO) in Agriculture. I was fortunate to have got into a very progressive and innovative bank which came out with a specialized setup Village Vikas Kendra (VVK) all over the country for comprehensive, well structured and schematic lending for agriculture, small business, artisans and micro service sectors in rural and semi urban areas.

Before this innovative structure, Muzaffarpur main office was financing in the villages. *Their experience was very bad in recovery.* The Umanagar Branch in Bihar was in operative in this most economically backward block for about a decade then.

This branch had been identified for VVK model III and VVK was opened in March 1978 at this branch. I was posted as incharge of VVK where I had been working since Nov 1977. I was 24, young and energetic, hailing from the state of West Bengal. I took the task as a challenge and virtually it was because of my initiatives the management identified the branch for VVK Model-III.

I carried out intensive survey of 24 adopted villages of the block and found the *predominance of money lenders and landlords/zamindaars in the area.* (1978)

I began with the formation of farmers clubs/farmers teams, formulated area-specific ARDC (Agricultural Refinance and Development Corporation) schemes for minor irrigation, dairy development etc for all the 24 villages. I identified a village which was most economically backward and where the farmers were subjected to exploitation.

On my own I approached DDA – District Development Agency – and the officials and collected the information that Akbarpur village was one of the most economically backward village with cent percent population in Below Poverty Line category. The Chief of DDA assured me all sorts of help besides subsidy for any type of venture to be financed by the branch. Government collaboration was ensured.

Without any loss of time I carried out in-depth survey of Akbarpur families covering their economic/social status, means of livelihood etc. The village was situated on the banks of river *Gandak* which is 9 km away from the branch and 10 km away from Muzafarpur town (Dist HQ).

There were 67 families with a total population of 405. Out of 67, 15 families were of marginal farmers having land holding of 10 to 15 cents. Almost all of them were eking out lives working as agricultural labour on the farms of land lords of adjacent villages.

They were all under-paid. They were working virtually as bonded labour for years together and had no opportunity to come out of it.

I organized a series of meetings in the village in the afternoon hours with head of each of the 67 families. A consensus was arrived at to form a village team with Sri Phuderi Sahani as Secretary and Sri Bhikari Sahani as President. The team included 10 members from all categories who *volunteered* to work for the betterment of village. It was decided that Sri Phuderi and Sri Bhikari would coordinate the entire development work beginning with opening of SB accounts, ensuring proper end use of bank loans, arranging for inputs, weekly review and finally timely repayment of bank loans.

The entire ground work took nearly one and a half months. At the beginning of May, 1978, an integrated credit plan was formulated covering each of 67 families according to the potential, aptitudes, scope/opportunity available and economic condition of each individual family in particular and village as a whole.

The first credit plan so prepared included several schemes. They vary from Crop Loans to Irrigation (pump sets) and self-employment schemes for dairy, grocery, tea stalls, vegetable vendors, cobblers, blacksmiths etc. The important thing is that they were all chosen by the Farmers Club formed by themselves for the purpose of availing facilities from the Bank.

The schemes were successfully implemented within July, 1978 and all families availed bank loans for specific purposes under DRI scheme (4% p.a. interest) and other schemes supported by subsidy @33% to 50% from MDA.

The subsidy element reduced the loan burden to a great extent. For instance for each irrigation unit costing Rs.3700/ provided to groups of 3 to 4 marginal farmers, Rs.1850/- (@50%) was as subsidy immediately credited in the loan account. Loan net of subsidy (Rs.1850/-) was further reduced by Rs.500/- as I *persuaded the dealer of pumpset to provide agency commission of Rs.500/-* and was subsequently credited in the loan account and the actual loan amount was reduced to Rs.1350/-.

There were fortnightly review meetings at the village mostly on Saturday afternoon, where Sri Phuderi & Sri Bhikari discussed the program and constraints, if any faced by any villagers. They tried to sort out the problem at their level, failing which they took help of Umanagar branch and MDA.

By mid 1979, it was observed that majority of villagers were not going to work as labourers to adjacent villages, rather most of them remained busy in managing their cattle, small business, farming etc. There were a lot of negative reactions by the landlords of adjacent villages. Incidentally, some of the aged farmers advised me not to move alone in motorcycle particularly during evening hours. However, I took the matter very lightly and told them, 'so long people of Akbarpur are with me, nothing will happen.' But the threat was not unfounded.

At the end of 1979, Officials from Banks ARDC & DDA visited the VVK and were satisfied to see the over all progress and got positive feed back about VVK. *The repayment was 100%.* I was thrilled to observe that my plan produced desired result. I sometimes got emotional and distributed chocolates to the kids of village, who used to run in the dust from the central entry/place behind the motorcycle shouting 'dadajee aa gaye, dadajee aa gaye'

and villagers looked at 'dada' (me being a Bengali) with broad smiles and sparkling eyes.

At the end of December 1979, Sri Phuderi & Sri Bhikari along with four villagers came to VVK and told that '*dada kal kuch sahib log aya tha, aur dinbhar gaon mey tha, hum logo ko bahut kuch pucha, likhke ley gaya*'

I took the matter lightly, thought it might be some State government or ARDC officials came to carry out some survey. But Sri Phuderi told that visitors were all white skinned persons, who were speaking in English and one/two Hindi speaking persons were doing the job of translation.

Surprisingly, in the first week of January 1980, Umanagar branch received a copy of 'New York Times', wherein the entire episodes of village were narrated focusing on the fact how *bank's*

assistance helped the downtrodden people meet their minimum basic needs. However, the name of bank was not mentioned in the report. Subsequently, when I showed the copy of 'New York Times' to DDA, they were pleased and informed that VVK of our bank was the only one who financed the villagers for their social/financial upliftment.

I sent a copy of 'New York Times' along with the certificate of DDA and a brief note on VVKs financial activities in village to Bank's Central Office. Bank's Executive Management Committee passed a special resolution appreciating the performance of VVK.

Farmers reporting white visitors

* * * * *

Case 30 – First Person Accounts SNS

I was sent on deputation as a Managing Director of Farmers' Service Society, Singoli (Mandalgarh)- Dist. Bhilwara – Rajasthan in July 1979. This society was merged with five PACS (Primary Agriculture Cooperative Societies) of District Cooperative Bank and taken by our Bank on experimental basis with objective to make it viable.

The Set Up

The society was headed by Managing Director and the Board comprised of one District Agriculture Officer, one Sub-Registrar and five other persons selected by the Share Holders. It had five Branch Offices (old PACS Centers) with an incharge called Secretary. All secretaries were from erstwhile PACs.

When I joined in July 1979

There was huge NPA and recovery was hardly 40 percent. Most of the agriculture land was rain fed. There was continuous natural calamity like drought. As the loan accounts were overdue the farmers were not eligible for getting fresh loans. The society was giving only short term crop loan to farmers and rural artisans.

Strategy evolved

I made an extensive tour of all the villages covering five PACS and interacted with the farmers and Secretaries. I motivated all the five Secretaries of branches and staff at Head Office that they should not only provide short term crop loans but also distribute essential commodities under Public Distribution System like sugar, control cloth, cement and other products. Society should also take up the activity for financing medium term loan for minor irrigation purpose i.e. digging of wells, electric / diesel pump sets etc. and long term loan for Tractors and other land development activities. I also advised them to think big and conduct credit need survey of the area. A proposal as to how the single cropped area depending only on rainfall could be converted into double cropped area was also mooted.

New Idea & Strategy

I knew that there is a deep perennial river named "BERACH" which flows through the catchment area. If the water can be lifted from this deep river and stored at highest place it can be used for irrigating approximately 400 hectares (1000 acres). The DRDA (District Rural Development Agency) provided 50% subsidy on such project. We had taken up the challenge and commenced this Community Lift Irrigation Project in record time of six months. This irrigation water was provided on No Profit-No Loss Basis.

Since farmers were having over dues and not eligible for fresh crop loan, their loan was re-phased and this made them eligible for fresh loans and fields were irrigated by charging hourly rate. We had provided all short term crop loans seeds, fertilizers and pesticides. The society also acquired two electric threshers for harvesting the winter crop i.e. wheat. After harvesting wheat, it was sold through Krishi Upaj Mandali Samities. After recovering bank dues, the balance proceeds were made available to the farmers. In a record period of two to three years, all farmers were regular in the repayment of the loans. The recovery percentage increased up to 90% and prosperity prevailed. This also solved the problem of drinking water in the vicinity. Every farmer was self sustained and acknowledged the contribution of FSS sponsored by the Bank. Pass-books were also given to all the farmers and there was a clear transparency in the loan delivery system.

The same experiment was repeated at another FSS sponsored by our bank at Sawaipur (Bhilwara)

Hence my tenure as M.D. of FSS at Singholi (Mandalgarh) and Sawaipur (Bhilwara) was professionally satisfying and I got State Award for 'Excellence' from the State Government for successful implementation of Community Lift Irrigation Project.

* * * * *

Case 31 – First Person Accounts KK

I headed a region for about two years. The region had 94 branches with 40 branches located in urban areas and 54 in rural area. About 20 branches were located in tribal areas.

There was no systematic effort to develop business. Branches were mainly dependent on walk-in-business. Being the oldest bank in the area with large network of branches, it had the advantage over other banks in business.

I planned:

1. Implementation of Government sponsored schemes: As usual, most of the government sponsored schemes were for financing dairy animals. The performance of these schemes was poor. In one of the District Consultative Committee, I had even suggested to the district administration to study the *SHG schemes* under implementation in Andhra Pradesh where the stress was mainly on creating employment and different activities were undertaken for this purpose. I had encouraged *Farmers Clubs* in the region which were playing a positive role in developmental activities and also in helping recovery.
2. I exploited the huge potential available for small scale and tiny industries in the area. While encouraging big corporates like Garden Vareli, IFFCO, textile machinery making industries and of course textile industry to seek higher limits from the bank and also utilizing the existing limits fully, *credit was extended to smaller units, new entrepreneurial ventures and tiny units in villages. The*

region was always in the forefront achieving the sector sub-sector targets for Priority Sector Advances.

3. Big umbrellas with bank's name inscribed on them were placed at the vantage points with couple of officers/staff manning a table placed under the umbrella distributing pamphlets and explaining salient features to the onlookers. As this was for the first time a bank particularly a PSB utilizing umbrellas for visibility and publicity, it was a great hit. I got 10 umbrellas from Bangalore and soon I had to order for 15 more on the demand from various branches.
4. Branch Visits: I visited all the branches once in six months and of course urban branches more frequently. This has helped me come closer to branch staff and the time spent with them was *most revealing to me*. Further most of the rural Branch Managers' review meetings were arranged away from the regional headquarters, many a times in picturesque resorts near Vapi River. It is not an exaggeration to say that I had developed not only working relations but also personal rapport with many of the Branch Managers who delivered goods. *I had few Branch Managers of rural branches who used to carry cameras with them to take photographs of the customers who came for opening of the accounts.*

Non-banking struggles

However, my story would not be complete if I do not talk about the worst nightmare I encountered at the fag end of my first year of my tenure. The landlord of one of the leading branches obtained a decree from the court to get the premises vacated by the bank. As branch failed to act on the notices received from the court, it resulted in the court passing the order ex-party in favour of the landlord. The landlord came with an army of ruffians at 5 pm one day and started throwing bank's property on to the road. It went on till 1 am. As there was no legal recourse available to the bank to stay the order, we became mere spectators. Meanwhile I along with other officers started searching for premises to keep the bank's furniture and fittings, safe, almirah etc.

We decided, come what may, my branch had to function the next day. The entire drama enacted by the landlord became an emotional issue for every one of us. Finally a premises was selected in consultation with the zonal head by 11 pm and the entire bank's property lying on the road was shifted to the new premises by 3 am. While the demolition was continuing, we called the software vendor and electricians to lay the cables in the new premises, arrange points for workstations, install server, etc. This entire operation went on up to 6 am. By 7 am everything was made operational. Even a telephone was installed. The new premises were made operational and transactions commenced sharp at 10 am. General Manager from HO visited the branch and was delighted at the uninterrupted services at the branch. It took three months for me to finalise and shift to spacious premises.

The entire operation involved almost 200 staff members drawn from Regional Office and branches. It was a *stupendous team effort carried out meticulously with instant planning*. As no one had eaten food, a team of staff went to nearby restaurants to pick whatever food that was available at 2am. A shop dealing in electrical goods was kept open throughout the night. Software/hardware vendor with his team of personnel was at the spot throughout the night and the next day. None of us thought of stealing a nap. I went home in the morning only to have a shower and change to come back and ensure that all was well. We ensured that the matter was not reported by the media. However, we placed an advertisement in the local news papers about the shifting of premises to new location. A notice board was placed at the old premises informing the customers about the shifting of the premises. *An enterprising staff member went to the residence of a painter and got a name New Microsoft Word Document Board prepared for installation at the new premises. I heaved a sigh of relief when the branch started functioning normally.*

The incident taught us many lessons in meticulous planning, mobilizing resources, and putting a plan into action, coordination, individual efforts and above all team spirit.

* * * * *

Case 32 – First Person Accounts AV

My career has taken shape in a set pattern. Having being born in a rural farming family my natural choice of studies has been graduation in Agriculture. Instead of going for M.Sc, I chose Diploma in Management in NIRD so that I could contribute to grass-roots rural development. First, I joined SERP– Society for Elimination of Rural Poverty and worked for six months. It was an opportunity well utilized. It gave me some training and gain in strengths both in terms of knowledge and skills.

Soon a better opportunity came in my path – DRO in a progressive public sector bank. Again it was my good fortune that I was posted to a rural branch with 4 decades of history in a forward district in Andhra Pradesh. It was opened in the compound of a sugar factory, serving the industry and the cane growers with tie-up with the factory. The bank's reputation has been very high right from the day one.

Growth of SHGs

Thousands of SHGs were formed by DRDA in this district.

I knew all about SHGs phenomena and Micro finance Fiasco in Andhra Pradesh. When I reported in the branch as an agricultural officer to take over the good work done by my predecessors, it had already over 600 SHGs.

In spite of good work the branch has been doing in empowering the women there was no due recognition or publicity for the bank. More over there was dissatisfaction among women groups because of inevitable delays and denials. The answer, I thought was planning.

The SHGs are represented by village officers or animators. Each animator is responsible for maintenance of 100 to 150 SHGs. They were visiting the branch and pressurizing the officers. Though there was intention to help, there was a failure of the branch on the delivery front.

I, therefore, organized the 'animators' who promote SHGs and maintain the records, into a committee. We were meeting at 2pm every Saturday to sort out problems of SHGs, formation and maintenance. Every Sunday we were attending to 20 SHGs on an average. Branch Manager and staff were also attending the Saturday meetings though they were not visiting villages.

We've also used SHGs as resources for recovery of bad debts in the villages lent directly. These women used to exert pressure on their husbands, brothers or sons. The strategy worked wonders. I had close liaison with DRDA and Agricultural

Departments. Even district collector called me to congratulate me on one occasion.

During my stay of 1½ years I have gained immense practical knowledge and experience. I could experiment with my ideas. I could feel I have grown as a person. Being alone in the place I used to work 7 days a week.Sunday was particularly exciting day with the staff working without any cadre difference. We used to process applications, check records of SHGs obtain documents at 20 SHG per day. No. of SHGs covered, amount disbursed and recovered is one thing; but what is the progress the members of SHGs made is a different matter. I was thinking of it. *'Upgradation' is the key issue.* I discussed those matters in mandal level, district level, and even state level coordination meeting. I could influence the decision making in my own way.

I have observed different group discussing. Formation is based on caste, creed, and affiliation. I think we should not interfere with the natural process of formation of groups. Social and economic factors play their part.

Once the group becomes cohesive after *storming* and *norming* stages there is the most difficult aspect of choosing productive activities and gradual upgradation. Production Vs consumption is a major issue the banker has to monitor with his superiority. Agricultural department & DRDA are on the job. Banker can influence the poor more than any government official or even NGOs because of money – power to lend.

Transferred to Regional Office

Now I am in Regional Office which guides, controls, and monitors the branches. With my operational experience I am in a better position in Regional Office. One thing I felt when I was in the village branch was the freedom I enjoyed in discharging my duties. The Branch Manager gave me full support. For example we extended our services beyond the 4 adopted villages because poorer sections approached us because of our dynamic approach towards SHGs. To accommodate them we waived minimum balance of Rs.1000 for opening the account. We accepted just Rs.50 for opening the account. I find sitting in Regional Office I may have to advise the regional authority to ratify similar or such other deviations from the norms by the branches. The Manager in turn kept his superiors informed, although orally. Now I keep same thing in my mind while controlling the branches. But still I feel I have superior information sitting in Regional Office than the branch. It will enable to give guidance to the branches in SHGs finance. We take a policy decision at RM level.

Empowerment

Encouragement

Entrepreneurship

Equal opportunity

* * * * *

Abbreviations used in Part I Elaborated

ADR	Agricultural Debt Relief
ARDC	Agricultural Refinance & Development Corporation.
ATM	Automatic Teller Machine
BDO	Block Development Officer
BLCC	Block Level Consultative Committee
DCC	District Level Consultative Committee
DDA	District Development Authority
DLCC	District Level Consultative Committee
DLRM	District Level Review Meeting
DPN	Demand Promising Note
DRDA	Director Rural Development Agency
DRI	Differential Rate of Interest (4%)
FDR	Fixed Deposit Receipt
FSS	Farmers Service Society
JLG	Joint Liability Group
KVIC	Khadi & Village Industries Commission
KYC	Know Your Customer
LAD	Letter of Acknowledgement of Debt
LMB	Land Mortgage Bank
MDO	Mandal Development Officer
NABARD	National Bank for Agriculture and Rural Development
NPA	Non-Performing Assets
NREGS	National Rural Employment Guarantee Scheme
OTS	One time settlement
PACS	Primary Agricultural Credit Society
RBI	Reserve Bank of India
SBC	Small Borrower Cell
SHG	Self Help Group
VDO	Village Development Officer
SFDA	Small Farmer Development Agency
VVK	Village Vikas Kendra
ZP	Zilla Parishad

* * * * *

MUSINGS OF

BAREFOOT BANKERS

PART – II

EMERGENCE OF BAREFOOT BANKER

EVOLUTION OF RURAL BANKER

Indian Banking and its concepts have come from UK thanks to the colonial rule. It is the British who gave us the term 'Prudent Banker'.

The courts used the concept as a yard stick in the judgements against the bankers. In 1830, a Massachusetts court offered a definition of prudence which became "the prudent man rule".., that he conducts himself faithfully and exercise sound discretion... He is to observe how men of prudence, discretion, and intelligence manage their own affairs.. in regard to the permanent disposition of their funds, considering probable income, as well as the probable safety of the capital invested'.[1] I repeat, the concept of prudence, built around 'risk aversion, predictability of income and preservation of capital, came to define a whole culture of managing other peoples money; but things have changed over a century and half. The new word 'sustainability' has to make us look at the word 'prudence' in the new light of eradication of poverty and sustainability of earth. E.F.Schumacher[2] has drawn our attention to the four cardinal virtues of Christianity: prudence, justice, fortitude, and temperance. He quoted from the book on prudence by Joseph Pieper (1960).

'He alone can do good who knows what things are and what their *situation* is. The pre-eminence of prudence means that so-called 'good intention' and so-called 'meaning well' by no means suffice. Realization of good pre-supposes that our actions are *appropriate to the real situation,* that is to the concrete realities

---

[1] 'Steering Business Toward Sustainability' by F.Capra & Gunter Pauli (1993)
[2] Small is Beautiful

which form the 'environment' of a concrete human action; and that we therefore take this concrete reality seriously, *with clear eyed objectivity'*. 'This clear-eyed objectivity', E.F.Schumacher wrote, 'however, cannot be achieved and prudence cannot be perfected unless by an attitude of 'silent contemplation' of reality, during which the egocentric interests of man are at least temporarily silenced. Only on the basis of *magnanimous* kind of prudence can we achieve *justice, fortitude, temperance* which means knowing enough is enough. Prudence implies a transformation of the knowledge of truth into decisions corresponding to reality'.

Money lender has always been an integral part of an ideal village habitat. There is a poem commonly known to Telugu family can be translated as: *abandon a village which does not provide a money lender, a doctor, wise man, and perennial stream.*

Money lender, the necessity, became the very anti-thesis; he exploited the poor with greed and usury. The British knew these money lenders' ways and they supported the British in the administration of the vast country. They played their part in sustaining the system of exploitation through 'wellfare' measures in the form of reliefs, grants, and loans. Banks were supposed to replace the usurious money lender by affirmative action. Money lender was never thrown out of business, he continues as pawn-broker, landlord, micro finance company etc. Next the doctor became town-dweller, with compulsory conscription for a couple of years and soon become part of super specialty, a new creature, ever growing monster. There are cases in Part I, the demand for medical treatment. When the banker responded; he was eulogized as god. There were barefoot doctors, who visited villages and served the masses and revered as gods. Similar is the position of barefoot banker in villages. Maladies and indebtedness are tackled by these men. There are epidemics when both these professionals are required to sacrifice personal comforts to serve people on a war footing.

The third element, the wise man is the assigned role of a teacher – educator. Both the banker and the doctor play the wise man role too. For prevention of maladies and debt traps the services of a teacher can be utilized 'catching them young'. What is left is water supply which is the role of the democratic government. Nehru called major dams as modern temples. These dams have become subject of controversy and *andolans* because they dislocate livelihood and habitat of people.

It is people's representatives who have to play the role of wise man in these matters which have become hot controversy and conflict for which the civil society and parliament have to join hands. In all these matters the banker who is looked upon as 'all-knowing' jack has to play his part.

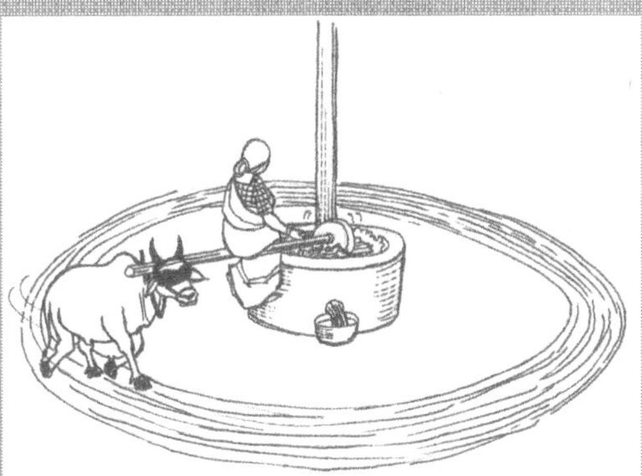

Before Nationalization

Bank clerk goes round and round with blinkers on doing what he or she is asked to do. 'See back and go forward' was the norm.'

Bank officer does what is proverbially known as buffalo cultivation–close and constant supervision. For every entry there is a check, a tick and several cross ticks.

After Nationalization

Barefoot Banker is the lucky guy free from proximate control. He capitalized on new-found freedom and autonomy to be creative and active.

On the other hand the up-down Manager took the rural posting as a punishment. Soon he is brought back to buffalo cultivation. It is like the fellow who committed theft and was sent to jail where he played cards and cheated inmates. He is kicked out of the jail!

Barefoot bankers and their branches operated like balloons in the hands of the vendor. Branch was both an administration unit and entrepreneurial unit. With the induction of Agriculture graduates there was a more systematic approach. Some banks created village development cells with simplified procedures and paper work. Greater emphasis was made on extension services.

Agriculture Assistant in clerical cadre was an innovation that worked well. Some of these Assistants and Cashiers who moved up the organizational ladder did much better when they became rural Managers. Some where down the line, the 'heat' was not sustained for the water to reach 'boiling point' or critical mass phenomenon, also known as Hundredth Monkey Syndrome* did not materialize. Probably from 1993 onwards the process has slowed down.

Now that we have the report on Financial Inclusion on hand, the new thrust Finance Minister is giving, the contents of the volume become relevant and hopefully trigger some more literature which will give pride of place to rural banking and paradigm shift.

* Discussed later

The career opportunities in banking will include a stint in semi-urban and rural areas when the incumbent will gain in personal growth fast.

However small and trivial the contribution might be, the cause for which it is made makes it laudable, recognizable and rewarding. Squirrel's story in *Ramayan* illustrates the point.

'Clear-eyed objectivity, an attitude of silent contemplation, knowledge of truth, justice, fortitude, and temperance' – self-restraint behaviour – these are the attributes, of the barefoot banker. One hidden attribute is 'absence of immediate gratification'. He knows the results of his actions do not flow in the short term.

'My Bank', an Identity

Our bank continued to retain its name and identity and the progressive outlook ever since its birth in 1908 as a bank in the service of the nation. It started with its focus on agricultural and rural development and had grown as international bank with largest number of foreign branches. Similar is the story of many other

Indian commercial banks. The Indian banks, more than 100 years ago were started with a national fervor and as a part of nationalistic movement. The strategy to keep the competition among banks worked well.

But government took measures to avoid duplication at least in the area of rural development. State level consultative committees and Lead Bank scheme were established. A structure outside the bank had its ramifications. Many Managers became independent of central management of banks and began making commitments on behalf of the bank.

New grass-roots Manager species emerged. It can be classified as the prudent, the dynamic, and the barefoot bankers.

Rural bank Manager is a JACK* of all trades and master of banking. Let us understand banking first. A bank is a financial intermediary. It borrows money from the saving public at a lower rate of interest and lends to investing public at a higher rate of interest to make profit to pay dividend to the share holders.

Commercial banks were lending short-term to traders against the pledge and hypothecation of goods. Trading firms fail in bad times creating bad debts and losses to banks. Thus banks who deal with other people's money have fiduciary responsibility and therefore, the Managers in banks have to be prudent, *cautions, analytical, traditional* and *systematic*. I call them CATS. Prudent-banker maintains secrecy about the clients' affairs. Even husband should not know what wife saved in the bank. Indian banking is based on British banking practices and principles. There are a couple of wise saws inherited from the British:

1. 'Banker must keep his eyes and ears open but mouth shut.'

---

* *Judicious, Agent of change, Considerate,* and *Knowledgeable*

2. 'Banker wears buckles, belt and braces, but his pants still slips down. Banks can become bankrupt.'
3. 'Banker gives umbrella when sun shines and takes it away when it starts raining.'

The Situation in Rural India

Life in rural India before colonization by the British was SIMPLE: Stable, Interdependent, Mutual, Productive, Leisurely and Ethical. Now it is MIRED: Miserable, Indebted, Ravaged, Excluded and Depressed state of life.

Banks in India were serving urban elite. It was left to the Cooperative Banks to finance for agriculture and rural folk. The cooperative movement which started in 1900 'has failed, but it must succeed'. Still it is struggling like the Indian farmer. There are some few pockets in the country where they succeeded but by and large, large sections of societies had no access to credit because of the principle 'once a defaulter, always a defaulter'. There are whole villages which were abandoned by the financial system. The indebtedness and poverty persisted.

All India Survey of Rural Credit (1951) produced a document of 1200 pages after a massive survey of lakhs of villages.

'Indian farmer is born in debt, lives in debt, and bequeaths debt' epitomizes the long report. Here are a few snippets from it.

- Indian farmer has no money sense, when to borrow and how to repay.
- He spends disproportionately large sums on festivals, marriages, and funerals

And then he borrows money to meet medical expenses and other urgent needs from the village money lenders whom he considers god for the timely help and benevolence shown. He was not aware that the interest charged was usurious. In to-days language he lacks *financial literacy* which is the cause of MFI fiasco in 2010 in A.P.

The money lender lends at usurious rates of interest which he justifies for most of the loan portfolio is irrecoverable. He thus hedges his high risk through higher interest rates. This is the argument put forward by MFIs, 'the money lenders in disguise', Ex. RBI Governor, Dr. Reddy said. He also said MFIs are sub-primes in the making.

It is said that it was the British who impoverished the country. British did their bit in the form of *taccavi* loans for asset creation – bullocks and wells.

End Use Verification by the Authorities

A Collector went for inspection to verify the end use of loans. He was shown the bullocks and appeared satisfied. But he probably did not know that a pair of bullocks went along with him! Even if he had known the deceit, he could do nothing. This has been the culture of rural finance.

What about wells? Even here there was ingenuity displayed by a farmer who dug well overnight and poured water on, to show that he struck plenty of water. The Collector jumped into the well to find its 3ft. deep! Some made good use of the loans and were benefited. Whatever might be the case the loans were rarely repaid. The 'benevolent' British government converted them into grants.

We need not complain about loan waivers, the modern replica – it has always been the case in the Indian rural drama. We, the early bank staff knew the state of affairs when we studied Indian Economics as a subject for our banking examinations.

But the cooperatives showed another way. Old loans were repaid by new loans. The new loans have to be invariably higher to cover the interest and other bank charges. There was no realistic repayment of debts even to this day. It is same as re-scheduling that the narrators talked of.

The Indian drama of poverty alleviation goes on. What happened at the grass-roots decentralised cooperative system? There are rich and poor in the village. The rich are also powerful. 'The rich cling to their privileges and the poor cling to their familiar miseries.' That is how the 'harmony' is maintained. The rich and the powerful corner all the cooperative loans and default and make the cooperative society defunct. 'All for each and each for all' principle failed. But it must succeed. SHGs and JLGs emerged on the same principle and seem to follow the trail.

CATS and DOGS among Bankers

Conservative Commercial Banks who had resources were nationalized and were asked to take care of the rural development. That was in 1969.

The prudent CATS – cautions, analytical, traditional and secretive were asked to play DOGS – dynamic, outgoing, go-getting, and strategic.

What immediately happened was haphazard response to the call for mass banking from class banking. There was pressure from politicians/bureaucrats. One collector remarked that banks were nationalized but not their Managers. Another said that he was devoting lot of time chasing the bankers to do what they should do.

Some well-meaning prudent bankers played DOGS, earned name, fame, and appreciation both from the banks and the government. They were called dynamic bankers, but the majority of their colleagues predicted doom and were happy when the dynamic paid the price for the mess created more due to poor change management in banks. One inspection of the branch was enough to find the name of the dynamic banker in the list of suspended Managers. The mass banking created a mess on a mass scale which needed an army of 'scavenger' staff to clear it. In the mean-time the suspended Manager was found honest and loyal except that he was 'over-enthusiastic'. That term itself the psychologists reject. According to psychologists it is addictive behaviour - deviant behaviour - and all enterprising behaviour is an addictive behaviour. They refer us to motivation theories. But systems thinkers have an explanation.

'Only variety absorbs variety'. Variety is a measure of complexity. What a Manager does is to manage the variety. When it is not managed, the Ashby's law, that is the name of the law, asserts itself causing hardship to people. If the organization incurs loss, the man loses his face. We have given a bad connotation to dynamism. David Rockfeller wrote a book, *Dynamic Banker* even before banks were nationalized in India. Dynamic Manager adapts to changes in the environment *strategically* not absent mindedly. Nationalized banks took time to adapt to change the government dumped on them. I say 'dumped' because the vast majority of the people in banks did not accept the change agent role whole-heartedly. They consulted management experts who had neither rural experience nor banking experience. Probably they think experience does not mean direct experience.

Practical Banker

The prudent banker had stored knowledge in the system, practical knowledge. Every budding banker had role models and mentors to guide him. He learnt everything at his desk under apprenticeship. He had a list of time tested values and principles. He grew imitating the models.

Now, after Nationalization, when he was sent to rural areas he had to shape his own roles in terms of personal knowledge, skills and values and the demands of the authorities which came to him by way of circulars. Some chose not to read the circulars and create work for themselves and their meager staff. They obeyed Ashby's law by shutting themselves like the ostrich. In the language of cybernetics it is called *attenuation.* Others took them seriously. These men did outstanding work but obeyed Ashby's law. Such men had inspired the confidence of controllers who gave whole hearted support whenever they needed. In the specialists language support is called *amplification.* The grass-roots Managers need amplification of variety by way of staff, structure, skills, systems, styles, and strategy. Above all the grass-roots entrepreneur-banker must have the amplification in the form of *shared values.* In the beginning those employees who did not share the mission and objectives of Nationalization put stumbling blocks through grapevine propaganda.

Analyzing Organisational Effectiveness The 7S McKinsey Model

Interconnectedness is an important feature of this model

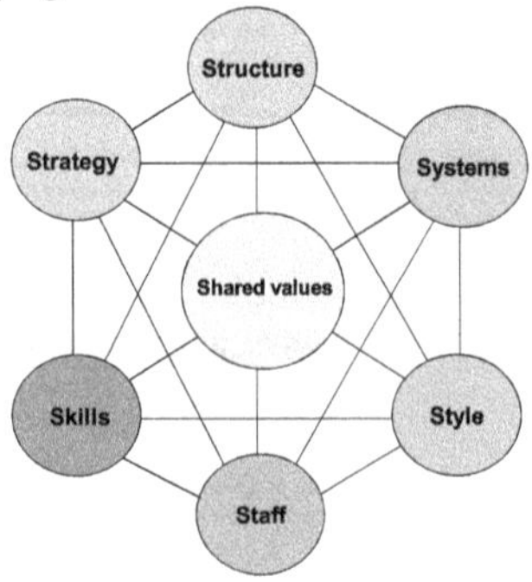

Advent of Agricultural Officers

Soon wisdom dawned on the management who recruited agriculture officers fresh from the university. These graduates found bank salaries better than what government offered. It was child's play to understand the rudiments of banking but they had the discipline to understand the problems of farmers and other rural poor. They had an edge over other graduates with regard to rural banking. There is a separate section for their episodic memories in part-I.

Identity of Barefoot Banker

Identity is the greatest motivator.

BAREFOOT banker is Benevolent, Audacious, Responsive, Evangelist, Futurist, Optimist, Open, and Transparent, individual playing the role effectively.

- Bank is not a charitable institution but the man in the rural Manager must have charitable disposition; he must be kind and compassionate and **Benevolent Banker. (B)**
- As Manager and employee of the bank he must follow the policies and procedures. He may follow policies but deviate from procedures for the procedures intended for class banking do not fit into the scheme of mass banking or rural banking. Hence his decisions are audacious; bordering on imprudence. **Audacious Banker.** (A)
- He is responsive and responsible to the needs of the rural poor and to his own bank. He acts with speed and takes spot decisions with conviction and courage. **Responsive Banker. (R)**

- He is like an evangelist-traveling preacher, preaching the gospel of self-help. Bank money acts as catalyst. He walks and talks and understands the problems of people true to *Rigveda*.

  He preaches that he has come to liberate them from the clutches of money lender, who acts with 'kindness' and feigns compassion. He also preaches banking principles and practices. If they observe the rules of the game they would continue to get help from the banks perpetually. **Evangelistic Banker. (E)**

- He is a futurist with long term rather than short term goals. He looks ahead for results correcting steps with objective feed back from the environment as a whole, as well as the individual cases. **Futuristic Banker. (F)**

- He anticipates with optimism. He sees opportunity in calamity than otherwise; he is in short an **Optimistic Banker**. **(O)**

- He knows he has to learn from experience and be open to the signals that come continuously from the environment. **Open-minded Banker. (O)**

- Openness demands transparency in all dealings with individuals both the beneficiaries and the others engaged in the rural development. **Transparent Banker. (T)**

In episode 1, case no.6, the duck-rearer refused enhanced loan to the surprise of the new Manager – new to the values of rural folk. There are a few honest borrowers whom even the proverbial money lender respected and charged less by way of interest. The honest borrower always dreaded default. Credit worthiness is a value in vogue in rural areas which this barefoot banker recognized.

The Manager is in a dilemma. He will always be in a dilemma. The Manager could have faced another, hypothetical, situation. If the man were to know that banks have scheme for education, he might have asked the Manager for a loan under the scheme. The dilemma of the Manager is how to bend the scheme, which is meant for higher education, for school or college education. The audacious Manager would grant and obtain confirmation. The principle that guides him is 'small man is better credit risk' because of smallness of the amount and largeness of honesty.

Yet another man might come back later with a proposal to buy land. (episode 11, case no.5). Sayulu's case is complex. The 'variety' is enormous. The Manager 'attenuated' the massive variety by 'trust the man,' the autonomous entity. Risk was small. But in future the banks were to formulate a scheme on similar lines to rehabilitate those who wish to go back to farming; they need to look into the complexity. The responsive Manager has to create a scheme which was never conceived by the policy makers. It is a long term loan which has longer gestation period. There is motivation from the farmer but does he have the know-how? What about the bargain, price, soil condition, water, power, and whole lot of other things. Should banker leave it to the man, because the Manager is no better in these things. An agriculture graduate can assist. Manager was audacious but what was the risk? It was small; the small farmer was shrewd not to take the deal. Manager was lucky? But he was responsive and futurist and optimistic.

I read an open letter in Feb, 2011 written by former CEO of Procter & Gamble to the Prime Minister of India in which he mentioned future of India is not in villages but in cities! Food crisis and food inflation has opened the eyes of such LPG* promoters that after all it is from the villages that we get our food and it is the millions of villagers who get their livelihood in agriculture or should science solve the problem with synthetic food?

Refer to episode 9, case no.5 loan mela and ground water clearance. How did this Manager pitch upon minor irrigation scheme, a complicated measure? He is an optimist and a friend. In his journey of learning more and more about rural problems of poverty he learnt, the stories of misuse and misapplication. If he were to be responsive he must respond to their genuine needs. It is not easy to identify the genuineness of the application for plough bullocks. He must be open and transparent to make people come out with truth. In rain fed and drought prone area buying and selling of bullocks is a regular affair. There is a distress sale of cattle because of dry climate and lack of fodder. When rains return the bullocks return when the farmers buy again. Bullocks are more or less most liquid assets next to cash in rural areas.

As already mentioned the British who did pretty little to solve the farmers' problems were happy to give small loans – taccavi - for purchase of bullocks and digging wells. Any how if they are the immediate needs of the farmers in rain fed drought prone areas, the banker can slip into the shoes of the village money lenders at cheaper rates.

Even after 40 years of Nationalization of major banks, the money lender rules the roost. On 13th Aug 2010, two days before we celebrated 64th Independence Day, an article appeared in The Hindu with the heading – *'How 'rural' is India's agricultural*

---

* Liberalisation, Privatization, Globalization.

credit' by Pallavi Chavan, a researcher. A snippet that should catch the attention of any rural Branch Manager in rain fed area is:

'Numerous studies and reports have argued that one of the major factors associated with the agrarian distress in the late 1990s and 2000 was an increase in rural indebtedness, especially to money lenders."

The article concludes: *"The increasing concentration of agricultural credit in the urban and metropolitan areas offers a missing link in the discussion on the persistence of agrarian distress despite the revival in agricultural credit in the 2000s.*

The other day I was talking to a rural Branch Manager who explained why Joint Liability Group (JLG) loaning is not taking off. It is a scheme for tenants loans for agricultural purposes without security. The land owners who live in urban and metro areas and who have left agriculture, borrow money from the banks at 5% and lend to the tenants at 24% as MFIs do. Managers are worried that it may result in double finance even though certificates are obtained that the owners have not borrowed on the same land. Producing certificates has become both art and science.

Arthur Koesler wrote, 'problem solving is bridging the gap between the initial situation and the target.' He also suggests a problem solving method: **Duncker Puzzle**

Shifting the Focus : "A good example is Duncker Puzzle about two trains and the bird. Two goods trains, a hundred miles apart; start moving towards each other, each at a speed of twenty miles per hour. A silly bird, frightened at the starting hiss of one of the trains, flies away at thirty miles per hour in a straight line along the railway tract until it meets the other train; it reverses its direction until it meets the first train again, and so forth.

What distance will the bird cover in its flight to and fro until the two trains meet? To compute sum of the series of flight-stretches is a rather complicated task. But if we think aside, forget about the distances covered by the bird, and compute the *time* until the two trains will meet–two and half hours–we see at once that the bird has also flown for two and half hours and hence covered *total* of seventy five miles."[3]

The Hundredth Monkey Effect (the critical mass)

Some anthropologists were studying the habits of monkeys on some islands in the ocean off the shores of Japan. They found one particularly smart little fellow washing its food before eating it. Soon other monkeys in the family also began to wash their food before eating it. Later this behaviour spread to other monkeys in the clan. One individual may acquire tacit knowledge from another without using language through observation imitation and practice. One day after 100th monkey learnt the trick every other monkey even monkeys in the neighbouring colonies began washing and eating potatoes.

[3] *The act of creation* by Arthur Koestler.

The same phenomena is true in humans as well. The Hundredth Monkey Syndrome hypothesizes that there is a point at which if only one more person tunes into a new awareness, a field of energy is strengthened so that new awareness is picked up by almost everyone.

This phenomenon is considered to be due to critical mass.

Another example of critical mass is switching on motor for pumping water. At first muddy water comes out of the well. If you switch off and switch on a little later the same phenomenon will be noticed. Instead if you keep the motor on, within a minute or so clear water will flow from the well.

Similarly if the bank experiments with financing a few borrowers they may end up with a negative experience of habitual defaulters. If on the other hand the bank continuous lending operations to every house hold in the village, the chances of positive experiences are more. This is what I attribute to the critical mass theory.

In the episode 15, case no. 5 the farmer reveals multiple needs, not just one asset or one land development or digging wells. Old pressing debts are the first priority. In the case the farmer says, 'I want money for deepening the well, replace a bullock and buy a pair, a bag of urea, and pay off hand loans.' Will our Manager respond and if so how? The evangelist-preacher who has come to liberate them from penury has to act fast on the spot. He pitched upon minor irrigation taking the cue from 'money for deepening the well' and investigated into it further.

Why are they not asking for wells? No bank is willing to give loans for wells because of cumbersome and time consuming process. Each area is different from other areas. We need situation basis appraisal.

To-day we have the concept 'situation based' extension. The evangelist has a lot to learn before he preaches to others. To-day we have another approach–*systems approach* or holistic approach. Each house-hold must be taken as one unit with integrated approach. Barefoot banker needs guidance and information on the latest development in the science of agricultural extension.

Kisan Credit Card (KCC) which was not there in 1970s is a right step, the audacious bank management had taken, of course with RBI's directive. It appears RBI is more liberal than public sector banks! In 1970s RBI was not at all in favour of outsourcing. But in 2006 they asked banks to recruit retired staff and ex-servicemen as business facilitators in villages. Rangarajan Committee on Financial Inclusion commented that Banks were 'slow in this regard'.

Leave it to the grass-roots Manager – everyman's JACK-*Judicious, Agent of change, Considerate,* and *Knowledgeable* about the rapidly changing developments on the rural front – distress, unrest, and half-hearted measures that he could read in the daily newspapers.

Evangelist, Educator and Extension Manager

Evangelist is a wandering preacher and enthusiastic crusader against all evils. Educator turns the head of the learner in the right direction. But the extension Manager shows the way. There are several cases in which agricultural graduates recruited by the bank in 1970s have done pioneering work which included the extension services which was their forte.

There is growing literature on extension. Our focus is on agricultural extension which has a long history. It was started in 1866 university of Oxford and Cambridge. Extension education was an innovation first used in 1873 by Cambridge University to describe what Mao Tse-tung put it in simple and practical terms.

> *Go to the practical people and learn from them; synthesize their experience into principles and theories and then return to the practical people and call upon them to put these principles and methods into practice so as to solve their problems and achieve freedom and happiness.*[4]

This extension service the pay back university people render, not out of charity –'If there are millions of people who want to better themselves but do not know how to do it, who is going to show them?'[5]

It is the educated and fortunate elite. They are in banks, in government and everywhere other than in rural areas. They are produced by the universities.

---

[4] Small is Beautiful
[5] Ibid

'Before World War II, the Chinese calculated 'that it took 150 peasant-work-years to keep a man for 5 years course in the university. He has to pay back what is due to the man, woman and child in the villages.'[6]

If you embark in this spirit it would lead you to the people to whom you owe 'having consumed the fruits of their labour.'

On the other hand if you care for your own comforts and join a mutual admiration society, a 'Trade union of the privileged' to see to it that his privileges not eroded by the great masses of fellowmen who have not been educated.[7]

'Tolstoy referred to it when he wrote:

'I sit on a man's back, choking him, and making him carry me, and yet assure myself and others that I am very sorry for him and wish to ease his lot by any means possible except getting off his back'.

'Education is not a passport to privilege; its purpose is to extend it to the needy.'

All educated people must see themselves as servants of the nation. They are soldiers saving the country. Extension education is practical, aimed at improving *farm and home.* It is turning the head in the right direction, not spoon feeding. Nor is it giving fish. It is teaching how to fish. It is to make people autonomous selves;

[6] Small is Beautiful
[7] Ibid

it is awakening them creating awareness. It calls for adult education, continuing education.

Get Off the Back

Buffet and Gates show open for private audience who do not want their names published. Media obliges. Who are these who accumulate wealth – 'bad money' as Buffet himself calls?

'India has tradition of philanthropy – Bill Gates' head lines screams.

"'Candid on his view that philanthropy was a way of converting *bad money into good money'* Mr.Buffett said". The report says, that if a vaccine manufactured from bad money saved a life, no one would inquire about the source of the money. However 'Mr. Gates sought to steer clear of the tricky question by saying it was the responsibility of the police and the governments look into these issues'. The philanthropists of 'bad money' owners are more guided by Mr.Gates than by Mr.Buffett.

'The US receives 2 percent of its GDP from philanthropy and hope it will increase... there are many in India having lot of money, ready to give but do not know how to give it back to society.. they are looking for a way out' probably without being caught by the police and tax authorities. 59 wealthy families in the US who have pledged *50 percent or more* of their wealth to philanthropic activities' says Gates.

We do '*punya*' to wash out our '*pap*'. It is same thing as I sit on the poor man's back and do everything except get off the back. The campaign started by the two great American friends of billionaires in India called, 'The Giving Pledge'. Tolstoy and Gandhi would have called the campaign 'Get off the Backs'. That is enough for meta-economics way and no trickery. Voluntary poverty is one way of getting off the back.

BPL families do not even understand the rhetoric. 'Their politics', Gandhiji said nearly a century ago 'is confined to bread'.

Adult Educators - TRIBES

Adult educators can be classified and grouped into TRIBES: Traditional, Re-educators, Inspirers, Builders of groups, Emancipators, and Self-actualizers. *Traditional* teacher taught–lectured, used chalk and talk method. See what a swamiji does and the teacher does the same with 'chalk and talk'. If we go back centuries, we had *upanishads*. Viswamitra and his disciples, Rama and Lakshmana walked and talked in the open air, sharing, enquiring, and learning.

This is what a *re-educator* does. Rama had learnt all crafts in the gurukula. Yet, Viswamitra's education was practical. That's the second tribe. Swamy Vivekanada quoted from scriptures.

Arise, Awake, and stop not till the goal is reached.' That's *inspirer's* way of educating adults. Rural masses are in deep slumber–ignorant of scientific advancement and technological innovation that are meant for bettering their lives. There, you need *builders of groups*. Group dynamics aid in teaching-learning process. They should be made SHGs. Help them stand on their own legs and take their own decisions. Nothing, not even education, can be thrust on the down-trodden. *Emancipation* has this meaning, helping people help themselves. Who are these *self-actualizers*? They believe that there is enormous potential in every human being and when they realized the full potential they become self-actualizers. The extension education's ultimate goal is self-actualisation of everyone.

Get off the back , Pay back and Reach Out

Report: Golden Jubilee celeberations of IIM (A) (2010). Mrinalini Sarabhai, wife of the late scientist Vikram Sarabhai, one of the founders of IIMA, in her address exhorted the students to try to fulfil her late husband's dream that the students of IIMA should not acquire only academic qualifications but should learn how to **reach out** to the poor and the deprived and become useful for the society.

M – Mal-nutrition

I – Ignorance

R – Ravage of calamities

E – Excluded from growth

D - Dejected

Crying for HELP: Health Education Living Peace

'O Mother Earth you know our needs. They are very minimal. We need good seeds and fertilizers, we need uninterrupted power supply, we need flexible loans... we need protection from middle men. We need reasonable price for our produce... above all good guidance' a farmer laments. (The Hindu)

Instead he gets ROPE – Rhetoric On Poverty Elimination – A Long Rope.

Extension is extending information

Information is data that which changes us. Facts that illuminate. Bank men may begin extension education with banking knowledge. 'Bank is a financial intermediary. It lends depositors money which is their hard earned savings. Banks have their primary responsibility to the depositors- Fiduciary Responsibility.

There are farmers and businesses who need money. Moneylender is a key character in the drama. A village which does not have a moneylender must be abandoned'. [Sumati Satakam]. The story telling is *Traditional.*

Banker must know the significance of Gram Sabha

Gram Sabha is a mini Lok Sabha where decisions are taken, policies are developed and implemented–true democracy. Panchayati Raj (1993) decentralization and self governance are two concepts that cannot be separated.

Gram Panchayat has been as ancient as Indian society. Ambedkar's speech may be recalled. In, November 1949, his last speech to the Constituent Assembly he said, 'It is not that India did not know what is democracy. There was a time when India was studded with republics, and even there were monarchies, they were either elected or limited. They were never absolute. It is not that India did not know Parliaments or Parliamentary procedure known to modern times.'

'They had rules regarding seating arrangement, rules regarding motions, resolutions, quorum, whip, counting of votes, voting by ballot, censure motion, regularization, *Res Judicata* etc..

Buddha must have borrowed them from the rules of the political assemblies functioning in the country in his time. This democratic system, India lost. Will she lose it a second time?' Ambedkar asked.

From 1949 to 2011 India progressed and regressed: Supreme Court of India (2011) brought "relief to young men and women determined to get married crossing caste barriers and harassed for that very reason by '*Khap Panchayats*'".

'Manmohan, calls for timely elections to Panchayats'. (April 2011). The 73rd constitutional amendment in 1993 on panchayati raj led to decentralization of political powers... social audit brought greater transparency...

'There is a need to strengthen gram sabhas on the lines of Lok Sabha and the Vidhan Sabha' Panchayat raj Minister said.

I.T, a necessary tool

'The road map sets out strategies and action plan for real devolution of functions and funds. I.T is necessary tool for transparency, disclosure of information, and social audit, efficient delivery of services and for improving internal management of panchayats' the Minister said. If CMD of the bank knows what is happening in parliament, the grass-roots CMD should know what happens in panchayati raj in his area of operation...

'Meetings of gram sabhas should be held regularly and women and deprived sections must, participate in them and place their views' UPA chairperson added. May be banker educates them in his own way.

Lok Sabha members are exposed to many presentations, well-prepared speeches by eminent men. Gram Sabhas too need such exposure. Some progressive panchayats may arrange meetings where the members are exposed to latest developments in agriculture, and initiatives taken by other panchayats elsewhere. A banker can look for opportunities to address the villagers in gram sabhas as a strategy, to educate them about credit discipline and marketing strategy or business strategy. He can go beyond banking and agriculture. It is not uncommon for the villagers to seek the advice of the banker living in the village. Health, education and even personal problems are brought to him. In case 22 a serious family dispute was brought to him. These personal matters can be generalized and the banker can educate them on prevention of diseases, planning for children's education and living in harmony in the family and community life.

Gram Sabha – Corporate Communication

Addressing Gram Sabha is an important function of a barefoot banker – evangelistic function. He educates and gets educated. Gandhi used '*padayatra*' for campaigns. A barefoot banker combines both: campaign for recovery or lending. He visits panchayat office and does field survey which is at once both general and particular.

There is a case in which a Manager was asked to celebrate deposit mobilisation week and campaign for deposits. He was actually bogged down with poor recoveries. He asked for permission from the Regional Manager to use the budget both for recoveries and deposit mobilization and also invited Regional Manager to address the gram sabha he intended to organize. Because of language problem, the Regional Manager deputed another Senior Manager who was known to be a competent speaker in Telugu.

It is important that the authorities know the multiple talents of the men working under them. The senior Manager conducted the meeting in such a manner that he could not only mobilize deposits but made even sizeable recoveries. Villagers were grateful that the higher management of the bank was really interested in the development of their area.

These communications go by the concept/subject Corporate Communication, an aspect of Corporate Governance. Not all Managers have seen the significance of visit of higher authorities. Some of the Regional Managers have learnt these things the hard way. One lesson was that they should not make a hurried visit but must have time to listen to the villagers more than his talking.

In gram sabha and loan mela the Manager needs to make more of extempore and impromptu speeches. At seminars organized by voluntary organizations, academic centres call for paper presentation if enlisted as a speaker. More often you may get opportunities to make the other two kinds of speeches.

Always the language and style of presentation vary according to the situation. Video films, audio cassettes, specially made for rural population where visual representation plays great part in influencing the rural audience. Right brain captures visual data better than facts and numerical details. Percentages and statistics do not impress them. At the end of the presentation the audiences are given handouts, colourful pamphlets. Even a pass book had impact on the farmers who hold it as a prized possession. The principle in marketing / selling is 'leave something tangible with the customer to help as memento. 'I hear I forget; I see I remember; I do I understand' is a well known Chinese saying. Add to it 'I carry a memento, I cherish it'.

Loan Mela is a marketing strategy to promote their own party initiatives devised by the politician. It was never a bank strategy. Both come under marketing communication, an aspect of corporate communication, as theory.

The same customer is wooed by different parties for different purposes. Soon individual Managers fell prey or enjoyed the rope trick. A clever banker with abundant soft skills converted the loan melas as opportunities for corporate communication and image building of the bank. The politician disappeared after the grand function leaving the banker and beneficiary to their ropes. The villagers understood the game and established and strived for long term relationship.

There are occasions when their own bosses visited the rural areas and welcomed publicity. When special cells are launched, they made the function grand accompanied by press meet for wider publicity.

All these events called for soft skills – human skills are needed for rural Manager – more than city Managers. 'Those of you who borrowed money from the bank have responsibility to repay so that bank could pay back the depositors. If the farmer or businessman has to repay the loans they must generate surplus from their own enterprises. How to increase the in comes is the crux of the problem ? Now you tell me your problems. Let's find out ways and means of increasing your income.'

That's turning the head in the right direction. That is the style of *re-educator.* Motivation to work adopting latest developments in science and technology requires inspiration. The bank officer must first educate himself. Read success stories and tell others to inspire them into action. These are *inspirers.*

It is time consuming and less effective educating one to one. Do it in small groups–homogenous or heterogeneous. It may start with one farmer across the table in the bank premises. Use his services to organize a meeting in the village. Gram sabhas are meant for extension work. If entire branch staff attend the gram sabhas, they too learn a great deal about group dynamics. The learning will be much more effective than any class-room training through the use of game theory. If the staff are given some theoretical inputs on group behaviour, they can learn much faster. Building groups and extending through them with the active involvement of the members is by far the best way. Tribals learn this way. Of course leadership is another element.

An Example[8]

Indonesian Farm Schools are examples of building groups. Teams of farmers are built to be taught in the open schools on their own farms. The lab, the class-room and the field are one and the same. Farmers are the experts, the extension worker is a facilitator. There is no teacher. All are learners from the

---

[8] Extension Management Literature

situation. (This is what Kolb's Model of Balanced Learning is all about. It is applied to farming situations.*)*

The school is a seasonal school. The annual crops have their seasons from land preparation to harvesting. The fodder production school starts in the dry season, when fodder is scarce. For tree plantation and soil conservation measures like hedge rows and grass strips, the schools are for longer duration.

Unlike the other schools the field schools function through regular group meetings according to the need. Number of instruction and learning periods vary according to the activity.

It is learning by doing by principle. But first there is understanding of cause-effect relationship. Then experimentations take place with alternative methods and inputs. Results are compared and the best technology is discovered on field-lab. It is then practiced-repeated and replicated in other fields/farms.

Typical example

25 farmers in a integral pest management programme in Indonesia in 1989 had the open rice field school for one full cropping season, met 12 times lasting four to five hours in the field. Each meeting had a set pattern

of activities: agro-ecosystem, field observation, analysis, and presentations, special topics and group dynamics. The first is the core activity and the rest are processes. They are divided into 5 groups of 5 each. Small groups ensure greater participation and allows for sufficient diversity of opinion. At the end of the school the 25 group become support group in the neighbourhood.

The 25 members are drawn from the farmers group. The larger farmer group is briefed about the field school process and purpose.

All farmers have been cultivating for years and generations mechanically without reflectively observing their own experiences. The farm school enables them to observe reflectively along with facilitators, who may be from the university.

The data collected for Agro-ecosystem analysis is on these lines:

- *Number of tillers per hill*
- *Varieties of insects and their populations*
- *Samples of insects and plants*

These data are collected from ten rice hills. Facilitator is with them guiding in the data collection. Discussions follow in each small group. One member from each group makes a presentation to all followed by questions and answers.

Thus the farmer owns the findings. Basis is Chinese proverb:

- *I hear I forget,*
- *I see I remember,*
- *I do I understand and discover and own for life*

Financial Literacy

'The Organization for Economic Co-operation and Development (OECD) started an inter-governmental project in 2003 with the objective of providing ways to improve financial education and literacy standards through the development of common financial literacy principles. In March 2008, the OECD launched the International Gateway for Financial Education, which serves as a clearinghouse for financial education programs, information and research worldwide. In the UK, the alternative term "financial capability" is used by the state and its agencies: the Financial Services Authority (FSA) in the UK started a national strategy on financial capability in 2003. The US Government also established its Financial Literacy and Education Commission in 2003.'

A banker has to be up to date with these developments in order to play the role of educator in the rural and semi-urban areas. This constitutes extension service. It is most likely that India also follow the example of OECD countries.

Another Case Study - Pragathibandhu model[9]

SKDRDP promotes small farmers self-help groups called 'Pragathibandhu SHGs'. There are about five to eight members in each group and every member owns anywhere from a few cents to two hectares of land. Predominantly made up of men, one or two women also join the group. The field workers of SKDRDP, after promoting such groups, train them on managing a group, documentation, handling of cash etc. –as routinely done in the case of any SHGs.'

In addition these groups also prepare a five-year farm plan based on the land holdings and cropping pattern of each member.

The farm plan is unique to each member and will consist of change in the farming practice, take up multiple cropping to generate continuous income, sustainable farming, mechanization, sustainable water supply and also ancillary activities such as home management, children's education, house construction, marriage etc.

Compulsory sharing of labour between the members of the group one day in a week is a new feature in his region. The members go to the house of another member and work in the farm without receiving any wages.

---

[9] The Hindu

Sharing work

The work to be done and the house to be visited are predetermined. On the day of the labour sharing, hospitality becomes the host's responsibility. The same day of the next week they go to another member's house.

As a result, each small farmer gets five to six free labour days in two months. The small farmers get the labour so essential for farming that too, without payment.

In the process, the affinity between the members of the group becomes stronger, they learn from each other, they help each other in times of crisis. "It is very common to see members working for eight to nine hours on a labour sharing day to complete the work," he explains.

There are two other tribes left. Emancipators and self actualizers. Tell the groups in gramsabhas that bank has come to uplift them and not make profit. Dictionary meaning of *emancipation* is: *a setting free or being set free from servitude, bondage or restraint.* Case no.29 and 32 are pertinent in this regard. The Barefoot Banker would address in the following manner.

"Banks have been nationalized for emancipation of rural masses. Mass banking should not become mess banking. Several types of bondages afflict the rural society. Indebtedness, fragmentation of land, loss of fertility of land, illiteracy, social inequalities and so on. Banks are here to liberate the people from usurious/and perpetual indebtedness. Why do you think we lend at ridiculously low rate of interest of 5%? Elsewhere the minimum rate of interest you pay is 24%. You do not know your strengths. Hanuman did not know. He knew his strengths when he started testing them."

Government of India Publicity

There is GOI ad which shows the *money lender* tapping the door of the farmer. Farmer's wife answers that her husband, Rajalingam, had gone to school.

Rajalingam who returns to explain what farm school does. At the end a bundle of notes in final settlement is tendered at the place of the money lender.

This should be changed to suit the future of financial services at the door step and repayment through B.Fs or B.Cs.

FIs collect at the door step; banks receive either at the counter or through the correspondent who makes himself available at *panchayat* office. Technology and transparency go together.

Attitudes, skills and knowledge that escalate continuously are all interdependent elements that a barefoot banker should keep honing up. He is a change agent in every respect.

Evolution through Caricatures

Snippets from Farmer's Note Book, The Hindu

A million dollar question

IFS… Integrated Farming System, an experiment.

'We selected 650 farm families chacked out a comprehensive and participative… Integrated Farming System IFS, to ease their debt problem'.

'… a drive to proper utilization of inputs, with willingness to take risks, ability to maintain a record of work being done, and provide feed back as and when required'.

'We found the reception is awesome… several farmers are demanding to be included… as income levels have doubled' says Dr.K.Jagadeshwara Associate Director of Extension, University of Agricultural Sciences (UAS), Bengaluru.

'The central government can try and replicate *this model…* at the national level… who is to decide? Not farmers nor scientists but the agriculture minister at Delhi… whether he acts or sits on it is a million dollar question' laments a bureaucrat of Secretary rank.

Focus shifts to guaranteed delivery service in IT – A Report

On 27th January 2012 another headline drew my attention: Replace IT with 'rural banking services' and read what Murali Gopalam says (page 12)

1. In the very last para he says 'far from playing a *reactionary role*, the IT companies were left to take proactive role… as 'idea partners' and not merely as service deliverers.

   This is exactly what the next decade of banking for rural development has to be and is going to be: 'idea partners' not farmers alone but partners to agricultural science, extension agents, NGOs etc. It is a collaborative service model that can deliver goods in future.

2. The more I empower the organization (farmers) the more I put the company (bank) in risk. 'The contradiction, however, needed to be addressed to expedite the decision making process in a dynamic environment, which required solutions to a client problem'. How true it is about bankers and farmers!
3. 'The second challenge' he says, 'relating to changing type of *work-requirements,* especially in a 'cloud environment.' 'Cloud adopting is happening faster in the US', than in India because of 'not-so-reliable network'. By network he meant a technical problem. But for banking it is poor networking with science, technology and extension agents and district administration. Bank services, extension services, science and technology services constitute BEST solution.
4. 'We need different kinds of *people as* opposed to *programmers*'. (bankers not as programmers!)
5. The cloud is dark and dirty he says, given the political economy, it is murkiest in India.

Many 'barefoot bankers' have managed under most adverse circumstances.

The Loan Mela

The day after

YAJNA, THE SPIRIT OF RURAL BANKING[1]

1.'*Yajna karma-samudbhavah'* (14/ch 3 Gita)

'*Yajna*, altruist actions is born of *karma'*

'Karma', ordinary action is escalated to '*Yajna'*

Altruistic action, opposed to egoistic, is unselfish concern for the welfare of others.

I am quoting from 'Gita for Modern Man' by Krishna Chaitanya (K.K.Nair) published in 1986. It was presented to me by a batch of participants in the Staff College, the most valuable gift. Interestingly I always received books of great value as gifts. They are like Bible to me.

What a barefoot banker does is performance of *Yajna* in its true sense, his day to day 'karma' is raised to the level of '*Yajna'* by his commitment. Our traditional theories are more powerful than Western, Modern Management theories if only we read them with an open and deep interest.

2. ***'Karma'*** *is physical action...* ***Yajna*** *is of conscious agent, man... for his work for others, for the world, for the society will yield benign results for all including himself...* ***ample for his genuine needs'***.

For his needs, and not greed. Gita's influence on Gandhi is visible in his words, *'there is enough in the world for everybody's need, not for everyone's greed'*. This was Gandhi's answer to

---

[1] ***'Gita For Modern Man' by Krishna Chaitanya (1986)***

Keynes's assertion that for another century greed and avarice must rule the world for everybody's happiness by Adam Smith's invisible hand. That century will be over in 2030. There are no visible signs of invisible hand working. The poor are relatively poorer and the rich abundantly richer. Hence GOI is harping an ***'inclusive society'***.

In 1776 Adam Smith in his 'Wealth of Nations' asserted that man cannot act except for the promotion of self-interest and Keynes was echoing same Western thought and Gandhiji opposed it vehemently.

3. *'God has not riveted man's motivation and action to the fruit of narrowly personal advantage'; he has made man capable of the altruistic act. However he has left man free to choose.. . if the man responds with the* ***yajna****, sacrificial, world conserving act,* ***tapas****, austere* ***disciple*** *by which the altruist character is stabilized...'*

The barefoot banker imitated God, Friend of all beings, by being friend of all in the rural society. No wonder, when villagers called the rural Managers gods, they were saying that they were friends of all!

4. *'Having been granted freedom, man can identify himself with his superficial self or his own deeper self. In the former he will work for his body* (Retirement benefits, ensure comforts, or just and stable income) *and its appetites. In the latter case, he will work for his own deeper verity* (reality)*, his actions will become sacred offerings (yajna)'.*

The barefoot banker who performed *yajna* did it without reading Gita or Krishna Chaitanyas. Later when he reads and relates his past accomplishments he finds peace within himself. What I am doing is to help them narrate all that they did to share with me, preferably, in writing. I believe, in writing the man finds his deeper self than by oral expressions. Chapter 16, Gita, yoga of the Discrimination of Divine and Demonic Traits has a long list of traits worth examining for our discussion.

5. *Fearlessness; purity of heart; integral congruence of wisdom and action; beneficence, (benevolence) self-control, altruistic deed* ***(yajna), personally undertaken and assimilated study****, (swadhyaya), austerity (Tapas) and uprightness; non-violence, truth,* ***freedom from anger****, renunciation, (of personal gain from action), serenity, refraining from fault finding, compassion, for all life (Bio-diversity), freedom from covetousness, gentleness, modesty, freedom from fickleness, vigour, forgiveness, fortitude, purity, freedom from malice and arrogance... the divine qualities (one who uses his birth in the world to realize them).*

For the purpose of writing a book, 'Successful Career Through Soft Skills', I searched for a list of soft skill in the Internet. I found the list endless. Compilers must have got tired listing what they call soft skills. Honesty, integrity, willingness to learn, work ethic etc do not conform to the definition of skills. Skill is action, what one does. *Vidura* told Dhritarastra that *panditha* is known not by what he thinks or what he says but by what he does, the performance. Self-study (Swadhyaya) is a essential acquisition of a barefoot banker.

6. *'Ostentation, arrogance, self-conceit anger, harshness and ignorance: these are acquired traits of one with demonic character... Grieve not, Arjuna, you are born to divine acquisitions'.*

Emotional intelligence, a fad at one time, refers to how anger has to be managed. Lack of E.Q. is demonic quality. When some of the personal accounts refer to threats from politicians or other elements, it was their emotional intelligence that came to their rescue-a divine heritage.

7. *'Fundamentalists, trying to annex Gita as a text that supports their stance sought to interpret terms, yajna, tapas, and swadhyaya as ritual sacrifice (pouring ghee in the fire and chanting mantras) and routine recital of scriptures... yajna is not a ritual sacrifice but* ***altruistic action'****.*

8. *'Yajna is satvic which is offered as imperative serenity accepted by the mind, without desire for reward (and performed as duty.) If it is done with reward in mind and for vainglory it is Rajasic yajna'. The rest all done mechanically, absent mindedly, and as routine ritual is all tamasic.*

In the last two chapters there is a distinction made of temperaments – *Satvic, Rajasic,* and *Tamasic.* Our interest is in **satvic**. The barefoot banker is a *satvic* human by traits and temperament.

9. *'Significantly out of the numerous synonyms used dwija*[*]*,* ***twice-born****, conventionally, this has reference to the sacrament of wearing the sacred thread*[*] *(upanayanam) when a boy (of the Brahmin caste) comes of age, which is supposed to make a* ***new man*** *of him.*

'But Vyasa is satisfied that no one has a monopoly to this second birth on the basis of heredity, caste, and that every one has to become a ***new man*** *by striving. All men must worship with work... such work has to be world conserving, not self-promoting. In Christian tradition of the new Being or New Man, which has same meaning of twice-born, refers to a reality that is new in the sense that it is the restoration of ontological (meta-physical) truth'.*

---

[*] Read the box at the end of this section

Dwija, twice-born, has always been bothering me as to how-to, translate into practical idea, the *upanayanam.* When I wanted to perform my son's thread ceremony an *upanayanam,* referred, the old pandith told that my son (16) is unfit for the ceremony because he passed eligible age for it. His explanation is not relevant here. But I have seen in many other castes this ceremony is in practice. Gayatri Mantra teaching is significant to this ritual. Any body and every body can recite Gayatri. 'In Gayatri, the greatest prayer of the Indo-Aryans, the man prays for the *light of understanding,* it ends with, 'May he endow us with pure intelligence'. It should not end with chanting. Its meaning and its significance to practice are important. Sri Aurobindo wrote mantras are *divine algebra* for intense practice. Formulae for action, **'For the art of expression was to the Rishi only a means, not an aim; their principal preoccupation was *strenuously practical,* almost utilitarian, in the highest sense of utility'.** ['Secret of Veda' by Sri Aurobindo]

'Sacrifice of the *vedavadin* is offering of desire directed towards material rewards, desire eager for the result of works ... Paradise'. 'Gita does not admit it.

Sacrifice is the very condition of life… the most important part of life... all works should be regarded as sacrifice, *yajna*, though by the ignorant performed without higher knowledge and by the most ignorant not in the true order, *avidhipurvakam.'* The highest knowledge (semantic understanding of *yajna*) is that which is done for *Lokasangraha.'*

Even the reluctant Manager who helps the poor and distressed under compulsion or mechanically without the intention of *Lokasangraha* is also rewarded. But the other who does as an altruistic action feels the reward in the act, when the beneficiary shows gratitude which one does not feel when financing rich man/enterprise. When he does it without the least concern/doubt of the recovery of the loan – he means it as only a means and that he is not the doer… he surrenders the result to society – that is *yajna*...If there is a drought which is not in the man's hands – floods or anything beyond him he would not regret his past action. Even when results are positive, he does not own it.

Recall what the bard said, 'A village which does not provide a money lender, a doctor, and a *'dwija'*, and perennial stream should be abandoned'.

I was translating '*dwija'* as a priest to avoid using the word 'brahmin' because a Temple or a Church is integral part of a village. This verse was quoted by the late Burra Venkatappaiah in his report, 'All India Survey of Rural Credit' (1951) to show inevitable and essential aspect of money lender in a village. Now the banker is asked to replace money lender.

Now that I have read Krishna Chaitanya quoted above, if twice-born is the *new-man* by virtue of practice of *yajna, tapas,* and self study. **Dwija is a transformed man**.

Every barefoot banker is a *dwija*, in the process of transformation. If you work in rural areas for two years or so, you will become a transformed man to occupy any position in the organization's hierarchy with ease and competence. That's my belief. But true to *satvic* sacrifice he dos not seek personal rewards. But they get elevated in status and stature by virtue of his or her transformation.

GOOD WORK NEEDS GOOD GOVERNANCE AND PROTECTION FROM EVIL DESIGNS

On the other hand the west gave us another concept – The Invisible Hand by Adam Smith (1723-1790)

As a boy he was kidnapped but rescued by his uncle. He was destined to become a great economist. Oft quoted idea of his 'the invisible hand' is reflected in his one line. 'It is not from the benevolence of a butcher, the brewer, or the baker that we expect our dinner, but from their regard to their own self interest.'

This is where we differ from the western thought. We in our philosophy do admit that the man's nature is self-interest; but we go beyond- that there is deeper and higher self-interest in '*Loka Samastha Sukhino Bhavanthu*'. Our self interest is very much tied to the larger society's interest.

There are other things Adam Smith said: 'the country is most successful if each member of it depended on himself and his own efforts. If every body developed his own particular gifts – doing what he liked doing and could do well – this would result in a great variety of trade and the nation would become wealthy'. What he was against was government's interference in people's initiatives. If everybody is 'selfish' everybody will have enough to be happy. This 'Invisible hand' idea meant different things to different people. In reality 'self-interest' has been equated with greed, competition, and envy.

GREED: Getting Rich Easily Eagerly Double quick

ENVY: Eliminating Notion of Values and Yeoman service.
Entirely No values and Yard sticks, for judging others.
Exceptionally Niggardly Vain Yard sticks.

DWIJA, SACRED, THREAD, WARE

Sacramental ceremony, *upanayanam,* popularly known as thread ceremony turns a boy into a *Dwija,* a transformed man more serious with a sense of purpose to life.

It has now become a ritual without purpose in majority of cases. *Dwija*, twice-born, not necessarily a Brahmin as it is made out to be is a title meaning, Devoted, Wise, Initiated, Jaunty (self confident), Altruistic person.

His hardware, the thread, symbolizes many positive qualities. A daily ritual of reciting greatest vedic mantra, splendour of mantras as declared by the Lord Krishna in Gita, Gayatri makes the man internalized the gospel of service.

SACRED – Sacramental, Always, Contemplating, Reciting, Ennobling, Discipline. Both SACRED & THREAD are software – programs in the bio-computer, the brain, recalled as situation demands.

THREAD – Tenacious, Hardworking, Resourceful, Enterprising, Altruistic, Dedicated.

WARE – Willing Always Resolute and Empowering.

Modern *Yajna*

In the box below there is an account of a lady scientist performing *Yajna* in the form of scientific discovery.

Dr.S.Adilakshmi won a national award for her research on jowar crop. A reporter who interviewed her wrote that it was her father who was an agricultural scientist who inspired her to take such projects that help the poor farmer improve his lot by raising, incomes from farming. It is '*Yajna*' in true sense her late father always said to do such research.

But scientist alone cannot change the life of the poor farmers. The extension Managers/worker who create awareness and provide guidance to the farmer to experiment and experience and take the fruits of research and technological innovations to them. But still it is the barefoot banker who supplies timely credit needed for such efforts, has to join hands in the combined *Yajna*.

Over all the **BEST** solution for the rural development problem is:

Barefoot banking, Extension management (Agl), Scientific research and Technology transfer in a integrated manner. In other sense it is *Yajna* performed by four modern *Rishis* – Barefoot banker, Extension Manager, Scientists and Technologists – together. Synergy in *Yajna*.

Loka samastha sukhino bhavanthu

* * * * *

TRAINING AND DEVELOPMENT

Banks spend huge sums on Training and Development and yet the top managements feel that the system of Training & Development has failed because they do not see any perceptible change in operations. Heads of Training system have a standard answer: Training is not a panacea for all the ills of the enterprise. Both are correct. The changes in the environment are rapid and responses are tepid. Transfers, job-rotations, special assignments have been in vogue since Nationalization of banks in 1969 than before.

Class-room instruction is necessary but not enough. The training system must work in close collaboration with other functions. Real learning happens or must be made to happen on the job with occasional, Induction Programmes, Refresher Programmes, and Role-Transition Programmes etc. 'Chalk and Talk' or 'Power Point Presentation' of concepts have their purpose and limitations. More and more successful operational Managers must be involved in these off job training programs.

Barefoot Bankers, the focus of this book, will have great deal to share their experiments and experiences. In this regard I wish to quote Schon (1991):

> 'observes that organizations are repositories of cumulatively built up knowledge: principles and maxims of practice, images of mission and identity, facts about the task environment, techniques of operatives, stories of past experiences which serve as exemplars for future.'

There is one assumption: the organization members share openly and freely their experiences with others. Authors like Chris Argyris feel that the organizational members do not share freely because of 'defensive routines'. Banks must create structures to capture the knowledge about the rapidly changing task environment and quickly adapt to meet the customer demands. In the context of Financial Inclusion, the bank's additional responsibility of creating demand to capture the 'missing market', (Rural Market) while increasing the supply of Finance for the Growth of rural economy. Educating and empowering the excluded categories keeping in *productivity* enhancement and *equity* is the new role a Barefoot Banker has to play.

Exposure Theory

Man learns through exposure to a variety of situations. Environment, education, and endowment (what one inherits) are the three factors that make up the personality. Exposure to situations enhances the mental material. The man exposed to city branch and city clients and who has also contempt for manual labour or rural poor may fail to deliver the financial services with the objective of financial inclusion unless he is duty bound to go out into villages, fields, outlying localities, thandas etc to see the plight of the poor, he would not change – his attitudes would not change, he would not acquire new skills, and his *axiology* would remain what it was. Class-room through documentary videos, may at best give him the vicarious exposure which have to be followed by concrete direct exposures and experience.

The word axiology was mentioned to me by a friend who had only a vague idea as something related to values. I looked up in my old dictionary. (Axiology: the branch of philosophy dealing with the nature of value and *types of value* as in moral, aesthetics, religion, and metaphysics). 'Words are vehicles of thoughts', wrote Arthur Koestler. The word meaning has triggered a train of thoughts in me. It is not an attitude alone is the issue; nor is it motivation. *It is absence of philosophical knowledge.* The Managers must be exposed to such words like axiology.

The cases in Part I can be discussed as the basis of axiology – moral, ethical, aesthetic, religion and metaphysical values. Each case can be used for deeper study of the man, in the case. After all it is the man who makes things different. They do ordinary things differently.

In the case no.6, episode no.7, the man with the blind eye was blind to axiology. The borrower saw with axiology glasses that the true eye was really blind to reality. He chose to quit.

Only to the man who is exposed to the real rural conditions, the images will change. He will not look at propositional data as much as the images of the penury and a wee bit improvement with the bank's help. His focus will shift to development and alleviation of hardships rather than on profit for the bank in books. 'A large proportion of positive activities', Lord Keynes said, 'depend on spontaneous optimism rather than mathematical expectation'. Most cases prove this assumption Keynes made.

The Summary of Recommendations by the Committee on Financial Inclusion stated categorically about the selection, training, motivation and *incentivising* the staff working in rural areas. The narratives in these pages reveal the personality type, educational background, up-bringing, training, self-study etc, of the narrators who gave first person accounts with a sense of pride and achievement.

The recommendation no. 14 of the report for commercial banks says, 'lending to low income groups and providing inclusive financial services need motivated staff… a system of incentives/disincentives put in place by the bank managements for special efforts/failures to achieve desired levels of financial inclusion'. What they are suggesting is 'carrot and stick' method. Recommendation no.21 says 'lending to the poor raises, *inter alia*, issues of *attitudes towards poor as viable and profitable customers*.. 'There is a positive correlation between training required by the Branch Managers and their overall attitudes'. Apart from attitudes the rural banker must have grit and guts to deliver financial services both literally and acronymically GRIT: Graciousness, Resilience, Integrity and Transparency. GUTS: Great Urge To Serve the needy. 'Prudent Banker' in the individual staff member may listen to the idea of 'profitable' customers. But he has been familiar with the word 'viable'. It is because of paucity of viable schemes sent from above he rejects many an application.

During 1970s and 1980s there have been training programmes on both hard and soft skills besides dealing with attitudes. Attitudes are most difficult to change. Banks could not make their staff live in the village. Allowing people to commute from city or town on daily basis became an incentive for people to accept the compulsory posting, for a period of 2 or 3 years. Most of the 'Bright Spots' are those who voluntarily took up the challenge of rural tenure and lived with family in the village. Even in *naxal* affected areas the villagers protected the Managers who lived in the village as one of them. Some cases in the book relate to this concept of living with people and sharing their troubles.

Smooth and Even Progress of a Rural Branch

A dynamic Manager turns around a branch which his successor finds it difficult to cope up with the work created by his predecessor. He may try to find fault with the Manager who handed over the branch and 'the mess'.

Controlling branches is like riding a horse in steeple chase. The riding calls for judgment, skill and nerve. Different horses have different ways of running. A few like to gallop along; some prefer to run at a slow pace. The rider must judge the different kinds of horses, horse power and horse sense. Modern management suggests smooth and even progress in a strategic and planned manner.

These are the aspects the training and development must take into account.

Identity, the greatest motivator–'Barefoot Banker'– an Identity

Give them an identity – Heath Brothers in their book *Switch* elaborate the concept of identity as a *motivational device.* They quote James March, Professor of Political Science at Stanford University, who says, 'when people make choices, they tend to rely on one of two basic models – the *consequences* model or *identity* model. Familiar to the students of economics, consequences model assumes that when we have to make a decision we weigh the costs and benefits of our options and make the choice that maximizes our satisfaction. Prudent Bankers follow this model. But there is no 'prudence' in financing the poorest of poor. There are only costs to the banks and no benefits.

There is one way to overcome this difficulty in using economic consequences model: to look for benefits outside the bank. Do you see a glow in the eyes of beneficiary? The money in the hands of the poor gives him power to decide what to do with the money. The wife influences the man's decision in a family of harmonious relations. In some cases the man may take autocratic decisions – good or bad. We assume that in most cases it would be bad. The assumption is to deny wisdom to the poor man which is not the reality. He is wiser than the urban lot. As regards the good or bad decision making in money matters poor are better than the rich.

But March's analysis is different. He advocates identity model. 'In the identity model of decision making, we essentially ask ourselves three questions: Who am I? What kind of situation is this? What would someone like me do in this situation?' There is no cost/benefit analysis. It is not identity that comes with birth, but by adoption. 'I'm an honest borrower'. 'In our family honour is a value'. In one of the cases a poor old farmer refused to take enhanced loan offered by the Bank Manager. His answer was, 'I don't want to be a defaulter'. He took a decision according to his own identity model, not according to bank's plans. As the farmer, poor or rich, 'develops and grows in that identity; it becomes increasingly important part of self image and triggers the kind of decision making that March describes'. Identity model is best suited to the rural Manager – Barefoot Banker–professional. I shall come to it a little later.

Committee on Financial Inclusion talks of motivating rural staff and training them in changing attitudes. Incentives and rewards the committee recommended may fail for as Heath Brothers affirm – 'any change effort that violates some one's identity is, likely, doomed to failure'. The Barefoot Banker gets his rewards and reinforcement from the environment in the form of the beneficiaries' gratitude and visible development in the economic sense – in the hinterland which is part of economic model. But what he cherishes is achievement and work done with the spirit of *Yajna.*

However, we can redefine prudence. Prudence and fiduciary responsibility built around 'risk aversion, predictability of income, and preservation of capital have become cardinal principles of the whole culture of managing other peoples money'.[1] The prudent banker was trained in this culture when major banks, which have grown to such strength, were nationalized in 1969.

Prime Minister Indira Gandhi nationalized major banks and soon after addressed the Chief Executive thus:

'I know banking is a conservative and staid profession. But the people's aspirations are rising and banks must meet their

[1] 'Small is Beautiful' by E.F.Schumacher (1973)

heightened expectations. I also know that expectations run ahead of capacities to fulfill them'.

She was right. But the Chief Executives were not fully convinced. They nodded the heads; had they not, the heads would have rolled, they knew.

Managing Change

'Banks were nationalized but not their Managers' was the remark made by a bureaucrat who was vexed with the task of making bankers give up their forte prudence and fiduciary responsibility. There was a need to change the attitude of the traditional banker, in keeping with the objectives of Nationalization, who should man the rural and semi-urban branches who have to serve rural areas? A TEAM–trust, esprit-de-corps, acceptance, meeting of minds–of dedicated people under a dedicated leader (Manager) with 'ownership and commitment', with an objective and strategy to translate the mission and with a clear vision; who possess diverse skills-hard and soft including banking law, rules, procedures, specialized technical knowledge of the computer age.

The leader – Manager must have ability to manage a decentralized organization with self governance. What should be the monetary incentives and non-monetary incentives for such a team and its leaders?

These aspects of change management have not been taken into account by the managements. All they did was to conduct training programmes and leave things to the individuals' initiative.

Lessons from freedom Movement and Insurance

In the wake of the Swadeshi Movement, a number of insurance offices were inaugurated in Bengal and some parts of India. Insurance also was regarded essential for the progress of the nationalist movement. Rabindranath Tagore said that the attainment of human welfare and prosperity by means of mutual aid and co-operative striving was the very essence of civilized life.

(Excerpts from Dr.A.Prasanna Kumar's book, 'Dr.Pattabhi Sitaramayya. A Political Study')

Researchers have identified several roles that change agents world over played. I used to discuss these roles in my class-room in the staff college in the programmes for branch Managers for attitude change. At that time I coined an acronym 'CREDIBLE' to present different roles requiring omnifarious social skills (present days soft skills). Collaborator; Re-educator; Diagnostician, Information specialist; Builder of teams, Leading light/liaison, Emancipator – these roles a self-explanatory.*

Participants of freedom movement who toured villages to spread prohibition and khadi soon developed skills while spreading welfare oriented messages in rural areas. The habit of leaving the house early in the morning to contact the rural folk before they left for their fields continued with them when they were absorbed as insurance agents after their return from jails.

---

* Read case No.32 for personification of CREDIBLE change agent.

In the language of modern management they developed *negotiating skills* like *personal disclosure, persuasive reasoning, co-operation* and *collaborative problem solving.* At times they used *articulating exciting possibilities* and *rewards & threats.*

Barefoot Bankers like all successful change agents must assume their work in rural areas is, infact, a movement.

Indian Banks and Indian insurance companies which started as a part of *Swadeshi* movement must continue to work for the empowerment, equity, productivity and sustainability in the same spirit.

* * * * *

BAREFOOT Banker as Corporate Communicator

Whether the Manager is conscious or not he does play the role of Corporate Communicator. If he is conscious, he may make deliberate choices assuming the responsibility for it.

Rural and semi-urban Branch Managers have more opportunities in that role than city Managers.

Training system in banks have to include 'Corporate Communication', a recent development in Management literature. In this section I presented some ideas from the emerging literature and related it to BAREFOOT Banker.

'All behaviour is communication, and all communication is behaviour'. In this sense corporate communication is corporate behaviour. Almost all cases in Part-I can be discussed as cases in corporate communication.

When a Manager talks to a prospective borrower in the office or in the village or to an audience in a loan *mela*, or in a Rotary Club or in the inauguration of a branch or specialized agricultural cell or Manager and staff attend a funeral of a poor, honest borrower in the village, and many more occasions he should realize that it is corporate communication function he is discharging.

It is said 'an ounce of practice is equal to tons of theory'. But tons of practice goes unnoticed and unappreciated. Both bankers and managements must recognize reward and encourage Managers in the organization to do corporate communication.

I realized the value of conceptual knowledge of corporate communication only when I was asked design and conduct a course in one semester for the students of PGDBM at Institute of Public Enterprise. That was in the year 2000.

A multi-disciplinary subject has evolved as an amalgamation of public relations, employee's relation, human relations, investors relations, internal communication linguistics etc. Under human relations, the group dynamics, motivating employees etc are included. These combinations are the result of paradigm shift in science, research, and management from fragmented approach to holistic approach. The whole is not only greater than but different from the sum of the parts.

Corporate communication includes oral and written, verbal and non-verbal; and what is true of individuals is also true of corporations. A bank is seen as a personality having identity and image.

'Recent times have seen great writers choosing titles like Corporate Image and Corporate Identity. There appears to be confusion in the use of terms.' (Van Riel, 1990-PGDM notes 2001)

Van Riel defines it thus: *'Corporate communication is an instrument of management by means of which all consciously used forms of internal and external communication are harmonised as effectively and efficiently as possible, so as to create a favourable basis for relationships with groups upon which the company is dependent.*

'...in-spite of their relationship, there is a fundamental difference between them. In general terms 'Corporate Image' can be described as the picture that people have of a company, whereas 'Corporate Identity' denotes the sum total of all forms of expression that a company uses to offer insight into its nature.

...the self-portrayal of an organisation, i.e. the cues and the signals which it offers via its behaviour, communication and symbolism.

Corporate Image is defined as: image is the 'set of meanings by which an object is known and through which people describe, remember, and relate to it.... net result of impression about an object.

In part, the Corporate image can be seen as reflecting the identity of an Organisation... (However) there are various external factors which also influence the image of organisation. These include the negative influence of the conduct of behaviour of certain company members; rumour formation; and most of all, the rational and (apparently), irrational ways in which members of the target groups select signals from those put out by the organisation.

On the inaugural day of the bank's branch grand publicity is given; some dignitary cuts the ribbon; speeches are made.. Some one from the senior management '*states*' the purpose of the branch and the bank. The invited guests applaud and laud the bank's gesture.

Imputed purpose is different from the stated purpose.

Stated purpose is what bank's superior says; imputed purpose is what the branch does.

The sentence on negative influence etc is most significant statement that a bank management must note: conduct of company members. The rural areas are much more sensitive to this than urban centres.

In the episode 1, case 5 several Managers criticized Nationalization of banks in the Rotary club, a public place; they have no exposure to 'corporate communication'; the subject evolved much later. Even otherwise they should have known the risk they had taken expressing their reservations. If they had made such remarks two years later 75/76 when the country passed through emergency, they might have been marked and shown the way by such thing as VRS. Alternatively they would have to be exposed to orientation programmes both in public sector management and a short course on corporate communication.

I am inclined to look at the plight of MFIs and their borrowers with corporate communication goggles: 'negative influence of the conduct of behaviour of' MFI recovery agents who used strong-arm tactics. They have done enough damage to the image of the whole 'Micro-Finance' industry.

Study the diagram showing the common starting points (CSPs) – Identity, Image, and Strategy.

Management communication
Marketing communication
Orgnaisation communication

The need to create favourable image in recent times has spurred on lot of research in corporate communication.

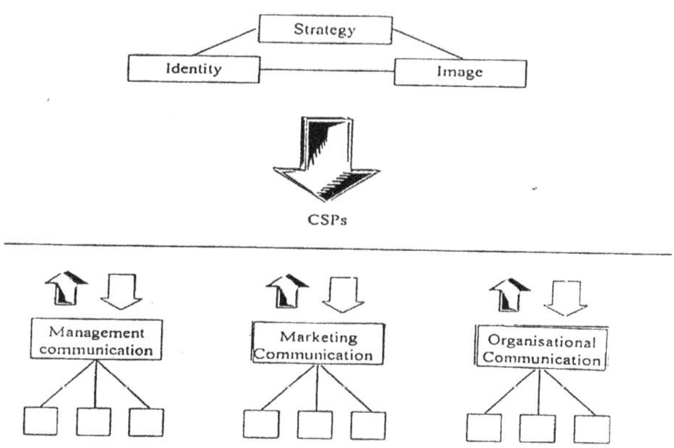

A bank, public sector bank, in particular must conduct its own research on an ongoing basis on its corporate communication system internally and externally to take steps to remedy the situation.

Management Communication

The most important is 'management communication', i.e. communication by (senior) Managers with internal and external target groups.

Management is often described as 'accomplishing work through other people'. Typically this includes functions like planning, organizing, commanding, coordinating controlling (Fayol, 1949). At the heart of all these functions lies effective communications.

Till recently it is seen as more or less one way communication by competent Managers / communicators / P.R.Officers. But now it is recognised that management is only possible with the consent of the managed. In other words, we cannot really manage anyone who does not want to be managed. As a consequence, one of the Manager's role is to continuously persuade individual subordinates that the goals of the organization are desirable. Communication, therefore, is vitally necessary to an organization, not only to transmit authority, but also to achieve cooperation (Timm, 1986).

Internal Communication

Every Manager, rural branch in particular, must accept the goals of the bank – desired goals. The senior management, internally communicate with all subordinates to that effect. That is part of management communication. Often in banks there is no express communication to reiterate the desirability of goals with the subordinates except forcing targets every quarter, half year, and annual reviews.

'*Management by the consent of the managed*' is what is lacking in management communication. Persuading should be based on 'data' on potential, competition, and capacity of the branch and past experiences.

The objectives of internal communication in the 21st century are mainly four in number :

1. *developing a* ***shared vision*** *of the company within the organization;*
2. *establishing and maintaining trust in the organization leadership;*
3. *initiating and managing the change process; and*
4. *empowering* ***and motivating employees*** *(Pincus, Robert, Rayfield and Debonis, 1991).*

This has to be accomplished through oral, written, and non-verbal communications by all Managers. The responsibility for communication stretches across all levels of an organization : senior management, but also middle and junior management.

In banks the problem is with middle level management. With exceptional growth of PSBs many subordinates were pushed up to bear bigger responsibility than they were prepared for. Orientation programmes in staff colleges could not make them any better. The vital apprenticeship was missing. Nor, there was any 'self development' efforts made. The promotion was seen as reward and power over people. At least in the present situation management students and other professionals have been entering the banking industry and it is in better shape.

By far the most difficult objective is 'developing a shared vision'. It is accomplished through oral and non-verbal (actions) than written. Written communication is drafted protecting the interests of the signatory!

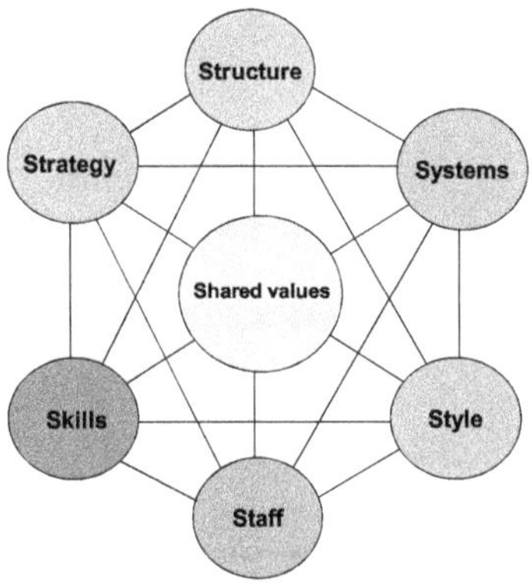

Actions, of course, speak louder. Even 'saying' orally lacked clarity. But clarifications are not sought.

Role of CEO in Management Communication

Talking to employees (Compassion)

Among other things the CEO has to 'talk' to employees. The questions to be answered are;

1. *Does CEO understand employees' communication and emotional needs?*
2. *Does CEO demonstrate his/her personal concern for employees' needs?*
3. *Do employees have accessible feedback channels to CEO?*

Role of other Managers

In addition to the 'symbolic' role of the CEO, middle and junior management play an important role in communication.

They must understand how those above them are likely to act because of their organisational position and how those below them are similarly motivated and limited by their placement in the organisational space. The critical task of middle and lower management is to interpret organisational goals, or guide subordinates to do so, in ways which optimise organisational functioning. Once the goals are determined and the principles understood, management (in discussion with communication specialists) must develop and decide upon a more specific set of communication strategies (Allen 1977).

Role of Specialists (support to Managers)

Communication appears to be too vital for organizational success to leave it solely to Managers. Experts both in marketing and in organizational communications are necessary to support Managers in improving the effectiveness of their communication responsibilities, by supplying developed programmes which increase the involvement of employees and elicit the support of external stake holders.

Conclusion

CEOs and General Managers should never consider hiring communication experts as the panacea of organizational communication, which has been the tendency in the past. A communication expert / specialist quickly becomes the resident expert and a feeling seems to creep over the rest of the management team that they no longer need worry about the problem. The danger is, of course, that it is patently absurd to expect one person (or department) operating out of one position, to solve a problem that is organizationally pervasive. ***This kind of lip service to remedy of organisational ills will not relieve anyone in the organisation of their own proper communication role, any***

more than the presence of a training executive relieves individual Managers of their responsibility for training. (Allen, 1977).

The highlighted lines in the end are significant. There have been no undue dependence on specialists in banks as of now regarding communication although advertisers pinch the purse of banks. It is difficult to arrive at cost/benefit ratio.

Marketing Communication

It is there in banks but the focus is on urban customers. Rural areas also need marketing communication. Business Facilitators are the sales promoters.

The element, the promotional mix, to which by far the greatest share of money is devoted is personal selling, or the directly related activity of sales management. The dinstinguishing feature of this from of marketing communication is the direct personal contact between the seller and the prospective buyer, ***which facilitates adjustment to the needs of the individual client.*** *Personal selling is defined by Kotler (1988) as 'oral presentation in a conversation with one or more prospective purchasers for the purpose of making sales'.*

This is what rural banker has to do.

Banks went to rural market. 'Expansion' was the idea. They sold existing financial products to a new segment – the rural segment without scientific *market research.* But they did develop a variety of innovative products to the city/town/trade/industry segments but by and large the rural segments were neglected.

`What they should have done was 'Diversification' strategy – new products to new segments. The attempts that were made in designing suitable products have been meager and minuscule. It took decades before they had kisan credit cards for example.

Marketing Research & Strategy : Marketing Mix

Products	Segments: Existing	Segments: New
Existing	(A) Market penetration	(B) Market expansion
New	(C) Product development	(D) Diversification

Even in the segmentation of market they have failed. Tenant farmer, by far the largest segment has been neglected mainly because security based products as opposed to clean cash credit which did not suit the segment at all. SHGs & JLGs are the new segments which deserver special market researches and product development.

Tangibility - Marketing Financial Products

To inspect the progress in minor irrigation project taken up by BOB with subsidy from SFDA and margin money from caste corporations the district Collector toured villages. In one of the villages, the Collector asked a beneficiary, a small farmer to tell him the name of the bank which financed the well-digging and electric motor. Unable to spell the name of the bank the man ran to the nearby tree where he hanged his shirt and brought the passbook the bank gave him. The Collector examined the entries in the pass book and asked the farmer a few questions and the answers the farmer gave tallied with what Collector found in the pass book. The Collector shared this episode in one of the DLCC meetings and asked all the banks to follow the same procedure.

In most banks in those days, there was no system of issuing loan pass books. Later I came across the concept of 'tangibility of a product missing in services' in a marketing book. Products are tangible because you can touch and feel. But services suffer from intangibility. To compensate for vital missing feature marketers innovated by adding something tangible to every service. The pass book, attractive and nice to touch, convenient to carry in the shirt pocket added tangibility to the information the book carried. Another marketing *guru* differentiated four types of product – generic, expected, augmented, and potential. Safety, liquidity, and return are features of generic product of savings bank service. A pass book with accurate information is 'expected' product. Even courtesy to the customer is an expected product feature. What could be augmented product? Micro-insurance linked to bank savings product will certainly serve as augmented product. Like technology if the augmented product becomes ubiquitous it will soon become expected product. Now the banker must search for potential product features which go by the name 'product innovation'.

Coming back to our story, the farmer always cherished it keeping it in his shirt pocket, probably the only shirt. We may consider B.Fs – leaving the versatile, tangible pass book at the end of the transaction with a smile, of course.

Organizational Communication

'Organizational communication' is used here as a general term to cover public relations, public affairs, investor relations, labour market communication, corporate advertising, environmental communication and internal communication. It denotes a heterogeneous group of communication activities which have only a few characteristics in common.

Their most important shared characteristic is without doubt the fact that all forms of organizational communication are directed primarily at so-called 'target groups', i.e. groups with which the organization has an interdependent relationship, ***usually indirect****.*

Unlike marketing communication, the various forms of organizational communication are less obvious in their attempts to influence the behaviour of groups on which the organization depends. Examples of such relationships are those with, say, public authorities (which may exercise the power to implement regulations unfavourable to the organization) or with financial journalists. When dealing with such groups (civil servants or financial journalists), it is unwise to employ styles that are, say generally accepted in other areas of marketing communication activity, e.g. expansive references to product benefits. ***A business-like approach is much more likely to be effective****. It will nevertheless be clear to all concerned that whatever forms of* *communication the company uses, it should strive to create for itself the most favourable position possible.*

Another characteristic of all forms of organizational communication, in the sense in which the term is used here is the fact that the different forms of communication manifested remain firmly rooted within the organization. It is obvious that they will not all fall within the functional management area of marketing. From this point of view, organizational communication could be described as ***'all forms of communication used by the organization, other than marketing communications or management communications.***

The rural or semi-urban Manager does all types of communication – Management, Marketing, and Organization which role has never been recognized and articulated or emphasized. The reward system has not taken into account these aspects. Of course it reflects in the balance sheet indirectly.

From the foregoing discussion on corporate communication it is clear that the total organisation - the individuals, the groups, and the departments must say what they mean. To bring about in the company wide change, it is necessary for the change for better should begin with day to day work place conversations and other communications like memos, reports, letters, etc., both oral and written forms of saying and meaning becomes very important.

A lot can be discussed on the role of barefoot banker as corporate communicator based on the foregoing notes.

Corporate Communication Illustrated. Caricatures–meaning and significance:

1. Lifeless Office (Case no.24)

An empty office with no customers and staff dozing is a non-verbal common communication without words, without intention. Message is 'not interested in business'. Previous Manager was doing commuting from city. Earliest he could reach was 11am and he leaves at 4 pm to catch the train at a distance of 10 km for returning home by 8 pm. Poor fellow has to 'struggle' for two years before he was 'liberated' from the punishment! It does not know which he really missed – opportunity to grow in personality

He is an organizational member who draws monthly salary. He is at times sent to an orientation programme which he avoids, if possible, and if he attends he is inattentive to the instruction. He thinks the instruction is indoctrination and must be resisted at any cost. Otherwise he would lose his freedom and would be exploited! Soon after Nationalization the banks had majority in this mould. Image of the bank suffered as a consequence.

2. Busy Office (Case no. 24)

Another direct recruit Agricultural Officer takes over. He lives with family in the village another non-verbal communication - management communication and a strategy. Villagers respond. It can

also be classified as marketing communication and advertisement of an *identity –we are a bank here to serve the people.*

Stated purpose without saying. It can be said a public relations strategy. The connection between concept and concrete action must be noted.

The new incumbent might not have studied 'corporate communication'; but he does it. 'Concepts come from concrete actions.' Result, busy bank and business development, reports to senior management, who reinforce and reward to escalate business further. Positive feed back is escalatory. The negative feed back has been corrected. Image gets boosts. A feed forward.

3. Shift-in Focus (Case no.11)

Recoveries are poor. Strategy: change man with instruction to improve recoveries. Puzzle solved by shifting focus. Here is the shrewd Manager who focused on lending, fresh lending. He shifted the office to the village proper. Corporate communication at work. There is publicity and advertisement to the whole village. Long queues and happy faces satisfied with the bank's work. This too is non-verbal communication to the defaulters. They all assemble to see whether they could interact with the 'god' – generous, open, dedicated – they get their chance to communicate verbally. The Manager listens more than talking. The villagers communication styles in groups is typical. One starts, another picks up and there is a chorus. The Manager must respond keeping his objective of recovery in mind. The narrator does not give details. A script writer can create a beautiful episode out of it. If the Manager were to record them in brief in his personal or official diary it would serve as 'knowledge at work' document. If the Manager is also a good story writer he could write a short story. The volume has a couple of such real life stories beautifully narrated.

The senior management had no idea of the process. If the process is known it can be replicated. Such things did not happen in the banks. Organizational behaviours deals with process and not products.

4. Loan Mela (Case 5, Episode 9)

It is a political affair and the politician will have control. A clever Manager may take it as an opportunity where he goes as a guest of honour leaving the event management to the administration and party workers and saves costs.

This is a case in which the Manager capitalized the event to the bank's advantage. Costs to government benefit to bank.

The politician is there to take credit for the work done by the bank. By its work bank already had the credit, acknowledged by people in-spite of politicians.

5. Addressing Gram Sabha a better approach

Gram Sabha is Lok Sabha in Panchayati Raj. Management communication includes Manager addressing gram sabha members, like Rotary Club members. Loan melas, credit or recovery camps are occasion when the Managers and senior Managers are communicating with external target groups.

The communication, well prepared speech, has to be the APT – keeping *audience* and *purpose* in mind and using proper *technique* and *timing*. The language, style and tactics vary according to the audience, their expectations, purpose. Multiple soft skills are developed by the incumbent during the tenure of rural posting which may not be vouched if he misses the opportunity

6. Addressing SHGs Federation at Mandal level, District Level & even State level (Case no. 32)

Public speaking

Public service

Public image

Publicity

Personality growth

7. Winning over an opinion leader (Case no.23)

Attending the wedding at mid night at any cost conveyed a great deal about the man's tactics and his sincerity of purpose - to establish positive relationship with an adversary. Cycling is symbol of overcoming obstacles to goals – the action speaks about the man.

Senior managements have no means to assess the man on the spot unless a mentor closely followed. We never had mentors in those days. Some of us had well wishers but most people sailed in the wrong boats.

8. Court advantage to the client

Banker meets the borrower in his own court. The borrower had the court advantage. 'Manager comes down to reach out to help – he 'stoops to conquer' the client to be ever loyal.

9. Red carpet for the poor

Farmer meets the Manager in high office. He will be overwhelmed if a 'red-carpet' is spread. Others watch with anxiety outside the cabin. Brief but graceful should be the encounter to satisfy large number of visitors. In an open office Manager is observed by most people. Usually the Managers may spend more time with the well-to-do or decently dressed at the expense of the poor.

Excluded and downtrodden may be given preferential treatment to send a message to the entire village that the bank does not exclude weaker sections and poorer or scantily dressed. I know instances when the poor visited the bank in a borrowed shirt.

10. Family as a whole (Case 5, Episode 15)

Question put to husband, wife answers; others watch Manager's reaction. Keep cool, allow the woman to speak. She has some vital information for Manager's decision making. An argument between wife and husband many emerge.

Everybody would be curious to know how the Manager is going to handle the situation. The Manager may encourage the women and empower her to speak.

Interviewing the family requires special skills which counselors develop. The problem is not just economic it is social, cultural practices… each time the Manager can learn and gain experience. Otherwise it becomes number game – how many applications cleared, how fast? How effective and so on.

* * * * *

BAREFOOT Banker and Communication Skills

Understanding Corporate Communication is conceptual skill or viewing communication at total organizational level. In viewing it we saw it as several roles–Management Communicator, Marketing Communicator, and Public Relations.

At micro level it is '*Human Skills*' variedly known as '*Social Skills*', '*Soft Skills*', and *Life-Skills* or *Relational skills.*

Customer Relations Management or CRM is a new dimension or long term relationships, fine tuning to the changing needs of customer by the enterprises.

Multi-Disciplinary Science – PSALM of Life

Communications was Engineering subject with its own development of Jargon–'Sender', 'Receiver', Encoding, Decoding, Channels, Noise, Feed Back, 'Correction' etc. This Engineer's domain has been occupied by Psychologists, Sociologists, Anthropologists, Linguists, and Media Specialists (PSALM) and thus become multi-disciplinary science and even art. The matrix below explains further the division.

	Verbal	**Non-Verbal**
Vocal	Oral	Para-lingual
Non-vocal	Written	Non-verbal SPATE

Let us start with Non-Verbal SPATE. As in 'river in spate' in the flow of communication the non-verbal is a 'flood' compared to verbal 'trickle'. A flood of messages are communicated without intention. The reader may be familiar with use of phrase 'Body Language' by the cricket commentators which is an aspect of non-verbal communication.

I have used SPATE and PAGEANT in the diagram below as acronyms:

SPATE		**PAGEANT**
Space use		Postures
Pageant	→	Attire
Appearance		Gestures
(physical)		Expressions
Time & Touch		Action
Environment		Non-action
		Tone

Non-Verbal SPATE

Space Use

Researchers divided 'space use', an element of non-verbal communication into (a) Territory (b) Personal Space. Bank office is Bank Staff's 'Territory'. They enjoy 'territorial rights'. Within the branch premises there are Manager's cabin and cash enclosures and are territories into which entry is restricted. The customer is the visitor who is made to observe certain protocol and decorum without 'saying'.

But the Manager and Bank staff, when they enter the village on bank work are in another's territory. The roles are reversed and norms of behaviour for the bankers and the villagers are reversed.

The reader may think that all this is 'commonsense'. Unfortunately the 'commonsense' is not so common in practice especially for the 'urbane' Manager and bank staff working in rural areas.

> Men must be taught as if you taught them not; and *things proposed as things forgot.*
>
> *Alexander Pope*

This topic too is discussed as *things proposed as things forgot.*

Self Development

We all learn to communicate at home, school, or college, long before we join service. At home and elsewhere we learn partly through observation and imitation of parents, teachers, friends, and superiors. The learnings vary from person to person for obvious reasons of exposure to different conditions. In this regard there is rural and urban divide. Managers who are born and brought up with rural family background have had an advantage over their urban middle class counterparts in serving in rural areas.

Competition among peers has increased in the modern organizations. 'Employability', a buzz word, compels every one to remedy, develop, or perfect their skills of communicating messages and skills of building relationships.

The focus has shifted from teaching and coaching to self-development for the simple reason coaching courses have become costly and time consuming. Time is precious in this competitive world. Everyone has to hone up and continuously review his or her own skills kitty.

Personal Space

Then there is the other aspect, 'personal space' or distance maintained between individuals interacting in bank office and in the field visits. Furniture in office keeps the visitors separated. The Manager who walks around his big table and receives a rich customer and shakes hands is reducing the physical distance. If he does same thing with rural poor client he closes the gap–the psychological distance, which is much more powerful than reducing the physical distance in building customer relationships.

Let us examine the operation of 'space use' when the Barefoot-Banker visits the villages. If he wears 'space use' gaugles he get spate of ideas for action. The Manager can win over the rural people with non-verbal communication itself. If he adds kind words, it will be complete. When he visits the village along with the Government officials, Sarpanch, and others, he gains the 'territorial rights' indirectly. The small man keeps his distance. If the knowledgeable banker knows the meaning and significance of 'Social Inclusion' and 'Financial Inclusion' and remembers that he has to bridge the divide and 'empower' the socially excluded he may have to find means to use his 'personal space' appropriately. He may do this when the banker visits the home/hut of the man. Visit is non-verbal message par excellence. He may keep the principles of *equity* and *empowerment* in mind and express it in non-verbal behaviour. The villagers are good at reading non-verbal cues and signs.

Pageant means deliberate display, a conscious effort to communicate non-verbally. PAGEANT, an acronym which keeps hidden in it many more elements of non-verbal communication will be taken up separately. Appearance, Touch and Timing, and Environment will be addressed now.

Appearance

Physical stature – tall and well built body has many advantages as an element of 'Non-verbal SPATE'. There was a problem in one of the rural branch. The District Coordinator was asked to sort it out. We had a Manager who brought disrepute to the bank. The villagers threatened to kill him. When the news came to the District Manager who was tall and imposing personality rushed to the village branch in his jeep and entourage. He could pacify the villagers with his imposing stature. Body language played vital part and it enhanced the oral-verbal negotiation and counseling.

Erect stance, gait, debonair, –all add to the dignity and help in winning over the rural folk. If he is soft-spoken and humane – the tone and tenor add value to the oral communication.

Appearance in office and appearance in the village have marked difference. Some researchers studied communication in terms of Attention, Intention and Commitment. In an interview when one interviewer puts a question to the interviewee, if the other turns away the interviewee gets puzzled whether to answer the question or wait till the 'disinterested' panel members comes back to the proceedings. This is much more true in interviewing the poor villagers than a job seeker in a multi-national company.

In a *credit camp* the Manager who sits along with other officers from Governments agencies is most observed by all. 'Right brained' illiterates make sense from the non-verbal clues– information from the Manager. At the same time the 'left brained' educated urban Manager interacting for the first time has to learn to study non-verbal messages from his rural audience. You have to show your honesty of purpose tactically and look for cues from the open and transparent rural folk. There must be meeting of minds through non-verbal exchanges. Communicate to the whole audience skillfully.

Loan mela is one occasion which will be dominated by the politicians of the ruling party. I have found it best to keep oneself at a distance from the motley crowd. I say 'motley' crowd because of the presence of retinue of the Minister who do not belong to the villages banks serve.

In the case 5 episode no. 9 the situation was some what different. It is the Manager's honest work that attracted the crowds thanks to spade work done by the S*arpanch.* All politicians should not be painted with the same brush however.

Timing

Banks have business hours and working hours for the staff the most unrealistic and arbitrary way of dealings with rural population.

Most Barefoot Bankers have deviated with established practices and made their work 24/7 schedule.

Timing and use of time have been found to be a non-verbal communication. When a Manager comes to the branch from the city at 11 am and leaves at 4 pm to catch the bus to city, it speaks volumes, in the negative sense. The villagers stopped coming to bank. (Case no.24)

When a new Manager changed the 'time management' the image of the bank changed for better rapidly.

Touch

Where 'personal space' ends touch begins. Barring shaking hands touch is rare in official life. Touch may be used sparingly but appropriately. It should be avoided lest he is misunderstood. For the Manager in the case 5 episode 6 when the poor man fell on the Manager's feet may warrant touch. When the Manager is overwhelmed with pity, his expression and action are more appropriate than touch. Probably he could call and caress the 10 year old boy. Still it may appear artificial. The principle involved is 'thus far, no further'.

Environment use: Environment is our surroundings. How we keep our surroundings – at home, in office and everywhere is part of our personal effectiveness. There are some who shape and control their environment with great care. At home, inside, everything is well organized, outside the garden is well maintained. In the office, our table, our files and papers and small space allotted to us must be in spick and span.

Researchers concentrated on office environment and ambience. But the barefoot bankers have yet another environment the village and open landscape. How does this theory of environment as non-verbal communication useful to the barefoot bankers. I leave it to the readers' imagination. Our rural society always emphasized keeping homes and public places neat and clean. This is one area we have to revive our tradition in improving health and hygiene. Temple culture and religious practices can be drawn upon.

PAGEANT: Manager's *posture* in his seat in office when he receives an affluent customer and the difference when he receives a poor ill-clad farmer tells a story about the man.

His *attire* in office and his dress and debonair in the village tells another story. The villagers read these signals much more efficiently than the urban people.

Gestures and gait play their part, the way he hails or calls a poor man vis-à-vis the influential persons communicate Manager's mettle.

Expressions – facial expression should be more natural than contrived. If you are not committed and compassionate your natural facial expression betrays intentions. Face is the index of mind. It is difficult to hide the mood. It is safe to make expression free and flexible. Learn to be expressive, cultivate the habit of responsiveness through non-verbal cues. Both *actions* and *non actions* speak louder than words. We had a Manager who brought disrepute to the bank.

Tone is equally important.

Para-lingual

Para-lingual refers to nasal sounds we make acknowledging and encouraging the speaker. It is an aspect of listening skills: ah, oh, yah, mm, mn etc.

Even short expressions like 'I see', 'Oh, I see', etc fall under this category which is a powerful way of motivating the speaker.

Traditional Bankers have a tendency to see keep their 'eyes and ears open and mouth shut.' They don't even use para-language which the villagers use liberally. The Banker can learn from them!

The foregoing is a cursory account of growing literature on non-verbal communication.

Remember that 80% of communication is communication without words. By effective display of your non-verbal communication, you can enhance your personal effectiveness guarding against the wrong ones.

In the end as 'Corporate Communicator' the Managers have to keep the bank's name higher and higher at every turn of events. Everything must be seen as an opportunity or threat to the image of the bank and bank staff.

Written Communication

'Writing Maketh an Exact man' (Bacon). Bacon's assertion is not less important to Barefoot Banker to share and document the episodic memories with the fellow bankers and world at large. But discussion is beyond the scope of this book.

ABCD of Oral Communication

Oral Communication can be further divided as Address (public speaking), Briefing, Conversation and Dialogue & Discussion

Address – One to Audience

One to many. There are 3 types of public speaking:

(a) Prepared paper speeches (b) extempore speeches (c) impromptu speeches. When the banker is invited to speak at a seminar with sufficient time for preparation, it belongs to (a). The invited speaker has no excuse for not preparing for the event which should be seen as an opportunity to project self-image and image of the bank. The second, extempore speech is a mental preparation or carrying the points in the pocket to be in readiness to speak in case he gets a chance.

The last, the impromptu speech is the shortest speech made on the spur of the moment. You may agree or disagree with the earlier speakers and make your point that is more radical and novel. This calls for alertness and readiness to make your presence felt on the occasion.

Prepared **Extempore** **Impromptu**

Public speech is a public service in public relations.

Public speaking is public service. If this is your motto, then you will be a successful speaker.

Once you get over you initial, natural, stage fear you have to really work hard to perfect the most sought after and satisfying skill. Many people remain at mediocre level or even become public bores because they do not develop the skills systematically. I have codified public speaking into three phrases:

STAND UP
To be seen,
SPEAK UP
To be heard
SHUT UP
To sit down.

STAND UP:

* Stance – Your debonair, poise and position from the moment you begin to walk up to the podium, till you begin the address matters a great deal. Your dress is equally important, 'Apparel oft proclaims the man', Shakespeare wrote. It holds good even to this day. The rule is, 'go by the audience's expectations'.

Use always the podium, on which you can keep your papers. You can hide most of your body behind it. Hiding the body is important because your body movement can distract the attention of the audience. For audience's attention you need to show only your expressive face and hands for appropriate gestures.

* Think of the opening sentences. Well chosen and well articulated opening utterances help relieve you from the tension. For the release from tension, you need to exhale. As you utter you exhale.

How do you begin?

Beginning with proper salutation like 'Mr. President, distinguished guests, ladies and gentlemen', is good enough for most occasions. Although it is customary to mention the names, designation and titles of VIPs on the dais, they are redundant from the audience angle. At times you might mix up and mess up the whole saluation. A bad beginning!

* Thank the organizers and the audience for the opportunity. Remember to thank the introducer. Although you may come prepared, pick up something from what he said. For this purpose you have to listen carefully to what the introducer is saying. You can even start with something he has omitted to say about you.

* **Audience – Contact.** Don't be a stiff-neck! Turn freely and naturally your head from left to right. Maintain the rhythmic movement. Don't stare at few faces and embarrass them. Refer to your papers now and then but don't read from them.

* **No Apology** – Apologising for coming late or not preparing is not to improve the rapport with your audience. On the other hand if you begin your address without any further delay it will be appreciated by them.

* **Delivery** - Your voice, your pronunciation, modulation and intonation constituting the delivery, is the most neglected part. There is considerable scope for improvement in this area. It demands hard work and diligent rehearsals. Standing before a mirror or friends and practising is not uncommon to many great speakers. They even use a tape recorder for the purpose. There is no reason why you can't do it. Now-a-days there is professional help available for those who want to develop their voice culture. Alternatively, you can listen to Radio and T.V. documentaries with particular reference to pronunciation, intonation, modulation and speed. (Refer to acronym SPEAK).

Unassuming. You should begin with confidence and yet display humility. You can speak of your strengths and also about the limitation of what you are going to speak.

Promptness. Long introduction is a curse to the audience. Begin the topic promptly. That is what your audience expect from you.

SPEAK UP

Survey and Preparation. If public speaking is public service, then you have to do justice to each engagement. Your audience come for enrichment, sparing their valuable time. Hence preparation is very essential. It may be necessary to survey the literature on the subject, the latest on it. The degree of survey and preparation may vary according to audience, purpose, and time. Time for preparation and time allotted to make the speech, both are important for survey and preparation.

The actual preparation involves writing down the speech (for the principles of writing refer to the section **"Writing Maketh An Exact Man"**).

Establish credibility. The audience-attention is the goal here. Credibility and importance of the topic to the audience have to be established to make them attentive. Next, establish your competence to talk on the subject. Your experience and knowledge form your competence. At the same time, acknowledge that there are many in the audience who have something to say on the subject. But the uniqueness you bring to bear on your speech is your own experience and opinions. Usually the introducer has to do this. If he fails, which is true in most cases, you have to establish the credibility of the topic and your competence yourself.

Audience-Acceptance: The entire body of the speech is aimed at audience-acceptance of your opinions. Your reasoning must be perfect.

Your speech contains facts, assumptions and your opinions. Your audience must accept them as such. When you state facts, quote the sources. Authenticity becomes important. To make assumptions valid is more difficult. Sometimes you are not conscious of the assumptions you make. Assumptions are bridges between facts and opinions. They have to be articulated and validated. What you take for granted, it may not be taken for granted by all in the audience. You will have to argue; give reasoning and validate it. There is the advantage in writing down. You can ask yourself whether the audience would accept the, statement readily or not. If not, you can support it with warranties, bring out possible rebuttals and back it up with evidence like the way a lawyer does. Ultimately what your audience want is your opinions, supported by verifiable facts, evidence and valid assumptions.

While preparing the speech provide for flexibility - either cut down or increase the text - according to the contingency. Remember also that the same subject will have to be put in different ways to different groups of people.

Keep the perspective: You present your speech as a coherent whole, not as disjointed pieces. You have to tie your ideas together. This is another reason why you should write down your speech. There are many things, many angles, many perspectives to each topic. Keeping the audience, purpose, and time in view you have to cut the coat.

Don't stray away from the 'central theme. Even if you have to digress a little, come back quickly to the main stream.

Use anecdotes and gadgets. Your anecdote should not digress the audience-attention. They have to be CRISP: Credible, Relevant, Interesting, Simple, Punch.

Use of gadgets like slides, public address system can mar the whole show if care is not taken. Every speaker must be ready for the contingencies with alternatives. While showing the slides what you speak should be consistent with what you are showing. In case you need to digress, switch off the slide projector.

Persuasion. In the ultimate analysis, public service is incomplete if you don't persuade people into acceptance and possible actions. For this remember you have to combine your reasoning with emotional appeal.

Gettysburg speech of Abraham Lincoln is an example worth remembering.

SHUT UP

Leave the political speeches to the politician. Politicians have difficulty with shutting up

Sum Up. Never end the speech abruptly. However small the speech might be, it must contain a summing up. This is necessary for refreshing the memory of the audience. Also, the last few statements are what they carry home. Again, writing the speech helps in preparing a short summary.

* Hark Back. Go back to the main points made earlier to pick up the trail. It is better if you can recall and reiterate the exact sentences.

- Use of Anecdotes. You can choose a small and simple anecdote or a famous quotation or a proverb or a catchy phrase or an acronym. You-can make an emotional appeal at this stage with a telling effect.
- Thank them again, if you had thanked the audience and organisers for the opportunity at the beginning, do it for the satisfying and memorable day at the end. Do it with gratitude writ on your face.
- Be Unassuming and Promptly sit down, the way you began the speech. Having said what you wanted to say, never linger longer than necessary. There are many things you might have left off. Never mind. Don't go back again, once you have begun to sum up. Promptly shut up and win the laurels, acknowledging due applause

Stance	**S**urvey and	**S**um Up
Think	**P**reparation	**H**ark Back
Audience-Contact	**E**stablish credibility	**U**se of Anecdotes
No-Apology	**A**udience Acceptance	**T**hank
Delivery	**K**eep the perspective	**U**nassuming
Unassuming	**U**se of gadgets and Anecdotes	**P**romptness
Promptness	**P**ersuasion	

of them.

Briefing – One To Small Groups

Be BRIEF. Lead with GRACE is the prescription in small group communications. Briefing is the most concrete aspect of leadership. You have to do it with GRACE.

Be BRIEF to brief

Bold	Behave naturally in front of the group.
Ready	Think ahead and plan your communication.
Informing & clarifying	Make it clear or understandable. Unravel the difficulties in your own mind first.
Enthusing	Make the subject come alive. Be enthusiastic and aim to enthuse the group. Use humour if possible.
Familiarizing	Render complex matter into simple forms. Summarise

We might add 'S' for Summarizing small group BRIEFS.

Lead with GRACE

G – Gate keeping

R – Reconciling

A – Asserting

C – Controlling

E - Energizing

The leader must keep the *gates of communication* open and shut to allow for free flow of thoughts and participation of all the members of the group, allowing and encouraging the silent ones and shutting the gate to the dominant others.

When arguments and counter arguments are presented, there can be a DEAD-lock: Defences, Evasions, Attacks and Denials. The leaders may have to reconcile the seeming opposite view points presenting holistic perspective.

It also involves *asserting* the leader's authority to impose order and decorum. He may watch over the language – the diction- when there is more heat than light. His own diction should be clear, appropriate, and effective and vigorous.

He has to, particularly, *control* the direction of discussion. At times the group may lose interest and become apathetic around tough issues. The leader may *energize* through emotional appeal. Combing reason with emotion calls for very high order of diction.

Conversation – One to One

Borrower Interview–rural situation; Art of Questioning to the rural folk

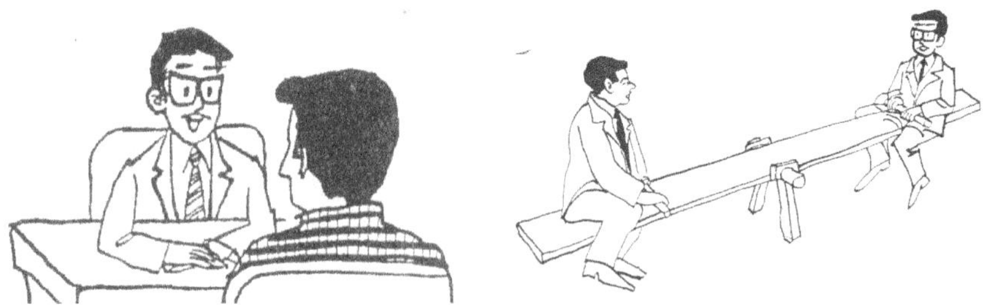

Conversation Style

ASPIRE for Social Skills

Social skills training has assumed importance since 1970's. The acronym ASPIRE puts compactly some of the training programmes conducted in the beginning. Now the focus of social skills training is mainly on Assertiveness training.

Asking questions
Sustaining conversations
Paraphrasing for active listening
Initiating and closing conversations
Reflecting and reinforcing
Expressing emotions

Asking questions is a separate module to equip the trainee to learn to ask questions. There are a variety of questions that you will find in the section which comes later. *Sustaining conversation* includes asking questions, initiating, reflecting feelings and reinforcing the speaker. *Initiating* a conversation includes asking questions. *Reflecting feelings* includes verbal and non-verbal communications. *Reinforcing* questions special effort (see later the acronym-ACCEPT).

These skills have to be practiced as diligently as one practices cricket or tennis strokes. With much practice the learner develops a repertoire of skills and sub-skills for using in the appropriate situations.

These aspects are general in nature whether the other party is from city or rural areas, farmers, literate or illiterate. However we have to consider cross cultural communication, psychological barriers and overcoming of barriers and negotiated settlements for recovery. In case no.12 the narrator writes that he has become an expert of OTS (one time settlement) of NPAs. Evidently he has mastered the social skills in all its aspects.

Tips for effective cross-cultural communication: remember they have to be SACRED.

These are not for only those who meet people outside India.

Speak slowly
Avoid idioms
Check understanding
Repeat more than once
Express clearly
Direct (to the point)

Within India we have cross-cultural communication problem. The rural folk have their own styles and tones different from urban people. We have north-south differences as well. Add to the complexity–the English speaking interacting with local people who speak several dialects.

For all the diverse situations the SACRED tips hold good.

Psychological Barriers to Communication : FIDGET

Filtering	(receiver hears what he wants to hear)
Inconsistency	(in thought and action of the sender)
Distortion	(receiver unable to decode messages)
Games	(both receiver and sender play-dishonesty)
Emotions	(of both the receiver and sender)
Timing	(by the sender)

Take the situation into your **STRIDE to overcome barriers**

Secure attention
Timing
Redundancy
Incorporating feedback
Directness
Empathizing

OTS Customer

Incorporating feed back in the next round is an important aspect in OTS- one time settlement of NPAs. The rules for feed back:

Specific
Tailor made
Agreed by the sender
Timely
Enabling
Descriptive

Banker has to learn to ask questions in a different mode to rural folk than the urban. The rural people use more of their right brains which is more intuitive than the analytical left which the urban elite use. They are inclined to ask questions to seek information and guage the intention of the Manager than answering probing questions. They evade certain type of questions. The banker need not conclude that they are dishonest, for generations of submission have inured them to a kind of style of answering questions put by the land lords and the revenue officials. Banker may gain by making the borrower in rural areas by what I call ACCEPT, an acronym: *Acknowledge, Confirm, Compliment, Endorse, Praise, Track on* (sustaining).

ACCEPT for reinforcement

Acknowledge
Confirm
Compliment
Endorse
Praise
Track on (Sustaining)

Answer their questions–confirming by a nod. While he does it with an embarrassed smile or giggle, don't hackle him or her. Treat women with utmost respect. Compliment whenever he/she speaks with pride and prestige or with confidence. Endorse their opinions whenever it is necessary.

Don't be tongue tied. Bankers have a tendency not to reveal what is due lest they be taken for granted. Praise comes from the others – villager elders confirming the statement. All that the banker has to do is to accept with liberal gestures. 'Track on' is an important element to show that the banker is not in a great hurry to wind up the interview. Ask 'anything else?'. It is possible that the other family member, for example wife, might add a word or two. Let the disinherited exit with excitement. They will remember the man in the banker for a generation. If the child is around, even next generation will remember.

Question in Question

Questioning is at once both a skill and art. It requires preparation, putting and the then pondering over the reply.

Questions are broadly ten types – PROMPTCALL, use 1,2,3 and 8 only with the rural poor. Instead of probing question (5) Use 'exploratory' questions.

Give the folk

enough ROPES

Recall question
Open question
Process question
Exploratory question
Social enquiry

1. **P**rocess question to start and maintain
2. **R**ecall question to refresh memory
3. **O**pen question to elicit more information
4. **M**ultiple questions to put down others
5. **P**robing questions to delve deep
6. **T**elling (Rhetorical) questions put to put down and not elicit an answer
7. **C**losed question to reflect feelings
8. **A**ffective question to reflect feelings
9. **L**eading question to lead to an end
10. **L**oaded question to tilt the conversation to one side

Sociolinguistic Approach – Turn Taking

Workplace conversation (borrower interviews included) involves the joint accomplishment of participants through *turn-taking,* where contingent meaning evolves only in the context of the interaction.

GRADES in turn taking – Discourse rhythm: Grades – Giving Receiving, Appropriating, Directing and Deflecting, Ending (Terminating), Sustaining (Maintaining).

Study of group behaviour truly has become multidisciplinary. Here I present from the sociolinguistic model the concept of *turn taking.* Turn taking is like a Seesaw – when one is speaking the other is listening.

Turn taking is a very useful concept for *discussion rhythm* also called discourse rhythm.

Turn *giving* : A yields the turn to B. Turn *receiving*: A yields the turn to B, B accepts the turn from A (B wants the turn, A does not). Turn *appropriating*: A wants to maintain the turn but B takes it. Turn *directing*: A allocates turn to B by asking a question. Turn *deflecting*: A appropriates B's turn in order to assign to C (Usually to prevent B from maintaining or sustaining it). Turn *ending* or terminating: A's turn comes to close. This may end the whole exchange or give the others the option (or the responsibility) to take it up. Turn *sustaining* or maintaining: A keeps the turn, whether B wants it or not.

Turn giving and receiving are self-explanatory. Turn appropriating is the classic case of competition for control of the floor. Turn direction has a number of basic functions. One is to ensure the development and continuation of a conversation/discussion. Another is to ensure that a particular person gets the turn (i.e., you give the person the turn). This can encourage democratic participation, to reinforce a particular position or to prevent someone else from gaining the floor.

Turn deflection is what a chairman or a leader of the group might do in order to prevent competition.

Turn ending or terminating often overlaps with the act of closing. In organisation it is the superior who has the privilege of ending a discussion exercising legitimate power.

Turn Sustaining: It will be obvious that turn maintenance will occur either where there is no attempt at turn appropriation or where such an attempt has failed.

Giving, receiving, and *directing* are helpful in maintaining discourse rhythm.

Appropriating, ending (undemocratically), *sustaining* without concern, not yielding chance to others are dysfunctional to quality conversations.

However *deflecting* may become necessary to ensure participation of all.

Dialogue & Discussion

> 'There was time when India was studded with republics.. Buddhists Bhikshu Sanghas were nothing but Parliaments.. (Buddha) must have borrowed them (the rules) from the rules of the political assemblies functioning in the country in his time. This democratic system India lost.. We must make our political democracy a social democracy as well. A way of life which recognizes *liberty, equality,* and *fraternity..* not to be treated as separate items in trinity…' (but) form a unity of trinity…'

Excerpts from Closing speech of the first Constituent Assembly of India (New Delhi, November 1949) Dr.B.R.Ambedkar.

In my view lakhs of SHGs that are formed are based on the 'union of trinity' of principles of ancient India.

SHGs, are infact a revival of ancient village system of 'responsible group life'.

Ancient system of deliberations in groups was 'Dialogue and Discussion' which the members of SHGs must learn to develop. Barefoot banker can slowly but surely help.

> Liberty cannot be divorced from equality, equality cannot be divorced from liberty. Nor can liberty and equality be divorced from fraternity. Without equality, liberty would produce the supremacy of the few over many'.
>
> *Dr. B.R.Ambedkar*

This is what is most likely to happen in SHGs & JLGs. To educate the SHGs the Barefoot Banker must educate himself/herself. Here is a humble attempt in initiating reader into 'Dialogue & Discussion'.

Recall - Schon (1991)

> Organizations are repositories of cumulatively built up knowledge: principles and maxims of practice, images of mission and identity, facts about the task environment, techniques of operatives, stories of past experiences which serve as exemplars for future.'

The above statement assumes that the organizations learn through meetings, group discussions and committees and so on. But the truth is 'meetings are where minutes are kept and hours are lost'. Reason being the discussions become debates and 'defensive routines' and do not result in organizational learning as Chris Argyris pointed out. If it has to result in organizational learning the members should learn the art of dialogue. I have included excerpts from my previous book on Dialogue and Discussion.

Some of the feature differences of Discussion and Dialogue

		Discussion	Dialogue
Nature :	1.	Occupational activity	Leisure activity
	2.	Time Bound	Ongoing
	3.	Purpose-driven	Philosophy-driven
	4.	Status	Status-Free
	5.	Competition	Co-operation
	6.	Spirit of Contradiction	Spirit of Inquiry
	7.	Adversarial	Camaraderie
	8.	Leadership	Facilitation
	9.	Win-Lose	Win-Win
	10.	Shallow	Deep
	11.	Algorithmic	Heuristic
	12.	Threat/Embarrassment	Congenial/Cordial
	13.	Predictable	Insightful
	14.	Convergent	Divergent
	15.	Explicit	Tacit-Explicit
Process :	16.	Preparedness	Spontaneous
	17.	Analytical	Intuitive
	18.	Exchange	Flow
	19.	Defending	Suspending
	20.	Advocating	Captivating
	21.	Review	Freshness
	22.	Questioning	Exploring
	23.	Critical	Creative
	24.	Breaking apart	Building up
Results :	25.	Heat	Light
	26.	Consensus	Emergence
	27.	Stimulation	Illumination
	28.	Problem solving	Problem-defining

29. Decision-making	Learning
30. Documentation	Absorption
31. Cognition	Cognitive Expansion

Note : For Living and Learning both dialogue and discussion are necessary. A combination works for work life.

Suspending Assumptions

Of all the points David Bohm made, this one is most crucial. Peter Senge laid great emphasis on this point and interpreted in a particular way keeping corporate Managers in mind. Bohm had in mind the society in general. Bohm says that people will bring to the group their assumptions. As they continue talking their assumptions will come up.

Tip of the Iceberg

Nine Tenth of our assumptions which are of things (or events), of ideas or of people are submerged in the subconscious. They need to be surfaced. These assumptions are usually about people. We stereotype them as women, workers, production people, and so on and apply our assumptions to them without verifying whether they are true or not. If I have, as marketing Manager some assumptions about production people, they will come up sooner or later in a dialogue, though not in the habitual discussion.

Then what is called for, says Bohm, is to suspend them so that you neither carry out nor suppress them; you don't believe them, nor do you disbelieve them; you don't judge them as good or bad; you hold it back, reflect back. The point of suspension is to help make proprioception possible, to create a mirror so that you can see the result of your thought. What is required then is that we notice the connection between the thought going on in the dialogue, the feelings in the body, and the emotions. Every body is much in the same boat, except that they are on the opposite side.

Let us see what Senge says on suspension of assumptions:

To suspend one's assumptions means to hold them as it were, 'hanging in front' of you, constantly accessible to questioning and observation by others.

Hanging in Front

Hanging in front so that they are constantly accessible. That is the significant point Senge is making. He quickly adds :

This does not mean throwing out our assumptions, suppressing them or avoiding their expression ... Rather, it means being aware of our assumptions and holding them for examination.

Peter Senge is echoing Chris Argyris's idea - among the set of Model II skills Argyris suggested - stating publicly the inferences that one makes about others with data and inviting others to correct if they are not accurate.

I think what they say is that behind our opinions there are assumptions which we must become aware, suspend them and not defend them. Usually we try to defend our opinions validating our assumptions. Sometimes we state the assumptions as if they are incontrovertible facts.

Inference Machine

It is said that mind is an inference machine reducing the complex to the simple, it leaps to conclusions. It is mind's both strength and weakness at once. It's strength can be best expressed in the words of Isaac Asimov. Comparing brain with computer he wrote in SPAN magazine thus :

"The business of brain is not number manipulation at all; it is that of creative thought, the trick of coming to reasonable conclusions before all the data is in. It has the knack of thinking imaginatively, intuitively, insightfully, and even fancifully".

Often opinions are inferences or leaps to conclusions without our being aware of the assumptions behind them. In dialogue people act as mirrors to each other helping each other seeing each others' incoherence in their thoughts. In a way in dialogue we are taking care of the weakness of inferring at the same time using it for its strength.

William Isaac's Dialogue Project

William Isaacs, director of Dialogue Project at MIT who conducted many dialogue sessions, and who himself participated in David Bohm's dialogue sessions in U.K., has this to say. "After some progress with dialogue, gradually people recognise that they have a choice : they can suspend their views, loosening the grips of certainty about all views including their own. They can observe the ways they have habitually made and acted upon assumptions".

I have a point here: when we defend we are truly not making a choice, we are being mechanical and absent-minded. To suspend is to make a choice, which is possible only when we are aware of what is going on inside us. By suspending assumptions we are breaking our ingrained habits of inferences and defences, without scarifying creative leaps, to conclusions.

Conversation in *being mode*

"In contrast are those who respond spontaneously and productively; they forget about themselves, about the knowledge, the position they have. Their egos do not stand in their own way, and it is precisely for this reason that they can fully respond to the other person and that person's ideas. They give birth to new ideas, because they are not holding on to anything. While the having persons rely on what they have, the being person rely on the fact that they are, that they are alive and that something new will be born if only they have the courage to let go and to respond. They come fully alive in the conversation, because they do not stifle themselves by anxious concern with what they have. Their own aliveness is infectious and often helps the other person to transcend his or her egocentricity. Thus the conversation ceases to be an exchange of commodities (information, knowledge, status) and becomes a dialogue in which it does not matter any more who is right. The duelists begin to dance together, and they part not with triumph or sorrow - which are equally sterile - but with joy" Eric Fromm.

How similar are the thoughts of Eric Fromm and David Bohm!. Probably they never met personally or otherwise.

Learn to SPIRAL up the Dialogue Ladder

If you eschew the wrong behaviours and cultivate the right ones you will shine in group discussions and find them rewarding to you and to the group as a whole. You can become a role model for others to imitate. But to graduate from discussion to dialogue you need additional qualities.

Suspending of Assumptions: To recap suspending is not defending nor suppressing one's views or assumptions, but to hold in front of you and everybody else in the group to see and examine together.

Participative Openness: is being candid, free and frank in putting forward your view point without any fear or ego. It helps each other in seeing the incoherence and fragmentation in each other's thoughts. What you contribute may be a piece that fits into the whole along with other pieces that constitute the whole. As long it is tacit, it remains a fragment.

Inquiry, the spirit of: Inquiry or spirit of inquiry is the heart of dialogue. Questions raised with genuine curiosity to know something beyond, to go deep into the matter become the heart of the matter. Learning to ask questions is an important aspect one should not neglected.

Reflective Openness: having made your point with sufficient clarity a need may arise to revise one's own opinion without the ego coming in the way, based on new evidence and examination of the assumptions.

Advocacy: after new evidence is produced, and clarified, as new information flows one has to put the facts together coherently supported by valid assumptions. This is called skilful discussion.

Listening: finally without listening there is no dialogue. Learn to listen without evaluation, suspending judgement. Whereas the speaker suspends his assumptions, the listener must suspend judgement on them. For this you may have to pay attention to what blocks communication while paying attention to the content of what the other person is saying.

Imagine a vertical spiral in which the bottom most ring collapses into next higher ring which in turn collapses into its next and so on. Similarly starting from active listening you may move up to suspending assumptions. In the final analysis the spiral is one and not many as one moves up, one can return to earlier level. In a sense, all levels are always present though one or more may seem more dominant at any movement.

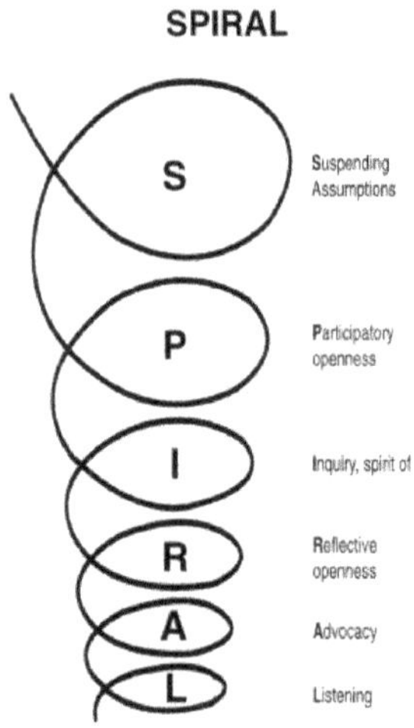

Om Sahana Vavatu Sahanau Bhunaktu, Sahaviryam karavava hai, Tejasvina Vadhita mastu, Ma vidvisa va hai, Om Santi Santi Santi hi

Kena Upanishad

(May He protect us both together, May He nourish us both together, May we work together with great energy, May our study be vigorous and insightful or illuminating, May we not dispute (no ill feelings. Let there be Peace, Peace, Peace).

* * * * *

MUSINGS OF
BAREFOOT BANKERS

PART - III

MANAGERIAL INSIGHTS

Reflections and Conceptualization

ORGANIZATIONAL BEHAVIOUR

First person accounts serve as cases in Organisational Behaviour for class-room discussion in MBA classes. They will be of particular interest to the students who wish to make a career in banking.

In the near future nearly 40% of the bank personnel are going to retire and the vacancies are to be filled by computer savvy youth. Banking has acquired a professional status –a calling which calls for competence, commitment, professional standards, a body of knowledge, master of banking and jack of many other disciplines. Now-a-days engineering graduates are applying for clerical posts while MBAs with HR, Marketing, and Finance are opting for Banking. Their natural inclination may be to work in urban centers serving corporate customers. But the future of banking focus will be rural house-holds with the governments' thrust on Financial Inclusion. That is where challenge lies. In my classes I was administering an instrument Work Preference Schedule–which brings out the motivation of the participants.

Rank the Following

R	-	Retirement benefits
E	-	Enough leisure
J	-	Just and stable income
O	-	Opportunities to learn
I	-	Independence & Freedom to work
C	-	Challenging work
E	-	Enjoyment of prestige in society

The boys were preferring challenge, opportunity to learn, and independence and freedom as reasons for choice of work experience. The girls generally choose just income, enjoying company of family, and enjoying prestige. There are very few boys and girls who give importance to just income, retirement benefits and prestige. The first category is high on Achievement Motivation, second Affiliation Motivation and the last showing Security Orientation. The trend is changing towards the concentration of the first. However 'challenge' in a job is far from '*kushi*' job. They have to overcome obstacles, negotiate at every stage of their career. It calls for exemplary soft skills. This is much more true of rural posting far away from superiors and mentors.

The cases reveal the independence and opportunity to learn in facing challenges. The young entrants to banking must opt for rural posting for faster personal growth.

Coming to the topic of O.B: 'the field of O.B is a field of both research and practice'. If the new entrant is research minded, he has an excellent field to search for solutions while practicing. 'O.B. is concerned with development processes in persons, groups, organizations, inter-organisational systems and community at large'. The bank staff is engaged in rural development and inter-organisational system. The cases can be studied from this angle. There are many agencies engaged in rural development– Governments, *Panchayatraj* system, NABARD, Agricultural University, ICAR, besides Farmers Clubs, SHGS, Tenant farmers, independent researchers and Micro Finance Institutions, other banks etc.

Rural Development Network

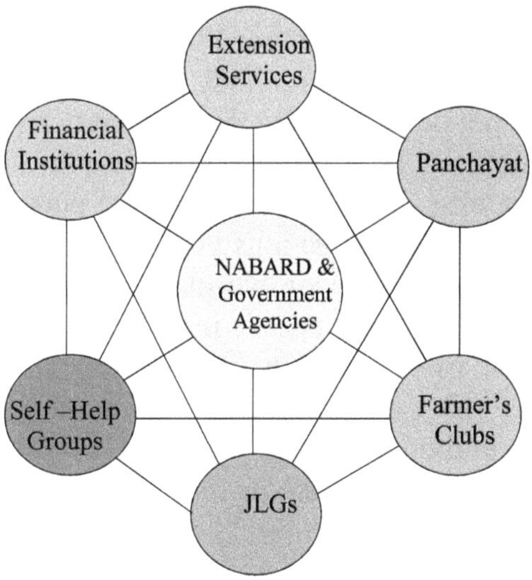

Reading carefully the cases–the first person accounts, in particular, reveal how the narrators interacted with the private, public, and panchayat institutions which calls for collaborative skills. 'The field thus stands out as a fertile synthesis of many lines of inquiry, inter-disciplinary area reaching across boundaries in its quest for comprehensive and in-depth understating'. The officer engaged with Government Agencies, scientific and technological communities in the common cause of emancipation of the farmers and farming will develop insights into the complexity of rural development. He will be liberating himself from the narrow vision of financing and follow-up. 'O.B. focuses on the action alternatives available to decision makers and helps them think through consequences of their choices of productivity, satisfaction and growth of individuals, groups,.. even the **community at large**'.

Service to Community

Rural life is community life. It is not like urban life where 'strangers' rub shoulders in crowded places without the community feelings. 'I care for no body; no body cares for me' kind of living. Bankers may not disclose anything about another customer. Secrecy is primacy. But the village comes to know everything about every one else. If you are transparent people will know. If you are transparent in your actions you need not say it, everybody will say it. You live in an open world. But this did not happen in banks. Nor did the banks permit individuals/employees to meet some of their own most important needs through membership in the rural branch. Though the management did not create the conditions, the individual narrators had their own needs – pride, prestige, gratitude etc – met as is revealed in their episodic memories.

CEO Vs Grass-roots Managers[1]

Academicians focus their attention on C.E.Os for role-models and case discussion in O.B. area and take the grass-roots Managers and staff for granted as mere followers of charismatic leaders. They say, *'...the Chief Executives have a profound influence on their organisations. Studies show that the fortunes of organisations go up or down with the kind of leadership at the top level... Employees observe... they interpolate what they really care about.'* They looked at their style of daily routine – 'in-basket, telephone, and calendar' (Pascal).

No body looked at the routine of the rural Manager. He has very little to do with three mechanisms Pascal proposed. No two days in the life of the barefoot banker are alike. No two rural

[1] 'Managerial Dilemmas' by S.Ramnarayan and M.Ram Mohan Rao.

bankers have the same routine. The branch is run on 24/7 basis. Most transactions take place in the early hours and in the evenings. There was a case when a Manager stuck to business hours-10 to 2 – the villagers resented so much that when he was transferred prematurely the local cable TV ran the scroll announcing the 'good news' of Manager's transfer.

Similar experiences could be found from other banks too. 'Role clarity and professional competence, dedication and commitment to the task and excellence are the contributing factors.' But the bank 'must focus on creating conditions that will facilitate a high level of performance *over a long period of time.* The conditions must be such that they might permit individual employees to meet some of their own important needs.'

The authors of 'Managerial Dilemmas' write: 'The first person accounts of Chief Executives presented in the section indicate that the senior Managers concern themselves with two kinds of problems: how to create effective organizational processes and how to deal with one or two general goals, which in turn subsume a large number of specific issues. Effective Managers pay a great deal of attention to organizational and interpersonal processes.'[2]

As said before high performers are motivated by (a) opportunity to learn by doing (b) independence and autonomy (c) challenging job. There are others whose main need is security and safety and working in safe and routine manner. These people are not likely to achieve the mandate of the bank in rural areas.

---

[2] 'Managerial Dilemmas' by S.Ramnarayan and M.Ram Mohan Rao.

a.

b.

c.

Daily Routine of CEO

a. Reading during travel

b. Efficient disposal of files in office

c. Preparing for the meeting.

a.

b.

Routine of Barefoot Banker

a. Receptive in office

b. Considerate in the field

c. Counsellor on all occasions

c.

Real HRD and Role Theory

The cases mainly represent the role played by some of the Managers/officers of the bank from 1969 to 2011.

The researcher must ask, how many miles the rural Manager walks; how does he talk and listen; how well does he understand rural world etc? How well the villagers understand the Manager and his team?

The C.E.Os real concerns–the cost, quality, *human resource development* or new product innovation – get picked up by the people *down the line* from these 'meta messages'. What C.E.O. does with his grass-roots Manager, the rural Manager does with the beneficiaries. If the C.E.Os concern is HRD within the enterprise, the grass-roots Managers concern is both HRD of his team members and more importantly the HRD of the rural people – the real HRD, the country needs.

'These accounts raise an important question: what is the role of a senior Manager in a dynamic environment.. not captured by static job-descriptions… Managerial roles cannot remain same in changing environment.'[3]

'The shaping of role behaviours is influenced by three sets of demands: personal, social, and organizational and situational demands.'

The cases in the volume are admirably suited to discuss role-theory.

When roles are not clearly defined by the managements how do individuals with professional competence, dedication, commitment to the job and excellence contribute in the *specific contexts* for *specific purposes,* informed by role-clarity on their

[3] 'Managerial Dilemmas' by S.Ramnarayan and M.Ram Mohan Rao.

own perform? There are many first person accounts shared with a sense of achievement and satisfaction decades after. There are lessons for future inquiry.

As Professor Edger Schein puts it, "... the deeper the psychologists delved into the behaviour of individuals within organizations, the more evidence they found that organization is a complex social system which must be studied as such if individual behaviour is to be truly understood.

Manager communicates individually as well as collectively, effectively

Even negative signals get picked up by the people *down the line* from these 'meta messages'.

Punctuality is the Casualty

Pending files speak for themselves

'There is, hence, a need for a greater understanding of how an individual's needs and responses are fundamentally affected by his motives, values, learning abilities and overall personality.'[4]

No such attempt was done, in my view, in public sector banks that I know, particularly in the context of managing for the purpose of rural development.

But now, in the context Financial Inclusion there is an urgent need to have re-look at the systems and styles of managing the barefoot bankers.

Re-call 7s Model

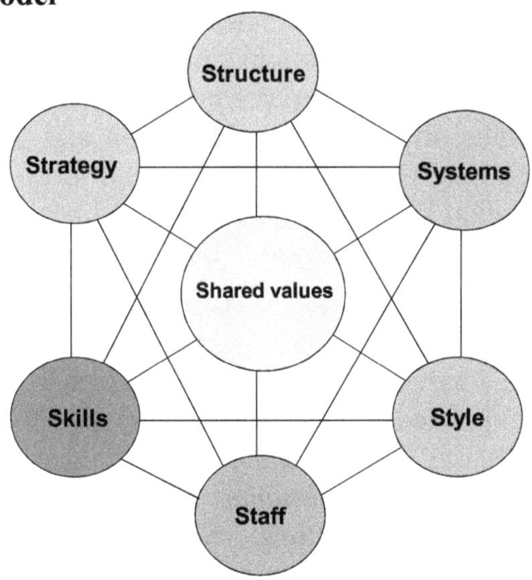

* * * * *

[4] 'Managerial Dilemmas' by S.Ramnarayan and M.Ram Mohan Rao.

KNOWLEDGE MANAGEMENT

Tacit knowledge is acquired through mechanical routine activities at work. One individual may acquire tacit knowledge from another without the use of language through observation, imitation and practice…

We all learnt banking – the class banking – at work in this manner. This is called socialization. What is tacit becomes explicit through a process of articulation into concepts. They become models. In banks 'Secrecy' and 'Prudent' have first become images–metaphors, analogies, hypotheses and they tend to become written down instructions in books of instructions and circulars. If the learners communicate to each other, which is not the case in banks, this promotes discussion and dialogue which leads to reflection… when banks were asked to go to rural areas, they had an explicit knowledge unsuitable to financing agriculture, artisans, and rural self-employed. Banks had similar problem a decade before Nationalization of 14 major banks.

When commercial banks started financing for industry, banks recruited Chartered Accountants to adapt to the change. A lot of explicit knowledge system was developed through massive training in Industrial Finance and Foreign Exchange etc. A new jargon emerged and new *semantic knowledge* was transmitted through 'documents, meetings, telephone or computerized communication networks' – the specialists are able to combine with the veterans of commercial banking. The explicit knowledge thus developed became 'collective tacit' through internalization–individual's tacit knowledge it became. They became shared mental models or material. Sparrow called it *Semantic understanding* about which I shall refer later. For organizational knowledge creation to take place, however, the tacit knowledge accumulated at the individual level needs to be socialized with other organizational members, thereby, starting a new spiral of knowledge creation. This has been the weakness of the public sector banks in India because of 'top-down' attitude of top people. Even the top management looked up to government and Central Banking Institution for guidance.

There was no spiral of knowledge creation because of top-down–setting targets to branches to meet targets set by the government – quarterly, half-yearly, and annual review and business meeting held routinely. The episodes narrated remained the private knowledge (explicit, not articulated) of the few individuals. The 'Bright Spots', as Heath Brothers, authors of 'SWITCH,' New York Times Best Seller (2010) called the '*successful efforts worth emulating*'. The cases reveal these Bright Spots. All these Bright Spots, at least, now after 40, 30, 20 years are worth emulating in the next decade of correction course.

From Tacit to Tacit – Socialization

Socialization is a process of **sharing** experiences and thereby **creating** tacit knowledge such as shared mental models and technical skills. One individual may acquire tacit knowledge from another without using language.

Through observation, imitation and practice, the key to acquiring tacit knowledge is experience, according to this model.

From Tacit to Explicit

Externalization is a process of articulating tacit knowledge into explicit concepts. It is a quintessential knowledge - creation process in that tacit knowledge becomes explicit, taking the shape of metaphors, analogies, concepts, hypotheses or models. According to Nonaka and Takeuchi, after we have conceptualized an image, we generally tend to express it in language. The process of converting tacit knowledge into articulate knowledge is facilitated through writing. When there are gaps in our understanding of these concepts as we communicate them to each other, this promotes discussion and dialogue which leads to reflection and differing styles of interaction.

From Explicit to explicit

Combination is a process of systemizing concepts into a *knowledge system.* The explanation given is that when individuals communicate through the various methods available such as, 'documents, meetings, telephone conversations, or computerized communication networks' they are able to exchange and combine knowledge.

Explicit to Tacit

Internalization is the process of embodying explicit knowledge into tacit knowledge. It is closely related to learning by doing. When experiences through socialization, externalization and combination are internalized into individuals tacit knowledge bases in the form of shared mental models or technical know-how, they become valuable assets.

For organizational knowledge creation to take place, however, the tacit knowledge accumulated at the individual level needs to be socialized with other organizational members, thereby starting a new spiral of knowledge creation.

* * * * *

KNOWLEDGE IN ORGANISATIONS[1]

Let me turn to the book, **Knowledge in Organisations. Access to thinking at work (*John sparrow (1998)*).** In the Preface he writes, *this book provides a framework to help individuals reflect on their own practices at work, and to help organizations understand and promote* ***sharing of considerations that influence employee thinking and action.***

This is a valuable book both for the rural Branch Managers in particular and the administrators controlling the performance of grass-roots Managers. The reader will get insights into what knowledge the decision makers use at work in arriving at the decision. There is risk and uncertainty in the decision making.

...a new form of management is emerging. This management by ***perception*** *requires greater recognition of organization participants' thinking in their decisions.*

(It) shows how knowledge that people use in the course of their action is a dynamic combination of particular ***kinds of mental material (5); two forms of thoughts and three types of thinking.***

Sparrow himself makes reference to other research material:

Capturing knowledge - *Schon (1991) observes that organizations are repositories of cumulatively built up knowledge: principles and maxims of practice, images of mission and identity, facts about the task environment, techniques of operatives, stories of past experiences which serve as exemplars for future.*

---

[1] 'Knowledge in Organization' by John Sparrow 1998.

Stock of knowledge is the essential purpose of capturing the stories/episodes of past experiences – to serve as exemplars for future that I embarked on this book.

He notes how through reflection a Manager 'draws on this stock of knowledge, adapting it to some present instance. And he also functions as an agent of ***organizational learning****, extending or re-structuring in his present inquiry,* ***the stock of knowledge*** *which will be available for future inquiry.*

These episodes that remained as individual mental material all these years did not serve as 'exemplars for future', nor it became 'stock of knowledge' and not *available for future inquiry.* The purpose of this work is to document, however cursory it might be, for the future inquiry. Had these friends not shared with me in writing, it would have been lost for ever. The present day Manager may benefit from the past experience by conceptualizing them into maxims and principles.

These intrapreneurs must possess knowledge–economic and financial literacy–skills and values in a greater measure.

I shall briefly touch upon ***kinds of mental material; two forms of thoughts and three types of thinking*** and apply the ideas to rural branch management which includes the Branch Manager and his superior office which seeks to control the branch operations via Manager.

The five kinds of mental material are tacit feel, recalling episodic memories, unconscious interpretation, semantic understanding, and talents or skills acquired through conscious practice. I have my own capsule (memory) in the form TRUST: Tacit feel, Recalling episodes, Unconscious interpretation, Semantic understanding, and Talents.

Unconscious interpretation is generations old mental material unknown to the individual decision maker. Semantic understanding is the result of education, training, and personal experiences at the conscious level that influence the decisions and actions in future. Books read are part of education and training.

A commerce, science or arts graduate promoted from clerical cadre trained in prudent banking is sent to rural area to finance for agricultural and the rural poor with no semantic understanding–knowing of rural economy, generations of poverty and perpetual indebtedness. He has no talent or tacit feel relevant to the task. He has some unconscious yearning and leanings partly personal, partly cultural. He has no episodic memories to recall. He might have studied the subject for his banking examination. But that was not deep, nor was it remembered. Images and fact finding are two forms of thought. I call them Imagistic or Data based. He has no *images* of what the banking could do or not do.

Autistic Thinking

Of 3 types of thinking, autistic thinking borne out of family background and childhood upbringing operates. Automatic ways of thinking to process the propositional data (a thought form) is an area of concern for managements. The Managers intuitively sense the people and the situation. This autistic thinking has no censors; 'it is free flowing'. The individual has no control over it.

Mental material –TRUST – is configured either in imagistic form if there are past exposures or unconsciously if there are no past episodes. Semantic mental material is used propositionally and rational thinking is applied.

On the spot decisions which the barefoot banker takes are 'autistic' than 'rational'. They are spontaneous rather than calculated risks. 'A large proportion of positive activities depend on spontaneous optimism rather than mathematical expectations'. (Keynes)

So, in sum, the bank Manager in small societies must be '*spot less'* clean, avoiding '*hitting spot'* knowing well when he takes '*on the spot'* decisions, it may put him '*in spot*' and others may look for '*sore spots*'. If he wants to be in *spot light* he should choose his company with care, caution and professionalism. Management must protect the bright spots.

The bright spots get into spot for on the spot decisions. Refer to case no. 20 for unique spot decisions not relevant to banking need to be also protected in the larger interests of encouraging bright spots.

Rational thinking is not much of help. The rationale of financing trade and industry may not serve any purpose in rural areas. It does not satisfy 'prudent man rule'. Finally, his *mood* plays lot of part in his thinking which is without semantic material. Yet, some of them had outstanding experiences. The book contains some examples. On the other hand the agricultural graduates hailing from rural areas have all the 5 kinds of mental material – tacit feel of rural life, episodic memories, about the hardships experienced directly, unconscious material is both personal and rural cultural, semantic understanding comes from education and field training. They have also skills of analysis with reference to farming.

In all cases the last type of thinking viz. Mood dependent thinking operates most of the time which cannot be altogether avoided. It varies from the feed back from the environment than from the higher ups.

Spot Light on the Spot Decisions

The phrases associated with the word 'SPOT' are interesting.

1. ***Spot light***: Strong light to illuminate; public notice or prominence.

A Manager may be *in spot light* and puts his organization in spot light.

2. ***On the spot***: when he is in the appointed place on time; when he is in trouble or danger. When a Manager takes a *spot* decision based on autistic thinking or mood thinking mentioned above, he may be *on the spot*.

3. ***Hit the Spot:*** His superiors may say that he '*hit the spot'*, meaning he satisfied his craving or need. The craving could be to reach the targets or improper urges -impropriety or imprudent or impudent or even insolent behaviour.

4. ***Hit the High Spots:*** in communicating a Manager may 'treat only main points or outstanding features of a topic' as in the case 5 episode 1 when the Manager took the main point that 'our credit with our advice' using the 'rope' metaphor.

5. ***Spot-less***: perfectly clean, no faults or defects, irreproachable. A Manager in rural and semi-urban areas- small towns and small societies must be spotless clear. Transparent – above board – appear above board like 'Caesar's wife' as the saying goes.

6. ***Sore Spots***: Sensitive areas. Managers do have their sore spots: the company he keeps. In small societies when the Manager is found in the company of un-holy characters, he is known for the *sore spots* which every one spots.

7. ***Bright Spots:*** They are successful efforts worth emulating as defined by Heath Brothers in a book 'Switch' (2010).

8. ***SPOT Quality***: I have coined an acronym SPOT to hit the high spots: Species Poverty* Obscuring Temperance – the quality / value that every one should adopt.

9. ***SPOT:*** Spontaneous Positive Optimistic and Trasparent.

The Elephant and the Rider[2]

'Virginia psychologist Jonathan Haidt in his wonderful book *The Happiness Hypothesis* wrote 'that our emotional side is an elephant and our rational thinking is its rider. Atop the elephant the rider holds the reins and seems to be in control of the elephant. Imagine 6 ton elephant disagreeing with the rider with regard to direction. The 'lazy and skittish, often looking for the quick pay off (ice cream cone) over the long term pay offs (being thin)'

Often managements drive the elephant in the Manager to produce results in the short term luring them with rewards rather than address the rider in him to plan for long term goals. Some of the bright spots in Part-I had no such pressure from senior Managers. But they built long-term relationship with villagers and when managements created structure and gave skilled staff and specialists, only then they produced outstanding results in a year or two.

Soon the branches suffered when teams were disturbed for administrative reasons. When rider in the man did not stir up the elephant and allowed it to be lazy nothing happened. The branches were on the verge of closure.

---

* 'SPECIES Poverty' is discussed in Part IV.

[2] Switch by Heath Brothers

Naturally the agricultural officers' first person accounts are much more vivid than others, who did not have the advantage. Nevertheless all recall with satisfaction and excitement.

Banks have been following traditional management styles: **F**ire fighting; **I**nternal orientation; **R**eacting to formal reporting system; **E**liminating cultural aspects and limitations – (FIRE) 'Modern management is shifting to a style characterized by **M**ultiplicity of perceptions; **O**penness to learning; **D**evelopment of mutual understanding; **E**xternal orientation; **S**ensitivity internally.' (MODES of control)

When something goes wrong, the administration notices in the reporting system, oral and written. Then the reaction is *fire fighting* ignoring the external factors and multiplicity of situations and cultural differences of place, persons and phenomena.

Modern science of management asks the management to use MODES to be sensitive to the image and identity – both external and internal considerations. The key lies in not in periodical and routine reporting but in *openness to learning* on an on going basis. What is important is what goes between the events. Gone are the days when management controlling and disciplining on the basis of outcomes – targets and achievements quantitatively and not quality of work, the process of decision making by the organizational member.

If you want quality, have a look at TRUST (mental material) and ID forms of thoughts (Imagistic or Data based – Id is the store house of all instinctive and irrational responses, and we are usually not conscious of it) and ARM (types of thinking)

'Managers must learn to operate in a less secure world requiring a **high tolerance for ambiguity** and a capacity for imaginative, flexible and speed of responses.'

FIST: **F**lexibility; **I**magination; **S**peed of Response; **T**olerance for ambiguity.

'They must view decision making as a continuous, exploratory, experimental, process with learning groups of Managers surfacing conflict, engaging in **dialogue publicly** testing assertions.'

My emphasis is on Dialogue. Monthly meetings of Managers' and the senior management must not limit to the deliberations and discussion; they must graduate to dialogue, where openness is primary.

Modern managements consider centrality of perceptions which vary according to the functional lines. Line Managers' experiences vary from the functional Managers experiences. Marketing staff differ from credit appraisal staff. In banks line Managers combine both, but at the administrative level there is separation of two. Now that banks are on the path of aggressive marketing and recruitment of MBAs poses new problems that they need to anticipate. Periodical meetings and discussions – sharing and learning from each other becomes significant. Insurance companies for long have had Agents, Development Officers, and Branch Managers, three roles interacting regularly. Banks have yet to gain the cumulative knowledge, shared and stored as collective pool of knowledge.

In a dynamic situation where one sees rapid changes, one can't wait for the manuals to be updated. *Manager relies on shared understanding acquired through socialization.* Instead of grape-vine exchanges, there is an urgent need to share all considerations of decision making, implementation, problem-solving, monitoring and evaluation among the groups of Managers at the regional level as often as necessary. These meetings are to be held proactively rather than as knee-jerk reaction. Recall the earlier statement – continuous, exploratory, experimental, process – dialogue in true sense – testing assertions/assumptions. Case no.31 in Part-I is an illustration of good governance.

Edward De Bono's Ideas[3]

The purpose of bureaucracy is to make rules and see no mistakes are made. 'A mistake hangs around', Edward De Bono wrote, 'a bureaucrat's neck for his or her's rest of the career'. 'Bureaucracy was never designed as a change mechanism but to implement things as they are. Many potential change mechanisms in the hands of bureaucrats are bound to fail. Many people with *vision* and *enterprise* are likely to get frustrated in bureaucracy and also likely to engender antagonisms that get them ejected'.

'Where change requires vision and enterprise but must also pass through bureaucracy the outcome is rather likely to be negative'. If the politician joins them,' the hope for change and innovative thinking is slight'.

Just as a rock has a definite shape, when we use *rock logic*' we judge whether something fits that shape'. But water takes the shape of its terrain-a bowl or a lake. It adapts to the terrain or landscape. *Water logic* is determined by the conditions and circumstances. If you add more water the new water becomes part of the whole.

In the case 5 in Part I there is an episode about a poor man who refused to take a poultry scheme, what the manager did was based on water logic. If he had used rock logic he would have told him, 'sorry we don't have a scheme'.

* * * * *

[3] 'I am write you are wrong' by Edward De Bono

ENTERPRISE, CREATION, DEVELOPMENT AND GROWTH[1]

'*Come to law as a well-read person.*' Justice Frankfurter advised young law students in his book 'Of law and of men'.

I read this in the book-review by Justice V.R.K. Iyer. Sri Iyer is in his 90s still contributing with his incisive analysis of judiciary as it is in vogue in 21st century. Every professional including a banker must read his work to become a full man–a fully informed man.

I have been an avid reader and read more for pleasure than for knowledge till I reached middle age which coincided with the Nationalization of 14 major banks. My bank is one of them. There after my reading has been purposeful and for insights and helped shape my career. The career continued even after retirement.

I was fortunate to come across an unusual book in the British Library by Tom Cannon, titled:

'*Enterprise, creation, development and growth*'. The very title attracted my attention. I was highly impressed by it and developed my own role model.

The author of the book, about whom any good reader, may read about on the blurb, Tom Cannon, was Director, Manchester Business School. I quickly went through the contents:

1. Images of enterprise

[1] Enterprise, Creation, Development And Growth by *Tom Cannon*

2. The entrepreneurial economy
3. The enterprise support system
4. Building an enterprise
5. Managing an enterprise – first steps
6. Managing the enterprise, the ongoing process
7. Management and larger enterprise
8. Public and voluntary enterprise
9. Personal development
10. Group work
11. Network and information
12. Individuality, enterprise and future

What more does a rural Manager of a public sector bank need? It is a pity the book was published in 1991 my last year of service in the bank from the bank's staff college. But I could find this book in British Library two years later.

I took the ideas and insights I got from the book to the class-rooms of public sector undertakings other than banks.

Now, for the purpose of this book, I searched and found the Xerox copy of the book in my home library and re-read with renewed interest , keeping the context in view.

I have a habit of translating the ideas into an acronym or two. Here is one: DRIVE: Desire, Responsibility, Initiative, Vision and Energy. These are the essentials of an enterprising man.

Snippets and Reflections

1. *Central to modern life, the concept of enterprise, personal endeavour lies at the core of every attempt to* ***create, shape or***

develop one self or one's community*. Individual and group initiatives supply the dynamics which drive society forward.*

Enterprise, reading between the lines, is not limited to building business. When we refer to certain communities as business-minded, we mean self-interested. But the right word is enterprise. ***What ails the rural India in general is lack of enterprise.*** When people migrate from the rural to the urban centre it is, in fact, flight of enterprising people. Those who risked and left, prospered while the rest languished in poverty.

A colleague who returned from Gujarat recently told me that the farmers are not keen in borrowing from PSBs. He tried his best to finance for agriculture but failed. He reasoned that the average Guajarati is business minded and self reliant. Their own farmer associations and cooperatives are very strong. What I deduced was 'enterprise'. He added A.P. is lacking in it.

2. *'This book extends beyond the conventional view that enterprise is building business and creating wealth. It is found everywhere, in every thing, from the wasp that builds a web, to the farmer who tills the land, the potter who moulds the clay, or to the scientist who visits the moon.* ***Enterprise is about building, not destroying.'***

There are Managers who built the image with steadfast patience of a spider building its web. There are those who destroyed it succumbing to temptations and transgressions and violations of moral code. Recall DRIVE: V also stands for *values---- moral, ethical and professional values* all must be in place. Age of the Manager is not significant. The 'streak' is important.

Raja Ram Mohan Roy, Mahatma Gandhi, Nehru and all other crusaders were entrepreneurs – recreated Independent India. They are gifted with Vision – looking beyond the obvious – unlike the frog in the well. It jumps from one end of the well to the other and thinks it has covered the whole world. The frog or the Manager cannot see beyond the obvious physically. He must have vision of the mind. He must know

'VISION LOOKS INWARD AND BECOMES A DUTY
VISION LOOKS OUTWARD AND BECOMES ASPIRATION,
VISION LOOKS UPWARD AND BECOMES FAITH.'

Arjuna did not see beyond the obvious. Krishna supplied the vision so that action took place. The Manager with entrepreneurial streak has to combine both the Lord and the man.

Responsibility in D**R**IVE includes responsibility to take risks – 'No venture, no win'. Responsibility to 'self'–self reliance allied to the talent is inherent in enterprise.'

The author concludes with a definition:

Enterprise is the characteristic of people, groups, and organizations which produces a disposition to self realization through achievement.

People and organizations showing enterprise have drive, energy, creativity and leadership to see the tasks through to completion by individual effort or successful team-work.

Here is a caution from the Arthur Koestler (1980):

'While exploratory drive may be adulterated by ambition and vanity the quest in purest form is its own reward.'

Do you see the echo of the verse no.47 in chapter II of Gita. There have been instances of ambition and vanity colouring the entrepreneurial drive. Bankers are no exception. Barefoot banker is the exception: his drive is the purest and it never craved for external rewards. It is unadulterated.

The individual drive can create problems as well as opportunities. The problems, the researchers attribute to lack of review and **appraisal** by the champions of the project. They tend to become intolerant of others.

There was a Manager who had drive and wanted to develop his branch with the special infrastructure created by his bank in a rural area. The enterprising farmers of this area had a tie up with a multinational cigarette manufacturing company and were already cultivating tobacco. The private company provided extension services to the farmers. Bank joined the partnership and provided the capital. Being the first branch in the area there was tremendous demand to which the *enterprising* Manager responded with speed and commitment. Image of the bank reached a new high and increased the demand. '*Positive feed back is escalatory*'. He worked and made his staff work day and night.

The Manager drove the branch system into high activity. The accountant who was responsible for house-keeping and procedures and internal administration opposed the high speed response. Manager overruled the subordinate because the seasonal opportunity should not be lost and image of the bank must be kept up. The staff worked 24/7 and still the documentation, the most important legal requirements fell into arrears. Result was a mess according to the bank's Internal Inspector who arrived soon after. Remember in those days there were no computers in banks.

Senior management stopped the Manager's discretionary lending powers. Situation came to a stand still with mounting pressure from the farmers. The situation demanded crisis management. How it was managed in 1978 will be dealt later.

It is surprising to hear the enterprising Manager can create problems to the project and be called intolerant of others. Single minded endeavour can lead to intolerance of others who lack the commitment. These men find it hard to understand others who fall short of their dedication. In banks, majority fall short of their dedication to rural development.

Solution to this problem is *team building*. The first step is to build consensus among the colleagues before undertaking any new work. Prior to that the Manager must gauge the level of dedication of each member. Ensuring the commitment and conviction from the team members is an aspect of team building.

In a large bureaucratic bank it is not enough if the Manager is successful in building teams ----he must get support from the senior management.

'*clash between the uncompromising demands of leaders and the desire of the team members, to follow a more normal life style*'.

In banks there are other problems: some one who joins the branch spoils the whole flock by design. Some times by design the senior management send such a fifth columnist. Politics can ruin the entrepreneurial drives. But one cannot ignore the reality. Assuming that the senior management is supportive, the local Manager may succeed with '*direction achieved through carefully/clearly worked out and effectively communicated* ***strategy*** *which is internalized by members of the team or organization.'*

In banking in 1970s Managers were not trained in leadership and team concepts. But some of them emerged as leaders and team builders by their natural disposition. Case 6 is a case in point.

"The first action of the CEO is to "clearly state his vision of the company's future" (Pinchat-1985)

Banks' direction came through circulars issued more as an obligation to RBI and government. The written communication lacks the emotion that is required in such matters as eradication of poverty and rural development.

Ronstad, R.C. 'Entrepreneurship' (1984)

"For Babson, the required intelligence, drive to achieve, energy, and necessary qualities of leadership were products of ancestry and, to a considerable extent, were outside our control".

Researchers wanted answers for deeper understanding. They have "*sought the* ***values, attitudes,*** *and* ***approaches*** *to life which lead certain people to take on challenges of initiating, organizing or developing which are generally associated with enterprise".*

It is really a challenge to classify bank's staff on these lines, while considering transfers, posting to rural areas, or promotions. When the branches to control were few, it was the personal knowledge of the superiors that helped. Large organizations have to manage through bureaucracy. By pure bureaucratic approach the banks' image suffered, the cost of which is of immeasurable enormity compared to loss in money terms.

David McClelland explicitly rejected the 'born or made' model. He believed and trained people to become entrepreneurs. Banks have rarely sent their Managers to such training programmes. But they were exposed to the idea because it was needed for them to appraise the self-employed and SMEs and their enterprises for sanctioning the loans. He talked of achievement motivation, creativity, risk taking ability and tenacity, all of which can be instilled through appropriate training and follow up. Others included 'traits-anxiety and neuroticism' and 'leadership aspirations'.

The case of the Manager who overruled the accountant, mentioned before, can be cited as an example of 'anxiety and neuroticism' or aspirations to move up the organsational ladder. It is said that he felt competition with his other colleagues who made their mark elsewhere through such drive.

But the senior managements who lacked understanding of the deviant behaviour suspected ulterior motives–graft. Far from it. It was soon proved: the investigator found beyond doubt no corrupt practices. The investigator was, an agricultural officer with extension as specialization. He was retained in the branch to control the situation without damaging the image of the bank. You need a shrewd Senior Manager to do such things.

Another who showed dynamism when cautioned went to the other extremity. Others ignored the warning and went ahead with their enterprise because they knew they were within the policy of the bank.

'In UK, for example, it is suggested that many self-employed entrepreneurs have a low 'comfort factor', i.e. once their business is established at a particular, acceptable level, they avoid risk and resist growth'.

*'Psychodynamic approach-proposition is based on the notion that enterprise in its, entrepreneurial form is a **form of deviant behaviour**.* It is really a challenge for superiors to control and still achieve.

Psychologists explain the deviant behaviour variously. It emerges in people whose attitudes are shaped by harsh, hostile or deprived background. They compensate by reducing depending on others... the individualism will express itself in several forms which will reflect the lessons learned during the period of deprivation.

An emphasis on personal achievement is in part a measure of increased control over destiny and an outward display of success in face of adversity.

There is a case of a tribal, a qualified agricultural graduate who saw poverty and deprivation in the childhood, who had a set back to his career because of deviant behaviour but he does not regret what happened to him. One of the allegations against him was that he unduly favoured his community belonging to deprived strata of the agricultural society of the service area. According to him all the previous Managers neglected this community people. He claimed that the richer and other communities complained against him and put him in trouble. His case is a clear example of what the author stated above. Let us recall A.Koestler's quotation above: *the quest in its purest form is its own reward.* His quest was to help his own down-trodden community which he did not see as favouritism but others saw it so. Koestler also adds--

'These people tend to produce aggressive behaviour and self-oriented approach to social discourse'.

This explains his defensive behaviour that annoyed, probably, the disciplinary authority who transferred him to a non-Managerial position in addition to stopping some increments.

Such men need counseling that a bureaucratic organization is different from self-employment. Apart from the Manager taking personal risk, there are risks to the bank which deals with other people's money. They must know and follow the concept **thus far, no further**.

There is, the author says, *however far less evidence that harsh, prior experiences are consistently linked with individual endeavour.*

There are bureaucrats hailing from reserved communities who have not put in such endeavour. On the other hand there are instances in banks, Managers doing evangelistic work in financing the socially and economically backward people–small marginal farmers and landless labourers for their upliftment Here is a beautiful passage:

*Glib and Ritchie have examined in some depth the 'antecedent influences' which are associated with personal enterprise. They place considerable emphasis on the **domestic, social, educational** and **work experiences** which affect the probability of a person or group acting in an enterprising way.*

Under 'education' we can discuss agricultural specialists recruited as DROs. I have seen differences on account of domestic and social back ground. Graduates with rural background hailing from rich families behaved some what differently from those who came from poorer class. Some favoured financing the rich land-lords whether they cultivated or gave the land under tenancy. It appeared to me that their concern was safety of bank money. But work experiecnce changed their behaviour when they learnt that the rich defaulted more than the poor.

The problem is complex. The people who monitor performance and behaviour have little time to analyse the complexity which an academician understands.

"The type of social development model highlights the impact of peers especially within the family, the value of positive reinforcements, through reward, role-models, and feedback as well as the contribution of particular type of work- life and educational experiences."

There do seem to be wide variations in the way people respond to those pressures, economic and social. Simultaneously, people faced with the same pressures will respond differently. This is ***specially notable in the type of semi-controlled environment found in large organisations.***

PSB is a large organization. Different Managers with different backgrounds – domestic, social, economic, and educational variations-face pressures differently.

People working, being educated or operating in this context will ***exploit, ignore*** *or* ***respond*** *in a wide variety of ways to* ***opportunities to demonstrate their enterprise.***

This is what exactly happened or will continue to happen in PSBs particularly in rural areas. There are gains and some losses- senior management has to **manage** in true sense.

Working together

A Very significant statement:

'Views of enterprise in an organistional context (Bank) are closely linked to how people ***work together****. Organizations are not fixed and rigid entities. They are made up of people who come together to achieve different things. Their motives differ and the way they interact depends as much on their expectations of each other as on any formal roles they perform and offices they hold'*

Senior Managers, line Managers, support staff, staff at operational branches and administrative officers have different roles to play.

The expectations are shaped by communication and reward system.

We will see in V.S.M how channel capacity and transducers function in control information system.

'People interpret signals in a variety of ways which may differ significantly from the objective of the individual sending the message. This will depend on the way it is sent, background 'noise' and perspective of the recipients.

A rural Manager exceeded, far in excess, the targets set for financing the weaker sections and won appreciation. He has evidently 'enterprise' in him. But other Managers who 'follow a more normal life style' receive the message in different ways. They expect a 'crash' in the former's life and, when it came later they had a good laugh. A few examples of such cases will settle peers at a much lower level or no enterprise at all. The whole bank will lose. There will be no trace of enterprise and the officers might opt for administrative position than operational / vulnerable jobs.

Managerial Enterprise

It will be quite some time for the banks to grow because there can be no creation, no development and no growth for a long time. The damage could be beyond repair. Hence managing 'enterprise' within the organization is the key to growth and success.

A firm which fails to recognize or reward enterprise may find enterprising individuals leave or seek recognition else where.

But this did not happen in the initial years of Nationalization, nor was significant till the dawn of 21st century. When VRS was offered not many sought re-employment in the banks. A banking system as 'society undervalues or denies access to enterprise is not likely to see many examples among its employees. This is what we see in the biggest organization–the government.

The pre-conditions include a ***sympathetic culture*** *(in the organization, large or small) awareness of the range and* ***diversity of situations in which enterprise can be expressed'*** *recognition and freedom to act.*

Sympathetic culture in banks means tolerance for mistakes and absorption of monetary losses, but keeping up of the flag of the bank.

Learning AID – A

Awareness, interest, desire, action. That is the process of learning. The cases of 'enterprise' that are presented in this volume have not become '*Awareness*' in the organsational system. Bank Senior Managers knew about some experiences but not about all enterprising performances. Even where there was awareness it was not documented. There was no *interest* to document.

There was no *desire* on the part of the members, majority of the members to emulate the examples. Even if awareness, interest, desire are there it did not result in action, future action.

In the same manner the cases where the deviant behaviour became delinquent behaviour or excessive enthusiasm, the action was limited to punishing the individual but not used for designing control mechanism that will take care to see the enterprise does not disappear from the organization. In the process the bank's image as an entrepreneurial bank should not be lost.

In 1980s there appeared to be a surge of enterprising behaviour, according to the book, in UK, Europe, and US. If India has to be an achieving society not only in the urban and metro areas but even in rural areas, banks have to play a vital role in showing the way in their own operation by way of example.

Conclusion – Communication and Reward Systems

*A recurrent question in the recent discussion of enterprise is, to what extent can enterprise be **taught or developed** in others?*

I had written a case of an enterprising bank Manager titled 'Snakes and Ladders'. Many academicians questioned the title which sends a wrong message. This Manager avoided snakes till the top man in the bank supported him; he even evaded responsibility for sometime.

The communication system failed because everyone was waiting for the top man's term to be over. Before that happened the Manager was promoted, reached a position where there are no snakes, but only ladders till another top man put a stop to his progress.

The members at large take the cues and read them differently. Some may aim at top man's support by hook if not by crook. Others may continue a sedentary life style – no enterprise, no snakes, no ladders. Be dead woods.

There are many in banks that may show no initial signs of enterprise to realize their potential. But opportunities prompt them. There are many who were sent to man or manage rural or semi-urban centres showed the enterprise unanticipated by the senior management. They could not rise in the hierarchy because of age constraints.

A passive worker may be the driving force behind a local dramatic society or sports club.

There are sub-staff, clerks, cashiers who had latent trait for enterprise had shown drive in rural branches. For the villagers Manager or chaprasi of the bank does not make any difference. Particularly the weaker sections approach the sub-staff or cashier with loan requests. The staff do not limit their performance for job descriptions. They do everything a Manager does except affixing the signature on cheque or sanction letters.

There is a case of an ex-service man who joined the bank as armed guard, rose to become a special assistant. What is more important is that he played multiple roles inside and outside. He saw several Managers come and go; he remained the sole representative of the bank in the eyes the villagers. The reason for his enthusiasm is that he is not taking risks that a Manager takes.

* * * * *

VIABLE SYSTEMS MODEL (VSM)

Small is Beautiful – Smallness in a Large Organisation

The following discussion is based on the writings of Stafford Beer who supplied series of diagrams for the design of structure of organizations and societies and is useful in diagnosing faulty ones.

'Viable' means able to maintain separate existence and a system consists of parts that constitute the whole which is greater and different from the sum of the parts.

Ever since there was a shift in the paradigm in the scientific field and other disciplines like management have adopted the same shift – in approach. Fritzof Capra investigated into the shift that has spread to all areas including economics and politics. He defined it as systems view--- a new view of reality, an inter-related and interdependent phenomena – psycho-social- economic and many other phenomena.

Stafford Beer was a cybernetic professional whose discipline is study of communication in all organisms and organizations. It is through communication an organization maintains its internal and external identity and image and thus remains viable. The viability is not merely economic but is the very existence of the organization. By definition a V.S. is capable of independent existence in a specified environment.

When banks were nationalized in 1969 their identity was kept intact and they continued to exist independently in its specified environment–financial and economical. They remain viable systems in every sense of the term.

A branch of such a bank can also be considered a viable system in a larger viable system. In fact even the parent bank is viable because the economy of the country is maintaining its own viability. The bank is as strong as its economy and the branch is as strong as its bank.

If the reader has understood the concept of V.S, then he should know how its independent existence is maintained in actuality. Cybernetics tells us that it happens because of effective communication with the external environment and internal milieu and relating the two-inside and outside.

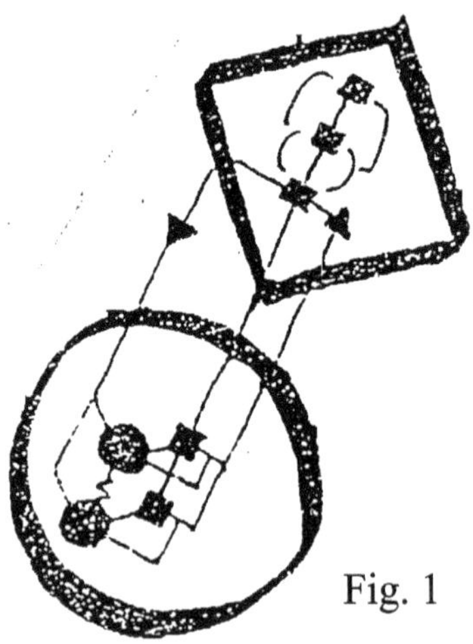

Fig. 1

Fig.1. depicts the V.S.M. It could be the bank as a whole or a branch in the bank. It represents internal milieu separated from the environment useful to understand the physiology of V.S.M. There is a square box–the brain–the ***management*** box containing 3 small boxes connected inside the box.

There is a circle representing the production unit–***operations*** where services are rendered. The box and the circle are connected by lines. Each line denotes to and fro communication channel. It is always two ways.

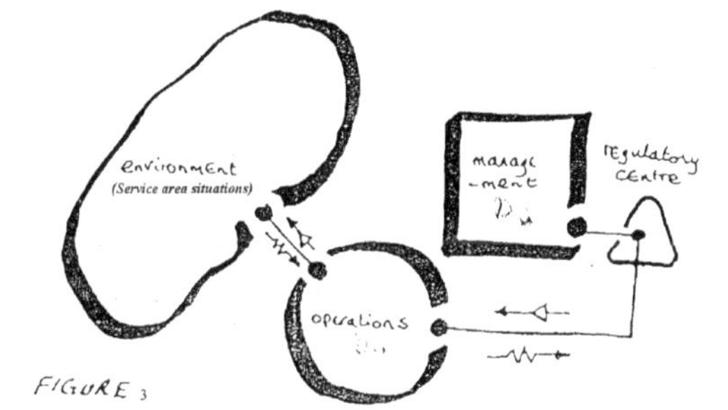

Fig. 2

1. The Square encloses all the Managerial activity needed to 'run' (whatever that may mean)
2. The Circle which encloses the relevant operations that produce the (total) viable System-in-focus.
3. The amoeboid shape represents the environment of all this
4. The arrows refer to the necessary interaction between three basic entitles: each stands for multiplicity of channels whereby the entities affect each other.

Fig.2. is a more elaborate one of the system and its environment, also connected with two-way lines of communication. Beer's notations are given as above.

The essential features of a V.S.M. are self-regulation, self awareness, self repair, self-maintenance, and the ***recursivity***, a procedure that can repeat itself indefinitely. Eg. Man, family, society, nation, world, the whole cosmos. One is within another larger system. A member in the branch, in the region, in the whole bank, in the banking system and so on are endless recursions.

Rural branch can have recursivity on many dimensions, one, branch in the bank in banking system etc. The other dimension is to see the branch in the rural society in the mandal, in the district, in the state etc. A third could be bank in rural economy in the national economy and world economy. There can be a social dimension–the staff in rural society and beyond. People who understand computer programmes have this definition of recursivity: 'a computer programming technique involving the use of a procedure, sub-routine, function, or algorithm that calls itself one or more times until a specified condition is met at which time the rest of each repetition is processed from the last called to the first.' Different from iteration.

Analogies are better than definitions. Man in the family in the community is good enough to understand recursive logic.

Just as a new born needs nurturing by the family, a new born branch of a bank needs nurturing to make it viable – capable of 'standing on own legs' literally and thereafter the child goes to school, learns more, goes to office, learns more, inter-acting with teachers and fellow students, and colleagues at office or extended families. *Interacting and learning are the means of growing.*

Similarly the branch as V.S. interacts with the environment for its own growth through interactions. The environment is a complex reality. A branch comes to know of its complexity gradually through interactions. It could be a mechanical and absent minded routine or it could be by strategy and structuring itself, gearing up to the needs of the hinterland. There is a cybernetic law which says, *'only variety absorbs variety'* where variety is a measure of complexity. It is a number we need to find out to know whether it is greater, equal or less of the interacting entity.

V_e, the variety of the environment, the hinterland where the branch is operating is enormous, much greater than what the bank's branch can absorb. Bank's variety is V_o – variety of its operations. So we have to begin with

$$V_e > V_o$$

It will become $V_e = V_o$ eventually whether by strategy or by absent mindedness. If it is by strategy everybody is happy and it costs less. If not the costs go up and men will be fed up.

V.S.M. recommends strategic approach by design.

To start with banks were surveying the area and applying for license from RBI. Later rural branch expansion was determined by District Consultative Committee under Lead Bank scheme, an outside agency. Bank managements give their concurrence. In any case the bank Manager never refers to the survey report, but *functions mechanically/absent mindedly.*

The interactions are piece-meal and not integrated or scientific. This is a major lacuna in the branch banking which caused hardship to inexperienced young Managers in several instances.

But in this volume there are some mature Managers who carried out surveys of their areas and had a strategy at the back of their minds though not on paper. Nor was it known to senior management.

CIS – Control Information System

Cybernetics is a science of communication and control. What flows is the information. CIS – Control Information System was missing in the control of rural branch which had been ad-hoc and showed only knee jerk reaction to troubles.

There was the case of Umanagar branch V.V.K. a thorough survey of 24 villages was done and the rehabilitation of bonded labour was implemented as a project. This success story obeyed V.S.M. and it was manned by the right person. (case no. 29)

V_o has been enhanced by a VVK structure and staff and vehicles etc and headed by a dedicated, competent and knowledgeable person. It was partly by choice, more by chance. The man was the chance happening in the case.

Survey and Identification

This is equivalent to market research. The communicative process starts in search of information. The communication can be via the district development agency which must be seen as an outside partner. Common objectives and goals bring the two together. The Bank officer phones the officer-in-charge of the agency with excitement at the senior management's decision to establish VVK at the branch; write an official letter to the agency– put them on readiness, fix a date for face to face discussions. For this to be effective, the man needs oral and written communication skills. Then he collects secondary information about the villages identified.

He must have visited the village to get hold of primary information. These interactions awaken the rural masses and raise their expectations. It proliferates the V_e. If the survey is to select and restrict commitment the result will be increased demand. That was increase of V_e. Market research has been found to be product promotion. There is a need for balancing the increase and decrease process. Stafford Beer has given terms for it. Inducing variety as *amplification* and reducing variety as *attenuation*. They are simultaneous activities. They are referred to as Harmony or Homeostasis or dynamic equilibrium. Bank must tread with caution and awareness of the two way processes.

We have cases of such balanced approach and exemplary results narrated as episodic memories. So, the first lesson that we might draw is something like 7S model, keeping in view 'only variety absorbs variety' and have project approach and time bound programme, monitoring, evaluating and reviewing and incorporating changes. Rural development is not child's play; it must be a systematic scientific and integrated approach in which every house-hold gets what it needs to improve its lot.

Management of V.S.

There is a similar link between management box and operational circle. It is again two-way, attenuation and amplification because $V_o > V_m$ and it must be equal. Homeostatic principle holds to make the ultimate equation as

$$V_e = V_o = V_m$$

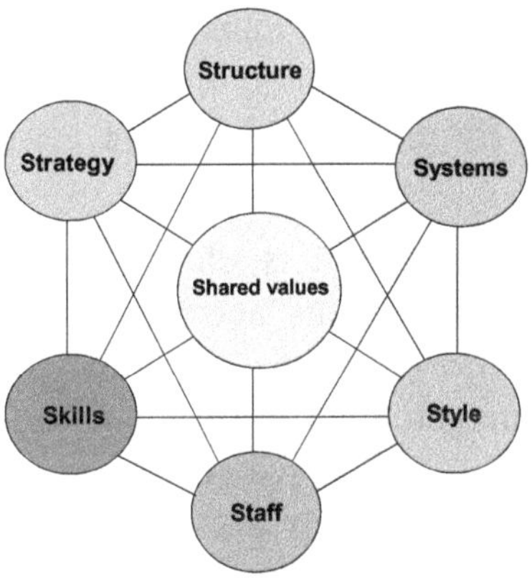

The management of the self-regulatory system hasn't got enough variety to absorb V_o. How do we make them equal? Leadership and teamwork is the short answer–the configuration of system, skills, styles, staff. For leadership the first task to create 'shared values'. All the members of the team must have same vision and mission and direction in their minds. VVK structure has a system of Credit Committee comprising of the Managers in-charge, and agricultural assistants (field staff). But there are other support staff drawn from main operations – cashiers, clerks, peons besides drivers.

NR (case no. 28) says 'another reason for the success of their model (VVK) was involvement of staff.' Where it is wanting there have been conflicts. It is the leadership which sorts out these conflicts. At week ends the entire staff must go to villages expressing solidarity and commitment with one and all. Another thing noticed in such teams was that there were no water-tight compartments.

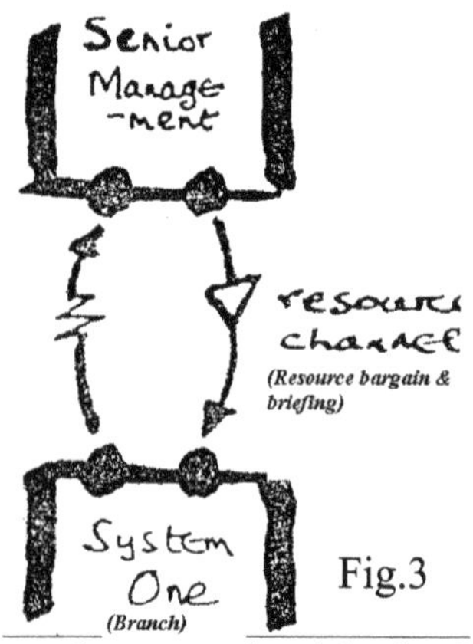

Fig.3

When there is greater demand from the hinterland, it must be seen as an opportunity and the management of the branch must enter into a new Resource Bargain to which we shall now turn. .

Branch management is charged with conducting operations according to a Resource Bargain *struck* with the senior management. Annual business meetings are not really Resource Bargains *struck* with the Branch Managers. They are more often than not simply targets *thrust* up on them; apportionment and distribution of targets set from the CMDs office. But there are exceptions. For example I was given a deposit target of Rs.1 crore for the branch where I was to go in the month of May. The target was to be reached, in those days (1978) for the December ending. The 1977 December figure stood at Rs.30 laksh after 6 years of the branch's existence. I made it a Resource Bargain in its true sense. I asked for establishment of VVK which means lot of resources in terms of men, vehicles, structure, new simplified procedure, field staff posting of agricultural officers – thus inducing enormous variety into the branch system. it was a negotiated settlement. It was readily conceded. It was my good fortune that the Senior Manager meant business. "Then the transmission of plans, programmes and procedures to operational circle should be regarded as act of regulation" (Beer). Now my branch should go according to a plan.

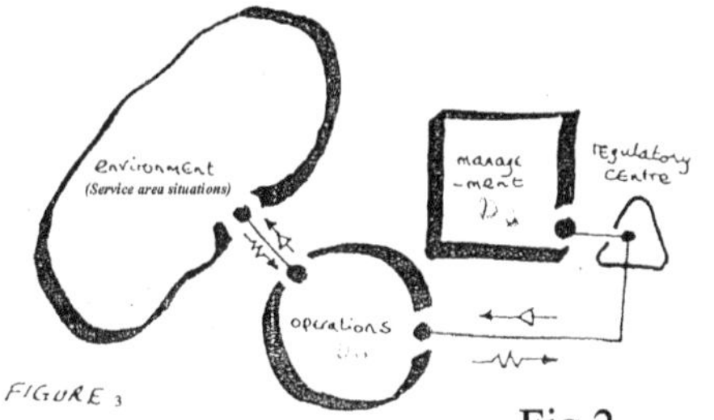

Fig.2

There lies the regulation. Refer to figure 2 in which there is a triangle with regulatory centre which lies in the branch system. The Manager cannot deviate from it without the concurrence of the senior management. There can be a mid-term review by the senior management and revision of targets, plus or minus. These reviews were not in vogue in those days. But now there is a review every 3 months. That is an improvement. But still who plays the shots is not clear. But it must be based on the flow of information and communicating, negotiations depends on the skills of the Managers whose strength is up-to-date information about the area of which he has better knowledge.

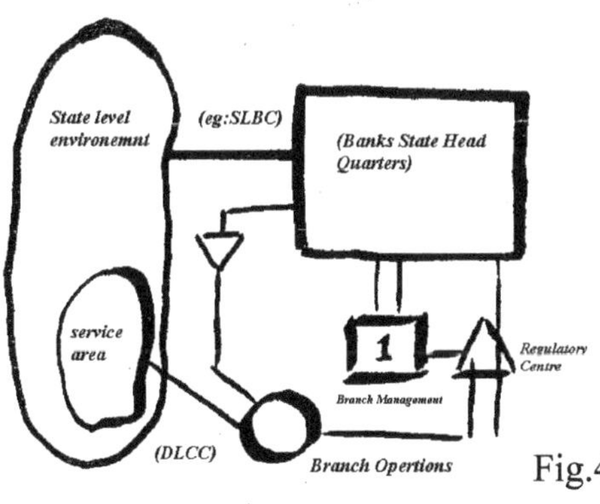

Fig.4

He may however, not have information about the future scene. The senior management is better placed in knowing about 'outside and future'. That brings us to the next figure 4.

Note the embedded environments. The larger one is the state level environment. SLBC in the State Capital reviews the performance bank-wise. Regional, zonal, or head quarters level managements represent in the SLBC reviews.

Similarly DLCC deliberations are not known to the interior rural branch unless there is a system of percolating important decisions taken at each of the levels. This calls for group discussion at various levels.

The preparation and dispatching of minutes or putting the minutes on the web sites may not be very effective.

I have used 'balcony view' for an analogy.

The Senior Management must have a *balcony view*: Imagine children are playing cricket on the road. You are watching and enjoying and clapping whenever a boy hit a four or six. You are not playing. Suddenly you see a truck on the road. What do you do? You shout and ask boys to stop the game and make the way to the truck.

You know the general condition of the vehicles and the drivers. But the children are lost in the game. Ideally they should have been playing in play grounds. Environments are far from being ideal. Your view is balcony view which is denied to the kids. *They are at a lower level and lost in the game. You are the man in the balcony–having a big picture /* distant view *you can see both environment and the play on the road.*

To have a 'balcony view' how should system be designed? It must have *information* which gives the picture–on going picture about the branch. That brings us to Control Information System. There is one more subtle point that we must note. From the balcony you have both the 'distant' view as well 'proximate' or current picture. You know the children are playing and their excitement. Do you know what is happening in the bank at the back of your mind. The Senior Management has no idea of the state of branch situation. How do we develop the information system that can give us the current situation in the branches at the time we are getting signals from the distance?

For example the Chief Minister expresses displeasure on the dismal performance in some areas. I read a report that CM regretted that JLGs for tenants scheme has not taken off. The problems of tenant farmers are becoming more and more complex with the passage of time. Bank Managers have other worries. No amount of pressure on the grass-roots Managers is going to sort out the issue. There must be some policy decisions required to motivate the Managers. These things take time. In the meantime politicians criticize the Managers as stumbling blocks to the progress. How many managements obtain feed back on the ground reality? They give lip sympathy, nothing concrete is going to happen.

In short, the rural Manager must know the mind of the bosses. They may say one thing in public, another in private. Write one thing and say something else. A third way is punishing people, or not protecting those who implement the stated policies. Yet another way is to reward the non-performers (actions speak louder than words). Under such hypocrisy, only fools tread the risky path.

Final figure cybernetic management no.2

'Cybernetics is the science of effective organization–was the science of communication and control–indicates the role of information in regulatory system'. (Beer)

A branch must be designed to be a self regulatory system; it needs the support of external environment and support and guidance of internal senior management to become such a, system.

'That the feed back of information is ubiquitous in regulation for every sort of system was a major discovery'. (Beer)

Feed back of information from the ground reality is the major casualty in banks.

Audit and inspection which is the watch dog of systems and procedures, checks and balances becomes blood-hound hounding bonafide performers more than the malafide delinquent elements. Rooting out deviant neuroticism is the function of Senior Management cybernetically – nipping in the bud. *It begins at the selection point.* It is a preventive measure, but often results in postmortem.

Box with 3 smaller boxes tells us all about the planning and control 'the central direction and local autonomy may be trying to disobey the cybernetic 'law of cohesiveness' inducing stress in men, groups and the whole organisation'. (Beer) Managing a large organization is not an easy, cozy affair.

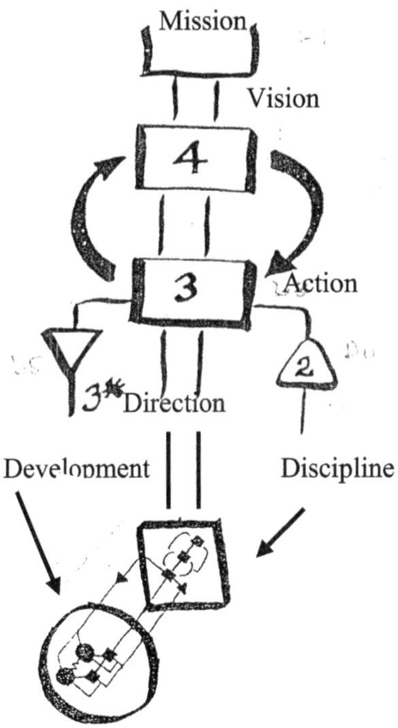

The three inside boxes which are interconnected represent the management that regulates. *First there is the mission and mandate from above.* One of the aspects is Rural Development with 60% of the branches in semi-urban and rural areas with primary responsibility of poverty alleviation, a curse of centuries. It is a Herculean task. Second is vision in constant touch with the outside and future, the eyes and ears of the bank. Vision system has its counterparts in every zone, regions and branch. At the branch level both mission and vision hats are worn by the same Manager.

These are sources of information to the top at all levels. Mission and vision are in constant interaction, because situation and scenario is changing. The essence of these interactions is the third hat that decides and directs.

The direction has two arms – besides the head. Head in the Senior Management and heads in the branches are put together in the Resource Bargain, discussed earlier. *The two arms are important. One is discipline or regulatory centre that acts with speed and corrective actions, short of fire fighting. The corrective is in the form answering SOS.* Reinforcing and dispatching information supply, revising instructions, recalling of Manager, in extreme cases, saving the bank's money and prestige. *The other arm is audit and inspection of the systems and procedures. This arm is also known as development system under the overall control of direction channel/system.*

Its function is to develop systems, structure, staff and skills and so on, on a continuous improvement mode.

This was the weakest link in the existing system of controls in the banking I knew. This acts directly on the circle (operations) where as the discipline channel works on the Managerial function in the branches. If we consider discipline as the function of personnel, then development is that of HR and audit. It is a function which was called in our time HRD and now HRM. Managing human resources are two different orientations. There are academicians who argue that the employment is a contract under hire and fire system and HR is not the responsibility of the employer. This is a western philosophy but not suitable to India, many aver.

Bank branches like the boats in the picture are bound to the bank by ROPE. 'Regular Ongoing Periodical Exchanges' with the Senior Management. The greater the length of the rope the greater the freedom and autonomy. Freedom and autonomy to respond to the 'tide and wind', rise and fall with the tides of fortunes; it is the wind and other climatic changes literally and figuratively affect the performance of branches. The 'post' represents the established

systems and structures. The fixed 'post' might suggest never changing systems and structures. They are fixed only for a period of time. When IT became ubiquitous the banks had adopted and adapted remarkably. Similarly they have to adapt to changing aspirations of employees and the customers they serve. 'Financial Inclusion' is a dramatic instance in the history of modern banking when both technology and HR systems and structure have to change. Branch – its staff, skills and styles of management must undergo drastic changes to suit the new mandate. Longer ropes and thinner thread are required; but firmness remains constant. Later in another context I discussed branches as balloons in the hands of street vendor. This is what cybernetics – the science of communication and control teaches us.

* * * * *

SECTION – II

EXTERNAL ENVIRONMENT

INTRODUCTION TO VOLUME II

I always felt that difference in performance at the operational banking level arises on account of conceptual knowledge and valid information both of which influence the decision making on day to day basis as well as strategic planning. Having spent a decade at the fag end of my career as senior faculty engaged in designing courses, topic planning, preparing handouts, writing cases particularly to facilitate guest faculty from IIM(A), I knew the value of knowledge and information.

The grass-roots operator needs the 'Big Picture' as the Americans call the holistic perspective. The 'Big Picture' is not a static picture; it keeps changing. To the rural manager most of the information comes from higher authorities in the form of letters, business meetings, visits of superiors etc. If he is a District level manager and member of DLCC, he would get information from outside the bank which is not usually shared with the higher management. There is some sort of adhocism. Even if the reporting system is streamlined, it is confined to files and does not become input to strategic management.

Volume II is divided into Part IV, & V.

Part IV & V have become necessary for making the bank manager appreciate the readiness with which he should adapt to rapid changes taking place in the largely populated democratic country with half of its population struggling and aspiring to improve their lot.

In 2008, a report on Financial Inclusion came into being. To read the report is one thing; to read it in the back drop of historical perspective is another thing. To give the dynamic big picture of 'the nation in the making' (Ambedkar) I have relied more on the News Daily (mine is The Hindu) than books. Yet one book '*Small is beautiful'*; is what I used more than any other volume.

Financial System

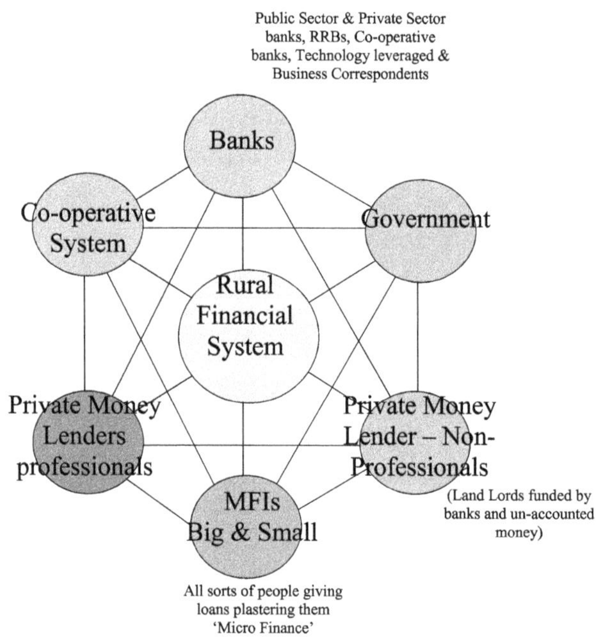

SPECIES Poverty

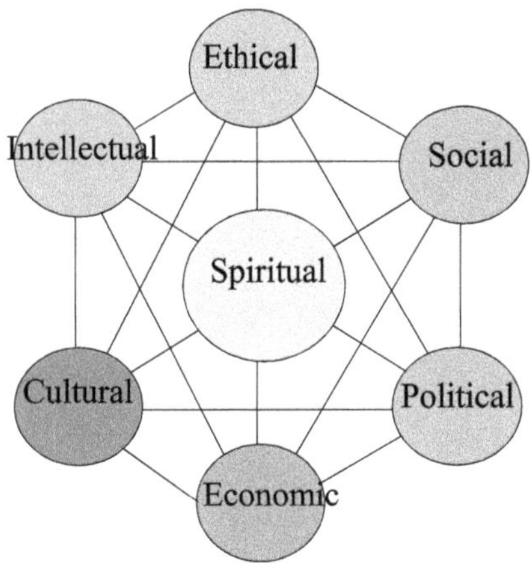

Ecological Literacy

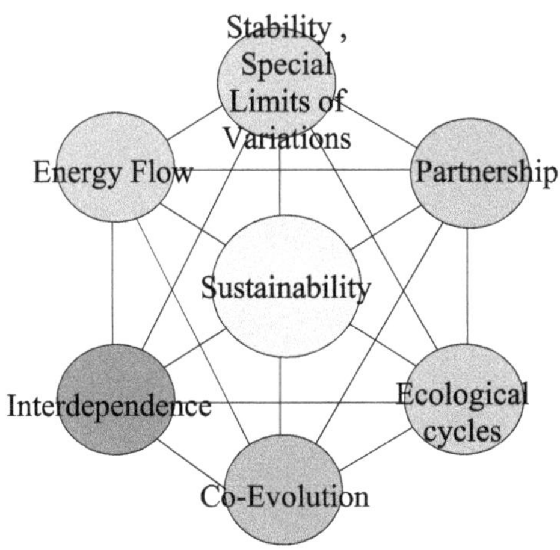

* * * * *

MUSINGS OF

BAREFOOT BANKERS

PART - IV

POLITICAL ECONOMY

RHETORIC

REALITY

READING MAKETH A FULLMAN

We read to find ourselves more fully and more strange than otherwise we could hope to find.

Harold Bloom

Political Economy

'Political Economy refers to the distribution of political and economic power in a given society and that influences the directions of development and policies that bear on the latter–policies'.

'In India a relatively small minority holds the power.. large and medium business houses, medium farmers, the upper echelons of the salaried class, and top layer of unionized labour hold the power'. 'The inequality in human capital (eg. Education) is much more than in physical and financial (assets) capital'.

Situation in Rural India

'As Amartya Sen has pointed out there has been no large scale famines in Independent India, unlike in colonial India, whereas, on the other hand, there is still a great deal of persistent and endemic hunger in the country'.

'Under-nourishment.. the record of 5 years.. the coexistence of starvation deaths, agrarian distress, rural indebtedness, farmer suicides in states like Orissa, Andhra, and Maharashtra, on the one hand with bursting public granaries, on the other, must be seen to be particularly unacceptable face of the recent regime of hunger and suffering'.

These are the statements one comes across in any standard text book of Economics in India.

'Reading Maketh a Fullman' (Francis Bacon)

Educate your self to Educate others

'Start reading a news paper which would help acquiring *knowledge* on different issues and read different books which would add value to the *knowledge* acquired'. A retired senior IAS officer said.

Role of banker in educating for financial literacy among children, youth, and all others is going to assume greater importance in times to come. There have been bankers in rural areas who have been doing some such thing as financial literacy since 1970s. That was an individual's choice then. Now it is going to be the norm and rule. Lending and promoting thrift are small part of his role henceforth.

Reading books and reading news papers efficiently assumes importance for the barefoot banker. The title 'Reading Maketh a Fullman' is derived from the oft quoted Baconian maxim given to us four centuries ago. Whether it is on the small screen of the laptop or a printed page on the desk top, reading is a skill less recognized by the modern youth.

Bacon wrote, Reading Maketh a Fullman, Conference a Ready man; and Writing an Exact man. All are pertinent to Barefoot Bankers' performance

Reading Habit

The officer of the bank goes to rural areas with a body of knowledge which varies from person to person depending on his university education and *reading habit.* Justice Frankfurter wrote in his book 'Of Law and Of Men', 'come to law as a well-read person'. It equally applies to bankers as lawyers whom the Judge addressed. He explained it further:

> Stock your mind with a deposit of much good reading, and widen and deepen your *feelings* by experiencing vicariously as much as possible the wonderful mysteries of the universe...

We all learn by direct experience if we care to reflectively observe our own experience as Gandhiji did. By reading books Frankfurter is suggesting learning through vicarious experiences reflecting on others experiences. What we miss by direct experience, we can gain through reading books and watching movies. Bacon's axiom became my beacon. I became an avid reader from college days. Initially I read more for pleasure whatever I found interesting and readable. It was only much later while in service I read for information and knowledge. Background knowledge of rural situation in India and information on initiatives and failures helped me in articulating my views. Thus 'Conference maketh a ready man' became true in my case. The third axiom, 'writing maketh an exact man' took shape only after my retirement from active bank service. Although I have been reading since college days without gap, it was only after my 50th year that I came across the book *Efficient Reading* which helped me 'swallow and digest' large amount of information and knowledge. Bacon wrote:

> Some books have to be tasted, others swallowed and very few have to be chewed and digested; that is some books are to be read only in parts, others, to be read but not curiously and some, very few to be read wholly and with diligence and attention.

There are books like 'Small is Beautiful' by E.F.Schumacher which must be read diligently with attention.

If the officer sent to rural areas had read, 'Small is Beautiful' or 'Ends and Means' of Aldox Huxley and the like critics who saw in 'Gandhi' what many Indian youth of the day fail to see, his approach to rural posting would be different. He would read the news paper reports, editorials, articles, and the latest developments in Agricultural Science and Technology and success stories in a different light. That light would serve as beacon to him. His decisions and strategies will be influenced by such 'good' reading.

Here is a sample.

> 'The virtue of massive public works programme for job creation have been extolled;'[1] 'if you can get new purchasing power into the *rural economy* byway of public works programme *financed from outside,* see to it that the fullest possible use is made of 'multiplier-effect'.

Schumacher adds,

> 'The people employed in public works want to spend their wages on 'wages goods', that is to say, consumer goods of all kinds.' 'If these goods can be locally produced.. do not seep away but go on circulating in local market the total employment effect could be prodigious,' 'If pump - priming must be backed by the indigenous production of additional wages goods, the additional purchasing power will flow into inputs'.

MFI's massive pumping money without the indigenous production of additional wages goods led to disastrous results

[1] Small is Beautiful by E.F.Schumacher.

To have multi-plier effect, '*pump priming must be backed by indigenous production*'. That is where MSMES and cottage industries need to be promoted by liberal lending in the service areas of the bank, the Manager must note. Though 'pump priming' refers to government investment bank lending has similar effect.

Report of the Committee on the Financial Inclusion-2008 headed by Dr.Rangarajan is a must read for all those urban educated fortunate. It casts shadows of the coming events – future of banking in the next decade. It is a great opportunity for the young educated to take up banking career to serve in the cause of rural development in a mission mode with a clear vision. After assimilating its meaning and significance the bank officers' attention will fall on those reports, editorials, articles, and developments in national English dailies published more and more in these days.

Unless the budding banker is knowledgeable and well informed at the macro level initiatives and micro level implication for implementation in a holistic manner, he will not be able to shape his role effectively and derive satisfaction as well as realize own potential. The inspiration to embark on this work comes from the readings.

What I found in these media reports and articles was that there was no mention of banks' and bankers' role since 1970s which deserved a place for drawing lessons from the past for the future banking, particularly, public sector banking and the selection of people to man semi-urban and rural sector branches.

RBI Governor said on 26th November, 2011 that 'MGNREGS is pushing up rural wages exacerbating price wage spiral', indicating '*pump priming must be backed by indigenous roduction*'.

Paradox of India's New Prosperity – A Report[2]

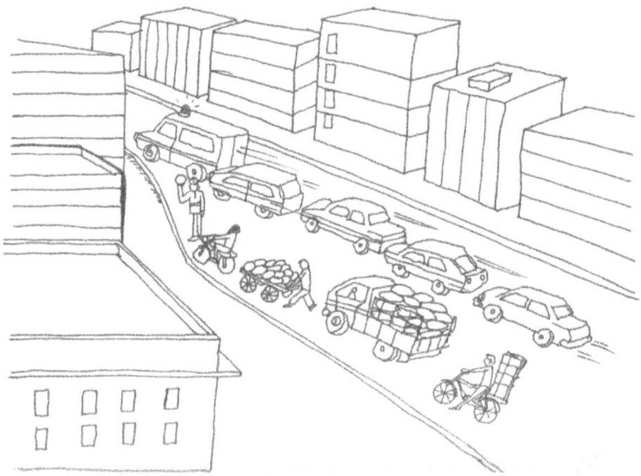

Imagine two traffic lanes both are stand still. After a while traffic in one of the lanes starts moving raising the hopes of those stuck in the next lane, they too, should be on their way soon".

Sunil Khilnani

Hence forth I use 'Lane 1' as the urban India's progress and prosperity and Lane 2 the 'rural India' stuck. When I read this report a scene in the film 'Gandhi' came to me in a flash. It was the trial scene about which Romain Rolland vividly described in his book *Mahatma Gandhi*. As I was editing this manuscript my grand daughter gave me 'The Great Speeches of Modern India' as a gift in which I found the full text of the statement Gandhiji made in that court in 1922. I don't know whether my grand daughter read it or not but it is a must read by youth of urban, educated India, those that belong to fast moving lane 1. I reproduced a small part of that historic statement in the next chapter. Gandhiji blamed towns people (Lane 1) for joining hands with the British administration in exploiting the rural masses. Probably we may have to replace 'British administration' with Government of Independent India!

A Better Analogy is Tandem Cycle

Notes & Acknowledgement

[2] Business Line.

I am Indian farmer, hear me out. O Mother! When our loan and other applications gather dust for months together, big companies are able to get full clearance in a matter of weeks.

TITIBITS[3]

Paradox of India's New progress

Lane 1 'Cities glitter because they corner much of the country's resources; graduates from our universities the urban elite- are in demand world over; it's 'youthful consuming middle classes attract investment from distant corners of the globe'; and its corporate giants stalk the world economy…'

Lane 2 'darkness, unfreedoms, despair persists, men, women and children toil long hours for meager wages.. millions are forced into degrading low paid work.. social stigma continues…

[3] The Hindu

Forest dwellers are driven out of their homelands dispossessed of agricultural lands, crushed by usury, displaced and uprooted by industry, dams, mines,…'

Harsh Mander

"In the last two decades, with the advent of liberalization and the neo-liberal policies, high-level corruption has become institutionalised. The neo-liberal regime has led to an exponential rise in corruption. Much of this corruption stems from the big business ruling politician-bureaucratic nexus which has been established."

"The main source of support for the Hazare-led movement is the urban middle class. Many of them were supporters of the liberalization policies and the reforms ushered in by the Manmohan Singh government. Now plagued by corruption, they want a messiah to get rid of the corruption that constantly affects their daily life. They would like corruption to end, while maintaining the economic regime that has conferred certain benefits on them. Hence *they are unable to see the organic link between the neo-liberal policies and the corruption that has been engendered.*

Prakash Karat

(Anna comes from Lane 2, his supporters belong to Lane 1 unaware of the root cause of corruption in high places. If they know they would know that they are sitting on the back of Lane 2 choking and refusing to get off the back)

TITBITS[4] (Lane 2 Dilemma)

Farmers would quit agriculture if they had an alternative

"Some years ago the National Sample Survey Organization (NSSO) reported after its study on agriculture that roughly half the farmers in the country did not wish to continue farming."

---

[4] The Hindu

"They would rather quit if they had an alternative. This shameful reality reflects the despair farmers feel and is based on the fact that agriculture is a loss making enterprise and the farmers are unable to either feed themselves or turn a profit," says Dr.Suman Sahai, Convener, Gene campaign, New Delhi in her blog (sumanasahaiblog.blogspot.com) on 'Why farmers don't farm'.

"Rural India is looked down upon by the well to do urban population, including the policy makers, who are seen as part of the urban elite. This discrimination strips farming and the farmer of his dignity and provides an incentive to the younger generation to move away from farming," she says.

"Raised on a diet of unreal aspirations beamed on television soap operas and Bollywood films, rural youth sees neither glamour, money nor dignity in farming."

"Why would they want to adopt it if there is nothing there for them?" she asks.

"Electoral politics plays with rice and wheat as gimmicks to get votes. The poor must certainly get the help of the state to overcome hunger and poverty but the way to do this should be *empowerment* and fostering self reliance – not creating dependency through doles," she mentions in her blog.

Many in the younger generation are forgetting how to farm. Two more generations of this kind of youth and we may not have enough people who can grow food in this country – and then?" she asks.

Speaking at the FICCIIB banking seminar, Dr.Chakrabarty said that the share of agriculture in GDP has fallen to 14 per cent from 50 per cent about 15-16 years ago. The sector also provides employment for about 60 per cent of population, he said.

Therefore, food processing industry and agro based industry need to be given necessary boost and impetus to improve productivity and employment opportunities.

Although agricultural credit has grown, it is from the urban and metropolitan branches of banks. This raises the question to which segments is this credit actually flowing to, Dr.Chakrabarty pointed out.

"This share of rural credit in agriculture has come down from 55 per cent to 38 per cent. The share of metropolitan credit has gone up. But that will not add to productivity. We need to see where the credit is going" he said.[5]

That's in spite of several measures to eradicate poverty one of which was bank Nationalization. Critics of government say the sorry state of endless waiting and living in hope is due to LPG – Liberalisation, Privatisation, and Globalisation that started in 1990s.

How long will the traffic in lane two wait? There is a dead line – *2020 when hunger and poverty will be eliminated.* That's hope of the 'growth' advocates.

Lane 1 is making rapid progress at 8 to 9% growth. All in Lane 1 are obsessed with growth with ever increasing number of billionaires and millionaires and are oblivious of the plight of the people in the next lane. The latest Forbes billionaires list[6] is out: 55 in India are with an average of 4.5 billions, an above global average. The net asset worth of these is around $246.5 billion (Rs.11,13,750 crore). This of course, does not include unaccounted income, or money stashed away from public gaze.' This years list is out.

---

[5] Business Line

[6] The Hindu

'Let us recall for a moment that 836 million Indians live on a daily expenditure of Rs.20/- or even much less.'

'Finance Minister is writing off in corporate income tax, apart from other freebies for 'struggling' billionaires. The freebies are in billions of dollars... for the efficiency challenged ethical deficit..'

Such strong words are used in the open letter to 'Gates and Buffet' on the 'Art of Giving' by P. Sainath. Mere 10 percent return on wealth of Indians in it would cover Health, Hunger, Education and MGNREGS.. These people in Lane 1 are unmindful of the plight of the people stuck in, the laggards. Some in Lane 2 are shifting to Lane 1 leaving Lane 2 worse. This migration is nothing new. It has been happening for over a century throughout the Western world. Result is food shortage because food is produced by the Lane 2.

The connection between Lane 1's prosperity and Lane 2's persisting poverty was beautifully put by Leo Tolstoy:

'I sit on a man's back, choking him, and making him carry me, and yet assure myself and others that I am very sorry for him and wish to ease his lot by any means possible, except getting off his back'.[7]

There is lot of lip service to the laggards – without getting off their backs. I discussed the matter in Part-II.

O Mother Earth My tribe is fast vanishing.. God bless my country... Why do they target agricultural land...? Government may earn money in the long run, everybody may have pocket full of money. But what about food?

[7] Small is Beautiful

Dreams[8] of the BLUE eyed: Born Lucky Urban Elite

Children of Lane 1 dream 'of a different future... in to-day's brand new world, children have different expectations of themselves and their lives. What role can parents and the family play in this changed scenario' of continuous growth of reform era?

The author of 'Dreams of a different future' asks this question in the Magazine Section on 14th November 2010, children's day. He concludes that 'Rajiv Gandhi's brain drain to brain bank prophecy is showing signs of turning into an *uncanny reality'*.

What the author wrote in the main text is not relevant to us. We are concerned with the unfortunate and inexcusable reality of Lane 2 last row.

You will find that reality on the next page of the same magazine on the same children's day; *childhoods of hunger and want.*

Tears of BLUES: Born Laggard Un-lucky Excluded Suffering

In much of rural India, hunger is still an every day reality and often the only way out is debt-bondage. He gave several tragic stories of that reality in 2010. One story is sufficient to highlight what BPL life means. 'Labani, a separated mother, grieves when her children 'see the neighbours' children eating biscuits, snacks or chocolate; "they come to me and ask me for it. If I have some money or rice to barter at the shop, then I give them something to eat; if not, then I try to explain my predicament to them and promise them something in the near future, a promise I know I will not be able to keep."

[8] The Hindu, Magazine Section

Still prevalent *Kutia* to *Halia*

'Even more harrowing for a parent than to send out a small child to work, is to send him into debt bondage, which is still not uncommon in many parts of rural, and especially tribal India. Indradeep earned his own food as soon as he was four years old, as a bonded *kutia* in the *sahukar's* home in Bolangir. He rose early to graze cows and bullocks and carry food to the fields, all seven days a week, every month of the year without any break. In return, his employers gave him tea and *mudhi* in the morning and a meal at noon and 12 kilograms paddy for a year as remuneration.

As he entered his 21st year, not much had changed except that he graduated into an adult bonded worker or *halia*.

Indradeep in time married, and only one son, Sadhu, survived.

Whenever they would walk past the village school he noticed how his little son gazed at it with interest and longing. He resolved that whatever it cost him, he would not send his son out to work as a bonded child labourer – as generations in his family had done before him, as long back as they could remember.

Instead, he and his wife would willingly shoulder his burden and send him to school. Life held together for them until Sadhu reached 14 years, and had passed class 7.

'Disaster again struck, when Indradeep was diagnosed with TB and nearly died. He was admitted in hospital for prolonged treatment. They sold the little gold which his wife wore in her ears, which had helped bail them out often in the past, when they had mortgaged it for loans at the doorstep of the money lender. They also mortgaged her gold nose ring. In the end, Indradeep could survive only with a blinded eye and a crippled body, with loss of normal functioning in one side of the body and heavy burdens of debt. He could no longer depend on his own hard labour, which had been his only wealth.'

M – Medical expenses

I – Indebtedness

R – Recurring of Misfortunes

E – Education (lack of it)

'His young son realized that it was his turn now to assume his responsibilities, which he did readily. On his own, Sadhu took the decision of quietly dropping out of school when his father was admitted in the hospital, and went to work like his father in the fields of landlords, and he grazed their cows. He then got in touch with other people in the village who regularly migrated, and left for the brick-kilns in Hyderabad when he was 14, for an advance of Rs.900. He has continued to migrate in bonded conditions after that every year. Slowly they were able to repay the loans and sustain themselves. We were witness to his tearful departure one year, when he migrated for an advance of Rs.8,000. Before leaving, he gave Rs.500 to his parents and released his mother's nose jewel from mortgage for Rs.1000.

It still weighs heavily on Indradeep's heart that the boy could not study. But he is proud that his son is responsible and caring. "He does not waste even a single rupee on himself, and saves it all for his family." (Financial Literacy is more self sacrifice and discipline).

'In this way, each generation valiantly but hopelessly battles hunger, both for the generation that has passed, and the one that is to come.'

Now let us turn to the first article.

'Rajiv Gandhi's "brain drain" to "brain bank" prophecy is showing signs of turning into an uncanny reality. Many people who went overseas to train are bringing in the best of Western education and returning to blend back into the fabric of India. Indian youth are increasingly turning to their own country for the very real possibility of better opportunity, better lives and a brighter future.'

Will these Lane 1 children returning from the west take on themselves *voluntary conscription* to educate and emancipate the rural poor or continue to choke them and not get off their backs?

These kutias and halias are the target group of beneficiaries for the barefoot bankers. To cover children the credit limits and banking products should cover the entire household's multiple needs. That's reading beyond lines.

Mansholt Plan[9]

Dr.S.L.Mansholt, Vice-President of the European Economic Community, launched the Mansholt Plan for European Agriculture. He believed that most of the farmers ought to get out of farming and become industrial labour because '*factory workers, men in building sites and those in administrative jobs*' – are better off with paid holidays etc. But E.F. Schumacher cautioned all such thinkers

[9] Small is Beautiful

saying that '*Dead matter enters the factory and comes out improved; but the man, the cog in the wheel, comes out corrupted,*'

> … 'Mansholt plan, accordingly, is designed to achieve, as quickly as possible, the amalgamation of many small farms into large agricultural units as if they were factories.. Aid is to be given 'which would enable the older as well as the younger farmers to leave agriculture'.

Similar arguments are heard in India:

***Fruits of Progress Have Eluded The Rural Poor* – A Report**

Make agriculture more remunerative: Narayana Murthy.

Addressing a policy forum at the International Conference on 'Eliminating hunger and poverty' hosted by the M.S.Swaminathan Research Foundation, Mr.Murthy said the dark side (lane 2) of India's growth story had been that fruits of progress in terms of GDP growth, rising exports or global recognition had not touched the rural poor dependent on agriculture for livelihood... Make Agriculture more remunerative ***even while reducing the proportion of people dependent on agriculture for livelihood.***

But it is worth comparing this statement with what M.S.Swaminathan said at the same conference at the end of the day.

'*Reversing the* ***paddy and poverty*** *paradigm was vital to addressing the challenge of* ***retaining farmers in agriculture and attracting youth for the occupation.*** *For youth to become interested in agriculture, farming has to be* ***intellectually stimulating*** *and economically rewarding',* an intellectually stimulating statement!

The challenge lies there both for the scientists and policy makers.

These are two opposite views that are prevailing in India, one of educated class and urban elite and those like M.S.Swaminathan. M.S.Swamiathan has better answers to India's poverty in my view. Bankers must hold the view of M.S.Swaminathan if they have to dedicate themselves for rural development. They must keep people in farming for the good of all.

In 2010 P.Sainath wrote an open letter to Prime Minister Manmohan Singh regarding suicide notes addressed to the Prime Minister about the policies adversely affecting Lane 2. In 2011 Gurucharandas, Ex-CEO of Procter and Gamble, India, wrote an open letter blaming the Prime Minister for not pushing through the reforms which he started 'heroically' in 1991. His plan was similar to Mansholt's plan. He reminded the Prime Minister that future of India lies in cities and not in villages.

Whom will the Prime Minister listen with maximum number of suicides of farmers reported in 2010? It has crossed a quarter of a million.

A snippet from the review of the book, *The Agrarian question in Marx and his successors*, by M.V.Nadkarni.

'The job market in non-agricultural sectors is not expanding fast enough to absorb those who are forced to give up farming.'

'In the Karnataka model a group of farmers in a contiguous area form a corporate body, with their land holdings as share capital, and manage the operations deriving the benefits that flow from such a large-scale exercise like setting up agro-processing units and warehousing facilities. May be it is too early to say if this will provide a solution, but surely it is worth a try.'

President Calls for Second Green Revolution

Another Report

Pratibha urges "out of box" thinking on agriculture. Banks must have 'out of box' thinking on agriculture finance and rural development.

Involve agriculture economy more proactively in growth process.

Banks have always been proactive; there have been 'out of box' thinkers among the rural Managers. But they feel the people in power do not seem to appreciate their initiatives.

Ms.Patil advocated "more intense frame works" encompassing "new technologies, better seeds, improved farming practices and better water management techniques" for closing the gap between farmers, the scientific community, lending institutions and the market.

She said higher agricultural income would improve the living standards of over 145 million rural house-holds which in turn will generate demand for growth in other sectors.

It was a more categorical statement linking Lane2 to Lane1.

These prepared speeches need not be taken with a pinch of salt. Take them as reminders lest we forget in our daily pre-occupations. They come as reassurances to the barefoot banker who is helping implementing the rhetoric. I think Lane 1 celebrities must reflect on the above highlighted statement.

'Globalization was introduced to eliminate trade barriers and for cost-reduction by the West at the cost of disturbing India's social fabric' said T.Scarlet Epstein, Professor, University of Sussex.[10] She added that '27% of the world's undernourished

[10] Education Plus, The Hindu.

population lives in India' (mainly in the Lane 2). By 2030 condition will worsen. The reasons she attributed to India's political and economic spheres and pointed out that the rural development in India was neglected over the years 'by the powerful and the rich riding on the fast-track', Lane1 on the backs of the poor. 'The negative aspects of Globalisation were outlined as more of the agricultural land being transformed into industrial land which will affect future food needs of the global population'.

On the same day appeared in the 'Online and Offline' column a heading – *Disturbing trends on food front: media watch.*[11] National Advisory Committee headed by Sonia Gandhi recommended that '75% of the people must be extended the benefits of statutory food security which includes both urban poor and rural poor'. It also asked the Government to identify priority groups (SCs and STs) both BPL and APL families, which was rejected by the Prime Minister's advisors simply because they can not procure that much of food grains from the Lane 2 which was neglected by the policy makers for the two decades.

Again on the same day there was an article titled, 'High global food prices but local solutions....'[12] the policy makers are looking at the problem merely as an economic problem while social ramifications could be more damaging. Fire fighting is going on for the long term neglect of Lane 2 growth.

Yet a disturbing news is conversion of Lane 2 into Lane 1 by official order. A recent government order of Chattisgarh turned a tribal village Panchayat into an urban municipality to facilitate starting of an industry which the villages have been opposing. It is Lane 1's *dadagiri.* Only Gandhigiri can save 3900 and odd population of the tribal village from losing their livelihood. The

---

[11] The Hindu

[12] Ibid

matter is in the court. Will the judiciary of Lane1 also join hands with politician – bureaucrat nexus?[13] The government wants to increase urbanization of all areas and they are trying to learn the process of urbanization from the Japanese.[14]

All politicians, bureaucrats, judges, professionals, bankers every educated person belonging to the Lane 1, do not yield any of their comforts and privileges without which Lane 2 would not move an inch forward. They are sitting on the Lane 2's back, and choking ..... carrying them. Mahatma Gandhi echoed it when he said, 'trace the source of the coin in your pocket you'll end up in a poor man's hut.[15]

Pay Back

E.F.Shumacher called upon the Lane 1 educated to pay back to the poor people what is due to them by serving them. He called it *voluntary conscription.*[16] The Lane 1 in India should heed Schumacher's advice for their own food security. The neglect of Lane 2 agriculture is similar to cutting the goose that lays golden eggs. There are many IITians, Software Engineers, NRIs who, having attained financial self-sufficiency are taking up rural projects, a way of pay back. Recently State Bank of India called for applications for fellowship to work in rural areas for 1 year with a stipend. Surprisingly 5000 applications were received all over India; the least qualified person was an Engineering graduate. The other candidates include B.Techs with IIM degree, IITians with

---

[13] Ibid

[14] Electronic Media

[15] Mahatma Gandhi 'By Romain Rolland' (1924).

[16] Small is Beautiful by E.F.Schumacher.(1973).

several years of service. That shows the young people have realized that they have to go to rural poor and serve them and experience the charm of such work which is really encouraging. Episodes in Part I of this volume reveal the charm and satisfaction the narrators had.

These young men can take up banking career and serve in rural areas as barefoot bankers to translate the initiatives taken by the government, NGOs, and other agencies in the cause of rural development, as sabbatical.

These young men and women who have offered their services, for more than one reason could be 'pay back' to society, a voluntary conscription. More importantly the aspiring youth are enriching their resumes and employability. The know it will result in their VIKAS – Values, Individuality, knowledge, Attitudes and Skills.

"Economic development is primarily a question of getting more work done. For this there are four essential conditions; motivation, know-how, capital and additional markets".

Youth for India fellowship program's aim appears to be to motivate and educate for know-how and markets leaving capital to Banks and Government and other private agencies like MFIs and money lenders.

They may also come across some negative feedback on banks and bank managers which may not be incorporated in their reports. If they do it it will be valid information for taking corrective measures.

* * * * *

PRE-INDEPENDENCE RHETORIC

The political rhetoric on poverty alleviation started in 1920 after Gandhi entered India's political arena. An extract from the film, Gandhi is presented in the box below.

Pages from History

'Since I returned to India I have travelled much of India and I could travel for many more years and still I could know much less. What we say here is nothing for the masses and the people of India are untouched. Their politics is confined to bread and soul. They may be illiterate but are not blind to see no reason to show loyalty to the powerful and rich who want to take over rule from the British.'

'This congress shall tell the world that it represents India.

My brothers, India is 700 000 villages, not a few lawyers in Delhi and Bombay. Until we join them in the field who toil in the hot sun we will not represent India, nor we would be able to challenge the British' said Mahatma Gandhi nearly 100 years ago and turned the freedom-struggle into a mass movement and liberated India.[1]

It is followed by the famous trial speech of Gandhi. He gave a new direction to the Indian National Congress.

[1] Film on Gandhi

Gandhi in 1922 – The Trial Speech*[2]

"Before the British advent, India spun and wove in her millions of cottages just the supplement she needed for adding to her meager agricultural resources. This cottage industry, so vital for India's existence, has been ruined by incredibly heartless and inhuman processes as described by English witnesses.

Little do town-dwellers[3] know how the semi-starved masses[4] of India are slowly sinking to lifelessness. Little do they know that their miserable comfort represents the brokerage they get for the work they do for the foreign exploiter, that the profits and the brokerage are sucked from the masses. Little do they realize that the government established law in British India[5] is carried on for this exploitation of the masses. I have no doubt whatsoever that both England and the town-dwellers of India will have to answer, if there is a God above, for this crime against humanity which is perhaps unequalled in history.'

'In my humble opinion, non-cooperation with evil is as much a duty as is cooperation with good.'

Those who saw Attenborough's film *Gandhi* must have moved in their seats when they saw this beautiful court scene and when Justice Broomsfield and Gandhi vied with each other in chivalrous courtesy.

The place of British rulers has been taken by the Government of India and that of town-dwellers continue to be the

---

* The speech made by Mahatma Gandhi in the trial court when he was charged with sedition.

[2] The Great speeches of Modern India (2011) edited by R.Mukherjee.

[3] Lane 1 India

[4] Lane 2 India

[5] Same is the case in Independent India.

Lane 1 urban fortunate and both continue to exploit and exclude the Lane 2 from the prosperity of the country.

Gandhi's Gram Swarajya

46 eminent personalities wrote in the book, 'Timeless Inspirer' edited by Dr.Mashalkar, internationally known scientist from India, about Mahatma Gandhi's relevance in 21st century.[6] He brought sense to the leaders and made the freedom struggle a mass movement and it was the masses who won the political freedom for the country but their own freedom is yet to be achieved!

Gandhi Tagore Controversy

In response to Tagore's article in which he wrote 'when the bird is awakened by the dawn, it does not only think of food'. 'Its wings respond to the call of the sky', Gandhiji replied:

The human bird under the Indian sky gets up weaker than when he pretended to retire. *For millions it is an eternal vigil or an eternal trance.* I have found it impossible to soothe suffering *patients*[7] with a song from Kabir...'

---

[6] Book Review, The Hindu

[7] PATIENTS: Poverty, Ailments, Trickery, Ignorance, Exploitation, Nakedness, Toil, Starvation

> **'Give them work that they may eat**! "Why should I, who have no need to work for food, spin?" May be the question asked. Because I am eating what does not belong to me. I am living on the spoliation of my countrymen. Trace the source of every coin that finds its way into your pocket, and you will realize the truth of what I write. Everyone must spin. Let Tagore spin, like the others. Let him burn his foreign clothes; that is the duty to-day. God will take care of the morrow. As it says in the Gita, Do right!'[8]

Indian Dilemma to-day is similar to Gandhi – Tagore conflict of ideas. 'Gandhi is nationalist and Tagore is a universalist'

[8] 'Mahatma Gandhi' by Romain Rolland (1924)

is not a correct statement. Both loved humanity abundantly. Only priorities varied in 1921. Tagore died in 1941 before India became independent politically. Gandhi died in 1948 before India attained Grama Swaraj.

We can extend the birds analogy further. In 1934 Tagore wrote extolling Cooperation: 'Imagine if all the small farmers farmed their land collectively, stored their produce in a common facility and sold them through a common mechanism… Only then can we prevent profiteering; only then can the farmer recoup the legitimate value of her labour'. The principle he was extolling was and is '*To-day the economic power has been captured by a small minority. But it has acquired this power only by accumulating the productive power of others. Their capital is simply the accumulated labour of millions of working people, in a monitised form. It is the productive power that is the real capital; and it is this power that latently resides in every worker'.*[9]

That reminds me of the story in *Panchatantra* in which birds of the same feather, flock together and fly in search of food and were caught in the trap laid by the hunter. They fly together using their natural strength of the wings although their legs were tied. Together with the net they fly in a cooperative effort to a place of safety. A friend, rat which had different kind of strengths i.e. biting and cutting the net to free the bonded birds, helped. Similar is the situation with the farmers who can collectively do farming in a cooperative venture to improve their lot. However they need external help which a banker can give. Banker can play RAT: Remove Awful Trap. The task of the rat is Herculean; it has to cut each knot of each individual trap. That is where 'plus' services–individual counselling, advising, guiding, and encouraging are really trying task to the bank Managers. Each one

[9] The Hindu (Year 2012 is declared as U.N. International Year of Cooperation)

of them has been trapped into perpetual indebtedness and fragmentation of land and surrender to the wily money lender. First banker has to redeem all the debts and liabilities of the poor farmer before he could make them stand on their own legs. He has another RAT role: Restore Abandoned Track of self-reliance through collective effort through bank credit plus, services.

The Great Escape

The birds in *Panchatantra* escaped from the impending *threat* by using their *strengths* (wings) and ignoring their *weaknesses* (the tied legs). They had an *opportunity* which they sought (a friendly rat, even the most unlikely resource) to free themselves. SWOT analysis!

Let us turn to Nehru-Gandhi dichotomy which is similar to Lane 1 and Lane 2 dichotomy.

'Gandhi Got Nehru'

"'Don't go near Gandhi, he will get you' was the warning given to the British administrators newly posted in India. Nehru, a Cambridge return, an aristocrat, who wore expensive clothes and moved in high society went near Gandhi and got converted: he took spinning wheel and shunned expensive living. His father Motilal pleaded with Gandhi to spare his only son. Instead of releasing Nehru, he got Motilal, his daughter and everyone of the family members one by one. That was the magic power he wielded.. Mahatma Gandhi saw in Nehru the future custodian of free India."[10]

[10] Gandhi, The Man by Eknath Easwarn.

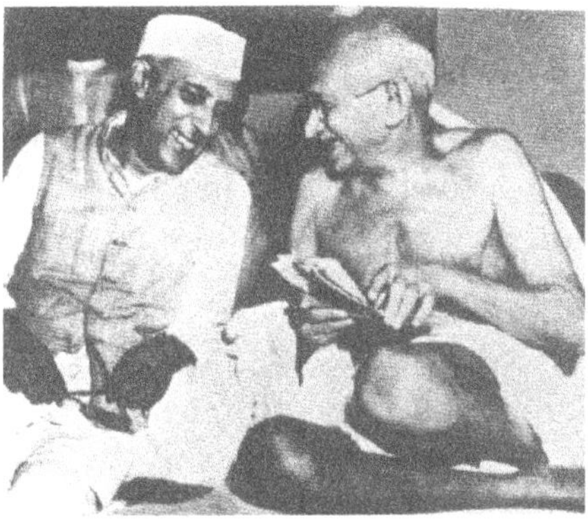

But both agreed on the problems of Indian masses but differed in the solution. Nehru was for growth through industrialization which will eventually solve rural poverty.

Gandhi was not content with political freedom. There is need to liberate the villages – Gram Swarajya. Decentralisation, self-rule and simple living etc.

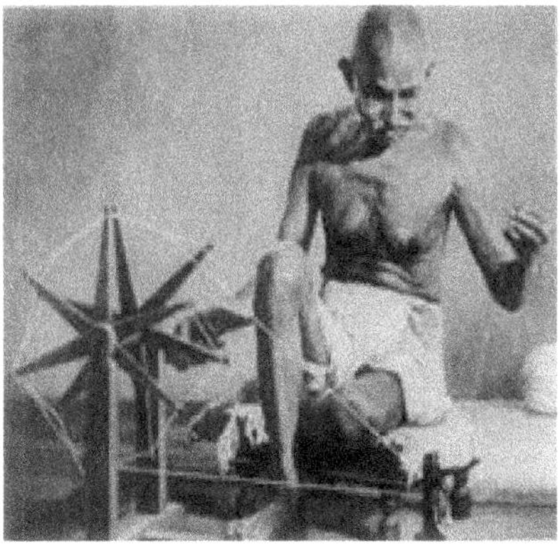

Symbols of The Spinning Wheel

S – Simple & Self-Reliant
P – Production by the Masses
I – Independent & Indigeneous
N – Non-Violent Technology

Gandhi always said that he was not interested in mass production but he was interested in production by the masses; and the technology has to be non-violent, simple, self-reliant and small scale – a technology with a human face. By burning the foreign cloth and relying on indigenous cloth we are becoming independent of the colonial rule.

The charka – spinning-wheel and spinning have become symbols of self-reliance, production by the masses, independence and indigenous economics, and non-violence (SPIN). He asked elite urban educated to shun foreign clothes, burn them in public – and spin and wear home made khadi.

The congressmen followed him in letter but few followed in letter and spirit. Gandhi produced several Gandhis and they are there even now – following non-violence, truth, fearlessness, voluntary poverty holding wealth as trust for the society. Right now when the country is polluted in every manner of life, Gandhism must re-establish itself. Barefoot banker must imbibe in spirit.

Poorna Swaraj (Dec, 1929 by Jawharlal Nehru)[11]

Great as was the success of India in evolving a stable society, she failed and in a vital particular, and because she failed in this she fell and remains fallen. No solution was found for the problem of equality. India deliberately ignored this and built up her

[11] The Great Speeches of Modern India (2011) etc.

social structure on inequality, and we have the tragic consequences of this policy in the millions of our people who till yesterday were suppressed and had little opportunity for growth....

We have three major problems:

1. The minorities, 2. The Indian states, 3. Labour and peasantry

The 3rd is the biggest problem. For India means the peasantry and the labour and to the extent that we raise them and satisfy their wants will we succeed in our task...

We must decide for whose benefit industry must be run and the land produced food. Today the abundance that the land produces is not for the peasant or the labourer who works on it; and industry's chief function is supposed to be to produce millionaires. However golden the harvest and heavy the dividends, the mud huts and hovels and nakedness of our people testify to the glory of the British Empire and our present social system. Our economic programme must therefore be based on a human outlook and must ***not sacrifice man to money***. If an industry cannot run without starving its workers, then the industry must be closed down. If the workers on the land have not enough to eat then the intermediaries who deprive them of their full share must go...

The industrial labour is only a small part of India...it is the *peasantry that cry loudly and piteously for relief* and our programme must deal with their present condition...I hope in doing so we may have the co-operation of some at least of the big land owners...who are our members of congress.

In 1930 India's population was 300 million. Now it is more than a billion. To create an awareness of the need of such magnitude you need barefoot professionals in all walks of life. Bureaucracy, businessmen and politicians nexus is creating the hurdles for the well meaning professionals, activists, NGOs and bureaucrats. A study on the governance revealed that plum posts to the corrupt officers are given by the corrupt ministers while the majority of the honest officers are being harassed![12] The same allegations are made against bankers of late. May be the good are waiting for new *avatar*. But this *avatar* will not be 'one person', one god in the guise of man; it will be in this form of mass movement of the righteous.

The barefoot banker tribe shall grow and take the lead for the economic poverty eradication keeping in mind the cultural change for better – the Gandhian path.

Padayatra – A Campaign (1930)

'Gandhi proposed March with 78 of his most trusted ashram followers to the little coastal town of Dandi some 240 miles away to make salt. When he gave the signals everyone in India was to act as if the salt laws had never been enacted at all. It was non-violent defiance.

He marched with the light, brisk step of an athlete covering about 12 miles a day stopping at every village on the way to preach the Gospel of ahimsa and the duty of non-violent and non-cooperation. By that time he reached Dandi 24 days later his non-violent army of 78 had swelled to several thousands.'[13]

[12] Times of India.

[13] 'Gandhi The Man' by Eknath Eswaran

It was a campaign by one man, an evangelist, the traveling crusader, to right the wrong. He is born timid to become a *brave, autonomous, responsive evangelist* that is what BARE stands for…

Gandhi was on march in March, 1930 by FOOT – *Forward looking,* set his journey covering 12 miles a day-slow-stopping at every village to preach the gospel of ahimsa – *optimistic*, hope and faith, an *outlier* an ordinary man putting out of the ordinary effort, *transparent,* for every body to see and learn.

> 'I claim to be no more than an average man with less than average ability… I have not the shadow of doubt that any man or woman can achieve what I have, if he or she would make the **same effort** and cultivate the **same hope** and faith', Gandhi said.[14]

This should inspire the Barefoot Bankers.

[14] 'Gandhi The Man' by Eknath Eswaran

So also a BARE FOOT banker is an average man who makes an extraordinary effort with faith and hope, an outlier.

There was no precedence for Gandhi's March. Similarly for the Barefoot Banker of 1970s there was no precedence.

A leader always ready to be led by anyone provided the path chosen is clear for everyone.

The same type of mass movement is called for in the next decade to eradicate poverty in the country. Report on Financial Inclusion has some guidelines and deadlines. In 1969 when 14 major banks were nationalized the intention was to make banking mass-banking, a shift from class banking.

Tryst with Destiny (Nehru, Aug,1947)

'Long years ago we made a tryst with destiny, and now time comes when we shall redeem our pledge, not wholly or in full measure but very substantially. At the stroke of midnight hour, when the world sleeps, India will awake to life and freedom...It is fitting that at this solemn moment we take the pledge of dedication to the service of India and her people and to the still larger cause of humanity.

That future is not one of ease or resting but of incessant striving so that we may fulfill the pledge *we have so often taken and the one we shall take today.* The service of India means the service of the millions who suffer, it means *ending of poverty and ignorance and disease and inequality of opportunity* To wipe every tear from every eye....may be beyond us, but *as long as there are tears and suffering, so long our work will not be over.*'

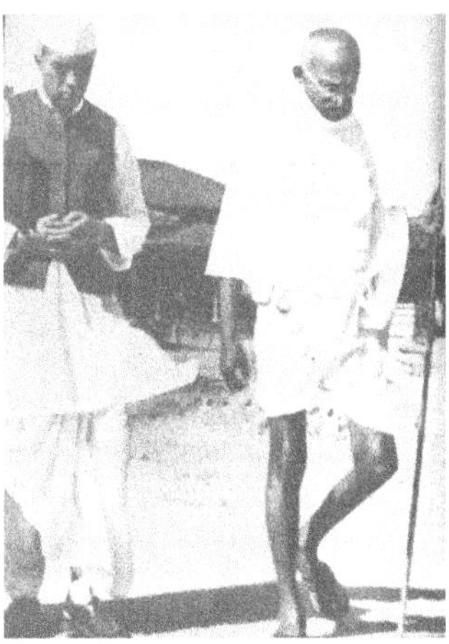

On 30th January 1948
Nehru felt lonely

The Light has Gone out (Jan,1948. Jawharlal Nehru)

The light has gone out, I said, and yet I was wrong. For the light that shone in this country was no ordinary light. The light that has illumined this country...will illumine this country for a thousand years...that light will still be seen in this country and the world will see it and it will give solace to innumerable hearts.

For that light represented something more than the immediate present; it represented the living, the eternal truths, reminding us of the right path, drawing us from error, taking this ancient country to freedom....

And while we pray, the greatest prayer that we can offer is to take a pledge to dedicate ourselves to the truth, and to the cause for which this great countryman of ours lived and for which he has died. That is the best prayer that we can offer him and his remains. That is the best prayer that we can offer to India and ourselves. 'Jai Hind.'

My Father, do not rest. (Feb, 1948.Sarojini Naidu)

...My father, do not rest. *Do not allow us to rest. Keep us to our pledge. Give us strength to fulfill our promise, your heirs, your descendants, your stewards, the guardians of your dreams, the fulfillers of India's destiny.* You, whose life was so powerful, make it so powerful –in your death. Far from mortality you've passed by supreme martyrdom in the cause most dear to you.'

Nov 1949–From Closing Speech of the first Constituent Assembly of India

'If we wish to maintain democracy not merely in form, but also in fact, what must we do? The first thing in my judgment we must do is **to hold fast to constitutional methods of achieving our social and economic objectives.** It means we must abandon the bloody methods of revolution. It means that we must abandon the method of **civil disobedience, non-cooperation and satyagraha.**

'When there was no way left for constitutional methods for achieving economic and social objectives, there was a great deal of justification for unconstitutional methods. But where constitutional methods are open, there can be no justification for these unconstitutional methods. These methods are nothing but the grammar of anarchy and the sooner they are abandoned, the better of us...'

'In India Bhakti or what may be called the path of devotion or hero-worship, plays a part in its politics unequalled in magnitude by the part it plays in the politics of any other country in the world. Bhakti in religion may be a road to the salvation of the soul. But in politics, Bhakti or hero-worship is a sure road to degradation and to eventual dictatorship…'

'These are my reflections about the tasks that lie ahead of us. They may not be very pleasant to some, but there can be no gain saying that political power in this country has too long been the monopoly of a few and the many are not only beasts of burden, but also beasts of prey. This monopoly has not merely deprived them of their chance of betterment, it has sapped them of what may be called the significance of life. These down-trodden classes must not be allowed to develop into a class war. It would lead to a division of the House. That would indeed be a day of disaster…'

We are not yet a Nation

'I remember the days when politically minded Indians resented the expression 'the people of India'. They preferred the expression 'the Indian nation.' I am of opinion that in believing that we are a nation, we are cherishing, a great delusion.

How can people divided into several thousands of castes be a nation? The sooner we realize that we are not as yet a nation in the social and psychological sense of the word, the better for us. For then only we shall realize the necessity of becoming a nation and seriously think of ways and means of realizing the goal. The realization of this goal is going to be very difficult – far more difficult than it has been in the United States. The United States has no caste problem. In India there are castes.

The castes are anti-national in the first place, because they bring about separation in social life. They are anti-national also because they generate jealousy and antipathy between caste and caste. But we must overcome all these difficulties if we wish to become a nation in reality. For fraternity can be a fact only when there is a nation. Without fraternity, equality and liberty will be no deeper than coats of paint.'

Talisman's from two great souls of India

1. Whenever you are in doubt, or when the self is too much with you, apply the following test.

'Recall the face of the poorest and weakest... person whom you may have seen, and ask yourself, the step you contemplate is going to be of any use to that person. Will that person gain restore him or her to a control over his or her own life and destiny?

Mahatma Gandhi

2. 'Feel, my children, feel. Feel for the poor, the ignorant, the down trodden, feel till the heart stops and the brain reels and you think you will go mad, then pour the soul out at the feet of the Lord, and then will come **power to help** and indomitable energy'.

Swami Vivekananda

One for decision and the other for action.

Many young men and women in any career will be moved hearing such words. This historical knowledge will enable them to serve the rural masses with confidence.

A talisman is a ring or stone engraved with symbols that are supposed to bring good luck, ward off evils and give magic power. A barefoot banker must have talismans to sustain his good work in a society i.e. turning bad to worse. While banking offers a challenging and exciting career to attract the youth, the youth must also be exposed to such rhetoric you find above.

* * * * *

POST INDEPENDENCE INITIATIVES & RHETORIC

Indian Drama

- 'British Imperialism produced poverty, or at least held India back while Europe went ahead partly from 1800 when the standards of living were about the same in all parts of Asia and Europe.

- In 1948 AICC avowed: A quick and progressive rise in the living standard of the people should be the primary consideration governing the economic activities and relevant administrative measures... The achievement of a national minimum standard in respect of all the essentials of physical and social well-being within reasonable period must be pursued as practical goal of all schemes for economic development.

- 'Nehru government provided both growth and welfare, not with much success.'

- There has been Gandhi-Nehru dichotomy in Indian initiatives – Development of Nehru and Welfare of Gandhi. Gandhi's emphasis was on villages and village development. Nehru's focus was capital intensive industrial development which he believed will have trickle down effect.

- Indira Gandhi, who from the beginning of her premiership had been a reluctant reformer, announced the Nationalization of India's 14 largest banks.

- Indira Gandhi told Chief Executives of these banks: I know banking is staid and conservative profession. But the bankers must rise to meet the aspirations and heightened expectations of people. I know expectations run ahead of capacities to fulfill them.
- Government did not rest with it. It set targets and initiated programmes. IRDP-Integrated Rural Development Programme – 20 point programmes.
- The Finance Minister said on the floor of parliament: What we aim at is not make-believe employment programme but a systematic and integrated utilization of human and natural resources in which everyone will engage himself or herself in some gainful employment and satisfy *basic minimum needs.*
- The financial resources to come partly from the government and partly from the banks.
- Under Lead Bank scheme introduced the district administration was entrusted with implementation of poverty alleviation programmes. DLCC-District Level Coordination Committee headed by the District Collector as Chairman–meetings were attended by the Managers of banks in district head quarters.
- The bank Managers were gaining new experiences which their superiors lacked.
- In the mean time there was pressure on the government for economic reforms.
- 63 years of independence and 11 five-year plans have helped the Lane 1. 'In the two decades of planning, it was hoped, that the implementation of *land reforms* measures

would transform the agrarian structure, release the productive energies of the long-suffering peasantry and usher in an egalitarian social order'. Nothing happened. 'The experience of the East Asian countries in this period (post Second World war) demonstrated that land reforms could indeed play a significant role in reducing rural poverty'. China's redistribution has been to the extent of 43 percent, Taiwan 37 percent, 33 percent in Japan, 32 percent South Korea'. 'Against these, the extent of redistribution in India was a negligible 6 percent! 'The Community Development programme aimed at the all-round development of villages' laying emphasis on agricultural extension, minor irrigation, education, comprehensive health care and other development activities' was launched in the second five year plan. 'It collapsed because of politics' said Mr.P.S.Appu, Chief Secretary of Bihar and former Director of L.B.Shastri National Academy of Administration in Massoorie.

- 'The framers of 6th plan correctly identified three cardinal failures of Indian planning: failure in full employment, failure to eradicate poverty, and failure to create a more equal society', the measures to remedy the situation proved inadequate.
- There were modest movers towards a more liberal economic regime in the early 1980s, more so after Rajiv Gandhi became Prime Minister. Growth did accelerate in the late 1980s and this was partly due to these liberalization measures but also to an over-expansionary fiscal policy.
- *Finally 'the newly elected Narasimha Rao government, with Man Mohan Singh as Finance Minister, responded to the*

balance of payments crisis by embarking on an extension programmes of liberalization.

- *'The financial sector was liberalized and banking supervision was strengthened'.*
- *After 1996 it was 'ending reservation policy for small-scale sector enterprise–a policy that has hampered growth and done nothing for social justice... and involvement in rural areas. [Computers for elite and Charkha for the rural]*
- *The truth was the Gandhi-Nehru mixture-growth with social justice-that it assumed marginalization of agriculture and rural life.*
- *Capital intensive investment and liberalization, privatization, and globalization (LPG) has reduced employment opportunities and poverty persists*

That's the summary of Indian Drama.

SPECIES Poverty

Dr.B.V.Parameshwara Rao of B.C.Trust, a Voluntary Organization described poverty as 7 fold. I have reduced it to an acronym – SPECIES Poverty and diagram below:

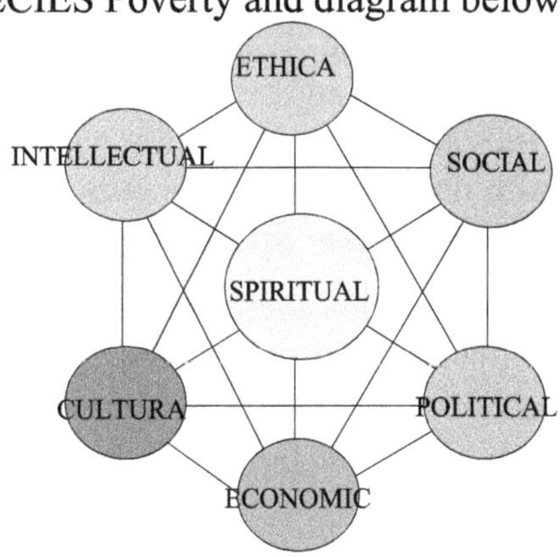

The diagram depicts the complexity of the problem. Poverty will persist unless all the inter-related dimensions of degradation is appreciated and the problem can be solved only holistically. Metaphysical awareness and ethical behaviour through education is called for.

SPECIES: Social, Political, Economic, Cultural, Intellectual, Ethical, and Spiritual. That explains why socio-economic poverty persists. We have been having fragmented approach to poverty alleviation as merely economic poverty. SPECIES looks at it holistically – 7 headed monster.

Social, Political, Economic Poverty

Scarlet Epstein, as already referred, said that globalization is 'disturbing India's social fabric.' Every body agrees that the Indian village is a swamp of inequity. Socio-economic aspect of poverty needs no explanation. Take political poverty; lack of political will, and policy poverty. That is not the end. Power, possessions, prestige, privileges, money power, corruption, competition, big fights in media and in assemblies and parliament go on while lakhs of Lane 2 suicides continue. Scams, scandals, fighting cases, defending corruptions are the features of Lane 1. Greed and envy rule the Lane 1. Here is a sample. While opposition stalls parliament for agreeing for J.P.C., the government and the political parties in power defend by showing scams in the previous regime. Both drag issues to the court. RTI act brings out skeletons in the cupboards of every political party.

Vigilance people say that there are enough laws to book the corrupt; no body has the nerve to book until a hue and cry is made. 'Discretionary land powers not meant for the rich,' says Supreme Court,[1] the head lines. 'If the poor benefited, it was ahead of

[1] The Hindu

elections, our babus always serve their masters'. Babus are bureaucrats who join hands with ministers to deny the Lane 2 poor, what is their due. Their ignorance is bliss of the corrupt. Political degradation starts once the elections are over. Poor man waits till next election when the politician embraces them and sheds crocodile tears.

I am reminded of the essay, *Art of Political Lying* written in 1710, two hundred years ago by Jonathan Swift still valid for the Indian context today.

Art of Political Lying by Jonathan Swift (1710)

- We are told, "the Devil is the father of lies, and was a liar from the beginning"; so that beyond contradiction, the invention is old: forced to exercise his talent in inferior regions among other fallen spirits, or poor deluded men, whom he still daily tempts to his own sin, and will ever do so till he is chained in the bottomless pit.
- But though the Devil be the father of lies, he seems, like other great inventors, to have lost much of his reputation, by the continual improvements that have been made upon him.
- When tumults and seditions are quieted, rumours and false reports are plentifully spread through a nation. So that by this account, *lying* is the last relief of a routed, earth-born, rebellious party in a state. But here, the moderns have made great additions, applying this *art to the gaining of power, and preserving it, as well as revenging themselves after they have lost it:*
- Adding some circumstances of its birth and parents. A political lie is sometimes born out of a discarded statesman's head, and thence delivered to be nursed and dandled by the mob. Sometimes it is produced a monster,

and *licked* into shape; at other times it comes into the world completely formed, and is spoiled in the licking. It's often born an infant in the regular way, and requires time to mature and often it sees the light in its full growth, but dwindles away by degrees. Sometimes it is of noble birth; and sometimes the spawn of a stock-jobber. *Here*, it screams aloud at the opening of the womb; and *there*, it is delivered with a whisper.

- It can conquer kingdoms without fighting, and sometimes with the loss of a battle: It gives and resumes employments; can sink a mountain to a mole-hill, and raise a mole-hill to a mountain; has presided for many years at committees of elections; can wash a blackamoor white; make a saint of an atheist, and a patriot of a profligate; can furnish foreign ministers with intelligence, and raise or let fall the credit of the nation. *This goddess flies with a huge looking-glass in her hands, to dazzle the crowd, and make them see, according as she turns it, their ruin in their interest, and their interest in their ruin.*
- There is one essential point wherein a political liar differs from others of the faculty; that he ought to have but a short memory, which is necessary according to the various occasions he meets with every hour, of differing from himself, and swearing to both sides of a contradiction, as he finds the persons disposed, with whom he has to deal. In describing the virtues and vices of mankind, it is convenient upon every article, to have some eminent person in our eye, from whence we copy our description.
- The superiority of his genius consists in nothing else but an inexhaustible fund of political lies, which he plentifully distributes every minute he speaks, and by an unparalleled

generosity forgets, and consequently contradicts the next half-hour. He never yet considered whether any proposition were true or false, but whether it were convenient for the present minute or company to affirm or deny it;

- And besides, that will take off the horror you might be apt to conceive at the oaths wherewith he perpetually tags both ends of every proposition: though at the same time I think he cannot with any justice be taxed for perjury, when he invokes God and Christ, because he has often fairly given public notice to the world, that he believes in neither.
- Few lies carry the inventor's mark; and the most prostitute enemy to truth may spread a thousand without being known for the author.
- if a lie be believed only for an hour, it has done its work, and there is no farther occasion for it. *Falsehood flies, and Truth comes limping after it*; so that when men come to be undeceived, it is too late, the jest is over, and the tale has had its effect: like a man who has thought of a good repartee, when the discourse is changed, or the company parted: or, like a physician who has found out an infallible medicine, after the patient is dead.
- Considering that natural disposition in many men to lie, and in multitudes to believe, I have been perplexed what to do with that maxim, so frequent in every body's mouth, that "Truth will at last prevail after the purpose of lie is served.
- It is only a short madness in the vulgar, from which they may soon recover.

A case study on political poverty

'Words come from the depths of truth'. The slip of the tongue is not truly slip but a flip-flippant remark – coming from deep troubled mind. When people rallied behind Anna Hazare, the press were pressurizing politicians to comment on the happenings. One Ex-Chief Minister of one party makes a flippant remarks and others are quick to attack him.[2]

The first one was reported to have said: 'if Mahatma were to be alive now, he would have either quit public life or become corrupt'. He also added: 'It is difficult to build any political party without being corrupt'. 'He said', the report said, 'his party received donations and it was a sort of corruption as those who make donations would *naturally* demand favours'. Logical enough. This logic, Gandhi never accepted.

He too collected donations and gifts from the rich and poor alike for the cause of freedom struggle. Women gave away gold bangles and chains to Gandhi without taking permission from the parents and husbands. They were spontaneous donations without expecting anything in return.

Several others refused to comment, except saying 'it speaks of the man'. One argued, 'It is *unfortunate* that such remarks had come at a time when the entire country has seen a movement against corruption after a long time and rallied behind Mr.Hazare'.

There was a spirited support from the 'accused' politician's father. He too said that 'Gandhi would have committed suicide seeing the present day politics. That was the spirit behind his son's remark.'

---

[2] The Hindu

Finally the originator of the controversy answered denying the remarks attributed to him.

'I was misquoted: I have not told that if Mahatma Gandhi was alive he would have been corrupt. That is not the word I said. In this situation, I think Gandhi would have run away from politics. Because, at present juncture, the way in which politics is going on, the way expenditure is going on for a politician.'

But his father said something more honest: 'no politician has any moral right to comment on Father of the Nation. But he was not after power.'

Anyway the Pandora Box has been opened.

Pandora

'Soon after the world has been created, Pandora Box, it was only inhabited by men.. there was no place for disease, no place for negative feelings. Zeus sent a woman to cause troubles to men. He called her Pandora – all gifted – gods and goddesses gave her gifts – beauty, charm and the art of flattery. But Zeus gave her a special box which she was forbidden to open. Pandora, the curious woman could not resist opening the box. At once a swarm of little winged monsters flew out. They were disease, envy, anger, revenge, and all other curses that brought happy times end and left all miserable. Pandora tried to close the box, but it was too late. *Only Hope was left,* all others escaped flown over the world.'

It was Greek story, and 'Opening of Pandora Box' became phrase apt for the situation 2010-11.

It was not politics that Gandhi shunned but – power, privileges, corruption and hypocrisy of politicians. It is the Gandhi spirit in masses that will drive away the corrupt politicians and their ilk in Lane 1 whose one goal in life is amassing wealth and displaying it as hard earned money.

Politics have become expensive because elections have become expensive because of envy, cut-throat competition. As long as half the population is hungry and dependent, the politics of money will win elections because, the poor man is asserting himself–bargaining for more and more dole-outs – politician might say, the poor have become too clever and greedy. Poor are aware that part of the bargain is pilfered. 'Let us make merry at least once in 5 years. By-elections come as bonus' they say. This is the lie, Gandhi's truth lies in the dignity of man, self respect. He was opposed to doles. 'Give the poor work that they may eat'. There is argument in favour of 'cash transfer' direct to the house-hold. It is easy to give 'dole-outs' than create jobs which is on the decline since 2 decades–the dawn of reforms and growth obsession.

Wherever Gandhi went he collected money for the Harijans (Children of God). Middle-class Indian women, particularly in the villages, used to wear every gold ornament they owned, and there was a saying that a man's best bank is his wife's neck. Gandhi found this a little ostentatious when so much of the country was near starvation, and he took every opportunity to appeal to such women to give up their gold necklaces, earrings, and bangles to be sold for Harijan service.

Not even children were safe from this prince of beggars. He was so irresistible that whenever his train pulled into a station, no matter what time of the day or night, great crowds of people of all ages would be waiting to press their money and jewelry into his outstretched hands. "We must step down from our pedestals and live with them–not as outsiders, but as one of them in every way, sharing their burdens and sorrows." Gandhi used to appeal to all philanthropists.

This is the heart of Gandhi's approach. He taught, above all, by personal example. He went and lived with the Harijans; and to encourage them to improve their health and sanitation, he himself became their servant. Hundreds of his followers made their homes in poor villages throughout India, living with the people, teaching and encouraging them by their own example to release themselves from the bondage of ignorance, squalor, superstition, and the utter poverty which followed three hundred years of foreign exploitation.

Gandhiji produced several Gandhis; they are there in the country even now without name and fame.

'Tens of thousands of hectares have been given away to corporations for commercialization in the guise of airport development, construction of highways, creation of Special Economic Zones and so on, at prices that are less than 10 per cent of the value of those tracts of land.'

'Apart from creating huge incentives for corruption, such policies have resulted in the involuntary displacement **of lakhs of the poorest people, leaving them on the brink of starvation and forcing many of them to join the Maoists,'** one critic wrote.

Anti-democratic & UnGandhian

'Many people believe that the hunger strike Anna Hazare undertook and the ultimatum he served were coercive in nature and have *no place in a democracy.* The attempt made by some of his followers to equate him with Gandhiji need not be taken seriously, as neither *his ideas nor his methods justify such a claim…*' writes K.N.Panikkar.

'Arundhati Roy says, 'Jan Lokpal Bill is unGandhian, concentrating power in the hands of a few.

Recall Ambedkar's last speech to the Constituent Assembly: we must abandon the methods of civil disobedience, non-cooperation, and satyagraha.. these methods are nothing but the grammar of anarchy.

'His agitation has been lionized by some people as a second freedom struggle. But it appears to have escaped general notice that the assertion of a few to represent the majority without any representative character is essentially *anti-democratic,'* concluded Mr.Panikkar.

K.N.Panikkar adds: 'The neo-liberal policies pursued by the ruling elite had opened up the possibility of corruption in the massive transfer of public assets and the promotion of corporate interests through political patronage… The unprecedented levels of corruption in recent times are a concomitant of the economic conditions created by liberalization.'

'Corruption is a complex issue that is embedded in bureaucratic rigidity and issues of economic access and political power. In this sense, the state is the main promoter of corruption. It cannot be reduced to a question of morality alone, nor can a solution be found by punishing individuals as a deterrent…'

'The aim of the bill is not to prevent corruption but to punish the corrupt… If *Jan Lokpal* is to live upto its *jan* character, its authoritarian and centralised structure should be dispensed with and it should be turned into an instrument of people's empowerment. **A beginning towards this end should be made at the formative stage itself by sending the draft bill to every**

panchayat for discussion, so that nation's conscience is truly aroused.'

In his new year (2012) message to the nation Dr.Singh said, 'with the economic reforms new forms of corruption have emerged which have to be tackled'. 'It is critical to eliminate corruption to support genuine entrepreneurship'[3].

One of the age old forms of corruption is the ROPE TRICK

ROPE TRICK: Rhetoric On Poverty Elimination
The Great Indian ROPE Trick

The rope is made to stand and a boy is made to climb it and disappear and reappear on the ground collecting coins. The Western magician tried to explain the act as a conjuring trick in which the onlookers in the street are hypnotized to create an illusion. The truth is the trick believed to be true by the Westerner was never seen, only heard.

While the boy is seen collecting the coins from the wondering public, the politician of today distributes notes collects votes.

Playing the TRICK –

Tantalizing
Rattling
Inducing
Conjuring
Knack

[3] The Hindu

PALM LEAF: Poverty Alleviation Legal Measures. Legal Entitlement And Food security.

Lane 1 people *Palm off greasing the palm* of the powerful having *itching palms* while the Lane 2 poor *yielding the palm.* Lane 1 people *bear the palm* alone palming off the lane2 and wearing the palm leaf in triumph.

Living under the shadow of PALM

Rope Palm: Poor are *roped* in with all types of lies. They are *Palmed off* easily. PALM is one way. Even if the LEAF is there they *know not the ropes.* They are given a *long rope* which comes handy to kick the bucket when they come to the *end of rope*: The long ROPE–began on 15th August, 1947: 'as long as there are tears and suffering, so long our work will not be over'. 'How long?', the man in the shadow of death asks!

'O Mother Earth every time our politicians disclose their assets their wealth has grown by leaps and bounds. I feel giddy reading. How do they do that? If that secret is known to farmers like me, we wipe out all our debts and look after agriculture peacefully.

O Mother Earth bless my country. We farmers are an umbilical cord who connect mankind with you, mother … My grandfather used to quote the great Tamil sage. Thiruvalluvar who has dedicated 10 couplets to us – agriculture was considered noblest professions. A satirist wrote.[4]

The secret is of course GREED!

---

[4] The Hindu

But the ROPE Trick I have in mind is acronym *Rhetoric On Poverty Elimination* that has been going on ever since Independence in India is a TRICK – *Tantalizing, Rattling, Inducing, Conjuring, Knack* the politicians have perfected in a way. To understand the knack we must refer to Jonathan Swift's satirical essay, 'The Art of Political Lying' written in 1710. After 300 years it is interesting to read and find the parallels in India.

Joseph Addison was a member of British Parliament, who never spoke on the floor of the Parliament on any day. But he wrote an article on the topics discussed in the Parliament on the next day in the Daily *Spectator* to the dismay of the members. On only one occasion he ventured to speak on the floor of Parliament at the insistence of some members. He rose to say, 'I conceive, I conceive… I conceive' and sat down inviting a comment from a lady member who said 'Sir Joseph conceived thrice and brought forth nothing,' to the mirth of all the members.

Similar but sad was the situation on the floor of Rajya Sabha, on 27th December, 2011, when two distinguished members of Rajya Sabha kept mum but articulated a few days later their views on corruption and Lokpal. One was Prime Minister whose new year message was already mentioned – *economic reforms, eliminating corruption* and *genuine entrepreneurship.* The other was Dr.M.S.Swaminathan who wrote *'Corruption-free India'* is a prerequisite for '*hunger-free India*' in an article in The Hindu on 3rd, January, 2012.

Putting the two divergent statements together we can say *genuine entrepreneurship is one which eliminates both hunger and corruption.*

Another form of corruption
Pearls to the powerful;
Peanuts for the powerless

In 1948 Indian National Congress AICC resolution was the first lie, a palter, insincere promise it proved. Most political lies are paltering making unreliable statements or insincere promises. That is the trick the Lane 1 politician, economist, social activists, intellectuals, scientists, corporate sector, marketers, and majority from urban elite have been playing on Lane 2.

Election time is the time when *swarms of flying lies are let loose.*

As this talking trick is not working, during election time, Lane 2 is showered with 'gifts'. The 'observers' or 'election watch' seem to come in the way of poor gathering what is their only right, to collect doles once in 5 years. Let all political parties freely dole out TV sets, cell phones, and laptops – the gifts are changing from clothes to articles in which corporate sector join hands. But the best gift is gold and silver not tarnished money in cash.

Some Examples – from the Horse's Mouth

1. Delivering Sir Sorabji Pochkhana Wala Memorial Lecture organized by Central Bank of India, the Finance Minister has another rhetoric: 'In the post crisis period, we have seen how unfettered growth of financial sector can have dangerous implications for both in developed and the developing world'. 'Financial stability and the banking system become an integral part of policy discussions.. the global crisis has compelled policy makers to *rethink* some of the principles of economic management'. '..well regulated, vibrant, fast-growing … matching with global' best practices in capital adequacy, risk management, business growth.. Indian Banking has done commendable job in meeting the vast banking and credit requirements of an economy which has a growth rate close to 9 percent in the last few years'. *'However, he regretted, the fruits of banking had not been*

distributed universally' ..Financial Inclusion is a key determinant of sustainable and inclusive growth which in turn, is essential for building an equitable society..

'A major unfinished part is to promote greater financial literacy and investor protection'.

'I see 'Swabhimaan' as a watershed in the evolution of Indian Banking'. 'Swabhimaan', a multimedia company designed to inform, educate and motivate people to open bank accounts.. business correspondents.

2. 'Work to ease disparities' Prime Minister tells scientists.

'the pace of reform in India will depend on how far the government policies meet the test of democratic consensus and take into account the *vulnerabilities of different sections of our population*' (March 26, 2011). He advised the companies undertaking green-field projects not to see their factories as 'bases' cut off from the needs and interests of the community around them.

'We need to work out more effective mechanisms and principles for the use of *land and other resources* that reconcile different interests, he said.

'The country still has to deal with the problems of mass poverty, hunger and disease and corruption'. 'We need to bridge the enormous infrastructure deficit, regional divide, and digital divide.'

'We have to upgrade skills, social services, boost manufacturing in order to provide employment opportunities for youth' and take advantage of Demographic Dividend.'

3. Finance Minister bats for financial inclusion (May 2011)

'Financial Inclusion is a key determinant of sustainable and inclusive growth, which in turn is essential for, building an equitable society.'

Lies, damn lies and statistics

One known drunkard in the village approached bank Manager for a loan for cart for carrying dirty linen of nearby Mission Hospital to the tank for washing and delivering back to the hospital on daily basis.

The villagers warned the Manager that the loan would not be repaid because the borrower will drink and waste the money and that he would never buy a cart.

But the Manager interviewed the applicant and promised to grant loan after verifying with the hospital authorities. He asked the Regional Manager whether he could finance for donkeys! Prompt was the reply from the higher authority that there was no scheme for donkeys.

Financing for donkeys instead of a cart was the Manager's idea to reduce the risks of financing a drunkard. He convinced the borrower for the revised project and granted Rs.300/- to buy 3 donkeys and 1 baby donkey – a family. Soon an inspector arrived and raised an objection for having granted the loan without a scheme. Manager's argument about the whole process of appraisal for economy i.e. viability and technical feasibility and pliability fell on the deaf ears. By the time he was called for explanation; the loan was repaid in full and the borrower gave up drinking and became active entrepreneur continuing his services to the hospital making him eligible by 'up-gradation' of credit worthiness and improvement of standard of living.

Enterprising Manager financing for purchase of donkeys

The Manager shared all this in his talk to the members of the local Rotary Club.

The foregoing is a real story. Now read the fibble.

The washer men in the area organized themselves and brought to the notice of the M.P. of the area that a scheme of donkeys under 'live-stock' programme should be approved by Government of India.

M.P. shot off a question as to how many donkeys were there in the country as on 31st March… Based on the reply by concerned Union Minister, M.P. thought he would put supplementary questions and fix the Minister.

So the Minister passed on the query to the Secretary who sent to all Chief Secretaries of the States who in turn passed on to the District Collectors. All the BDOs and VDOs were alerted. VDOs and sarpanches go on '*padayatra*' in search of donkeys in the villages. They count and get tired and stop search and simply add 10 percent to the count.

10 percent is the standard long established practice and the number given at each stage is increased by 10 percent till it reached the Union Minister. He glanced at the figure given by his Secretary to the last digit and told him that the figure was incorrect. He broke the surprise within a minute: 'add two to the figure. One is you and the other myself,' the Minister said.

It was a donkey's work to collect data and answer questions in Parliament, he thought. So you know why the saying 'Lies, Damn lies, and Statistics' in that order has gained currency.

'Facts plus' become data. The data becomes information for the planners, policy makers, and politicians. On the way the 'data' undergoes so many changes and the final product has no resemblance to the fact. You may not agree but read the box below.

Spruce up the data (Editorial)[5]

'Reserve Bank of India Governor Duvvuri Subbarao's recent critical observations on the authenticity and quality of key economic data will be widely endorsed by those who rely on the data for myriad purposes both official and non-official. Coming from the head of an institution, which is the most significant user of such data for policy making, the observations are particularly noteworthy…'

'For instance, the advanced estimate made in February 2010 pegged GDP growth for 2009-10 at 6.8 per cent. Three months later, it was revised to 7.7 per cent and again, in February 2011, to 9.1 per cent, a staggering 40 per cent variation in what is the most important number on the economy. Policy making based on such inaccurate, provisional data can lead to "sub-optimal results"…'

[5] The Hindu

'Dr.Subbarao's critical comments extend to the entire gamut of economic statistics... It is not first time that the reliability of official statistics has been publicly called into question.' (Report)

.. Statistics

Data collection for answering arliament question.

'Please add 10% to the figure.'

There are 100 crows on the tree; one of them was shot how many are left. The school boy who gave the answer 'zero' failed!

Loan Mela – A campaign or a political lie?

Credit camps are a characteristic of mass banking where large number of loan applications are cleared. The applications are stereotyped small amounts for small borrowers identified, the whipped up government official a target based approach. Small Farmers Development Agency, caste based SC, ST, and BC corporations collected and presented the lists to the bank for consideration and sanction.

The banks were taking their own 'sweet' time to take up these weaker section schemes. In the mean time the peoples' aspirations and expectations are aroused and they pressurize the peoples representatives. To avoid individual MLAs or MPs taking up the case with individual banks the political party in rule devised what is called *Loan Mela* where and when the minister or bureaucrat would distribute sanction letters in an well organized mass meeting.

This became a worry to the grass-roots Manager in the beginning. He reconciled to the idea when the higher management joined hands with the executive and legislature two wings of democracy.

This gave rise to accumulation of pending sanction letters without delivery of loans. Again it is the turn of the politician and bureaucrat to pressurize and censure the grass-roots Manager who tried to demand strengthening of the systems, staff, skills and structures from their own management. These were considered as teething problems till over jealous party politics made a mess of loan melas organizing them on a grand style in sports stadium with widest possible publicity.

The whole idea of 'awareness, advertisement and publicity' campaigns have become 'lies' in the eyes of the poor and they played their part in the games – psychological games – dishonesty of transactions – and ROPE TRICK. In the case no.18, story 3, the minister and the bank's zonal Manager hand over the rope to the beneficiary of diary loan symbolizing the loan sanction.

Photos are taken and prominently published in the local dailies. Photographs are important. Why not Manager's photo who is directly accountable to all such loaning? Well, now he gets legitimacy of such 'melas'. The zonal Manager and minister may repeat at another place in another state. But the local manger does the trick again and again till the next inspection followed by investigation and implication of imprudence or impudence are pointed.

All this constitute TRICK – paltering. Barefoot bankers were never a party to these short terms measures which are anti-thesis of eradication of poverty.

Victim of Loan Mela

The case 5 episode 9 is about loan mela in 1977. Managers were generally shy on those occasions. But some shared the dias with Ministers and enjoyed the politician's praise. The positive feed back by way of appreciation have made some Managers unwittingly fall prey to the TRICK and landed themselves in trouble because of jealousies and competition for the lime-light and career progression. There are others who kept the people's representatives at a distance and earned the appreciation of the rural people but also earned the wrath of local politicians. There was a time when one Union Minister in his enthusiasm to impress the party bosses had organized Loan Melas in big stadiums and on a mass scale. The beneficiaries were loyal to the political party leaving credit discipline to winds. These events have made many a good banker withdraw from the sincere attempts in poverty alleviation programmes. The bright spots were put in a spot, fix. What was going on smoothly in 1970s and 1980 had a set back and more and more honest Managers had to suffer. Others who came later looked at the negative side of the whole affair. Even collectors were unhappy about the political interference. We can't paint all politicians with the same brush. Politics, Politicians, and Diplomacy – If you do your job well and are transparent you can manage political interference.

Cultural and Intellectual Poverty

Culture means cultivation of soil/agriculture; it means raising, improving, developing plant, animal, and human beings. It also means tastes, manners and habits. There is cultural poverty in soil, plant, animal and human due to corruption everywhere.

The economist who follows Keynes is an example. In 1930, Keynes wrote that for another 100 years we must pretend that 'foul is fair, because foul is useful'.[6] During these 100 years he speculated that the 'invisible hand' of Adam Smith of 18th century, will operate when everybody will be rich by being selfish, greedy, and usurious and self-protecting as right principles. That prediction will have to end in another 20 years. There are no signs of its happening. Every economist is predicting that hunger and poverty will disappear by 2020. 'Not more than average Gandhi with less than average ability – showed the way in 1930 itself. 'Earth provides enough for every man's need, but not for everyman's greed'.[7] What ails lane 1, I repeat, is Greed: Getting; Rich; Easily; Eagerly; Double quick devoid of ethics and ENVY: Eliminating Notion of Values and Yeoman service.

The rich 'must be intelligent enough from time to time to help the poor because this is the only way by which they will become richer still' and free from in-security born out of fear psychosis. They must be intelligent enough to see that peace and permanence which they seek are not found in economic prosperity but in keeping 'the inner house in order'. The intellectual poverty lies in the belief that material prosperity is the road to peace and permanence'.

Proper use of Land[8]

'Man has despoiled environment that sustained him all along. He forgot that he is child and not master of the world, whether savage or civilized.' He is slowly learning that he must conform his actions to laws of nature if he has to remain viable – able to maintain independent existence in a specified environment, obeying the natural laws. *The proper use of land* is one issue. 'The

---

[6] Small is Beautiful
[7] Ibid
[8] Ibid

proper use of land', E.F.Schumacher said, 'poses, not a technical nor an economic, but, primarily a metaphysical problem'. Land is not a 'factor of production' but is a sacred gift to mankind for its own survival and one and half million other species.' For Indians it is God. We use the term land as if it is man made. 'A farmer is considered simply as a producer who must cut costs and raise his efficiency by every possible device, even if he destroys – the health of the soil and beauty of the landscape, and even if the end effect is the depopulation of the land and overcrowding of cities'. That is the result of our thinking that land is a factor of production and not as life giving and generous earth. 'In our time, the main danger to the soil, and there with not only to agricultural but to cultivation as whole, stems from the towns-man's determination to apply to agriculture the principles of industry.' *Agriculture is not a paying proposition. It is a living proposition.*

Ethical Poverty

That brings us to the 6th element in poverty – Ethical poverty. Lack of ethics or ethical behaviour, which is hurting lane 2 people stems from the spiritual poverty – not being aware of the metaphysical origin of man. It is not religious but secular spirituality that is being addressed.

Mr.Narayana Murthy of Infosys was conferred the World Entrepreneurship award for the year 2003 for "*Running the company philosophically, spiritually, ethically and financially in an outstanding manner in an industry which is dynamic and volatile*".

Where are such entrepreneurs in India?

'If the laws suitably modified and efficiently *implemented*,' it may be possible to eradicate poverty. The problem is in implementation – the ethical poverty has to be first managed with a firm hand because it cannot be eradicated.

Political poverty is policy poverty plus ethical poverty that brings us to the spiritual poverty.

Spirit –Centered, Ego-Transcending Leadership

'The only work that spiritually purifies that which is done without personal motives, without desire for fame or public recognition or worldly greatness, without insistence on one's mental motives or vital lusts… without vanity or crude self-assertion or claim for position or prestige, done for the sake of the Divine alone and at the command of the Divine.[9]

Sri Aurobindo (1873-1950)

'All work done in an egoistic spirit, however good for people in the world of the Ignorance, is of no avail to the seeker of the yoga.'

A Few Precautions[10]

'Spirituality cannot be asked to prove its credentials before the tribunal of economic growth, enterprise bottom line, shareholder value, and the like. Rather, it is technology, economics, business, and their cohorts which have to pass the test of spirituality. Spirituality has to be the remedy for the growing malignancy in our secular affairs.' (Chakravarthy).

[9] 'Against The Tide' The Philosophical foundations of Modern Manager by Prof. S.K.Chakravarthy.(2003)
[10] Ibid.

'Spiritualized management would mean *Business Ashram* instead of Business casinos, when ego-hunt ceases, when everyone in the *Business Ashram* become free 'liberated from the in-born ego-centricity in the responsible group life–team work–where calm dialogue, rather than fierce debates, defenses, and denials give way, then 'man gets his first chance of achieving spiritually in his inner and outer life'.[11]

On the other hand Self-centered Organisations are defined by Competition, Speed, Consumption of resources particularly non-renewable resources and all sorts of corruption and foul play.

India and China – Race or Journey together?
'Growth and other concerns,' by Amartya Sen in the Hindu 14/02/2010

- While economic growth is an important boon for enhancing living conditions, its reach depends on what to do with the fruits of growth.
- There is little case for confusing (1) the important role of economic growth as a *means* for achieving good things (2) growth of inanimate objects of convenience being taken to be an *end* in itself.
- ...more worryingly this group (Lane 1) of relatively privileged and increased prosperous Indians can easily fall for temptation to treat economic growth as an end in itself, for it serves directly as the means of their opulence and improving life styles without further social efforts.
- In fact, however, that India cannot be seen as doing splendidly if a great many Indians–most Indians–are having very little improvement in their deprived lives.

---

[11] S.K.Chakravarthy.(2003)

Somebody compared China's progress with Hare's speed and India's that of Tortoise. If we adopt Hare's strategy we may allow the traffic in lane 1 to speed up to catch up with China. It was tortoise which completed the 'race' ultimately.

The Winner-3D Approach for Success in Life

The Hare challenged the Tortoise. Tortoise accepted the challenge. Knowing full well its own limitations why did the Tortoise accept the challenge? Hare took it as a race. Tortoise, took it as journey towards a **Destination.**

Hare looked behind at the competitor. Tortoise looked ahead towards the destination. It had right **Direction.** It moved ahead with commitment.

The Hare was proud of its own performance compared to its competitor. Soon it became tired and complacent. The result was deep slumber. Tortoise went ahead unmindful of Hare's behaviours at its own pace in the right direction towards the destination with **Determination.**

Tortoise was the winner who accomplished its declared purpose by adopting **3D Approach – Destination, Direction, Determination.** A new meaning for an old fable.

There were counter attacks on Amartya Sen in the media by some NRI intellectuals who claim that they, with great difficulty, made GOI accept 'growth momentum' but they were sorry a Nobel Laureate had this to say.

India's **destination** can be *inclusive society*; its **direction** is agricultural development and rural employment. Its **determination** lies in the policies and the vigour with which the policies are *implemented.*

The article ends in a cautious note:

In terms of human resources, it is not enough to have lots of young people – these young people need to be properly educated to fully contribute to the new economy.

India can do better, suggests OECD – A Report

National savings could be channeled into areas such as poverty alleviation, says report.

Structural transformation in labour markets had made the services sector a key source of employment

Further in comparative terms China appeared to have better realized the link between poverty alleviation and agricultural growth, while India's modest achievements in poverty reduction may be associated with the relatively poor performance of its agricultural sector, the report noted.

Citing the rapid rise in labour productivity as a key factor driving this growth the study noted that in the case of India structural transformation in labour markets had made the services sector a key source of employment unlike China, where manufacturing appeared to dominate.

India and China Can Learn From Each Other

I – Tsing, the Chinese student studying at the ancient university Nalanda for ten years and returned home to write in 691AD about *medical practices* and *health care* in India and China and compared them. He wrote, 'much can be learned by both the countries from each other.'

Lin Yutang the Chinese philosopher in his book 'The Wisdom of India'[12] had written unforgettable truths: *It is characteristic of Indian thought that, in India, religion and philosophy are inseparable. In India no 'link' between philosophy and religion is necessary, and the problem of finding the fatal missing link in the modern world does not exist.*

Hindu philosophy and the knowledge of God are inseparable as, Chinese philosophy and the questions of human conduct are inseparable.

That is where we in India can learn from the Chinese. *There is too much religion, in India and too little in China,* Lin Yutang lamented. *The trickle of Indian religious spirit overflowed to China and inundated the whole of Eastern Asia.*

It would seem logical and appropriate that any one suffering from a deficiency of the religious spirit should turn to India rather than any other country in the world. That the Christian doctrine of turning other cheek could be turned into a national movement, practiced ***by the masses,*** *only in India and in no other country in the world. India's paradox is the pacifist's paradox the world over. But peace, can come only from non-violence and disbelief in force, and non-violence can come only from India, because Indians seem really to believe in it.*

---

[12] 'The Wisdom of India' by Lin Yutang, 1956.

These words were written in 1956 after studying the fabulous animal fables in *Panchatantra* and Budhist literature, the legacy of India and also *Epics, Puranas*, *Upanishads* and *Rigveda.*

Let us emulate the Chinese in the questions of human conduct, the inseparable element in Chinese philosophy. Peasants come first.

In short we suffer from SPECIES poverty and economic poverty will end only when we turn to Gandhi's socialism which stems from spiritual values – Truth, Non-violence, Simplicity, and Voluntary poverty, need based living, the immortal preaching and *Loka Samastha Sukhino Bhavantu* and start showing the path to the West. Globalisation in reverse order-East to West.

Schumacher, an economist, who wrote 'Small is Beautiful' had to write 'Guide to the Perplexed', to clarify that 'Small is Beautiful' but 'Big' is not ugly. But he emphasized Bigness and unlimited growth is meaningless. 100 years of growth has left a billion people below poverty line. Half of them live in India in spite of the fact the protagonists of growth hope to eradicate poverty. He gave two parallels.[13] 'My grandson must grow, but not myself. It will be disastrous if I grow.' He tells a story about longevity. A boy went into woods and there he met God. The boy asked God, 'is it true that 'one day' to you is equal to thousands of years to the mortals.' 'Yes', God replied.. 'By the same token', the boy asked that 'one dime for you is millions to us.' 'Yes my boy', God replied. The clever boy asked of God, can I borrow a couple of dimes from you?' 'Sure,' God replied, 'but I don't have it on me, wait for 5 minutes I will get back to you'. That's the significance of long term – in the long term we are all dead.

[13] 'Guide to the Perplexed' by E.F. Schumacher.

Schumacher called Gandhi one of the greatest economists of all times. Again he gave a comparison. If you ask any westerner, who is the greatest musician of all times, he would reply, Beethoven, the famous pianist. That's uppermost in his mind. If you ask, how about Mozart, the same person will reply, 'yah, yah, he too is equally great'. Mozart does not come to mind readily. Similarly if you ask the same person who is the greatest economist of all times, pat comes the reply Lord Mynard Keynes. If you draw his attention to Gandhi, he would agree. That is how he described Gandhi as an economist of all times. Average student of economics remembers Keynes, not Gandhi. Schumacher advised in 1960 itself that Indian planners must read Gandhi, the greatest economist, India produced.

That is the relevance of Gandhi an economist who will bring sense to the planners and policy makers in India belonging to the Lane 1 intellectuals followers of Keynes.

Planners want to learn lessons of urbanization from Japan. Their problem has been lack of natural resources – land and water; they are compelled to import and export and grow crops on roof tops. Their strengths lie in patriotism, discipline and team work which we are lacking. There is a saying individually Indians excel while collectively they fail. We have ample land which we are surrendering to industry.

Race or Journey

I thought of some more metaphors from the track events in sports and put my observations in the boxes below!

Sports Metaphor - Track Events

1. Flat Race – The Sprint

'Flat race short distance sprint – long distance running, steeple chasing, and hurdling. Sprint, short distance dash calls for physical stamina and endurance, training and practice. 'The most important thing for good sprinting is 'driving power' which is obtained from powerful leg muscles or strong thick leg muscles for the tall and the short respectively'. LPG is giving the driving power to Lane1.

Sprint is unsuitable metaphor for economic growth with inclusive society. Also the surface for the flat race is not well made out road to prosperity.

2. Marathon – Long distance run

Marathon, a character in Greek Mythology who ran 24 miles to deliver the good news of victory over Persian invaders, to the citizens. 'Rejoice Victory, we conquer' so saying he dropped dead before the feet of watchers'.

'In the long run' we're all dead, Mynard Keynes said.

So Marathon is not suitable for economic growth with inclusiveness for it is too long. We have completed six decades and 11 five year plans and poverty persists.

3. Hurdles

'The most interesting and spectacular event is the hurdles race, short distance than marathon, longer than sprint. Ten obstacles or hurdles are placed to be cleared. In the beginning of 20th century the participants 'jumped over hurdles and lost time recovering from the jolt of landing;

Whereas the modern method is to take hurdles in the stride moving smoothly and evenly throughout the length of the race.' Our hurdles are – man made, god made. Still it is not a race between states, castes,, educated and uneducated or between Lane 1 and Lane 2, the hurdles are artificially created.

4. Steeple Chase

'Riding a race horse calls for judgment, skill and nerve. Different horses have different ways of running. A few like to gallop along in the front; some slow down immediately they are in the lead and must only be brought there a few yards from the winning post; some prefer the race to be run at a slow pace, for this allows the jockey to save them for quick bursts of speed at the finish; some require a strong gallop to set to make their stamina

tell. The 'rider' is the democratically elected government which wants faster, more inclusive, and sustainable growth. It must judge the different kinds of 'horses' and 'horse power' and horse-sense. Industry, business, large, small, medium and micro enterprises, agriculture, allied activities as also educated highly motivated with 'driving power' money power etc etc. the 'jockey' the executive must have knack, 'skill and a nerve'.

Rider is to be blamed when foul play is noticed. It is the millions of watchers who judge the judge and cry foul. All this obstructs the 'smooth and even' run.

5. School Events

Sack race, 3 legged race, leap frog.

Sack race is a handicap race. Learn to live and shine with handicaps – some in-born and others created by social inequalities and generation of backwardness. They must learn a new technique of 'jumping' holding onto the sack. It requires motivation and encouragement and incentives, subsidies, and reservations – democratic affirmative action. Let every one run with the sack on.

Let Lane 1 boy and Lane 2 boy be tied together, inhibiting the stronger, smarter, one to slow down using all his strength. Let the other, the weaker boy put extra effort. Ultimate success depends on how they combine the strengths and weaknesses to meet the challenges before both of them.

A game in which each of the players takes a turn jumping with legs spread wide over the bent back of other players. The important point is 'taking turns'. It is not one person 'sitting on the back and choking' the other always. Everyone will jump and also bends. In military two units advance –one unit is kept in action and the other moves past the first unit to a position farther in front ... by passing.

Lane 1 faster growth is 'leap frog' or bypassing Lane 2. inclusive growth is mere rhetoric or lip service.

***6. Tandem Bicycle** is a better metaphor. First bicycle is a green concept. It does not use non-renewable resources of the earth. It is good for humanity and nature's health, ecologically non-violent technology. simple, small, cheap, and non-violent, ideal for small distances.*

Tandem cycle is for two persons one sitting behind the other. Close coupled axles acting in conjunction. Two sets of pedals placed tandem –

one behind the other. Lane 1 in the front and Lane 2 pedaling from behind.

In my school days ordinary single pedal cycles were used by two sitting tandem. The stronger and senior sits at the back actually pedaling.

The fellow, smaller or weaker fellow, sits on leather seat doing nothing excepting holding bar balancing.

***7. Cross country running -** 'the ideal course containing many types of ground – grass lands, ploughed land, marshland; hills,* *water, fences, stone walls, hedges and so on'. This is typically Lane 2 running. They are running out of their energy and patience. This is winter sport. But for Lane2, it is life long, all through the year, running and staggering.*

Fun in turn-taking

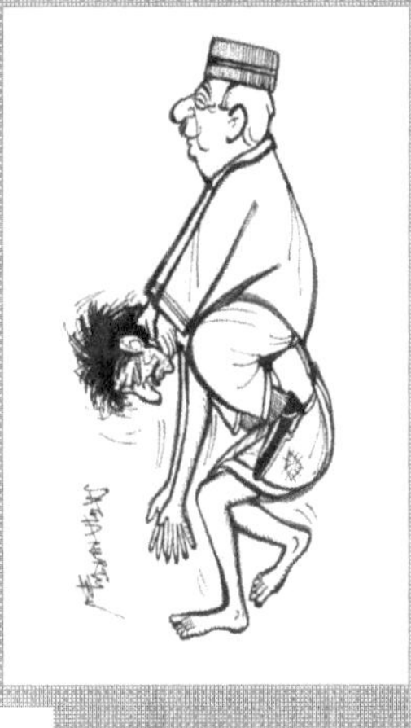

No Fun of turn-taking

The only running village urchins know is to chase vehicles

Inclusive and Sustainable Growth (A Report)

- 12th plan (2012-2017) 9-9.5% growth.
- The objective must be faster, more inclusive and also sustainable growth: Manmohan.
- Special focus on policy and governance reforms and re-designing of government programmes.
- 100% literacy, inclusive growth, and development of physical and social infrastructure.
- set monitorable targets related to different dimensions of inclusiveness…
- For faster, more inclusive, and also **sustainable growth**… we need to identify the critical areas where existing policies and programmes are not delivering results and should, therefore, be strengthened or even restructured… it called for new *initiatives* to meet *new challenges.*
- Citizen feed back reveals general unhappiness with governance and *public delivery.*

'Public Delivery' includes banking services to every citizen at door step. 'They believe that corruption is built into systems of public service delivery' the plan panel said.

Sustainable Growth

The objective must be faster, inclusive and also sustainable growth: Manmohan.

The word 'sustainable' seemed to have been used in the sense of maintainable growth from the fiscal angle.

Sustainability has assumed greater significance for the past few decades. In 1993, Paul Hawken, in his book *The Ecology of Commerce* discussed the central role of business in global environmental destruction.. He wrote 'There is no polite way to say that business is ravaging the world'.

In 1993, Fritjof Capra and Gunter Pauli,[14] wrote in their book, 'the great challenge of our time is to create sustainable forms of business, embedded in sustainable communities'... 'Stabilizing world population will only be possible *when poverty is reduced world wide'*.

'Business activities are responsible, directly or indirectly, for most human impacts on the earth's ecosystems – and business operations today are conducted with too little thought as to their sustainability – that is the satisfying of our own needs without diminishing the chances of future generations'... 'Hence, business people have a strong self-interest in minimizing the ecological damage of their operations.'

It applies to all those in Lane 1 businesses, industry and services equally.

Jamshyd N.Godrej in the Foreword wrote 'I can only end by saying that with its power outreach and its characteristic verve for expanding its domain, business has to don a societal responsibility as the caretaker of Planet Earth.' We have been saying financial literacy is pre-requisite for financial inclusion. Financial Inclusion and inclusive society considerations must have bearing on ecological literacy.

'Ecological literacy', they said, 'is pre-requisite for sustainability.' 'What is good for business', they quoted Paul Hawken, 'is almost always bad to nature'. 'By disregarding this principle of ecology, our political and corporate leaders again and again endanger the health and well-being of millions around the

[14] Steering Business toward Sustainability by Fritjof Capra & Gunter Pauli in 1993.

world' and the authors proceeded by enunciating principles of ecology.

Principles of Ecology:[15]

1. Stability: The stability of an ecosystem depends on the degree of complexity of its network of relationships; in other words, on the diversity of the ecosystem.

1a. Special Limits of Variations (Flexibility): Ecological cycles have the tendency to maintain themselves in a flexible state, characterized by interdependent fluctuations of their variables.

2. Partnership: All living members of an ecosystem are engaged in a subtle interplay of competition and cooperation, involving countless forms of partnership.
3. Ecological Cycles: The interdependencies among the members of an ecosystem involve the exchange of energy and resources in continual cycles.
4. Co-evolution: Most species in an ecosystem coevolve through an interplay of creation and mutual adaptation.
5. Interdependence: All members of an ecosystem are interconnected in a web of relationships, in which all life processes depend on one another.
6. Energy flow: Solar energy, transformed into chemical energy by the photosynthesis of green plants, drives all ecological cycles.
7. Sustainability: The long-term survival of each species in an ecosystem depends on a limited resource base. Ecosystems organize themselves according to the principles summarized above so as to maximize sustainability.

[15] Steering Business toward Sustainability by Fritjof Capra & Gunter Pauli in 1993.

'Ecological awareness is spiritual in its deepest essence'. 'Being ecologically literate means understanding how ecosystems organize themselves so as to maximize sustainability. This is the lesson we have to learn to build sustainable human communities. We need to revitalize our communities – including our educational communities, business communities, and political communities – so that the basic principles of ecology become manifest in them as principles of education, management and politics. Today, this is especially important for business, which has been designed without any attention to the basic principles of ecology.'

Go back to Gandhism.

Principles of Ecology

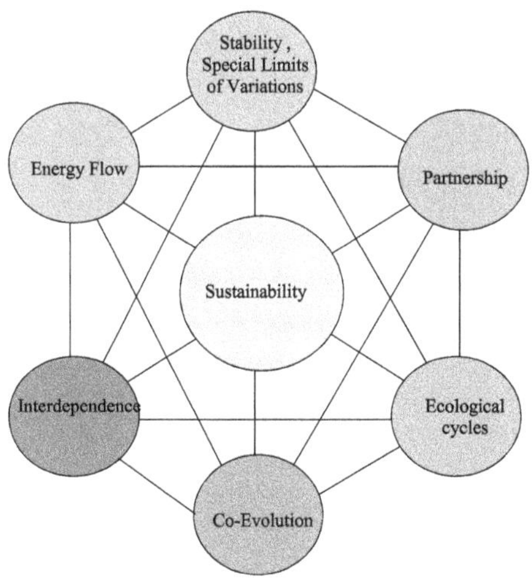

Ecologically literate SPECIES. The above diagram brings to focus the principles of ecology: *partnership* (interplay of competition and cooperation) *interdependence* (web of relationships) and *co-evolution* (interplay of creation and mutual adaptation) and sustainability etc.

Justice Markandeya Katju speaks:

'Nobody needs to be poor. It is the state's duty to ensure it... economic growth has benefited only a handful.' He quoted French thinker, Rousseau: *It is obviously contrary to the law of nature for a handful of people to gorge themselves on superfluities while starving multitude lack the necessities of life.*

'Surely' justice Katju lamented, 'a system in which a quarter million farmers have committed suicide in the last 15 years and vast masses live in poverty is unacceptable.'

* * * * *

MUSINGS OF

BAREFOOT BANKERS

PART - V

FINANCIAL INCLUSION & CHALLENGES

'As long as there are tears and suffering, so long our work will not be over' – Nehru

Tall Rhetoric Tame Reach

FINANCIAL LITERACY

Economic literacy for the rural banker and financial literacy for the rural people are the pre-requisites of financial inclusion in inclusive society.

Financial literacy is to use of financial services to maximise the effectiveness of these services. Before the banker educates the beneficiary he's to educate himself: he needs economic literacy – the meaning and significance of financial services. Economic literacy does not stop with the Uiversity education. The application of conceptual knowledge needs updating of economic information and the growth of economics in the dynamic world. The other day I read a report:

Financial Literacy Key to Financial Inclusion: Mukherjee.

Whatever Finance Minister says it must attract the attention of the barefoot banker; these statements cast their shadows on the coming events. Knowing coming events gives the banker breathing time for preparation.

'Mixed outcome from priority sector lending system', Finance Minister felt.

Opening sentence: 'Financial literacy is a prerequisite for effective financial inclusion, which will ensure that financial services 'reach the unreached, and under-reached sections of the society' the Union Finance Minister Pranabh Mukherjee said here on Monday (Bangalore)

Delivering the inaugural address at an international workshop on 'Delivering financial literacy: challenges, strategies, and instruments' organized jointly by RBI and the Organization for

Economic Cooperation and Development (OECD), Mr.Mukherjee observed that the 'outcome from elaborate system of priority sector lending in India is mixed'.

One can expect new thrusts in P.S. lending. Rural Bank Manager must anticipate and be ready – be proactive, take them as feed forward.

He complimented the RBI for launching a financial literacy project among school children in the state (Karnataka). The efforts to improve literacy should take into account 'the divergence and multi-lingual frame work'... marked differences between rural and urban areas are also important issues in India ...The perceptible variation in the ***penetration of banking*** *across regions' was also an important factor..* A meaningful rhetoric.

Financial Literacy – Some Definitions

'Financial Literacy also referred as financial capability, is the ability to use knowledge and skills to manage financial resources effectively for a *life time of financial well-being. It is a life time security measure*'.

A More comprehensive definition is given by the Institute for Socio-Financial Studies.

'Personal financial literacy is the ability to read, analyse, manage and write about personal financial conditions that effect *material well-being.* It includes the ability to discern financial choices, discuss money and financial issues without (despite) discomfort, *plan for the future*, and respond competently to *life events* that effect every day financial decisions, including *events* in the general economy'.

The comprehensive definition given by the Institute of Socio-Financial Studies reminds me of my grandfather's financial (mis) management in the late 19th century and early 20th century. The story is in the next box.

Life, Events, and Life time Financial Management of my Grandfather

Hailing from a rural poor Brahmin family migrated to the city of Machilipatnam, studied under street lamps grew to the position of District and Sessions Judge in late 19th century. He was living a frugal life saving more and spending less. He invested his savings in gold ornaments and silver ware till his friends and colleagues among the white men advised him to invest in joint stock company, Arbuthnot & Co. That was the first financial literacy lesson he had. Investing in business boosts economy and employment. They ridiculed the Indian culture of investing savings in wife's jewellery.

'Arbuthnot & Co. was strongest commercial organization in the 19th century. Sir George Gough Arbuthnot was the head of Arbuthnot & Co. at the time of the crash. He was a member of the Madras Legislative Council and a prominent figure in Madras society at the time. Sir George's social eminence had not a little to do with the travails of the firm. He brought in numerous deposits but used them for speculation and personal advantage. Much money was spent on searching for gold in the Nilgiris and Annamallais, on investment in American railway projects, on new South African gold fields and in the plantation crops of the West Indies. Arbuthnot & Co. was drained dry. When P.Macfadyen, senior partner of P.Macfadyen & Co., London, Arbuthnot's correspondent and associate in England, and an old Madras hand, committed suicide in October 20, 1906, the crisis broke. Both firms petitioned the courts on the 22nd to be declared insolvent.

'The auditors appointed by the Official Assignee estimated Arbuthnot & Co.'s liabilities at Rs.27 million and its assets at only

Rs.7.½ million! The firm had 2,300 operating accounts in India with balances of Rs.2.75 million and about 4000 fixed deposits with claims amounting to over Rs.25 million. With the assets being described as being only on paper and "beyond all belief, worthless, which crumble to dust when touched," there was no way to meet the claims of the depositors, who were almost any and everyone in Madras who had savings or some money to invest.'

'In the aftermath of the crash, several things happened. Sir Arthur Lawley, Governor of Madras and himself a victim of the bankrupt company, launched a public fund to raise money to help the weaker sections who had lost everything in Arbuthnots'.[1]

At the family level my grandmother took over the financial decision making. She, being from landed gentry started investing in landed property, while the joint family members spent lavishly on weddings and other occasions. They never used cash for anything, nor did they have any accounting literacy. During those days of inflation there was no dearth for creditors. What happened to Arbuthnot & Co. happened to judge's family. The judge became bankrupt. But the pity is there was a change in General Economy in 1930s which hit this family very badly. That was The Great Depression when the land prices fell drastically. That financial literacy is a dynamic concept much depending on the state of *general economy*, was the lesson we can draw from the real story.

Old is Gold

Women saved some part of family income in the form of gold ornaments which became their exclusive property. In emergency situations they pledged them with the pawn-broker. Villagers saved in silver and other metals too. They knew saving, investing, and borrowing. Nothing is new.

---

[1] 'Hundred Years of The Hindu'.

Every house-hold rich or poor do discuss money income, expenditure, plan future (may not be distant future) - children's education, marriages, sickness, agricultural operations, and other life events etc. (refer to comprehensive definition in the previous pages). They may not be able to read, write, or operate technology based products.

They may not plan for events in general economy which even the educated class are not good at. Their financial planning goes hay wire during calamities in the family and nature's fury. (There was no insurance cover. Hundred years back life insurance policies or products could be sold to only the educated with great difficulty. Insurance agent was a bad Omen!)

Money lender need not tap the door, the borrower against gold will pay promptly and redeem the gold, the woman's property.

Even bankers preferred to give gold loans.

No need for recovery camps and frustrated experience for the bankers.

One *'dandora'* – drum beating that the gold will be sold to adjust the loan account is enough.

Cash to redeem gold loan even in the evening at the bank employee's home was not uncommon.

She had no gold to pledge or the bank did not have 'gold loan' scheme. Otherwise she would have preferred 'no-fills' credit. (case 5, episode 12) Security minded bankers would not bother to know the purpose for gold loans – the golden products.

BPL families need clean clear cash credit linked to insurance and gradual up-gradation to the growing needs. The need has become urgent because of falling rate of employment in organized/formal sector.

Mutual Trust is the essence of rural finance. More than financial literacy and 'social heart and 'financial acumen' there are values that mattered. As in the case 6, episode 8 the farmer doubts the very generic feature – liquidity of savings product. Can 'Trust' be a major feature of all bankable products. The farmer had his own definition of 'bankable' scheme. Can he bank on this bank? That brings us back to the concept of corporate identity, corporate image and the strategy to bridge the gap between the two.

Right now what is the image of a bank? It is not a poor man's bank; it is not for rural illiterate; it is not for those who are technology illiterate. The committee on Financial Inclusion admitted that the technology based product development has actually increased financial exclusion. What can banks do to change the image? Change the mind set of the staff, all sections of employees from top to bottom? Attitude change is not the answer. The answer is cultural change – shared values in the entire bank. At least a critical mass – the hundredth monkey effect has to be reached in quick time. Only then performance parameters' have any significance.

A modern trend is the investment in land – plots in cities and towns expecting rise in prices. There is risk involved in this. Here is a case when the investor tried to locate his plot after 20 years found somebody already constructing a house in his plot.

Looking at the muscular power of a land grabber, he had to settle for whatever money he was prepared to pay in exchange to the legal documents. Between them it is the lawyers who make money without risk.

A Report: '4.8 lakh ha of public land encroached on in Karnataka'. Task force report uncovers 'greed and connivance' of politicians and officials... ..only 4% of this total land in its 20 months tenure could be recovered... it is proof of this collusion'

There is an urgent need to educate women groups in financial literacy and lifetime management of money.

Empowerment
Equity
Productivity
Sustainability

The key elements of educating the SHGs. (Refer to case 32)

Book Review

On August 9th 2011, I saw in The Hindu a review of the book, The 'Financial Inclusion Imperative and Sustainable Approaches' by Deepali Pant Joshi, a senior RBI official. The reviewer writes, 'As it turns out however, the thrust of the policy initiatives aimed at financial inclusion has been on the supply side. The demand side has not received adequate attention. For instance, the RBI's effort to spread financial literacy among the rural population and stimulate the demand for banking services is yet to gather momentum. Joshi has elaborately and somewhat repetitively in patches, dealt with the various policies and programmes initiated for reaching the bank services to the rural parts. Moreover, since the 'last mile' is critical for financial inclusion, the value of the book would have been enhanced considerably, if the author had drawn material from field studies rather than rest content with summarizing official reports.

I am sure the studies referred do not refer to impact of banking services.

That is where the role of barefoot banker becomes significant and relevant. 'Musings of Barefoot Bankers' becomes meaningful in the context. My point is that you need a barefoot banker to give the push from the supply side and also pull from the demand side by spreading financial literacy among rural population.

Life Literacy

I discussed what I termed as SPECIES Poverty. To eradicate SPECIES poverty we need SPECIES literacy: Social, Political, Economic, Cultural, Intellectual, Ethical, and Spiritual literacy. The last includes Ecological literacy.

Indian ethos coming from ancient times took care of cultural literacy which subsumes social, economic, intellectual, ethical and spiritual literacy as well. It was holistic and metaphysical. The 'material well-being' is not the end of all things in life. In spite of the ancient ethos, there has been degradation (poverty) in social, economic, ethical aspects of our ethos. All though many claim to be religious they are not truly spiritual. It is ethics in behaviour or values driven behaviour that communicates one's spirituality. Right conduct is prerequisite to spirituality. Fortunately majority in Indian society are spiritually literate in the sense of right conduct at home and in public. 'Win at home and win in public' meant right conduct. Right conduct includes financial management. Voluntary poverty was the life's literacy of our people. The vulgar display of riches is really lack of life's literacy. Plain living and high thinking are two wheels of vehicle of life.

'Comprehensive Financial Inclusion' (CFI) - SCRIP PLUS

S-Savings 'products suited to the pattern of cash flows of a poor house-hold'.[2]

C-Credit 'facilities both for productive and personal purposes'.[3]

R-Remittances & payments

I-Insurance (life and non-life). 'Banks can play a vital role by distributing suitable micro-insurance products.'[4]

P-Product innovation

PLUS services are 'financial counseling/advisory services by the formal financial system – all at affordable cost.

P-Perennial – all the year round

L-Lasting – durable and reliable/literacy services

U-Universal – applicable to all

S-Specific – 'particular' requirements of the poor need to be evolved.

There is a 'missing' market because of mismatch between 'products' offered and 'needs of the beneficiaries.'

* * * * *

[2] Report on Financial Inclusion
[3] Ibid
[4] Ibid

REPORT ON FINANCIAL INCLUSION

'Access to finance by the poor and vulnerable groups is a prerequisite for poverty reduction and social cohesion. This has to become an integral part of our efforts to promote inclusive growth.'[1]

Extent of Exclusion The poorer the group, the greater is the exclusion.

> "NSSO data reveal that 45.9 million farmer households in the country (51.4%), out of a total of 89.3 million households do not access credit, either from institutional or non-institutional sources. Further, despite the vast network of bank branches, only 27% of total farm households are indebted to formal sources (of which one-third also borrow from informal sources). Farm households not accessing credit from formal sources as a proportion to total farm households is especially high at 95.91%, 81.26% and 77.59% in the North Eastern, Eastern and Central Regions respectively. Thus, apart from the fact that exclusion in general is large, it also varies widely across regions, social groups and asset holdings. ***The poorer the group, the greater is the exclusion.***"

Data are facts recognized. There are many more facts not yet recognized by the officials. Even this much should change the heart of policy makers. The committee admits its focus is only supply side, not demand side '*which depends on motivation,*

[1] Report on Financial Inclusion (2008).

markets, know-how, besides credit supply.' A barefoot banker's task includes motivating the slumbering rural majority to improve their lot with credit availability at affordable cost. Motivation and mobilization of the generally conservative rural community especially in backward areas is daunting. '*To get out of the rut requires greater effort than what people are ready to make*'. Also '*the poor cling to their familiar miseries as tenaciously as the rich cling to their privileges*'.[2] Thoreau, American Naturalist wrote long ago that '*if you give money to an Irish beggar he will buy more rags with it*'.[3]

In 1970s the credit disbursement even in adopted villages was meager. To-day the case is different. Profit and growth hungry MFIs have gone to the other extreme to make the Committee Chairman 'shocked at the unethical lending and coercive methods of recovery' that led to dozens of suicides in A.P. in September, 2010. The committee took into consideration the role played by RRBs and Short Term Co-operative System which have 'covered much larger areas than the commercial banks.' In this regard they had the following comments to make regarding Micro Finance Institutions. The committee wrote in 2008:

Micro Finane Institutions - NBFCs

> 'Micro Finance Institutions (MFIs) could play a significant role in facilitating inclusion, as they are *uniquely positioned* in reaching out to the rural poor. Many of them operate in a limited geographical area, have a greater understanding of the issues specific to the rural poor, enjoy greater acceptability amongst the rural poor and have flexibility in operations providing a level of comfort to their clientele.'

---

[2] 'Ends and Means' by Aldus Huxley (1937)

[3] Walden Pond by Thoreau.

The Committee has, therefore, recommended that greater legitimacy, accountability and transparency will not only enable MFIs to source adequate debt and equity funds, but also eventually enable them to take and use savings as a low cost source for on-lending.

The sentence can be redrafted as: 'the banking institutions ***must*** play a significant role in facilitating inclusion as they are uniquely placed in reaching out to the rural poor.'

> "There is a need to recognize a separate category of Micro finance – Non Banking Finance Companies (MF–NBFCs), without any relaxation on start-up capital and subject to the regulatory prescriptions applicable for NBFCs. Such MF-NBFCs could provide thrift, credit, micro-insurance, remittances and other financial services up to a specified amount to the poor in rural, semi-urban and urban areas. Such MF-NBFCs may also be recognized as Business Correspondents of banks for providing only savings and remittance services and also act as micro insurance agents."

PSBs may recognize MF-NBFC as their Business Correspondents provided there are barefoot bankers among them who may be allowed credit dispensation in a limited way. Collaborative marketing is already in place in other spheres.

In November, 2010, after MFI mess and suicides in A.P. in September, the Chairman of the Committee said, 'MFIs have to reform themselves and they are already linked to the banking system…. But if this link is to become strong MFIs need to mend their lending practices.' However he felt 'there is need for multiple systems of operation in the micro finance field'. (Co-operative system, RRBs, Commercial banks, MFIs and MF-NBFCs – all institutions must co-exist). But, 'repercussions on banking will be serious if the MFIs fail'.[4] All may not fail, still there is a market if they reduce the rate of interest and control their collection agents who behave like mafia. World over MFIs are criticized for making tons of money out of the poor. At the end of the day the poor become poorer even if somehow suicides are prevented. No private company will work without profit maximization and growth in mind. It is certain that many MFIs will find it not worthwhile to continue the business without the kind of profits they have been making. Micro Finance Institutions on Verge of collapse (Head lines on 31st Oct, 2011)

Making Money out of poor people (Report)[5]

"Some banks are charging interest rates of 100 per cent or more from the customers."

"Drawn by the prospect of hefty profits from even the smallest of loans, a raft of banks and financial institutions now dominate the field, with some charging interest rates of 100 percent or more from their impoverished customers."

"Micro-credit should be seen as an opportunity to help people get out of poverty in a business way (sustainability way), but not as an opportunity to make money out of poor people."

Business community had their scruples in India traditionally.

Debating micro-loans' effect

'Underlying the issue is a fierce debate over whether micro-loans actually lift people out of poverty, as their promoters so often claim. The recent conclusion of some researchers is that not every

[4] The Hindu

[5] Ibid

poor person is an entrepreneur waiting to be discovered, but that the loans do help cushion some of the worst blows of poverty.'

A cash transfer in effect. Not sustainable.

"The lesson is simply that it didn't save the world," Dean S.Karlan, a professor of economics at Yale University, said about micro-lending. "It is not the single transformative tool that proponents have been selling it as but there are positive benefits'.

'Still, its earliest proponents do not want its reputation tarnished by new investors seeking profits on the backs of the poor, though they recognize that the days of just earning enough to cover costs are over.'

A few days later there was a complaint from the District Collector against MFI in Khammam district in A.P. that they were exploiting the tribals. The principle of long term survival of MFIs is at stake.

"Making pots of money from micro-finance is certainly not illegal. (but immoral) 'CARE, the Atlanta-based humanitarian organization, was the force behind a microfinance institution it started in Peru in 1997. The initial investment was around $3.5 million, including $450,000 of taxpayer money. But last fall, Banco de Credito, one of Peru's largest banks, bought the business for $96 million, of which CARE pocketed $74. CARE expected to use the money to extend its own reach in other countries."

They want to become global mega micro finance company! Greed for mega growth!

'The microfinance industry, with more than $60 billion in assets, has unquestionably outgrown its charitable roots. Elisabeth Rhyne, who runs the Centre for Financial Inclusion, said in congressional testimony this year that banks and finance firms served 60 per cent of all clients. Non-governmental organizations served 35 per cent of the clients, she said, while credit unions and rural banks had 5 per cent of the clients.'

Potential to become bigger and bigger–big is becoming ugly

'Private capital first began entering the microfinance arena about a decade ago, but it was not until Comparatamos, a Mexican firm that began life as a tiny nonprofit organization, generated $458 million through a public stock sale in 2007 that investors fully recognized the potential for a windfall, experts said.'

'According to the Microfinance information exchange, a web site known as the Mix, where more than 1,000 microfinance companies worldwide report their own numbers, Compartamos charges an average of nearly 82 percent in interest and fees.'

Money lenders in disguise of MFI.

'Part of the problem, however, is that all kinds of institutions making loans plaster them with the "microfinance" label because of its do-good reputation.'

SHG – Bank Linkage Scheme

> 'The SHG - Bank Linkage Programme can be regarded as the most potent initiative since Independence for delivering financial services to the poor in a sustainable manner. The programme has been growing rapidly and the number of SHGs financed increased to 29.25 lakhs on 31 March 2007. The spread of the SHG - Bank Linkage Programme in different regions has been uneven with Southern

States accounting for the major chunk of credit linkage.'

There are in 2010 in A.P. 9.5 lakhs of SHGs with 10 million membership but many of them not linked to Banks because of individual Managers' reluctance to add burden to the work load. That is one reason for the groups going for MFIs loans. In a way the politicians were right. There is an interesting case no.26 when a Manager, an agricultural graduate took charge of a branch the first thing he did was to identify SHGs in his area and linked them to the bank credit in a big-way. He got praise and appreciation both from the district administration and bank management. But soon he landed himself in trouble. There were complaints against this officer who happens to belong to tribal community and attributed misuse of authority to favour his community people. The complaints came from the villagers who, it is alleged, were instigated by the staff of the branch and the successors. This is not an isolated case.

The pictures depict the reality – the obstacles to financial inclusion.

One such case is enough to spread rumours which deter other Managers to venture into the area of finance and jeopardise their careers. It is better to bc blamed for omission and non-performance than getting into trouble. This happened in 2005. Non-performers in the micro-lending have good laugh at the dedicated lot; this way the population of 'non-performing assets' – asset standing for staff, increase. Had the management dealt with the problem of the damages of grapevine deftly, the banks would have accomplished financial inclusion long ago.

> 'Many states with high incidence of poverty have shown poor performance under the programme'.

The case I quoted belongs to one such backward district in A.P. In every state there are places with high incidence of poverty. 60 per cent of the cultivated area in India is under rain-fed and drought prone area where backwardness is glaring. The Committee could have gone into it more deeply at this phenomenon. When I asked some of the Managers from Coastal Andhra (forward districts) to share their experiences in SHGs finance, I found that there was excitement in their tone on phone for the excellent work they had done. They had hundreds of SHGs – even more than a thousand SHGs financed by them with excellent recovery experience. But sadly their counter parts in backward areas have nothing exciting to share. They didn't mince words: 'It is a thankless job. Recovery is a big headache. To work here is a punishment.' I saw bitterness in their replies. I chose not to bother them any further.

> 'NABARD must upscale the programmes in the identified states'.

No, they must identity the rain-fed and drought prone areas in all states and do something to increase the incomes; only then the bankers will be encouraged to serve better. Lack of productive enterprises in SHGs to generate sufficient income is most important reason for failures. The committee did mention it when it said, 'there is a need to evolve SHG models suited to the *local context* of such areas'.

Such areas are there in every state.

SHG Movement & Mal Practices -Sri M.Ramakrishnaiah[6] [7]

> 'Although SHG movement has, no doubt registered significant successes', 'to me, this is not surprising considering the rapid spread of the programme, the target-pushing attitude of the relevant government officers, the inadequacies in the training of the women participants, the lure of matching government grants, varying social contexts of villages etc. - at the same time, I have seen evidence of *certain mal practices and distortions* creeping into it in the same manner as in the case of cooperatives'.

SHGs or JLGs fail the way cooperatives failed. And MFIs accelerated the process of decay, in my view.

Mal practices to corrupt practices

Report: 'Rs.260 crores swindled in Indiramma housing scheme... To the dismay of everyone it is also found that umpteen members of SHG (women) are also involved in the irregularities, encompassing as many as 3 lakh dwelling units.

Training and preparing women on such a large scale is a daunting task instilling financial discipline and ethics. I have a personal experience with regard to a cooperative society of taxi drivers. Each member was liable to all the 12 members of the society. When some errant members started defaulting on repayment, other good members also followed suit. When we seized and auctioned the vehicles there were pathetic protests by the disciplined members of the society. I could do nothing but sympathise with their condition.

---

[6] BCT Journal

[7] Read Cases 26 & 32

Let us focus on SHGs and not MFIs. SHG bank linkage was replaced by SHG – MFI linkage with disastrous consequences. The time will come when the SHG – bank linkage should be reestablished. This is my firm view. It is a welfare measure and it should rest with the public sector banks. There is another aspect I wish to present. We thought money in the woman's hand will be spent on the family and money given to man will be spent on wasteful and harmful drinks and drugs. Now some of the SHGs (W) experience is as bad as money in the hands of men.

Both men and women groups are vulnerable to get into debt trap. They need vigilance of Barefoot Banker.

'At the meeting 'India Desk' in the World Bank, the officer asked Dr.BVP the secret of success. BVP told them 'you are backing the wrong horse'. He explained: whatever money you spend is not going to give any return. He told them that it is women who manage the house hold. You are backing the men who waste the money. Women will spend on the family welfare. For men, family is small part. For women is everything.'

The result was Dwacra – self help women's groups.

'But there was one mistake, a grave mistake. The programme was 'giving money' as if money is everything. Thrift as the source of investment in records, obtain loan – matching amount – Loans to repay loans to repay loans'. 'None of it was spent on productive ventures, but spent on houses, house-hold articles, cars, motorcycles. Men did not change their drinking habits either. Children are getting spoiled with easy money habits. Riches without culture.' laments Dr.BVP in his book.

This is true even now. Self help groups an ideal solution could go wrong ways. Micro finance, Government finance, pension funds, bank loans to them–every body is happy–excellent recoveries–Borrow from one source and repay another–multiple finance at usurious rates!

'Where are we going? God alone save the country' is sum and substance of Dr.BVP's book. But he started well in 1970s as some of the cases presented in this book illustrate in 1970s and 1980s.

'There is a need for multiple systems of operation in micro-finance field'. Whether we like it or not, the biggest in the multiple systems is with the private money lender, who is not the traditional one but almost every one who wants to make money out of the poor.

'These episodes contain facts recognized and retold out of memory. Memory contains only what we registered and held in the long-term memory. Theoretically mind recalls things happened in that space and time. Only small fraction is captured recalled and narrated. Yet, they contain some messages which I earnestly wish to convey through this medium. Essentially every writer writes first for himself. But this is not fiction which may not be questioned. But readers of shades of different views may read them with excitement, wonder or with a pinch of salt. 'Take it or leave it' is my mood in writing.'[8]

Yin Yang Swings

For the past 30 years the shift from masculine to feminine has taken place. We must shift to the other side, Yang. Self-help groups and development of women and children in rural areas is showing signs of disaster.

Man and wife participating in the interview

Family as a Unit

Can we take family as a unit instead of dividing it and trying to rule/control. Both genders failed. I've interviewed way

[8] 'My Experiences in Villages' by Dr.B.V.Parameshwar Rao

back in 1977 entire family while sanctioning loans for purposes, and limits etc. I used to keep aside technical feasibility and economic viability, end use; purchase committees etc and discuss simple need identification and involving the family members as a whole (episode 15, case no.5)

Complementarity –Yin and Yang. Opposites are interrelated in a polar, or complementary way – man and woman are part of family. If there are women's groups and men groups they have to be made complementary.

Yin and Yang are related – an essential property of natural systems – family is a natural system in that children need both parents for healthy growth. We'll be creating cultural imbalance preferring one for the other ignoring, interrelatedness and interdependence of all phenomena.

'Self-assertion (male or female) – is achieved by displaying Yang behaviour, by being ***demanding, aggressive, competitive, expanding*** *– as far as human behaviour is concerned'.*[9]

Integration is furthered by Yin behaviour-*responsive, cooperative, intuitive* and *aware of one's environment.* Directionality seems to be crucial. Having failed with focus on male member, turning in opposite direction has helped and gave immediate results upto a point. Now swing must move towards opposite direction–male concern.

In HUF, there has been male domination. Women, therefore, have to be empowered. To that extent SHG (women) & DWACRA have served their purpose, but not for economic and social development. Let's follow 'the pendulum example'.

---

[9] 'The Turning Point' by F.Capra

When we talk of creating assets to the family Yin and Yang, both aspects of the family have to be integrated – cyclically. Oscillations. Give rest to women and turn to masculinity. Ecology principle no.3 – cycles: the interdependencies among members of an ecosystem involve exchange – Yin-Yang exchange of energy and resources in continual cycles.

Women are good for thrift to begin with. As money begins to pour in they find it difficult to balance savings and investment. They are poor Managers. Look at shopping malls. Whom do you find? Women. When basic minimum needs are met, they have improved nutrition, health, and education of the children. But credit-worthiness they might lose sight of.

In 1975, 76 & 77 we financed small borrowers both males and females. Both repaid regularly. But they do not have long term plans. Wife wants to spend on the repairs to the house. Husband wants to buy an electric motor. One wants immediate gratification and another looks at long term. It is masculine Vs feminism quality, but not male and female dichotomy.

Keep them together. But sickness, poor health, malnutrition, child labour whatever are the decisions both should be involved as far as intervention is concerned.

'The natural order is one of dynamic balance between yin and yang[10] *of the Chinese are two opposite poles.'* They correspond:

[10] The Turning Point by Fritjof Capra (1988)

Yin		**Yang**
Night		Day
Feminine		Masculine
Responsive		Demanding
Cooperation		Competition
Conservative		Aggressive

The list is long.

'In Chinese culture (and Indian culture) yin and yang have never been associated with moral values – one is good and the other bad – but the dynamic balance between the two; what is bad or harmful is the imbalance.[11]*'* SHGs for women have helped us in empowering the women and not in financial management. Financial literacy, as the Finance Minister emphasizes again and again, is the prerequisite for financial inclusion.

What the rural house-hold needs is money sense, when to borrow, how much, and when to repay and how. The up-gradation has to be gradual and varies from situation to situation.

As in the case of Dunkers example let us shift our focus on self help groups, the borrowers or the demand side. Let us leave the reformation of the business model of MFIs to themselves. Let us reform the self help groups that have helped us in empowering women to a good extent. In this regard let me quote from Shashi Tharoor's book:[12]

'The poor rural women have proved, if given the opportunity, they know how to wisely invest their money for economically viable and environmentally sustainable income generating activities, repay their loans almost at 100 percent

---

[11]The Turning Point by Fritjof Capra (1988)

[12] The Elephant the Tiger the Cellphone (2007).

repayment rate and become masters of their own destiny without the interference of their men. The idea was tested first and proven in Bangaldesh by the Grameena of Dr.Mohammad Yonus who was awarded the 2006 Nobel Peace Prize for his achievements. Dr.Prabhakar (of SRI) has taken the same idea and successfully replicated.. in Kerala's Palakkad district'.

Tharoor also admits that '*when money given to men seldom trickles down to the family; the toddy shops of Kerala* (any where in the country) *flourish on self indulgent spending habits of men*'. This was the point made by Dr.B.V.Parameswara Rao a nuclear scientist to the UN officials. 'Empowering women is empowering the family' all are agreed. The problem of micro-credit is something else. Read Shashi Tharoor:

'*Of course poverty alleviation is not simply throwing money into the hands of the poor women and enforcing repayment*' – nor is it forcing them to commit suicides to get compensation to family in lakhs! That's what happened in A.P. 4 years after Tharoor wrote these lines. Read further.

'This is also done by unscrupulous agents who go from door to door in the villages opportunistic people who lend money to the poor women at exorbitant interest, exploit their vulnerable situation and addict them to perpetual indebtedness / borrowing. They are called 'Blade Companies' (in Kerala), because of their cut-throat interest rates'.

He did not foresee that the women cut their own throats with the blades in the form of too much loans like too much alcohol of their men.

Tharoor writes SRI is different '*it seeks to build social assets along with economic assets. SRI is breeding a new generation work force, imbued with professionalism and a sense of customer service*'. All the activities SRI engaging women in were in place for almost 4 decades in the BCT activities. I reiterate that one of the earliest voluntary organization, BCT remained small restricting its activities to 100 villages in 3 mandals. There is a tendency to grow larger and larger among micro-credit companies. In V.Os and MFIs the principle should be 'Small is Beautiful'. The moment the 'grandness' enters in the minds of these men it will soon become victim of greed, growth, profits and more profits. They become big sharks in the words of Dr.Mohamood Younus who is himself in trouble.

The rate of interest will not remain 24 or 30 percent. 'Expenditure rises to meet the rising income'. The bubble will burst. Micro-credit should remain the function of democratic government in my view.

Malegam Committee gave its report. A bill in the Parliament may be introduced soon.

Joint Liability Groups[13]

> "SHG-bank linkage has emerged as an effective credit delivery channel to the poor clients. However, there are segments within the poor such as share croppers/oral lessees/tenant farmers, whose loan requirements are much larger but who have no collaterals to fit into the traditional financing approaches of the banking system. To service such clients, Joint Liability Groups (JLGs), *an up-gradation of SHG model*, could be an effective way. NABARD had piloted a project for formation and linking of JLGs during 2004-05 in 8 States of the country through 13 RRBs. Based on the encouraging response from the project, a scheme for financing

[13] Report on Financial Inclusion

> JLGs of tenant farmers and oral lessees has also been evolved. The Committee has recommended that adoption of the JLGs concept could be another effective method for purveying credit to mid-segment clients such as small farmers, marginal farmers, tenant farmers, etc. and *thereby reduce their dependence on informal sources of credit.*"

Is MFI an informal or formal source? That was the doubt I got in my mind because of their methods of lending, rate of interest and other charges and above all the method of recovery. Former governor RBI felt MFIs are money lenders in disguise.

Banks have been objecting to it because of the oral leases. Financing for crop loans is the issue. Ever since Nationalization of banks, banks have been financing small and marginal farmers for wells and minor irrigation. But they neglected production finance which is the issue now. Crop loans were given without collateral both by the primary agricultural societies (PACs) and banks. Most of them became defaulters and had to forgo production finance for which they had been depending on money lenders. (informal sources is the dignified name given to them). The principle in cooperative societies, SHGs, and JLG is 'all for each and each for all'. When individuals are given the joint liability of all of the members it demands extraordinary discipline of collective responsibility which means internal policing. Responsible group life is no easy matter. BCT taught the *Mahila Mandalis* to learn to deliberate on many issues concerning self-governance.

Role of NGOs – Small is Beautiful

> 'NGOs have played a commendable role in promoting SHGs and linking them to banks. NGO with their low resources are finding it difficult to expand in other areas and regions. There is,

therefore, a need to evolve an *incentive package* which should motivate these NGOs to diversify into other backward areas.'

I am afraid there is problem in this suggestion. Take the NGO, Bhagawatula Charitable Trust in Vizag district. They don't want to expand at all beyond the 3 *mandals* they are covering. Dr.B.V.Parameswara Rao is a Gandhian who believed in 'Small is Beautiful'. Reading his auto-biography-'my experiences in villages'–though he was sounding cynical with the kind of obstacles he had to face since 1976[14] when he founded BCT. He was the first man to start Mahila Mandalis (SHGs) in 1976, although Dr.Mohammad Yunus, got Nobel Prize in 2006 for something similar.

THEN

Locked inside by the Male member

NOW

Locked outside by the recovery agent aided by SHG members

It was thrift groups of women who were not willing to go for work in the fields or construction activity. They were in fact

[14] 'My experiences in Villages Development' in Telugu by Dr.B.V.Parameswara Rao.

locked in their houses when the men went out to field work. He really liberated these *pardah nisi* women in villages to engage them in some productive activity – generating income. It was empowerment of women in true sense. In the initial stages he faced problems from the government staff who saw threat to themselves. He could get the help only from bankers who found charm in the uplifting programme.

I met him in 1977 when he told me that bankers were creating further indebtedness and blame the villagers for defaulting by giving loans recklessly. His approach is to start with thrift– small amounts and make a loan available certain times more on the thrift. Even that loan is linked to training given on how to use the asset acquired. He was running a Dairy Training School for poor women before a graded buffalo or cow is given on loan. There is gradual upgradation of loan and the know-how and further an assured market. This is what exactly E.F.Schumacher[15] argued. Motivation to uplift themselves comes with upgradation of know-how and assured market; only then capital works. Without market and know-how there won't be motivation. Only then bank finance will serve any purpose. No NGO should try to become big– expand. According to one study in an ideal situation a VO (NGO) should not operate its activities in more than 5 villages; then it can work at grass-roots with people's participation.[16] It can be a very small group of volunteers who can aid credit delivery system. NGOs which expanded have paid the penalty of mismanagement. Schumacher argued the essential thing of all large scale organization to do is to create smallness in large organizations. He gave the analogy of balloons in the hands of the street vendors as opposed to Christmas tree.

---

[15] Small is Beautiful.

[16] Aligning Human Resources Process. Challenges and Development (1996)

The CEOs at the bottom of the Pyramid

'A man holding a large number of balloons in his hand.. Each balloon has its own buoyancy and lift… the balloon is not only an administrative unit but also an entrepreneurial unit.

The monolithic organization, by contrast,' he argued, 'might be symbolized by a Christmas tree, with star at the top and a lot of nuts and other useful things underneath. Everything derives from the top and depends on it. Real freedom and *entrepreneurship* can exist only at the top.[17]

Branches under the administrative control of Barefoot Bankers behaved like balloons – an entrepreneurial unit.

Some of the Bank branches, by default, behaved like balloons, the entrepreneurial units. Banks did not make use of these experiences of the CEOs at the Bottom who were neither nuts nor nitwits. There were STARS among them: Single-minded, Team, Autonomous, Resilient, Service oriented.

---

[17] Small is Beautiful

NGOs have been in existence but it was only in 1995 onwards GOI gave green signal to their involvement. In 2008 report the emphasis is more on suggesting incentive packages to motivate them to diversify. Former founder Chairman of NABARD M.Rama Krishnaiah, IAS who was also associated with BCT after his retirement has this to say. *'BCT's role as a nodal agency for several small NGOs engaged in Non-formal Education was a resounding success.' 'The prestige of BCT, its resourcefulness and impartial and professional handling of the affairs stood it in good stead. I believe that several local leaders with aptitude for rural development have been helped to stand on their own feet and strike out on their own in due course.'*

'There is a clear case for encouraging some NGOs to develop into nodal agencies, depending on the dedication and experience of their leadership. I believe that the concept of nodal agency has great relevance and utility from the stand-points of both the government and the voluntary sector.'[18]

BCT Experiences

Case 1 - A woman entrepreneur

Kasulamma of Gokiwada village was leading a hand-to-mouth existence until a few months ago when she approached the mahila mandali and got a loan of Rs.100 to make and sell *jentika,* a dry flour snack.

Every evening she sat by the roadside and sold her ware to the farm workers returning from fields. Instead of money she accepted sugarcane from them which she sent to the jaggery mill in bulk. With that she again bought flour, made more *jentikas,*

---

[18] Two Decades with NGOs – M. Rama Krishnaiah, BCT Journal.

collected more canes, got more jaggery. Today she claims to have a savings of Rs.1,100.

Kasulamma has repaid her loan and can look forward to a loan of Rs.1000 and buy a few sheep or goats which she can fatten and sell at a profit in a few years. She would be making a few thousands.

And all the while she need not worry about the health of her sheep. The village para-vets of BCT will be there to advise her. And she can always take her animals to the veterinarians in Haripuram farm.

BCT enters a village through thrift. The women in the villages are encouraged to save small amounts by raising saplings and selling them to BCT or by stitching *adda* leaves (used as eating plates which BCT sells to the Tirupati, Simhachalam and Annavaram temples and also to local people for marriage feasts etc). The savings are collected by thrift workers.

Case 2

If you had gone to Marripalem village 10 years ago, you would not have seen the women. If you go to Marripalem today, you may not see the men. Ten years ago when Dr.Parameswara Rao visited the flood-affected village, he was told that the men did not allow their women to venture out of their homes. Some of them even locked up their women when they went out for work.

The men did every outdoor work, including fetching water. When the women travelled, the bullock-carts were heavily curtained. "If you visit the village again tomorrow after 10'O clock when the men are away in the fields, you may meet some of the women", someone told Dr.Rao. The next day he met a few women who almost whispered to him their plight.

Rao knew that merely talking to the men would do no good. The first and most harmless step should be something that the men did not resent. He could give them *adda* leaves to stitch. The nearby Kothakotta village could supply the leaves which the women could stitch within the cloisters of their home and the Trust could market the finished eating plates. The men would not resent their women knitting at home and supplementing the family income.[19]

Solitary confinement to freedom and empowerment

Farmer's Clubs

Sri Rama Krishnaiah himself, in NABARD introduced 'Farmers Clubs' which his successors abandoned only to be revived later and are a great success in several places, but in other places they have become defunct or non-starters. The reasons can be attributed to purely local situations. It is here some bank Managers took initiative to start, to revive and grow. One reason I

[19] The Week – Dec, 27-Jan 2, 1988.

heard was the land owners stopped cultivation and the tenants had no organization.

'There is a lot of conceptual confusion', wrote K.K.Upadhyaya CEO of the Charitable Trust (a V.O) Bhoruka Charitable Trust. The projects they had undertaken were health, family welfare, education, woman and child development and sanitation etc for improving *quality* of life. However the benefits of these projects could not reach the common people, especially the remote and backward areas. One problem was 'largeness' and the consequential bureaucracy'.[20]

In this regard I wish to present E.F.Schumacher's analysis[21] '...

> 'dangers to the integrity of the individual when he feels as nothing more than a small cog in a vast machine and when the human relationships of his daily working life become increasingly dehumanized; productivity, stemming from ever growing parkinsonian bureaucracies.' '... with a hatred of authority from below and a contempt of people from above... sharply divided between **us** and **them**, torn by mutual suspicion. Undoubtedly this is all a problem of communications.'

He quotes from Franz kafka's novel, The Castle.

> ... no body likes to be ruled by rules... people say, 'I did not make the rules: I am merely applying them. The fundamental task is to achieve smallness **within** large organization.'[22]

---

[20] Aligning Human Resources Process. Challenges and Development (1996)

[21] Small is Beautiful

[22] Ibid

Similar is the plight of all grass-roots Managers be in banks or NGOs as nodal agency.

A Case of NGO

The Chairman of the Committee on Financial Inclusion, Dr.C.Rangarajan commended the work of BCT (Bhagavatula Charitable Trust) when he was Governor of A.P. State.

"The Bhagavatula Charitable Trust is truly bringing about a rural transformation which has been the goal of people like Mahatma Gandhi. In a dedicated way, the Trust has devoted itself to build the confidence of the people. The people themselves have become the instruments of the change with the Trust playing the role of an adviser.

The Trust has involved itself in all aspects of rural life – education, agricultural development and growth of allied activities."

Dr.C.Rangarajan, Governor Andhra Pradesh.

"Our Mission (BCT)

Create opportunities at the door steps of the villagers

Continuous self-improvement in the quality of their lives

Generating their leadership in solving their problems & utilizing their resources most effectively.

Our vision

To transform 100 villages in 3 mandals, viz. Yellamanchilli, Atchyutapuram and Rambilli of Visakhapatnam District, Andhra Pradesh into model villages in such a way that all able bodied persons are gainfully employed, that substantive improvements in the state of literacy, health and economic sustenance take place and that local leadership and facilitation is fully developed.

Our values

Our attention is the poor villagers

Our motto is concern for the other person

Our belief is the intrinsic capacity of every person, even the poor to help one self.

Our approach is participatory

Our role is motivating and facilitating Honesty of purpose, openness and truth, upholding human dignity and being fair to all will be guiding principles of our conduct."

100 villages in 3 *mandals* and nothing more. BCT in spite of its success recognized not to get into the trap of largeness which afflicts Lane 1 people. Even after 4 decades the task is incomplete to expand into new areas whatever may be the *incentive package* (Report on Financial Inclusion). Apart from smallness the man at he top and its governing board is a vital factor.

'In the sixties, for a person who returned from the USA after completing higher education in Science and Technology, well-paid job opportunities, with assured career advancement, were many. It was unthinkable for such a meritorious youngster to plunge into rural development straight away spurning lucrative job offers. It was all the more unthinkable to the wife, father and other family members to support a financially bleak way of life chosen by the idealist and brave through all the tribulations that inevitably come up in such a pursuit of life,' wrote MR. G.Ramdas, a retired bureaucrat.[23]

[23] BCT Journal

'In rural development there is no fixed goal after the attainment of which you may celebrate the success. It is a continuous struggle in which the goal is set higher after every stage of achievement. You have to modify your strategies taking into account the changing social and economic realities without ever compromising on the ultimate objective.

All the principles of modern management, public relations, individual and mass psychology have to be pressed into service to achieve the desired goals.'

'Be it adult literacy, Wasteland development, encouraging and supporting rural artisans, social forestry, income-generating and employment oriented ventures like Prawn Culture, Salt-manufacture etc, BCT implemented all of them long back.'

'One important thing must be borne in mind. Rural development is a community effort. Its success cannot be judged merely by statistics and balance sheets. It is judged by the changes it brings forth in the attitudes of the people and the initiatives they take for their own advancement. From this point of view, the success of BCT is phenomenal.'

'In a fit of idealism some people of charitable disposition take to rural development or other area of Social work out to give up sooner or later either because of setting in of charity-fatigue or because of the depressing ground realities. One can only marvel at the tenacity of purpose of Dr. Parameswara Rao in whom burns brightly the spirit of rural development even after more than 35 years of uninterrupted service.'

Is it not the same thing Lord Keynes said? I repeat 'A large proportion of positive activities depend on spontaneous optimism rather than on mathematical expectation.

All these aspects apply to – Barefoot Banker. He may not have charity fatigue for two reasons: one he is employee and the other is his tenure is limited to 5 years at the most. The man is integral, both the leader and followers. Gandhi produced thousands of Gandhians with Gandhigiri like Spartacus. 'I am Spartacus, every slave said. 'I am Gandhi' every one engaged in rural development must identify himself/herself. Dr.B.V. Parameswara Rao is one such Spartacus.[24]

'One important thing must be borne in mind. Rural development is a community effort. Its success cannot be judged merely by statistics and balance sheets.'

This sentence taken from Mr.G.Ramdass remarks on the previous page applied to all Barefoot Bankers.

* * * * *

[24] Spartacus was leader of slaves who revolted against Romans

CHALLENGES

Twin challenges before the government are to increase production and productivity–yield per acre so as to provide food for all. The crude materialist view sees agriculture as '*essentially directed towards food production*'. When we focus on agriculture as a measure of food security we try to hand over agriculture to corporates for large scale farming–mechanisation and profit maximization and drive out millions from the legitimate occupation and livelihood. By-product of this step is to increase factories which will need more land. Both land and labour goes for industry uprooting farming and farmers.

> 'Principle' of agriculture is that it deals with *life,* with *living* substances. Its products are the result of processes of life and its means of production is the *living* soil'. (Lane 2). 'The fundamental principle of modern industry, on the other hand, is that it deals with man-devised processes which work reliably only when applied to man-devised, non-living materials,'

E.F.Schumacher reminds us when he adds,

> 'human life can continue without industry, where as it cannot continue without agriculture' – 'the difference between life and death'.[1]

> 'Man's management of land must be primarily orientated towards three goals – health, beautify, and

[1] Small is Beautiful

> permanence. The fourth goal – productivity – is a by-product.'[2]

'Natural farming is becoming popular among ryots', a report. Community managed sustainable agriculture (CMSA) is spreading in A.P. in 22 districts covering 8225 villages benefiting 25,77,877 acres of land owned by 10,47,093 farmers –CMSA-aims at bringing down excessive dependence on chemical inputs in agriculture and help farmers revert to natural farming; it reduces cost of cultivation and increase net income'[3] – both economics and meta-economics are taken care. They are locally available natural resources and taking advantage of natural processes – building soil health by considering soil as a living organism and a bank for crop nutrients.

GOI has increased the fertilizer subsidy. In 2011-12 budget it is proposed to transfer subsidy directly to the farmer. '*Obviously the fertilizer industry is happy*', wrote R.P.Singh, former Union Minister of rural development in an article[4]. '*But hardly there is a discussion on what is good for the farmer and the farm*! The huge investment in chemical fertiliser production '*has always been under criticism as it was promoting an over use of chemical fertilizer there by catalising soil degradation*', resulting in decline in production threatening food security of the country.

'*The dry lands have never received the benefits of the crores of money being given out as fertilizer subsidy; as most farmers in these regions are, by default, organic – cannot use chemical fertilizers, water being limited factor.*'[5]

---

[2] Small is Beautiful.

[3] The Hindu

[4 & 5] Ibid

Soil degradation, farmers' view[6]

'Farmers are aware of the crisis, the deteriorating soil even though the government seems to be oblivious of it. But the farmer is helpless. Green peace India report, 'of soil, subsidies and survival' based on social audit conducted in 5 states, has revealed that 96 percent out of the 1000 farmers surveyed were of the opinion that the use of chemical fertilisers led to soil degradation but they continue to use them as there was no option. 94 percent

www.ingramcontent.com/pod-product-compliance
Lightning Source LLC
Chambersburg PA
CBHW071235230926
51849CB00001B/110
9789385433221